WOMEN, FAMILY AND SOCIETY IN MEDIEVAL EUROPE

Historical Essays, 1978–1991

———————— ✦ ✦ ✦ ————————

Women, Family and Society in Medieval Europe

Historical Essays, 1978–1991

✦ ✦ ✦

David Herlihy

ed. with an introduction by
A. Molho

Berghahn Books
Providence • Oxford

First published in 1995 by

Berghahn Books
Editorial offices:
165 Taber Avenue, Providence, RI 02906, USA
Bush House, Merewood Avenue, Oxford, OX3 8EF, UK

Library of Congress Cataloging-in-Publication Data
Herlihy, David.
  Women, family and society in medieval Europe / by
David Herlihy.
      p. cm.
  Includes bibliographical references and index.
  ISBN 1-57181-024-2
  1. Women--Europe--History--Middle Ages, 500-1500. 2.
Family--Europe--History. 3. Europe--Social life and customs.
4. Women--Italy--History--Middle Ages, 500-1500. 5. Family--
Italy--History. 6. Italy--Social life and customs.   I. Title.
HQ1147.E85H47   1994
305.4'094--dc20   94-39212
                                                                  CIP

British Library Cataloguing in Publication Data
A catalogue record for this book is available from
the British Library.

Printed in the United States.

ACKNOWLEDGEMENTS

—— ✦ ✦ ✦ ——

Permission to reproduce the following articles is gratefully acknowledged to the holders of their copyright.[1]

I: "My Life in the Profession."[2]

II, 1: "Women and the Sources of Medieval History. The Towns of Northern Italy," in *Medieval Women and the Sources of Medieval History,* ed. by Joel Rosenthal (Athens, Georgia, 1990), pp. 133–154.

II, 2: "Did Women Have a Renaissance?: A Reconsideration," *Medievalia et Humanistica,* 1985, pp. 1–22.

II, 3: "The Natural History of Medieval Women," *Natural History,* 1978, pp. 56–67.

II, 4: "Women's Work in the Towns of Traditional Europe," in *La donna nell'economia. Secc. XIII-XVIII.* Atti della "Ventunesima Settimana di Studix" 10-15 aprile 1989, a cura di Simonetta Cavaciocchi (Florence: Le Monnier, 1990), pp. 103–130.

II, 5: "Making Sense of Incest: Women and the Marriage Rules of the Early Middle Ages," in *Law, Custom, and the Social Fabric in Medieval Europe. Essays in Honor of Bryce Lyon,* ed. with an appreciation by Bernard S. Bachrach and David Nicholas (Kalamazoo, Michigan: Studies in Medieval Culture, XXVIII, 1990), pp. 1–16.

III, 6: "Family," *The American Historical Review,* 96, 1 (1991), pp. 1–15.

1. The following chapters are here published for the first time: no. 12, 14, 15.
2. This title is the editor's. The Italian version bears the title: *Il discorso del vincitore.* This essay was published in an Italian translation in the program of the ceremony in which David Herlihy was awarded the Premio Internazionale "Galileo Galilei." The English version included in this volume is published here for the first time.

III, 7: "The Making of the Medieval Family: Symmetry, Structure, and Sentiment," *Journal of Family History,* 8 (1983), pp. 116–130. Permission granted by JAI Press, Inc.

III, 8: "The Family and Religious Ideologies in Medieval Europe," *Journal of Family History,* 12 (1987), pp. 3–17. Permission granted by JAI Press, Inc.

III, 9: "Santa Caterina and San Bernardino: Their Teachings on the Family," in *Atti del simposio internazionale Cateriniano-bernardiniano. Siena, 17–20 aprile 1980,* a cura di Domenico Maffei e Paolo Nardi (Siena: Accademia senese degli Intronati, 1982), pp. 917–933.

III, 10: "The Florentine Merchant Family of the Middle Ages," in *Studi di storia economica Toscana nel medioevo e nel rinascimento in memoria di Federigo Melis* (Pisa: Pacini Editore, 1987), pp. 179–201.

III, 11: "Medieval Children," in *Essays on Medieval Civilization. The Walter Prescott Webb Memorial Lectures,* ed. by Bede Karl Lackner (Arlington, Texas, 1978). Used by permission of the Walter Scott Webb Memorial Lectures Committee, the University of Texas at Arlington.

III, 13: "Age, Property, and Career in Medieval Society," in *Aging and the Aged in Medieval Europe,* ed. by Michael M. Sheehan, CSB. Papers in Medieval Studies 11 (Toronto: Pontifical Institute of Medieval Studies, 1990), pp. 143–158. By permission of the publisher, copyright by the Pontifical Institute of Mediaeval Studies, Toronto.

III, 16: "The Problem of the 'Return to the Land' in Tuscan Economic History of the Fourteenth and Fifteenth Centuries," in *Civiltà ed economia agricola in Toscana nei secc. XIII-XV: Problemi della vita delle campagne nel tardo medioevo* (Pistoia: Centro italiano di studi di storia e d'arte, 1981), pp. 401–416.

III, 17: "Tuscan Names, 1200–1530," *Renaissance Quarterly, 41* (1988), pp. 561–582.

III, 18: "The Rulers of Florence, 1282–1530," in *City States in Classical Antiquity and Medieval Italy,* ed. by Anthony Molho, Kurt Raaflaub, and Julia Emlen (Stuttgart: Franz Steiner Verlag, 1991), pp. 197–221.

Appendix: "The American Medievalist: A Social and Professional Profile," *Speculum,* 58 (1983), pp. 881–890.

CONTENTS

✦ ✦ ✦

INTRODUCTION

✦ ✦ ✦

Early in October 1990, just a few months before his much too premature death in February 1991 when he had barely passed his sixtieth birthday, David Herlihy traveled from his home in Providence, Rhode Island to Pisa, there to receive the Premio Internazionale Galileo Galilei. Annually awarded by the Italian Rotary Clubs to a non-Italian scholar who made a distinguished contribution to an understanding of the Italian past, the Premio Galileo Galilei was one of a series of prestigious awards—among which perhaps the most notable was the Presidency of the American Historical Association—bestowed by the scholarly community upon Herlihy in recognition of his extraordinary scholarly career. At the time of his trip to Pisa, Herlihy was aware of the gravity of the illness which doctors had diagnosed only a few weeks earlier. It is perhaps this knowledge which explains the decidedly autobiographical tone of his comments during the solemn ceremony in the *Aula Magna* of the University of Pisa. His speech on that occasion was unusual and not quite true to his style. A prodigiously productive scholar, Herlihy had never tried to draw attention to himself. His personal trait which most often struck his colleagues and students was his bemused, understated, even diffident style. Whether in his classes, or in his writings, he had always focused readers' and students' attention onto sources and analytical problems. And always, especially when boldly presenting the hypotheses which became the trademark of his article- or book-length studies, he had pointed his interlocutors' attention to the fragility and provisional nature of his findings. Uncharacteristically, if only momentarily, in Pisa, Herlihy changed the subject matter and adopted a different tone. The subject matter became his own scholarly experience, his reflection on "the reasons why I chose the economic and social history of Italy in the Middle Ages." In his categorical statement that "today, looking back over more than thirty-five years of research, I can easily give answers" one catches a self-conscious tone of closure, a wistful glance backward onto the traces of an intellectual voyage about to be drawn to an end.

Herlihy's speech on that Sunday morning in Pisa forms an ideal introduction to this volume. The object of his exercise on that occasion was to review his scholarly life and explain to a mostly Italian audience the reasons which had led him—a first generation Irish-American born in San Francisco—to devote most of his career to the history of Italy in the Middle Ages. There is no need to review Herlihy's scholarly self-portrait here. With his usual economy of expression and penetrating insight, he presented to the Pisan audience a clear guide to the principal events and intellectual influences which marked his life, from 1948 when he was enrolled for his first university degree at the University of San Francisco, a Jesuit university, where, as he notes, "the *ratio studiorum*" had not changed since the Renaissance, to 1978, year of publication of *Les Toscans et leurs familles*, his and Christiane Klapisch-Zuber's *magnum opus*. Interestingly, he passed over in silence the last thirteen years of his life. No doubt, in late 1990 he shared the general view that the publication of that great book marked the high point of his career, that his name and that of Christiane Klapisch-Zuber would be linked in the minds of current and future students of medieval history with their great, jointly authored book.

Yet, it would be an error to view Herlihy's work following the publication of *Les Toscans* merely as an appendage to the preceding dozen or so years of extraordinarily intense and fruitful work, to think of it as a period when he simply worked out variations on themes which he had first explored before 1978. To be sure, many of the essays he wrote between 1978 and 1991 harked back to questions, sources, and methods which he had refined in the preceding years. But there is no doubt that in the last thirteen years of his life Herlihy displayed the same level of prodigious intellectual energy, unrelenting curiosity about the past, and inventiveness and imagination that had marked his career's preceding stage. What sets the last years apart is the fact that his life came to an end just as he

was on the verge of defining the outlines of two substantial historical problems to each of which he planned to devote a major book.
Of course, there is no telling how that career might have developed—what unexpected intellectual breakthroughs, or refinements
in his questions or methods might have marked his thinking—had
he had the gift of another dozen or so years of healthy life. The fact
that that gift was withheld from him means that a casual student of
Herlihy's career has greater difficulty in identifying his accomplishments following 1978, for these are less evident and striking. Yet, a
closer look at the record suggests that these last years produced
scholarly foundations which were as solid as anything he had put in
place in the 1960s and 1970s. The evidence for this claim is contained in the pages of this book.

The essays gathered in this volume were written in the last thirteen years of Herlihy's life. In reality, one of them (ch. 16) was con-
ceived and presented to scholarly audiences in 1977, although its
revised version was not published until 1981. Two more were published in 1978 (chs. 3, and 11), one (ch. 14) was written in winter
1978, delivered at Wellesley College in March of that year but never
published, and a fourth one (ch. 15), also unpublished, can be dated
from internal evidence to between 1979 and 1985.[1] One essay
included in this volume (ch. 12) was left incomplete at the time of
his death, although Herlihy had circulated it among specialists for
their comments. The remaining essays appeared in print between
1981 and 1991, with a strikingly crescendo tempo of publication in
the last few years of his life, four essays appearing in 1990, and three
in the first two months of 1991, preceding Herlihy's death in February of that year. One should add to these the two books Herlihy produced in the 1980s, and the projects he left incomplete to get a
sense of the unrelenting energy and unflagging enthusiasm which,
to the very end, he brought to his studies.

1. Regrettably, I reached the conclusion that a very important essay of Herlihy's,
never republished since its original appearance in Italian in 1978, had to be excluded
from this volume. Dealing with "Florence's Economic Relations with its Subject
Cities," this piece was originally written in English, and then translated into Italian.
Unfortunately, the original version could not be located among Herlihy's papers. Its
inclusion here would have presented the awkward problem of retranslating this piece
from Italian to English, a choice discarded. This essay will be included in the Italian
version of this volume.

It would be a mistake to categorize the themes on which Herlihy worked following publication of *Les Toscans*. His mind spanned a very wide field, just as it had done in the first two decades of his scholarly career. Yet, it is possible to identify in the essays included in this volume at least two major themes on which he was working very hard in the last few years, and which, it is reasonable to suppose, he intended to continue cultivating in the years to come. Above all, there is the history of the family. In 1985 he had devoted a book to this subject. Even so, he lingered over this topic until the very end. His presidential address to the American Historical Association, in late December 1991 barely a few weeks before his death and when his illness had almost completely sapped his strength, was also devoted to this theme. Its title, "Family," in its stark, but ambiguous simplicity, conveys a sense of the force which Herlihy attached to the concept—one suspects both as a subject of historical research, and an institution to which he, exemplary *pater familias* that he was, felt an especially abiding commitment. If his earlier studies on the family had dwelt on demographic, and more generally quantitative dimensions of this institution's history, it is clear from his later essays that he was progressively drawn to questions one might define as qualitative, gender roles within the family, spiritual forces which shaped the behavior of the family's components (hence that wonderful article contained in this volume on Tuscan names), religious inspiration provided by men and women of exceptional spirituality whose lives could also be read as expressions of contemporary family life. Even his unfinished essay on History and Sociobiology seems to me to be an attempt to approach the topic of the family from yet another angle—however unusual, difficult, and controversial it might be to negotiate that approach. It is altogether likely, therefore, that, given the constancy of his interest in this subject, and the variety of approaches with which he sought to approach and analyze it, that, at some point, Herlihy would have written another book on it. The extensive notes he left behind, on a project which he tentatively entitled "The Seven Ages of Man," lend support to this hypothesis.

Alongside (indeed, part and parcel of) his interest in the history of the family was his continuing fascination with the history of women. It is perhaps important to remember here that, in his Harvard years,

Herlihy had been one of a tiny number of scholars responsible for the introduction of instruction on women's history in that University. The first cluster of articles in this volume shows that his commitment to this subject matter remained strong to the very end. His appreciative, yet critical response to Joan Gadol's provocative question ("Did Women Have a Renaissance?") was fair, balanced and set the tone for much of his writing on the subject. It was a writing which eschewed polemical statements, but did not shy away from expressing critical views toward certain exuberant claims made by a few overly enthusiastic proponents of women's history. For his part, Herlihy sought to uncover the reality of women's vital contributions to many manifestations of medieval life, even if extant medieval records are notorious for obscuring those contributions—just as these records often minimize, and even altogether overlook the roles of the poor of both sexes. One suspects that Herlihy's ideological commitment—assuming that even this way of expressing oneself does no injustice to his thinking—to the study of women's history was comparable to his interest in the common Tuscan folk, whose lives his study of the catasto did so much to illuminate. The key in studying groups whose lives had been so very often passed over in silence by traditional historiography was to discover documents which had been largely ignored by historians, to invent new ways of analyzing them, to imagine new questions one could ask of them. One could thus enrich one's field of vision with insights drawn from these documents, while at the same time perceiving the distortions and interpreting the silences of much documentation which historians, traditionally, had relied upon in their study of the past. The point was that the study of women's histories made it possible to gain a better understanding of society as a whole, capturing the lives both of men and of women, of rich and poor, of dominant and subordinate groups—as these lives were reciprocally intertwined with each other.

If his fascination with the history of the family and of women linked the last phase of Herlihy's career to the years preceding the publication of *Les Toscans,* his second clear interest in his last years—for a certain kind of political history—seems to me to represent something of a break, an opening toward questions which had left him largely indifferent in his earlier years. The most evident manifestation of this interest was his staggeringly ambitious project on the Florentine electoral records *(Tratte)* during the two-and-a-half centuries of the Republic's history. At the time of his death, he had nearly completed the task of coding and inputting the tens of thousands of names contained in these volumes, and had written one relatively short essay based on them. It is difficult to escape the impression that his goal was to write a history of Florence's ruling class based on this mountain of information, collate the electoral records with data on the catasto he and Klapisch-Zuber had collected, and with other records which he had in mind studying in the future. As his one article based on this data clearly shows, the project on the *Tratte* was slowly directing his attention to questions on the articulation and distribution of political power, and on the history of Florence's dominant class. Not the least regret caused by his premature death is that we shall never know how he would have used this information, what shape he would have given to his book on the social history of power in Renaissance Florence.

But his interest in politics—and in the expression of power—was not confined to his project on Florence's electoral rolls. His wonderfully suggestive article on Mantua shows an especial sensitivity to the bearing of political organization upon cultural manifestations in signorial courts. And his piece on city and country-side in Renaissance Tuscany casts this problem in terms which historians of political institutions in fifteenth century Italy—one thinks of Marino Berengo, Giorgio Chittolini, Elena Fasano, and in the United States of Judith Brown and James Grubb—would greatly appreciate. Herlihy's description of economic ties between center and periphery of the Florentine state tends to linger upon those very relationships of power which were instrumental in creating the territorial states whose fates political and institutional historians of renaissance Italy have recently described. In short, in the last several years of his life, the phenomenon of power, and its articulation both at a level of local and of regional politics had begun to exercise its fascination on Herlihy, a complement to his long standing and abiding interest in the history of the family, of women, and of what, conventionally, we tend to define social history.

Beyond the scholarly themes which attracted Herlihy's attention, there is another element of his career which merits some attention here: It is what I can only call his scholarly temperament, his attitude toward his studies, which, in many respects it seems to me, remained constant over the decades. Samuel Cohn's anecdote about Herlihy's boast that he was the first to have published a graph in *Speculum* strikes me as significant, not only because it bespeaks Herlihy's intense interest in breaking precedent, in being, if one will, "modern," but also because it illustrates his continuing interest in and commitment to quantification. Counting was a vital part of Herlihy's method, whether it was the number of people in a tax census, or a population's age and gender distribution, or the consumption of wheat, or the number, gender and provenance of saints per century. And such counting—in simple, or extremely complex, sophisticated ways—imparted upon his work an extraordinary solidity, gave it a dimension that very few works of medieval history—certainly of Italian medieval history—had until Herlihy showed the rest of us the way.

If for Herlihy counting was an essential ingredient, his work's other, inseparable, ingredient was the big question. With the passage of time, the initial big question about the nature of Pisan capitalism in the thirteenth century was refined and redefined. But there is not one of the dozens of essays, written by Herlihy in nearly forty years of publishing, that did not address a significant question. There was something adventuresome and ebullient about Herlihy's incessant quest for questions to ask, for new ways to examine new and old evidence, for interesting angles which might reveal new and unexpected insights. There is no better illustration of his approach—that playful inquiry of a seemingly dry-as-dust data base, with suggestive and important results emerging from such analysis—than his Presidential address to the Medieval Academy of America, in which, using the Academy's mailing list as a source, Herlihy, in a particularly shining demonstration of his analytical skills and of his gentle, if impish, sense of humor, presented his audience with a collective portrait of north American medievalists. Lest someone be tempted to think that this was merely an academic exercise, a bravura, but idle demonstration of his analytical skills, let that person reread Herlihy's conclusions about the geographic and age distribution of American medievalists to realize that, just as in everything else that he wrote, big issues and big stakes loomed just immediately below the surface.

Then, there was what I like to call Herlihy's "modernity," his sensitivity to what was going on in other fields, his capacity to follow the technical and often arcane explorations in other disciplines—sociology, economics, statistics, even, as one of his unpublished essays shows, sociobiology. More so than any other of Herlihy's works, his book on Pistoia, published a quarter-of-a-century ago, showed his extraordinary inclination to learn from other disciplines, modernize the questions which medievalists could ask, strike up a dialogue and strive to create a community between medievalists and scholars working in other disciplines. For more than one young scholar at the time of its publication, that book was an exhilarating experience, a sign of the potentialities which our field of inquiry held. Compare Herlihy's Pistoia, for example, with an equally impressive and important book, published the year after. Nicolai Rubinstein's *Florentine Studies* contains a number of beautifully crafted essays, written by some of the leading Anglophone (and one Francophone) historians of the 1960s. These essays are models of erudition, each represents important contributions to knowledge, all are based on extensive and intelligent archival explorations, they bespeak the enormous additions to knowledge made in Florentine studies since the last war. But, from the point of view of method and of the questions asked, every single one of these essays could have been written twenty years before, or twenty years after. That, surely, could not have been said of Herlihy's book on Pistoia, a work of its times, and for this reason a heroic work, which conveyed not only the excitement of new knowledge, but of new ways of organizing and conveying that knowledge.

If Herlihy spent the 1960s and 1970s mastering the computer, learning programming languages, and exploring the methods of statisticians, geographers and economists, by the 1980s he was beginning to look for new tools used by other disciplines. The search was slow, but by the middle years of the decade it was becoming clear to him that biology might offer new and fruitful avenues of exploration. Just as he had done in earlier years, it was not enough for him to gain a smattering of this new knowledge. His earlier approach to computers had taught him that if he was to use them effectively he had to learn not simply to apply programming languages written by others. And so, he learned to write his own programs, suitable to the specific research campaigns that he was preparing to launch. The same with his new interest in biology, more specifically with sociobiology. He read in the subject assiduously, began an active correspondence with a number of biologists, and by the late 1980s felt that he was approaching a level of mastery to begin writing his first essays. I have no doubt that this angle of vision—the application of biological concepts to the study of medieval society—would have been one of his distinctive contributions to the study of medieval history. As it is, the only evidence of all that studying is a nearly finished essay, a lonely testimonial to David Herlihy's constant search for an *aggiornamento,* for seeking to go beyond the boundaries of his discipline. Only such a commitment to continue searching not only for new evidence but also new ways of analyzing that evidence could offer him the chance to continue enhancing his understanding of the past.

There are of course problems with Herlihy's work. His two biographic sketches of other scholars—of Yves Renouard and Raymond de Roover—show that Herlihy was as well aware as any member of our profession that no scholarly work can be perfect, that a fatal flaw inevitably accompanies and in the end undermines even the most accomplished and technically refined reconstruction of the past. That surely is the case with his writing, even if I do not quite share the views of those who claim that his most striking flaw was his lack of interest in the theoretical dimensions of scholarly discussions. To the contrary, theories of all sorts permeated and defined his reflection from beginning to end. Rather, in my estimation, the problem lies elsewhere, and, interestingly, it is a problem evident from his book on Pisa (1958) to the essay on Florentine office holders (1991). It is this: It does not appear to me that very often Herlihy had thought through with sufficient rigor the links between his vast data bases and the ambitious questions which he posed of them. There is a kind of looseness, a surprising sort of fuzziness in some of his work, especially in some of the answers which he provided. One example will have to suffice here: Does the demographic structure of the Florentine population—which he and Klapisch described with clinical precision—really prove the psychological links of dependence of Florentine young men on their mothers? These ties of dependence may well have existed—here, it was Herlihy's piercing intelligence which enabled him to develop that insight—but it does not appear to me that the insight itself rests on the bed of that empirical data which he had analyzed.

I am convinced that Herlihy himself was aware of this weakness. But he recognized that such a weakness was an integral part of his method, that to correct it he would have had to follow a different path, abandon his intense and sustained search for new questions and new methods. One would be justified in wondering what interior strength—of a spiritual and intellectual sort—allowed Herlihy to recognize with a frankly surprising openness the problems which he, before any one else, spotted in his own work. Alongside his "modernity" and the untiring quest for new questions and new methods of analysis, David Herlihy possessed an internal strength which allowed him to pursue his work in the conviction that, all its imperfections notwithstanding, it was his best and most honest effort. It was at once an expression of his pride in his craft—the historian's craft—which demanded of him much hard and skilled labor, but also of a profound and genuine *quiete dell' anima,* an inner strength and spiritual peace which I am tempted to call religious.

In his Presidential address to the Medieval Academy, having put forth a series of hypotheses about the significance of women's entry into the field of medieval history, he paused to muse: "These then are the trends hidden within the Academy mailing list ... The computer detects their presence; it is an accurate observer. It remains for us to judge how well its conclusions correspond with our own memories and perceptions of what was happening." Even more poignantly, in his *Medieval Households,* published in 1985, in which he presents a breath-taking overview of European history from antiquity to the late Middle Ages, aware, no doubt, of the fragility of some of his conclusions, he addressed his reader: "At a minimum, he or she should acquire a broad view of the evidence available (and lacking) for the study of the medieval household. May many readers be inspired (or provoked) to enlarge substantially, or interpret more persuasively, the data laid out in these pages." And he closed with a quotation from Horace: "If you know something more accurate than the things written here, then openly share it; if not, use these with me." This was Herlihy's hallmark, as a scholar and as a man. He openly shared with us the fruits of his impassioned and intelligent studies of the past. That sharing has made us more sensitive students of history, by bringing to our attention dimensions of the past experience which, it would be fair to say, few other historians could have imagined. It also gave us at once an unusually high and a profoundly humane standard by which to measure our own and our colleagues's scholarly accomplishments.

In bringing this volume of essays to the attention of the scholarly community, I cannot help but recollect once more my deep friendship and admiration for David Herlihy. Our first encounter went back to 1967, in one of the annual meetings of the American Historical Association. In the following years, the two of us often met, most often in Florence, to talk of work, while a deep friendship grew between our two families. These meetings became more frequent, the discussions more intense, and the friendship more profound following the Herlihys transfer to Cambridge, Massachusetts, a short drive from Providence. It was in the course of these visits, that an initially improbable suggestion slowly came to maturity: Since our scholarly interests overlapped so clearly and we found each other's company so congenial, why shouldn't we try to become colleagues? To our astonishment, this seemingly fantastical proposal was realized during the course of the academic year 1985-86, when the members of the History Department and the senior administration of Brown University gave their enthusiastic endorsement to this plan. Logistical details were worked out relatively easily, although, for the historical record, one rather amusing incident should perhaps be recounted here. Because of legal difficulties encountered in the preceding years by Brown University, Herlihy's appointment as Professor of History at Brown, had to receive the approval of U.S. Federal Judge Raymond Pettine, who, over a period perhaps of more than a decade, oversaw all new senior appointments and promotions made by the University. As a result of this awkward situation, on a spring morning in 1986, accompanied by a bevy of the University's lawyers, I appeared in Judge Pettine's court, was duly sworn in, and was asked to testify, before this distinguished jurist of Italian parentage, on David Herlihy's scholarly qualifications. The issue was quickly resolved when it became apparent that an Irish-American had devoted his scholarly life to the study of Italian history, and that he was considered by his peers among the very greatest historians of his generation. With an understanding smile the good judge dismissed me, and soon thereafter approved Herlihy's appointment. And so, starting in late summer 1986, the Herlihys, in addition to being close friends, became colleagues and neighbors, living as they did directly across the street from my family's home.

For all the brevity of David Herlihy's tenure at Brown, his influence on his colleagues and students was profound. The combination of his kindness and *auctoritas* made him a wonderful colleague, whose judgment was often solicited by the rest of us. The publication of this volume of essays is a testament to David Herlihy's scholarly vitality, imagination, and originality. It is also an expression of the deep affection his colleagues and students nurtured for that wonderful man.

Anthony Molho
Keene Street, Providence
May 1994

Editorial Note

In preparing this collection of essays for publication, the format of the notes was standardized. But I made no effort to check their contents. In one instance (ch. 4, n. 19), David Herlihy had not provided a reference for a passage cited in the text. Regrettably, I was unable to locate this reference.

PART I

MY LIFE IN THE PROFESSION

─────── ✦ ✦ ✦ ───────

I would first of all like to express my gratitude to Professor Bolelli, to the Galileo Galilei Prize Foundation, and to the Italian Rotary Clubs for the great honour shown me today.

I have been asked to reflect very briefly on the reasons why I chose to study the economic and social history of Italy in the Middle Ages. Today, looking back over more than thirty-five years of research, I can easily give answers. It is less easy to explain why, as a young student, I entered upon the path that I have followed.

There are four reasons why today I do what I do: the dazzling wealth of Italy's historic tradition; the importance of the Middle Ages within that tradition; the special interest of economic and social history; and the extraordinary documentary wealth of the Italian archives.

It is hardly necessary for me to emphasise, before this audience, the wealth of the Italian historical experience. This is the capital country for two institutions that have powerfully shaped Western civilization: the ancient Roman empire and the Latin Christian Church. The art of the Italian Renaissance redirected and reeducated the aesthetic tastes of Europe. Its thought and philosophy of the same period taught all Europeans to look at themselves, their societies and their social institutions in novel ways. This list of achievements could easily and endlessly be enlarged.

I have often wondered how it was that this peninsula came to play so large a role in European cultural history. Here are a few, unformed thoughts.

Italy was and is a land poorly endowed by nature. But that poverty may also have given a psychological stimulus to its peoples. To compensate for material deprivation, these peoples were perhaps led to cultivate their spiritual endowment, their intellectual and artistic culture. In the biographies of many great persons, it has often been noticed that seeming disadvantages of birth, wealth or relationships often over the course of long careers prove to be advantages. So it may also be with nations.

The cultivation of a rich intellectual culture may also have equipped the Italians to make good use of what is, undoubtedly, their one great natural resource: Italy's location on the globe. Set in the middle of the Mediterranean Sea, the peninsula enjoys relatively easy contact with the three continents of Europe, Africa and Asia. In history it has served as a bridge connecting the regions to its west and north with those to its south and east. This location formed the physical basis for the extension of the ancient Roman empire, and equally for the commercial empire of Italy's medieval merchants. Goods as well as ideas flowed into and across this land. Economically, Italians have traditionally taken in raw materials from abroad and by virtue of their skilled labour have turned them into finished products, which they in turn export abroad. Trade and high human skill thus compensate for a poor natural endowment. But where goods move easily, ideas do too. Italy has often served as the cultural intermediary in the flow of ideas. We need only think of Greek philosophy or Christianity itself in the ancient world. Both these cultural traditions reached the rest of Europe mediated through Italy. In the late fifteenth century, Italy similarly received and transmitted Greek scholars and Greek texts emanating from Byzantium. Italy, it seems, has fared best at times of open frontiers and of free movement of goods and ideas—in the ancient world, in the Middle Ages and Renaissance, and today. For this reason too, it has served as a cultural bridge of another sort: a bridge into the past. For those who wish to know the origins of Western civilization, Italian history also offers a wide highway back through the centuries into the great formative periods—classical antiquity, the Middle Ages, and the Renaissance.

In Italy's long history, the Middle Ages constitute a major segment. In America, the Italian Middle Ages have traditionally attracted far less interest than the ancient empire or the Renaissance. The study of Western civilization in America traditionally progresses in the following order: first ancient Rome is considered, then the barbarian invasions, the Carolingian empire, then the German empire. Medieval Italy and indeed all the European south are conspicuously absent from this sequence. Italy reclaims the attention of students only in the Renaissance period. And the Renaissance itself has been traditionally presented in America almost exclusively as an artistic and intellectual movement.

In my own education, I learned almost nothing about the Italian Middle Ages. They were for me as for most Americans of my generation a *terra incognita.* But for that reason they have held for me a special interest. All scholars hope to discern something new, and the chances of doing so are enhanced when the territory has been only lightly traversed.

Economic and social history appeals for a similar reason. Until the present generation, historians largely dealt with great events and the great persons who participated in them. They largely ignored the uneventful lives of ordinary people. They ignored too the processes by which those men and women earned their bread, married, made their homes, and reared their children, and prepared for death. But a major change in the orientation of the historical disciplines has now occurred and is visible in all epochs and areas of history. Many historians now investigate exactly the processes of ordinary life. They do not ignore the great and the powerful, but they seek to see them too within a context of the total society. By studying the *popolo minuto* as well as the *popolo grasso* and the *magnati,* they hope to achieve a picture of the human past that is both more balanced and more humane.

The records of medieval Italy are especially suited for an investigation of ordinary people doing ordinary things. From the seventh century there have survived in huge numbers private acts. Most are contracts of various sorts. Most of these record land transactions—sales, leases, exchanges and the like. But many also mark events in the cycle of personal lives—marriages, emancipations, wills and inventories. From the twelfth century in ever greater numbers commercial records appear. We are given the first full view of what is now called the commercial revolution of the Middle Ages. There are surveys as well as serial records. From the middle thirteenth century, the governments of Italian city states took surveys of their populations in ever greater detail. In this age, when the common people of the past have a particular attraction for historians, the common people of medieval Italy enjoy visibility that is probably unique in Europe.

These reasons for the study of Italy's economy and society in the Middle Ages are apparent to me now. But I was not at all aware of them thirty-five years ago. I came to do what I do largely by luck, but also under the influence of several memorable teachers. I was born in San Francisco in the state of California. I was slow to appreciate that the city of my birth was named for a medieval saint. Not having seen Italy, I did not recognise how much the Californian landscape, with its Mediterranean climate, resembles that of Italy. Even the place names of California, though given by the Spanish, echo those of Italy. These things I realised only when I first visited Italy in 1954. But the recognition made gave my first visit here the value and the satisfactions of a return to home.

I was educated in San Francisco in Jesuit schools, through to the reception in 1951 of my first university degree, called in America the baccalaureate of arts. The curriculum that Jesuit schools then followed was very traditional; it was virtually the same *ratio studiorum* which the Order, founded in the Renaissance, had first devised out of Renaissance values. It stressed the ancient classics in Latin and in Greek. I carried from that training a good technical knowledge of those ancient languages and also a deep appreciation of ancient and Mediterranean culture.

In entering upon graduate studies, I decided to leave my native city in order to study on the eastern seaboard of America, which is still the cultural heart of the country. I first intended to study Byzantine history, and for this purpose I entered the Catholic University of America in Washington, D. C. Although I admired ancient Hellas, medieval Hellas, or Byzantium, seemed to me a neglected field, and I was eager to explore what I took to be untrod realms. I spent one year in Byzantine studies, and received what in America is called a master's degree. Although I am not now a Byzantinist, I found this visit to the east a broadening experience.

I was, however, warned that university posts were few in Byzantine history, and that I should look to a different field, if I hoped to find employment. Reluctant to abandon the Middle Ages, I decided to study the history of that successor state to medieval Byzantium, Russia. For this purpose I enrolled at Yale University.

There, I quickly discovered that the surviving sources of medieval Russian history are very few, and also very difficult. Ideally, the proficient student should know not only Greek and Russian, but Old Church Slavonic, Arabic and Turkish. Moreover, archeology, even more than philology, seemed the subject's real frontier, and archeology was then precluded for Americans.

In 1952 I met at Yale a professor from Italy, Roberto S. Lopez. Lopez, as many of you doubtlessly know, had left Italy in 1939 when fascist racial policies threatened his career. After receiving an American degree, which as an established scholar he hardly needed, he found employment in the United States and was eventually invited to join the faculty at Yale University, where he would spend the remainder of his long and productive life. He brought with him to America and to Yale the then new interest in the medieval economy, particularly in its commerce and its towns. He also brought an infectious enthusiasm for what he was doing. While I, still a student of medieval Russia, was lamenting the paucity of Russian materials, he was lamenting in his own seminar the insurmountable volumes of medieval Italian records. Scholars had barely penetrated their mass, particularly those relevant to economic history. Not only the force of what he said, but even more the enthusiasm he radiated for the field, finally persuaded me to change my principal field of concentration to the economic history of medieval Italy.

On Lopez' advice, I came to Pisa in 1954 to study its notarial chartularies which he had first explored. I and my wife Patricia, and son Maurice, who celebrated his first birthday here, spent one year in Pisa. We were the only Americans in the city and were known as "gli Americani." The experience confirmed us all that Italy was a land to be treasured for its present as well as its past.

The research done at Pisa was the basis for my doctoral dissertation, and I received the doctoral degree, in America known as the Ph.D., from Yale University in 1956. The dissertation was later published in English and Italian. My experience in Italy had not only convinced me of the wealth of medieval documentation but also of the need to develop efficient methods of interpreting their content. It ought to be possible to show certain changes over time in the large runs of private acts out of the central Middle Ages. Were payments made in coined money or in money substitutes? Were rents set in money, in kind or in labour? Were the lands sold or traded isolated fields or complete farms? Were the principals in the contracts male or female? Did they identify themselves by means of a patronymic or a matronymic? Were landowners mentioned in the acts men, women or ecclesiastics? By tabulating the answers to these and similar questions, one could illuminate, I believe, long-term trends over time. One could objectively establish trends. These illuminated trends would lay the basis for surer inferences concerning changes in the economy.

I began this work simply by tabulating by pencil in a documentary series the number of payments in money as opposed to those not in money, and so forth. By the 1960s, two changes lent me encouragement in this work. The first was the growing application of quantitative methods to historical materials. While the methods I was using could only suggest trends and not establish outputs, nonetheless the new methods were showing that a greater variety of documentation was susceptible to statistical analysis than was formerly believed. The second novelty of the 1960s was the advent of the computer. It promised relief in the supremely boring tasks of tabulation. It was still necessary to convert the documentation into machine-readable form, but once that was accomplished, the computer allowed the data to be viewed in almost unlimited ways. The joining of the computer and the propensity of the medieval Italians to generate documents was a marriage made in heaven.

A culmination in this use of statistics in the analysis of medieval records was a project undertaken in 1966, to study with the aid of a computer the great Florentine Catasto of 1427–1428. The document was well known to historians, but its very size was an obstacle to its efficient study. It surveyed 60,000 households and 260,000 persons across nearly the entirety of the Tuscan lands ruled by Florence. I first encountered it myself while working on a study of Pistoia in the Middle Ages and Renaissance. I remember how amazed I was to find recorded in its pages not only the names of the Pistoiesi but also their ages, relationships within their households, and belongings. When I finished my study of Pistoia, I decided to undertake an analysis of the entire survey. But this would obviously require money and support. Through a chance meeting in 1966, Fernand Braudel, then president of the VIᵉ Section of the Ecole Pratique des

Hautes Etudes, proposed a Franco-American joint enterprise. I was spending with my family the year in Florence, and all of us were driven from our home by the Arno flood of November 1966. My wife was expecting a baby, who when born in February would turn out to be our first daughter and the last of our six children. She was named Irene Fiorenza, in honour of the city of her birth.

The catastrophe of flood and the expectation of a baby halted scholarly work of any sort for several months. But in early 1967, I reached an agreement with the French to study the Catasto by computer. Christiane Klapisch-Zuber became director of the French part of the enterprise. The major task was the conversion of the Catasto into machine-readable form. The work of accomplishing this and of interpreting the results took ten years. We published the results in French in 1978, in English in 1985 and in Italian in 1988.

One curious result of this enterprise deserves mention. The information on people and wealth which the Florentines of the Quattrocento collected was so vast that no contemporary, to our knowledge, was able to add up the final totals. A final summation of the number of Tuscans and the worth of their holdings required the aid of a modern computer. This fact alone—that the computer was able to calculate the totals of a medieval survey when contemporaries could not—offers convincing proof that the machine has a role to play even in medieval history. And I hope that our analysis also shows that quantification too has much to offer in medieval research.

In closing, let me publicly state my profound thanks to those who directed me especially in the early stages of my career. I owe a particular debt to the late Roberto Lopez. I treasure the technical training he gave me, his astute guidance, and especially the enthusiasm and love for his work which became, in a real sense, my work also. I try to pass on these qualities to my own students. I would count myself fortunate, if I succeed half as well as he.

PART II

1

WOMEN AND THE SOURCES
OF MEDIEVAL HISTORY

The Towns of Northern Italy

✦ ✦ ✦

In the history and civilization of northern Italy in the Middle Ages, towns hold a special prominence. Even the violence and tumult of the early medieval centuries only weakened and did not erase a significant urban presence. The economic revival from about 1050 carried with it a full rebirth of urban life. From the late thirteenth century to the end of the Middle Ages, towns included within their walls probably one in five or one in four northern Italians.[1] Throughout the central and late Middle Ages, towns dominated the political and cultural life of the Italian north, and their residents produced a prodigious amount of records and documents, many of which have survived. For the historian of women in the Middle Ages, these historical sources hold a special interest. What do the sources of these vigorous communities reveal about women?[2]

The great strength of the Italian medieval documentation associated with cities is its sheer volume.[3] Several factors made urban

1. In the regions of Lombardy and Tuscany, persons living in the ten largest cities constituted between 19.1 percent of the entire population in Milanese territory, 23.4 percent in the Veneto, and 26 percent in Tuscany: see J.C. Russell, *Medieval Cities and Their Regions* (Bloomington, Ind., 1972), p. 235, table 32.
2. For a general introduction to the historiography of women in the Middle Ages, see S.M. Stuard, ed. *Women in Medieval History and Historiography* (Philadelphia, 1987), and especially the essay by D.O. Hughes, "Invisible Madonnas ...," pp. 25–50, with its bibliography on medieval Italian women on pp. 143–59.
3. For a guide to the collections of the Archivi di Stato, see *Guida generale degli*

dwellers prolific producers of records. The traditions of Roman law gave to the written instrument a special priority in determining what the law was and in proving facts in dispute. Perhaps the supreme expression of this respect for writing was the notarial act, the exact nature of which I shall presently consider. More than six hundred notaries were practicing at Florence in 1336–38.[4] In the late Middle Ages, notaries typically represented a large and often the largest profession in the Italian cities.

The urban milieu, in which roughly a quarter of the population lived, supported a highly literate culture. According to the manuals that guided him, the mark of a good merchant was "to write everything ... almost always to have pen in hand."[5] He should keep a record of "everything, every purchase, every sale, every remembrance and contract, every gain and loss, in the shop and outside the shop ... And this is necessary, since by failing to write it and entrusting it to the pen, things are forgotten and grow stale."[6] After all, he could never predict what items of information would later prove of value. So important were literacy and arithmetical ability in the urban economies that some towns maintained public schools, where the young could learn the vital skills. According to the Florentine chronicler Giovanni Villani, some 8,000 to 10,000 children, both boys and girls, were learning to read in the city grammar schools in 1336–38. Older boys learning the abacus in six schools

Archivi di Stato italiani, directed by P. d'Angiolini and C. Pavone; ed. P. Carucci, A. Bentoni-Litta, and V. Piccioli Sparvoli, 3 vols. to date (Rome, 1981–).

4. The number comes from G. Villani, *Cronica*, 8 vols., 6 (Florence, 1823–25), p. 185. In 1427 in Tuscany, notaries constituted the largest profession at Florence and ranked second after the shoemakers at Pisa. They ranked third at both Pistoia and Arezzo, fifth at Prato, and fourth at Volterra and Cortona. The larger the city, the more numerous notaries were likely to be. See D.Herlihy and C. Klapisch-Zuber, *Tuscans and Their Families: A Study of the Florentine Catasto of 1427* (New Haven, 1985), p. 128, table 4.7.

5. "Dimonstrava essere officio del mercatante e d'ogni mestiere, quale abbia a tramare con più persone, sempre scrivere ogni cosa ... quasi sempre avere la penna in mano." from L.B. Alberti, *I libri della famiglia*, in *Opere volgari*, ed. C. Grayson, 1, pp. 1–341. *Scrittori d'Italia*, no. 218 (Bari, 1960), p. 205.

6. "O'inteso più volte da' savi e antichi mercatanti ch' egli sta così bene al mercatante avere sempre le mani tinte d'inchiostro, perché dimostra essere officio di mercatante essere sollecito di scrivere ogni cosa, ogni compere, ogni vendite, ogni ricordo e contratto, ogni entrata et uscita, in bottega et fuori di botega sempre avere la penna in mano. Et questo è necessario, perché indugiando lo scrivere et fare credenza alla penna, le cose si dimenticano et invecchiano" from G. Rucellai, *Zibaldone*, Vol. 1, *Il zibaldone quaresimale: Pagine scelte*, ed. A. Perosa, *Studies of the Warburg Institute*, no. 24 (London, 1960), pp. 6–7.

numbered 1,000 to 1,100 (girls did not continue formal education beyond grammar school). Some 550 to 600 other boys were studying Latin and logic in four schools in preparation for the university.[7] The community nurtured a large pool of educated persons, from which the urban governments drew scribes and clerks, to staff their big bureaucracies. The active merchants and the busy officials in turn generated massive documentation.

But in spite of their abundance, the records of these urban communities scrutinize women much less thoroughly than they do men. There are several reasons for this. The legal traditions imposed on women numerous disabilities that made it difficult for them to act independently of male tutelage.[8] The Lombard law, which prevailed in most of the north, placed the woman under a permanent wardship, called the *mundium*. Initially under the authority of her father, she passed at marriage into the *mundium* of her husband. The woman without a living father or husband remained in the wardship of the king. No other code of Germanic law was as restrictive on women as the Lombard. But even Roman law required that a woman live under the *tutela* of a male, although this was in practice often fictional and there were legal ways by which she could become a person *sui iuris*. Still, the common practice of the cities required that any woman entering into contract must obtain the express approval of a male relative. This limited women's initiative, and they do not appear as independent actors as often as their numbers would lead us to expect.

A second institutional obstruction to the visibility of women in Italian medieval documentation was the republican form of government under which the free communes principally lived. In areas of Europe, principally in the north, where a hereditary nobility dominated politically and socially, women often gained offices and influence through the play of inheritance or through service as regents for minor sons or absent husbands. These routes to preferment were closed to female residents in the republican communes, for only males served in communal offices. Even the public ceremonies associated with the city governments were closed to women. Not until late in the Middle Ages, with the emergence in Italy of princely

7. Villani, *Cronica*, 6, p. 184.

8. M. Bellomo, *La condizione giuridica della donna in Italia* (Turin, 1970), offers a survey of the juridic position of women in medieval Italy.

lines and a flourishing court life, did women acquire the social visibility and influence they had long held within the northern nobility.

Still another institution that obstructed women's active participation in public affairs, and therefore their appearance in medieval sources, was the guild. In many cities guilds were central to the economic and even the political systems. The guild almost everywhere limited the participation of women in the trade it represented; usually, if grudgingly allowed only the widows and daughters of masters to practice the art. And women were altogether excluded from guild offices. As a result, it is difficult to judge the exact economic role of women under the free communes.[9]

Finally, Italy and other Mediterranean lands nurtured a strong cultural prejudice against feminine participation in all forms of public life. About 1420, Christine de Pisan, a native of Italy though living in France, asked the allegorical figure Reason why women did not appear in courts as lawyers or advocates. Reason explained that women could not exercise force or coercion and that public roles would at all events give them a "brazen appearance."[10] In Italy, virtuous girls past the age of puberty were expected to limit their contacts with the world beyond the household. When Catherine of Siena reached the age of twelve, she was kept at home "according to the local custom, for at Siena it is exceptional that single girls of that age are allowed to leave their homes."[11] But even married women were repeatedly admonished against unnecessary contacts with persons outside their immediate families. Women did not move easily through Italian urban societies.

In sum, men and women in the medieval towns operated within widely separate social spheres. Men held a near monopoly over public affairs, and the formal acts of governments—the promulgating of laws and statutes, the imposing of taxes, the making of peace and war—were almost always the work of males.

9. For example, the matriculation lists of the Florentine guild of Por Santa Maria, preserved in the *Manoscritti* deposit of the Archivio di Stato, record hundreds of matriculants from the early thirteenth century on. I have found not a single woman. The guild included the silk trades, in which women held a special importance. But they were not allowed representation in this organization of workers—or of masters.
10. Christine de Pisan, *Book of the City of Ladies*, trans. E. J. Richards (New York, 1982), p. 30. Christine died in about 1431.
11. *Acta sanctorum quotquot toto orbe coluntur*, (Paris, 1863–) *III Aprilis*, p. 863. Hereafter this work will be cited as *ASS*.

Women, on the other hand, presided over the activities that were carried on within or were centered upon the household. To be sure, even in domestic affairs males decided how resources should be allocated and made the important decisions that affected the family fortunes and the marriages and careers of offspring, but women still directed the household in all its quotidian activities. They supervised the early education of the young, of boys as well as girls. They set the tone of domestic culture, and they took leading roles in the rituals of the home and in the practice of charity and private devotions. Although these activities were rooted in the home, they sometimes opened for women access to a wider world. This is especially noticeable in regard to religious practices. In medieval urban Italy, there were few women statesmen but many women saints.

The levels of visibility that women attained in medieval sources therefore differed radically according to the type of record and the person or institution that produced it. The typology I use in the following survey of Italian medieval documentation is as follows: prescriptive literature; administrative records; account books, memoirs, and correspondence; narrative accounts (chronicles and biographies); and imaginative literature. The sources may further be classified according to the entities that produced them: the church, to which we owe the oldest documents; governments; and private individuals. Finally, some of the categories admit a further division into literary or statistical documents, depending on whether the information they contain is principally verbal or numerical.

Prescriptive literature either commanded or counseled people how to behave. The church, of course, was the chief source of moral exhortation, but large numbers of persons, authorized or unauthorized spoke in the name of religion. Women were often targeted. They may have been only half citizens in a political sense, but they were fully and completely moral persons, the agents or objects of moral or immoral acts. They had souls to save and were involved in the salvation of others—family members, lovers, friends.

Much church legislation (chiefly expressed in conciliar enactments) and many works in moral theology refer to women in both the religious and the secular life. But the genre that contains perhaps the richest materials on women is the sermon.[12] The rise of the mendicant orders from the early thirteenth century lent a powerful stimulus to preaching, which the mendicants construed as a major part of their mission.[13] A series of great preachers—Giordano da Rivalto (or da Pisa), Iacopo Passavanti, Bernardino da Siena, Cherubino da Siena, Girolamo Savonarola, Bernardino da Feltre, and others—addressed big congregations in which women constituted a large, perhaps often the largest, part. Some sermons were addressed directly to women.[14] The preachers often dwell on the moral failings they regarded as common among women: vanity, immodesty, bickering and nagging, and sexual sins, such as contraception and abortion. And they sometimes congratulate women for the virtues in which, in their estimation, women were superior to men: modesty, compassion, charity, and piety itself.

Bernardine of Siena (1380–1444) was probably the most outspoken of all the great preachers. Before his time, preachers allegedly spoke in vague and abstract terms about the moral ills of the day.[15] Bernardine, in contrast, called a spade a spade, and his frank and clear messages attracted and enraptured huge crowds.[16] Once, he directed mothers to come to the church with their daughters alone so that he could talk to them frankly about sexual abuses in marriage. He addressed many social issues: the reluctance of men to marry; the confinement of unwilling girls into convents, as if they were "the scum and vomit of the world"; homosexuality and contraception; and the duties and

12. On medieval sermons in general, see E.C. Dargan, *A History of Preaching from the Apostolic Fathers to the Great Reformers, 70–1572* (New York, 1968), an informative if not especially profound survey. Recent works based on Italian sermons, though not particularly concerned with women, are D. Weinstein, *Savonarola and Florence: Prophecy and Patriotism in the Renaissance* (Princeton, 1970); and J. O'Malley, *Praise and Blame in Renaissance Rome* (Durham, N.C., 1979).

13. On the rise of the Franciscan order, see F. de Sessevalle, *Histoire générale de l'ordre de Saint François: Le Moyen Âge*, 2 vols. (Le Puy-en-Velay, 1937).

14. See, for example, Giordano da Pisa, *Quaresimale fiorentino, 1305–1306*, ed. C. Delcorno (Florence, 1974), pp. 255–59, 430–34. See also Cherubino da Siena, *Regola della vita matrimoniale*, ed. F. Ambrini and C. Negroni, *Scelta di Curiosità Letterarie Inedite o Rare dal Secolo XIII al XVII*, no. 228 (Bologna, 1888), for an especially frank treatment of sex in marriage.

15. On Bernardine's style, see C. Delcorno, "L'ars praedicandi' di Bernardino da Siena" in *Atti del Simposio Internazionale Cateriniano-Bernardiniano*, ed. D. Maffei and P. Nardi (Siena, 1982), pp. 419–49.

16. See Bernardino da Siena, *Opera omnia*, Patres Collegii S. Bonaventurae, 9 vols. (Florence, 1950–65); Bernardino da Siena, *Prediche volgari*, ed. L. Banchi, 3 vols. (Siena, 1880–88); and I. Origo, *The World of San Bernardino* (New York, 1962).

claims of various family members, including wives and mothers. Finally, he often made concrete and colorful references to daily life. He described the inept bachelor, who left his quarters in squalor, and the good wife, who maintained the cleanliness of her home and the physical and moral health of her family.[17]

Women were not supposed to preach in churches, but they could and did serve as sages and spiritual counselors. A French scholar, André Vauchez, speaks of the feminization of piety in late medieval Italy.[18] (We shall return to this when we consider hagiography.) In Italy late medieval women saints were not only numerous but also influential. None was more influential than Catherine of Siena (1349–80), who wrote devotional tracts, letters, and sermons or at least dictated them to her male secretaries, as she had never learned to read. In her letters to women, she warns them against an excessive commitment to their husbands, children, and families; they had their own souls to save. Catherine Vigri of Bologna (1413–63), a Poor Clare and a renowned mystic, wrote a book entitled *The Seven Spiritual Arms*.[19] Catherine Fieschi Adorno, known as Catherine of Genoa (1446–1510), who entered the religious life after the death of her husband, composed a vivid meditation on purgatory.[20] Concern for the suffering of others, in this life and after, was a mark of the period's feminized piety. These tracts from Italy are exceptional sources for investigating the cultural world of women in the late Middle Ages; no part of Europe offers richer materials. In religious matters, Italian urban women spoke with exceptional strength and clarity, perhaps because they were silenced in almost every other cultural sphere.

In contrast to the religious literature prescribing modes of behavior for women, the public legislation of the town govern-

17. See Bernardino da Siena, *Opera omnia*, 2, p. 83, for the reference to the girls deposited into convents, and pp. 306–18, Sermo 48, "De honestate coniugatorum," for the descriptions of domestic life.

18. A. Vauchez, *La Sainteté en Occident aux derniers siècles du moyen âge d'après les procès de canonisation et les documents hagiographiques* (Rome, 1981), pp. 243–49.

19. Her life may be found in *ASS, II Martii*, pp. 35–89, and in G. Sabadino delli Arienti, Giovanni, *Gynevera de le clare donne di Joanne Sabadino de li Arienti*, ed. C. Ricci and A. Bacchi della Lega, *Scelta di Curiosità Letterarie e Rare*, no. 223 (Bologna, 1888), pp. 204–45. For the most recent edition of her Seven Spiritual Arms, see Catherine of Bologna, *Le sette armi spirituali*. [incomp. cit.]

20. See Catherine of Genoa, *Purgation and Purgatory: The Spiritual Dialogue of Catherine of Genoa*, trans. S. Hughes (New York, 1979).

ments is singularly poor in what it tells us about women. This is true in spite of its volume. Every free town had its statutes, many of which have survived and have been published, sometimes in repeated revisions. The enactments of the urban governments, usually called *provvisioni*, are still lengthier. The governments legislated on many matters affecting women—ages of marriage, amounts of the dowry, crimes of abduction and rape, and prositution.[21] But they tell more of the legal constraints on behavior than of behavior itself. As a great historian of the Italian family, Nino Tamassia, wrote, they illuminate very well the *mala vita* of the conjugal couple but say little of its good life, the contentment with which probably most husbands and wives passed their days.[22]

One kind of legislation did have a special relevance to women. These were the sumptuary laws, which were multiplied over Europe from about 1300. The laws were directed against the supposed waste embodied in lavish social events (weddings and funerals) and expensive attire—for men but primarily for women. Authors of *novelle* poked fun at these laws and congratulated the adroitness of women in evading them.[23] The issue was not exclusively one of extravagance and waste. Ostentation in dress was one means by which some women, otherwise muted, could make public statements. What those statements were is now a fascinating topic of research and discussion.[24]

Much more yielding than the public laws in information about women are private tracts on good manners and the management of the household. From the early fourteenth century there have survived *Avertimenti di Maritaggio*, instructions or rules supposedly given by mothers to their newly married daughters, on how to

21. Bellomo, *La condizione giuridica*, includes much material from statutes bearing upon marriage and the dowry. For an old but still valuable bibliography of northern Italian statutes (including unpublished statutes), see L. Fontana, ed., *Bibliografia degli statuti dei comuni dell' Italia superiore*, 3 vols. (Milan, 1907).
22. "I coniugi che vissero dolcemente insieme nulla hanno lasciato alla storia e agli storici" N. Tamassia, "La famiglia italiana nei secoli decimoquinto e decimosesto," *L'Indagine moderna*, no. 15 (Milan, 1911), p. 196.
23. "Come le donne fiorentine, senza studiare o apparare leggi, hanno vinto e confuso alcun dottor di legge," F. Sacchetti, *Il libro delle trecentonovelle*, ed. E. Li Gotti, (Milan, 1946) no. 136, p. 338.
24. See, for example, D.O. Hughes, "Sumptuary Law and Social Relations in Renaissance Italy," in *Disputes and Settlements: Law and Human Relations in the West*, ed. J. Bossy (Cambridge,1983), pp. 69–99.

become good wives.[25] Francesco da Barberino, who died in the plague of 1348, wrote a long poem "The Deportment and Customs of the Woman," in which he gave advice on all stages of the woman's life.[26] Similar works of admonition and instruction proliferate after the Black Death. The revival of classical studies in the humanist movement greatly enriched the fund of materials that could be exploited for the purposes of moral exhortation. Among the humanist tracts extolling marriage is *De re uxoria*, written in 1415–16 by the Venetian humanist Francesco Barbaro in celebration of a Florentine marriage. Less erudite tracts on household management remained popular, and women figure prominently, if sometimes passively, within them. In the first decade of the fifteenth century, the Florentine Dominican friar, Giovanni Dominici, wrote the *Rule of Government and the Care of the Family* specifically for a woman.[27] She was Bartolomea Alberti, who was rearing her four children alone during the exile of her husband. In part a devotional tract, the book gives many detailed instructions on the training of children. Probably the best known of these tracts on household management is Leon Battista Alberti's *Four Books on the Family*.[28] About one-half of the work is devoted to the choice of a wife and the running of the household. The essay shows an extreme condescension toward the wife, but this is an accurate reflection of the prejudices that the young commonly encountered and had to overcome.

Prescriptive literature primarily preserves the commands or recommendations of a legislator or counselor; in contrast, administrative records, often referred to as "documents of practice," record better than do the laws and counsels what actually was happening. These administrative documents may further be classified into surveys (inquests or censuses) that describe a situation at a given moment in time and serial records distributed over time (minutes of meetings, lists of court decisions, or lists of payments of rents or taxes). The information recorded may be primarily verbal, as in

25. See I. Del Lungo, *La donna fiorentina del buon tempo antico*, 2nd ed. (Florence, 1926), pp. 93, 105–9, for an example of this popular genre.

26. Francesco da Barberino, *Del reggimento e costume di donne*, ed. G.E. Sansone, Collezione de "Filologia Romanza," no. 2 (Turin, 1967).

27. G. Dominici, *Regola del governo di cura familiare*, ed. D. Salvi (Florence, 1860).

28. Alberti, *I libri della famiglia*.

inquests or court decisions, or numerical, as in censuses or counts of deaths or baptisms.

Church archives yield the oldest deposits of administrative records of special interest, though often concerned with rural monasteries and churches, are deposits of charters or collections of transcribed charters known as cartularies. The oldest charters date from about 750, and even before 1200 they are numbered in the tens of thousands. Italy, moreover is distinguished by the wealth of its episcopal, which is to say urban, archives. The see of Lucca, for example, possesses the oldest and richest run of such charters antedating 1200 in all of Italy and probably all of Europe.[29] Those dating after the year 1000 are still not completely published. Deposits of charters have survived from many other urban institutions—cathedral chapters, collegiate churches, monastic orders, and, from the thirteenth century, mendicant houses. Some of the religious communities were female, though these were again few in relative numbers.

The charters typically record conveyances of land—donations, sales exchanges, and leases. They often involve either urban property or urban residents. Copies of wills giving land to churches appear occasionally, as do marriage and dotal agreements that helped establish title to lands subsequently acquired by churches. In showing how the laws were followed (or ignored) in practice and in clarifying inheritance rules and marital conveyances, the charters cast invaluable light on the legal and social status of women. They also illuminate changes in kin organization. In about the year 1000, an association of heirs, holding property in common and known as the *consorteria*, appeared in Italy; historians track its appearance and development principally through the funds of charters. Still another novel form of kindred is the agnatic lineage, or patrilineage; it made its appearance at a slightly later date, the eleventh and twelfth centuries. Again, the charters provide the most detailed picture of its formation and functioning, and both new forms of kindred organization had profound repercussions on the status of women.

This voluminous charter material illuminates the experiences of women in other ways as well. It is possible to assess how often

---

29. See "Raccolta di documenti per servire alla storia ecclesiastica di Lucca," ed. D. Barsocchini, in *Memorie e documenti per servire all' istoria del Ducato di Lucca*, vol. 5, pts. 1–3, 1837–44, repr. (Lucca, 1970).

women appear as principals in land transactions. The charters also identify pieces of land by naming the contiguous owners, and this offers another way of investigating the relationships of women with property. In identifying the principals in a contract the scribe usually uses a patronymic, but he sometimes uses a matronymic: "Peter, son of Mathilda," for example, instead of "Peter, son of Bernard." The use of matronymics, which again can be measured over time, offers an indirect but still useful index to the social visibility of women.[30] Until the surge of lay documentation from the middle thirteenth century ecclesiastical charters and surveys are our principal sources for both legal and social history, including the history of women.

As government and private records grow in volume from about the middle thirteenth century, the ecclesiastical charters lose importance, but other types of serial records associated with the church retain interest. Since ancient times, churches and monastic houses had kept necrologies—lists of deceased members or benefactors for whom prayers were offered upon the anniversaries of their deaths.[31] Appearing later are baptismal registrations: registrations at Siena survive from 1381, at Pescia from the end of the fourteenth century, at Florence from 1450, and at Pistoia from 1471.[32]

In addition to the administrative records produced by the church are those produced by the town governments. Among the most illuminating records generated by town governments are fiscal surveys, variously called *libbre*, *estimi*, or *catasti*. The towns of San Gimignano and Prato in Tuscany, for example, possess surveys for both city and countryside from the late thirteenth century.[33] Over the course of the fourteenth century, these surveys became even more detailed. An *estimo* of the population of Bologna, dated 1395,

30. See D. Herlihy, "Land, Family, and Women in Continental Europe, 701–1200," *Traditio*, 18 (1962), pp. 92–101.

31. See, for example, "Nomi di uomini e di donne seppelliti in S. Maria Novella, tratti da un Libro di cartapecora esistente nelle mani de' Fratri di detta chiesa," in *Delizie degli eruditi toscani*, ed. Ildefonso di San Luigi, 9, (Florence, 1777), pp. 123–203, the great necrology of laypersons, including many women, buried in the Dominican convent of Santa Maria Novella.

32. See D. Herlihy and C. Klapisch-Zuber, *Les Toscans et leurs familles* (Paris, 1978), p. 351, n. 4.

33. See E. Fiumi, *Demografia, movimento urbanistico e classi sociali in Prato dall'età comunale ai tempi moderni*, (Florence, 1968); and E. Fiumi, *Storia economica e sociale di San Gimignano* (Florence, 1961).

gives even the ages of the residents.[34] The city of Verona possesses eight surveys of its population between 1424 and 1502.[35]

The greatest of all these population surveys is beyond doubt the Florentine *catasto* of 1427–30. It describes nearly 60,000 households and gives the names and ages of 260,000 persons settled in both the Tuscan cities and the countryside.[36] It also describes the households' assets and liabilities. It is therefore possible to trace quite precisely the life cycle of Tuscan women (and men), establishing their ages of marriage and their changing status and fortunes as they aged. Though there are problems associated with these registrations and especially the registrations of women, this survey is unsurpassed in the information it supplies about the life cycles and the social and economic status of Tuscan women, including those of Florence. (A copy of the coded survey is available at nominal cost from the Data Program and Library Service at the University of Wisconsin, Madison.)

The fiscal needs of the communal governments also generated serial records, which primarily reflect the income and expenditures of various entities. One such serial record of particular interest for women's history is the *monte delle doti*, a special fund created in 1425 to aid Florentine families in accumulating dowries for their daughters. A father deposited a sum of money in the fund at the birth of a daughter (he could make the same provision for a son), and the sum would be returned to him with interest when the daughter married, entered the religious life, or died. Julius Kirshner and Anthony Molho are currently engaged in a systematic exploitation of the massive serial record associated with this fund.[37]

34. P. Montanari, *Documenti sulla popolazione di Bologna alla fine del Trecento*, Fonti per la storia di Bologna, no. 1 (Bologna, 1966).
35. D. Herlihy, "The Population of Verona in the First Century of Venetian Rule," in *Renaissance Venice*, ed. J. R. Hale, (London, 1973), pp. 91–120.
36. See D. Herlihy and C. Klapisch-Zuber, *Les Toscans*, and *Tuscans and Their Families*.
37. See J. Kirshner, "Pursuing Honor While Avoiding Sin: The *Monte delle Doti* of Florence," *Studi senesi*, 87 (1977), pp.175–256; J. Kirshner and A. Molho, "The Dowry Fund and the Marriage Market in Early Quattrocento Florence," *Journal of Modern History*, 50 (1978), pp. 404–38; J. Kirshner and A. Molho, "Il Monte delle doti a Firenze dalla sua fondazione nel 1425 alla metà del sedicesimo secolo," *Ricerche storiche*, 10 (1980), pp. 21–48; A. Morrison, J. Kirshner, and A. Molho. "Life-Cycle Events in Fifteenth-Century Florence: Records of the *Monte delle doti*," *American Journal of Epidemiology*, 106 (1977), pp. 487–92; A. Molho, "Investimenti nel Monte delle doti di Firenze: Un'analisi sociale e geografica," *Quaderni storici*, 61 (1986), pp. 147–60; A. Molho, "L'amministrazione del debito pubblico a Firenze nel quindicesimo secolo," in *I ceti dirigenti nella Toscana del Quattrocento* (Florence, 1987), pp. 191–207.

The courts of the communal government and its associated institutions, such as guilds, also preserved records both of criminal prosecution and of civil litigation of all kinds. The recorded testimony of witnesses provides one of the few occasions when women are directly quoted. (Gene Brucker's recent account of a Florentine marriage is based on the trial minutes of an ecclesiastical court, preserved in notarial cartulary.)[38]

The oldest administrative records generated out of and directly reflective of private life are notarial acts and the bundles of notarial acts known as cartularies. Between 1154, the date of the earliest surviving notarial acts, and around 1300, when other types of records begin to slowly replace them, they yield almost all that we know of citizens' transactions not directly involving church or government. The notarial act in Italy acquired, probably from the middle eleventh century, the special quality of public faith. This means that a document drawn up by a licensed public notary could prove in court the existence of a contractual obligation, even after the death or in the absence of the principals, witnesses, or the notary himself.[39] The notary received his commission from the universal heads of the Christian commonwealth, the emperor or pope, or from those (usually the communal governments) to whom they had delegated the authority. The act, in other words, was a valid means of proof accepted throughout Christendom. Given the solemn importance of the acts they witnessed and redacted, the notaries very early entered copies of the agreements into cartularies, and it is chiefly in cartularies that they have been preserved.

The great port city of Genoa possesses the oldest series of cartularies, which date from December 1154.[40] Many deal with commercial investments; these are the only quantitative sources in the whole of Europe that bear on business affairs before 1200. From the thirteenth century, particularly after 1250, cartulary deposits survive in numerous urban archives. They contain nearly every conceivable type of document: contracts for sales and exchanges of land or of

38. See G.A. Brucker, *Giovanni and Lusanna: Love and Marriage in Renaissance Florence* (Berkeley, 1986).

39. The standard introduction into the juridical character of the notarial instrument is H. Moresco and G. P. Bognetti, *Per l'edizione dei Notai liguri del sec. XII* (Genoa, 1938).

40. On the Genoese sources, see E. Bach, "La Cité de Gênes au XIIe siècle," *Classica et Mediaevalia*, no. 5 (Copenhagen, 1955), pp. 11–29.

animals, records of loans and business investments, letters and commissions, apprenticeship agreements, appointments of agents and procurators, marriage contracts, acts of emancipation, wills, and every other sort of binding agreement or contract. Their volume and variety tend to diminish after 1300 and particularly after 1350 (for reasons that I shall mention), but even in the late Middle Ages, Italians who wished to record a particularly solemn agreement went before a notary. Notaries also served both the ecclesiastical and the secular governments in recording, for example, the testimony of witnesses in litigation. Notarial acts, written in a formulaic Latin that only slowly gave way to Italian, rarely betray feeling or sentiment. Nonetheless, especially for the late thirteenth century, they are our principal window looking out upon the private life of the period and upon the role of women within it.

Notaries have a special and continuing importance in regard to marriage and dotal agreements. The parties anticipating marriage or their representatives appeared before a notary more commonly than before a priest. (Not until the Council of Trent were Catholics required to make their marital vows in the presence of a priest.) The notary was needed to record the *instrumentum sponsalitii*, or formal betrothal, and a *confessio dotis*, or dotal agreement. (The *ductio ad maritum*, or procession that took the bride to the groom's house, confirmed the marriage and led directly to its consumation.)

Women figure prominently in many kinds of notarial acts: contracts of apprenticeship or of household service, litigation of all sorts, betrothals and dotal agreements, and many last wills and testaments, both as testators and as beneficiaries. They were often litigants in trials and were just as often summoned as witnesses. The cartularies further illuminate women as property owners and business investors. To be sure, the factors mentioned above that limited the public role of Italian women reduced their visibility here as everywhere. But the researcher who sets out to explore the vast sea of the notarial archives can be sure that women will be encountered in impressive numbers.

From about 1300, the apparently rising levels of literacy within the urban populations made the services of the notary dispensable. Moreover, the literate citizens, apparently pressed by mounting volumes of transactions, seem to have found it troublesome and expensive to have continuous recourse to notaries. They therefore recorded more and more of their transactions and agreements in other forms. One of the most common means of registering transactions was the private account book. The governments obliged by accepting entries in the private account books as proof of the existence of an obligation or of its satisfaction.

Women were only rarely direct and active participants in economic exchanges and are only occasionally noticed in account books. They are much more visible in a kind of source closely related to account books: family memoirs, or *ricordi*. In recording moneys received and given, many heads of household also recorded other events affecting their families, such as marriages, births, and deaths. By their wealth of observations, some writers made of their *ricordi* true domestic chronicles or family histories.[41] Many also often included advice and counsel for their expected readers, their own descendants. The most revealing *ricordi* thus combine characteristics of a statistical record, narrative account, and prescriptive literature.

The authors were, to be sure, all of them male. But many were also diligent observers, and they describe in detail all aspects of family life, from the physical structure of houses to domestic rituals. They often describe the experiences of or comment upon their female relatives. The memoirs rarely directly record feminine voices, but they brilliantly illuminate the milieu in which women lived and the attitudes with which their fathers, brothers, husbands, and sons viewed them. Christiane Klapisch-Zuber's studies of Italian women of the Renaissance and the various symbols and rituals that marked their existence are based in large measure on the *ricordi*.[42]

Also from the early fourteenth century, high levels of literacy within the urban communities, characteristic of women as well as men, enabled the urban dwellers to communicate by writing letters. In particular, Italy's far-flung merchants often wrote letters to and received letters from their wives, mothers, or other female rel-

41. F. Pezzarossa, "La tradizione fiorentina della memorialistica," in *La "Memoria" dei mercatores: Tendenze ideologiche, ricordanze, artigianato in versi nella Firenze del Quattrocento,* ed. G.M. Anselmi, F. Pezzarossa, and L. Avellini (Bologna, 1980), pp. 39–149, discusses Florentine ricordi. Florence offers by far the richest numbers of these domestic accounts, many of them still unpublished.

42. See C. Klapisch-Zuber, *Women, Family, and Ritual in Renaissance Italy,* trans. L.G. Cochrane (Chicago, 1985).

atives. The Datini archives located at Prato, the largest of all the collections of private mercantile records, include from 1381 exchanges of letters between Francsco di Marco Datini, then at Pisa, and his wife, Margherita.[43] These letters are an exceptional source in recapturing the spirit of a medieval Italian marriage. Notable too are the letters written in the middle fifteenth century by a Florentine matron, Alessandra Macinghi-Strozzi, to her exiled sons;[44] these letters, remarkable for their content and also for their rarity, are unexcelled for the insight they offer into the social world and social values of a middle-class woman in quattrocento Florence. Letters survive from several noblewomen of the Renaissance, including Lucrezia Borgia, whose correspondence with Pietro Bembo constituted, in the opinion of its editor, "the prettiest love letters in the world."[45]

The same limited public functions that women fulfilled won them limited notice in the narrative accounts—the many chronicles and histories that tell the history of the free commune.[46] They are better represented in another narrative form—biographies. In 1111-15, a priest named Donizo composed a metrical biography of Matilda of Tuscany, patroness of Pope Gregory VII.[47] It is a rare example of a medieval biography dedicated to a woman who is not a saint. In the fourteenth and fifteenth centuries, the new humanist scholars favored the genre, as the lives of virtuous persons would presumably inspire emulation among their readers. Giovanni Boccaccio supplemented the available lives of famous men by publishing a collection of the lives of famous women.[48] The women he remembers are taken either from ancient literature or from folklore; he includes,

43. See the description of these letters in I. Origo, *The Merchant of Prato: Francesco di Marco Datini, 1335-1410* (1957), reprint (Boston, 1986), pp. 165–87.
44. A. Macinghi-Strozzi, *Lettere di una gentildonna fiorentina ai figliuoli esuli*, ed. C. Guasti (Florence, 1877).
45. This is the title the editor gave to her edition of their correspondence; see L. Borgia, *The Prettiest Love Letter in the World: Letters between Lucrezia Borgia and Pietro Bembo, 1503–1519*, trans. H. Shankland (Boston, 1987).
46. For recent comment on the chronicles of medieval Italy, see G. Zanella, ed., *Storici e storiografia del medioevo italiano: Antologia di saggi, Il Mondo Medievale*, no. 14 (Bologna, 1984) [a collection of reprinted essays].
47. Donizo presbyter, "Vita Mathildis," ed. L. Simeoni, *Rerum Italicarum Scriptores*, nuova edizione, vol. 5, pt. 2, pp. 3–106, 118–27 (Città di Castello, 1931–40).
48. G. Boccaccio, *Concerning Famous Women*, trans. G.A. Guarino (New Brunswick, N.J., 1963).

for example, the fabulous biography of a lady pontiff, Pope Joan. Vespasiano da Bisticci, a book dealer turned author and perhaps the most famous biographer of the Renaissance, included in his *Vite* the life of one woman, Alessandra de' Bardi.[49] In 1483 the Bolognese writer Giovanni Sabadino degli Arienti composed the biographies of thirty-three women, one of them still living. Most were queens and duchesses, but he also wrote about Joan of Arc and his recently deceased wife.

Even more numerous than these secular biographies are the lives of women saints. An incomplete list of women saints would include Umiliana dei Cerchi of Florence, Clare of Pisa, Angela of Foligno, and Margaret of Cortona.[50] Many of these women saints were ter- tiaries, that is, members of the "third orders" associated with the Dominicans or Franciscans. In other words, they spent all or most of their lives outside of a cloister, and they interacted intensively and frequently with the lay world. But as tertiaries, they also attracted male biographers, who often also served as their confes- sors. Margaret of Cortona (d. 1297) was married and widowed young. Her father and stepmother would not take her back into the paternal home; for a while she supported herself as a prostitute.[51] Angela of Foligno (l248–1309) dictated her life to a Franciscan friar named Arnaldo or Adamo, who recorded her accounts in the first-person singular as direct quotations. Her life, rich in realistic details about her extraordinary career and written with passion, is one of the richest surviving testimonies we have, one that is osten- sibly from the mouth of an urban woman of the Italian Middle Ages.[52] The biographer of Catherine of Siena, Raymond of Capua, was also her confessor and thus acquired an intimate knowledge of this extraordinary woman.[53]

For some women saints, such as Francesca Ponziani of Rome, the patron saint of the city, we possess not only contemporary lives but

49. See Vespasiano da Bisticci, *Renaissance Princes, Popes, and Prelates: The Ves- pasiano Memoirs. Lives of Illustrious Men of the Fifteenth Century,* trans. W. George and E. Waters (New York, 1963).

50. Bibliographies on all these women may be found in *Women in Medieval History.*

51. The life of Margaret of Cortona is in *ASS, III Februarii,* pp. 302–63.

52. The life of Angela of Foligno is in *ASS, I Januarii,* pp. 186–234.

53. An English translation is found in Raymond of Capua, *The Life of Saint Cather- ine of Siena,* trans. G. Lamb (New York, 1960).

the minutes of their canonization processes, in which those who knew these "friends of God" testify as to their characters.[54]

Many of these holy women had been married and had adopted a religious life only after the deaths of their husbands. Their biographies thus give vivid information about the training of little girls, courtship and marriage, the tasks of running a household, relations (including even, as with Francesca, sexual relations, which nauseated her), and, of course, religious culture. These lives are yet to be fully mined for what they reveal about urban women in the late Middle Ages.

In regard to the information it yields about women, the imaginative literature of late medieval urban Italy shows the same strengths and weaknesses found in the entire body of historical records. First in poetry and then in prose, literary output grew rapidly beginning in the late thirteenth century. On the one hand, in all the genres, depictions of women or allusions to them are plentiful, and they offer to the historian an inexhaustible mine of materials for social history. On the other hand, the number of women authors is exiguous, hardly more than a handful.[55] And the dominant interest of women authors was, as we have mentioned, religion.

Love is, of course, a constant theme in refined and learned poetry though the poet's mistress is usually an unreal figure, an icon, in a genre dominated by stilted conventions. Often more revealing are oblique allusions to women. Even the exalted poetry of Dante Alighieri contains realistic and colorful vignettes of women: of girls married at too young an age; of the merchant's wife who sleeps alone while her husband is in France; of the old grandmother relating to her grandchildren as she spins tales of Troy, Rome, and Fiesole.[56] The traditions of popular poetry contain carnival songs, supposedly sung by masques during the carnival time.[57] Some of the

54. For the Latin lives of Francesca Ponziani, see *ASS*, II Martii, pp. 89–178; see also P.T. Lugeno, ed., *Il processo inedito per Francesca Bussa dei Ponziani* (Santa Francesca Romana), 1440–1453 (Vatican City, 1945).

55. See the critical remarks, bibliography, and selections compiled in N. Costa-Zalessow, ed., *Scrittrici italiane dal XIII al XX secolo: Testi e critica* (Ravenna, 1982).

56. See Dante, *Paradiso, Le opere di Dante: Testo critico della Società dantesca italiana*, 2nd in (Florence, 1960) canto 16, lines 25ff; these vignettes are taken from the celebration by Dante's ancestor Cacciaguida of the virtues of old Florence and the failings of contemporaries.

57. See "Canti carnascialeschi del rinascimento," ed. C.S. Singleton, *Scrittori d'Italia*, no. 150 (Bari, 1936); and *Nuovi canti carnascialeschi del rinascimento*, ed. C.S. Singleton (Modena, 1940).

masques are women—nuns, the unhappily married, peddlers, and the like—and many more songs are addressed to women. They are, of course, burlesques, but they have the truth of many things said in jest. Even the learned Latin and Italian poetry of the humanists is rich in social references. The whole tradition of elegiac poetry, represented by such masters as Angelo Poliziano (1454-94), flourished in these centuries when ancient forms of expression were assiduously imitated. Many elegies remember women. Of the Latin poets, the Neapolitan Giovanni Pontano (1426–1505) deserves special notice.[58] In his *De amore conjugali*, he celebrates conjugal love at every stage, from betrothal to the wedding to the giving of a daughter in marriage. He also composed lullabies (*naenia*) and nursery songs. His poems are amongst the most elegant expression of family sentiments that the age has bequeathed.

In regard to prose, the period's many collections of short stories (*novelle*) have a special interest for social history. The *Decameron* of Giovanni Boccaccio is the recognized masterpiece of the genre. Although the plots of these often ribald tales hardly represent common occurrences, their settings, both social and material, are certainly realistic. Even the commonly encountered triad of beautiful young wife, aged and ineffective husband, and eager and unattached young man set on seducing her reflects the prevalent pattern of urban marriages. One of Boccaccio's tales, that of the patient Griselda, offers a model of feminine submissiveness that would be cited for centuries.[59] Boccaccio also presented in his *Il Corbaccio* one of the most vicious portraits of a woman extant in medieval literature.[60] It seems hardly necessary to review other genres, such as drama, for the common pattern holds everywhere: abundant survivals, rich and often realistic in circumstances, if not always in plots, but scarcely a handful written by women.

Perhaps we can summarize the reasons for the low visibility of women in medieval Italian urban documentation in the following fashion. Documents are born out of an effort to communicate.

58. Representative selections of his large output can be found in Pontano, *Carmina.* [incomp. cit.]

59. See the chapter entitled "The Griselda Complex" in Klapisch-Zuber, *Women, Family, and Ritual*, pp. 273ff.

60. For an English translation, see G. Boccaccio, *The Corbaccio*, trans. and ed., A.K. Cassell (Urbana, 1975).

Certain circumstances made it necessary or likely that communication be recorded in writing. The message conveyed might have been especially solemn or formal, such as a law or an administrative decree. It might have created a future obligation, as, for example, a notarized contract did. The originator of the message might have been seeking to reach someone at a distance; thus, a traveling merchant sent a letter to his agent in another city or to his wife at home. Or the author of the message thought that its contents ought to be preserved; they might later prove instructive, whether for the author or for a successor or a descendant. Now, in generating these solemn, seemingly important, and usually written communications, men were much more active than women. They were the legislators, administrators, merchants, and diarists. The archives therefore overflow with documents written by male hands, out of male interests. But historians must recognize that the written documents preserve only a small part of the communications that actually occurred. The messages, requests, and conversations that were carried on informally and at close range, as among members of the same household, depended almost exclusively upon the spoken word. And women were active and often the leading participants in the conversations of private life or in those reflective of private, mundane, but continuing interests, such as the day-to-day supervision of households, instruction of children, or religious life within the home. Unfortunately, however, their words are largely lost to historians. The written documents, focusing on other matters, serving other functions, catch those conversations only rarely and echo them only distantly.

But historians cannot assume that the surviving written records are an exact projection of reality. Women's low visibility in the documentation does not indicate their low importance in shaping the culture of the day. On the contrary, they seem to have dominated major areas of cultural life, most notably mystical and charismatic religion. The historians of medieval Italian urban women are not well served by the surviving written records, though neither are they totally denied. But they must learn to be alert, patient, sensitive listeners.

2

DID WOMEN HAVE A RENAISSANCE?

A Reconsideration

———— ✦ ✦ ✦ ————

Interest in the history of women now forces historians to reexamine the large epochs into which they have traditionally divided the past. Conventional divisions, such as medieval or modern, which have long seemed valid and valuable in the light of masculine doings, seem quite different when measured by the experiences of women.

Of all conventional periods, the one that has proved most vulnerable to feminist reassessment has been the Renaissance. In the old and familiar view, the Renaissance of the fifteenth and sixteenth centuries, beginning in Italy and then spreading to all Europe, transformed European culture through the revived appreciation of classical learning. Supposedly, too, it was an age of individualism. It liberated men, or some men, from the social and intellectual trammels of medieval society. It liberated men, but what did it do for women? In a seminal article published in 1977 and entitled "Did Women Have a Renaissance?" Joan Kelly-Gadol gave a forthright answer: this supposedly progressive period did nothing for women.[1] And most feminist historians have agreed with her. By many social

1. J. Kelly-Gadol, "Did Women Have a Renaissance?" in *Becoming Visible: Women in European History*, ed. R. Bridenthal and C. Koonz (Boston, 1977). The theme is expressed in several of the studies presented in *Women in Medieval Society*, ed. S.M. Stuard (Philadelphia, 1976). Kelly-Gadol and others were in part reacting against a famous section (Book five, Chapter six) in Jacob Burckhardt's classic work, *The Civilization of the Renaissance in Italy* (New York, 1929). In one of the weakest parts of this great book, Burckhardt quite unrealistically lauds the freedom and equality of the lady in Renaissance Italy.

indicators—access to property, power or knowledge—the position of women deteriorated across the long centuries of the Middle Ages. Women in fact fared better in barbarian Europe of the sixth or seventh centuries than they did in the cultured Europe of the fifteenth and sixteenth. In her recent study of early medieval women, Suzanne Wemple affirmed that as early as the Carolingian empire in the ninth century, "women of the aristocracy faced a decline in the number of social options open to them."[2] The Renaissance with all its overtones of progress and improvement is thus judged meaningless when applied to women and their history.

In this essay, I will reexamine this now widely shared assumption: that women lost status and visibility from the beginning to the end of the Middle Ages. To encapsulate the history of approximately one-half the members of an entire civilization, over more than a millennium of human history, is clearly a formidable task. To apply a fair test to the thesis, we need some sort of yardstick that will allow us to compare how women fared in the various periods of medieval history. There is one documentary genre that might permit such comparisons: the lives of women saints, whom these Christian centuries produced in abundant numbers.

WOMEN AND SANCTITY

Hagiographical records are, to be sure, notoriously difficult to use.[3] Few of the early hagiographers, fewer still of the earliest, had a personal knowledge of their holy subjects. Lacking direct observations, the authors had ready recourse to legend. When even legends could

2. S. Fonay Wemple, *Women in Frankish Society: Marriage and the Cloister, 500-900* (Philadelphia, 1981) p. 194.

3. For the early cult of saints and its relation to the veneration of heroes in pagan antiquity, see the stimulating essay by P. Brown, *The Cult of Saints: Its Rise and Function in Latin Christianity,* Haskell Lectures, n.s. 2 (Chicago, 1981). For introductions to the study of women and sainthood, see the collected essays *Women of Spirit: Female Leadership in the Jewish and Christian Traditions,* ed. R.R. Ruether and E. McLaughlin (New York, 1979); and *Religion and Sexism: Images of Woman in the Jewish and Christian Traditions,* ed. R.R. Ruether (New York, 1974). More specialized is O. Reber, *Die Gestaltung des Kultes weiblicher Heiliger im Spätmittelalter: Die Verehrung der Heiligen Elisabeth, Klara, Hedwig und Birgitta* (Hersbruck, 1963). Biographies of women in early medieval sources, including saints' lives, are reviewed in M. L. Portmann, *Die Darstellung der Frau in der Geschichtsschreibung des früheren Mittelalters* , Basler Beiträge zur Geschichtswissenschaft, 69 (Basel, 1958).

not serve, they stitched together clichés and commonplaces. Many saints' lives are little more than compilations of edifying *topoi*. On the other hand, these sources offer some singular advantages to the social historian. They are, to begin with, numerous—even for periods, such as the early Middle Ages, not well served by source survivals. While the particulars of the narratives are rarely to be trusted, the lives undoubtedly reflect common social situations, common attitudes and assumptions. Finally—and this is the crucial consideration—they pay attention to women. In the lives of saints, women make more than token appearances. Most medieval writers, in depicting a woman, adhered to the advice given by the ghost of Hamlet's father: they ignored her; they left her to heaven. Hagiographers did so too, but also charted her ascent.

We shall try to use these lives, antedating 1500, to illuminate the fluctuating fortunes of women. To be sure, our test applies to only one sector of social life, religious experiences. But it is a fair assumption that visibility among the blessed paralleled visibility in the secular world as well. Even the pursuit of sainthood required resources. The dumb priest, according to an Irish saying, never got a parish; the repressed and ignored woman, however holy, never won a cult.

To permit comparisons, our census of medieval saints must include men as well as women. The counting of saints has in fact become a popular exercise among medieval historians, but these efforts differ quite a bit from each other according to the sources used and the time and space surveyed.[4] Our basic source will be

---

4. Recent examples of a quantitative approach to the study of saints are the following: J. T. Schulenburg, "Sexism and the Celestial Gynaeceum, 500–1200," *Journal of Medieval History*, 3 (1978): 117–33, which examines women saints in the *Bibliotheca sanctorum* in 12 vols. (Rome, 1961–69); M. Goodrich, "A Profile of Thirteenth Century Sainthood," *Comparative Studies in Society and History*, 18 (1976), pp. 429–37; D. Weinstein and R. M. Bell, "Saints and Society: Italian Saints of the Late Middle Age and Renaissance," *Memorie Domenicane*, n.s. 4 (1973), pp. 180–94; A. Murray, *Reason and Society in the Middle Ages* (Oxford, 1978), pp. 338–49. In their 1973 study, Weinstein and Bell classified 485 saints by sixty-five variables for the period 1100 to 1425; their basic source was A. Butler, *Lives of the Saints*, 2nd ed., ed. H. Thurston, S. J., 4 vols. (New York, 1963). See also, by the same authors, *Saints and Society: The Two Worlds of Western Christendom, 1000–1700* (Chicago, 1982), which examines 864 saints. Murray made use of the *Oxford Dictionary of Saints*, ed. D. H. Farmer (Oxford, 1979), to study saints who died between 900 and 1500. Many statistical tables are given in the large study by A. Vauchez, *La sainteté en Occident aux derniers siècles du Moyen Age d'après les procès de canonisation et les documents hagiographiques* (Rome, 1981).

the standard bibliography of medieval hagiographical writings, the
Bibliotheca Hagiographica Latina, the two volumes and supplement
published by the Bollandist society.[5] In making our census, we
count as members of the court of heaven only individually named
saints. Groups are ignored. Otherwise, the 11,000 virgins martyred
with St. Ursula would throw our sex ratios hopelessly awry. We
enter the name of the saint by date of death assigned by the Bollan-
dists, and we make no effort to screen out mythical from historical
figures. We shall not usurp St. Peter's functions. When the death can
be dated only by century—as for example, the seventh century—we
enter the death in the middle year of the period, 650 (see Table 1).

Table 1

Saints by Periods

Period	Men	Women	Total	Sex Ratio (men to women)	Density Women	Men
1–313	767	158	925	4.85	.51	2.45
313–475	327	51	378	6.41	.32	2.01
476–750	755	111	866	6.80	.41	2.76
751–850	102	13	115	7.85	.13	1.03
851–999	112	21	133	5.33	.14	.75
1000–1150	217	18	235	12.06	.12	1.44
1151–1347	255	69	324	3.69	.35	1.30
1348–1500	63	24	87	2.64	.16	.41
Not given	156	57	213	2.74		
Total	2754	522	3276	5.28	.35	1.84

Source: *Bibliotheca Hagiographica Latina*

The total number of named saints for the period of Church history,
dead before 1500 and entered into the *Bibliotheca,* is 3276. Of
these 522 are women. The sex ratio among the blessed is thus about
five males for every female.

To illustrate changes in the distribution of saints across the Middle
Ages, we can further divide this lengthy span into eight shorter periods, commonly used in ecclesiastical history.[6] We can then calculate

5. *Bibliotheca Hagiographica Latina antiquae et mediae aetatis,* ed. Socii Bollan-
diani, 2 vols., Subsidia Hagiographica, 6 (Brussels, 1898–1903); *Supplementi,* Subsidia Hagiographica, 12 (Brussels, 1913).
6. Many of the dates are approximations, but embrace recognizable periods of
medieval history: the late Roman empire, to its fall in the west in 476; barbarian
Europe, to the election of the first Carolingian king, Pepin, in 751; the Carolingian
empire, to the mid-ninth century (850); the disintegration of the empire and renewed

a kind of density index—number of saints divided by number of years in the period. The results of this exercise are also presented in Table 1. Although the index shows wide fluctuations, the overall trend is nonetheless clear. Saints become markedly fewer as the Middle Ages progress. Saints of both sexes are numerous during the age of persecutions, ending in 313, when the Edict of Milan brought peace to the Church. They are numerous too under the Christian Roman empire, lasting in the West to 476. But perhaps most unexpected is their continued, or rather enhanced, importance in the barbarian Europe of the early Middle Ages, which we date from the fall of the Roman empire in the West in 476, to the establishment of the Carolingian dynasty by Pepin the Short in 751. This epoch yields more saints per year than any other age of the ancient or medieval Church.

After 751 and the establishment of the Carolingian empire, the relative number of saints falls continuously, to reach its lowest levels in the closing century of the Middle Ages. For several reasons the ranks of recognized saints grow thin as we approach modern times. It was fairly easy to establish a cult during the early Middle Ages. A reputation for sanctity during life and a few opportune miracles performed at the candidate's tomb after death usually sufficed to inscribe a new name on the liturgical books of a local church.[7] Then, too, the tumultuous times of the early Middle Ages favor cultivation of heroic virtues. The local churches were contending with a deeply ingrained paganism; they were eager to identify and celebrate champions, of whatever sex.

But the uncontrolled proliferation of cult figures created problems too, and from the eleventh century, the universal Church sought to impose strict controls over local cults. From about 1200, the papacy reserved to itself the right to canonize saints, and the procedures it gradually laid out took on all the aspects of a trial, replete with judges, lawyers, experts, and witnesses.[8] To promote the cause of a servant of God now required a lengthy and expensive process. Typically, only big religious orders, or prominent lay fami-

invasions, to 1000; European recovery and reorganization, to 1151; the height of medieval civilization in the "long" thirteenth century, to the outbreak of the bubonic plague in 1348; the crisis and transformation of medieval society, to 1500.

7. For a recent, full survey of the development of the cult of saints in the early Middle Ages, see the first part of Vauchez, *Sainteté*, which is entitled "La discipline du culte des saints dès origines au XIIIe siècle," pp. 13–68.

8. *Ibid.*, pp. 39–67, with abundant bibliography.

lies, had the resources needed to initiate and carry through these proceedings. It is understandable, therefore, that the total number of saints drops precipitously over the late Middle Ages.

But even as the totals were falling, the relative proportions of male and female saints were shifting too. Women saints are numerous among the martyrs of the early Church. More surprising is the continued importance of female saints even after the persecutions ceased. They are especially common in the period of barbarian Europe, between 476 and 751. Indeed, the density of women saints then surpasses that of any other of our eight periods, saving only the age of persecutions. The social and religious prominence of early medieval women is confirmed.

After 751, as the Carolingian empire grew and then disintegrated, the relative number of female saints registers a marked decline. Women saints are at their fewest right in the middle of the Middle Ages, from about 1000 to 1150. During that span of 150 years, male saints outnumber female by 12 to 1.[9] Powerful movements were then transforming Western society: the Gregorian reform of the Latin Church, which sought to extirpate clerical marriage and win for the clergy freedom from lay control; the rise of effectively governed feudal principalities; the beginnings of commercial revival and the rebirth of towns; the expansion of Europe, through crusades and colonization. And yet the visibility of women was fading, according to our index. Here, again, the experiences of men and of women in the past seemed not to be congruent.

The thesis, that the status of women deteriorated across the Middle Ages, is thus partially sustained. But not entirely: after 1151, the relative proportion of women saints begins again to expand. Over the years 1348 to 1500, although the number of saints is small, still the sex ratio drops to the lowest levels so far attained.[10] In other words, the trend marked out by women's involvement with holiness is not linear. Rather, the relative distribution of female saints lies like a slack rope across the medieval centuries, high at the beginning and at the end, but drooping low in the middle ranges of this millennial span.

9. For similar conclusions, see Weinstein and Bell, *Saints*, p. 220.
10. Vauchez, *La Sainteté*, p. 243, goes so far as to speak of a "feminization" of sainthood, most visible among the urban saints of late-medieval Italy. Weinstein and Bell, *Saints*, p. 221, also note this pronounced trend.

It can further be argued that women, while becoming relatively more frequent among late-medieval saints, were also moving upward in the heavenly hierarchy. What male saints of the four-teenth century, for example, rival Catherine of Siena or Bridget of Sweden in spiritual, or even political, influence?

To explain these shifts in the relative number of female saints, we must look more closely at their personalities and careers. Here we shall develop a crude typology of sainthood. We can distinguish those who owed their elevation, at least in part, to high status or connections with great and powerful families, from those who earned their reputations through personal charisma, through going the way of prophecy and mysticism.

In our census of saints it is easy to identify women associated with great families and to trace the frequency of their appearances across the centuries. It is less easy to sort out the charismatic fig-ures. To measure their appearances we must use proxy types, that is, identifiable categories of women saints likely to include many charismatic. Martyrs can serve this purpose, as martyrs were ven-erated for their personal courage and commitment, not for high office or even high achievement. But martyrs are rare after the age of persecution. In the late Middle Ages many female mystics were associated with the new mendicant orders, the Franciscans or Dominicans. That association was often loose. For example, St. Christina of Stommeln, a thirteenth-century visionary from the Rhineland, spent most of her career as a beguine, a religious woman following no recognized rule, before she entered the Dominican Order and, incidentally, found a biographer.[11] St. Catherine of Siena, perhaps the greatest mystic of the fourteenth century, was a member of the sisters of penitence of St. Dominic.[12] But she was not cloistered and remained free to travel widely, to Florence, Pisa, Avignon and Rome, where she, the daughter of a cloth dyer, instructed and exhorted the mighty of the world. Her

11. Christina fled her native village to escape an unwanted marriage and lived by begging in Cologne. See *Acta Sanctorum* (henceforth *ASS*), IV *Junii*, p. 431: "Cum autem esset duodecim annorum cum eam parentes ipsius matrimonio tradere vollent, Christi ancilla hoc renuens et parentibus ignorantibus fugiens, perrexit Coloniam, ubi pauperibus sociata, et fame atque siti cruciata, petiit alimoniam."

12. Blessed Raymond of Capua, *Vita di S. Caterina da Siena (n. 1347-m. 1380)*, trans. P.G. Tinagli, O. P. (Siena, 1934), Classici Cristiani, 47–49. An English transla-tion is *The Life of St. Catherine of Siena*, trans. G. Lands (London, 1965).

extraordinary career would have been inconceivable had she been tied to a cloistered community. At times the association of these holy women with the established orders was entirely fictional. The mendicants posthumously coopted them into their ranks, even though they had never during their lives been formally associated.[13] Table 2 shows the distributions over time of these principal types of female saints: martyrs, queens, abbesses and mendicants.

Our basic distinction, between status (family connections) and charisma (personal magnetism) evokes this further comment. These two routes to sainthood were not easily combined, whether by men or by women. High office or a high place in society carried weighty responsibilities, which tended to dampen or suppress mystical exuberance. A prelate or prince who received, or thought he was receiving,

Table 2

A Typology of Medieval Female Saints

Period	Martyrs	Abbesses	Queens	Mendicants
1–313	136	0	0	0
313–475	17	1	1	0
476–750	12	36	6	0
751–850	1	2	1	0
851–99	11	3	2	0
1000–1150	0	1	3	0
1151–1347	3	10	2	23
1348–1500	0	1	1	4
Not given	31	0	0	0

Source: *Bibliotheca Hagiographica Latina.*

direct instructions from heaven could easily rock Church or society. On the other hand, freedom from administrative or social responsibilities conveyed evident benefits on the charismatic or mystic; such duties were likely to demand time and divert psychic energies. St. Francis of Assisi never received Holy Orders; the responsibilities of the priesthood might well have repressed his mystical vision. Catherine of Siena, although she attracted a "joyous brigade" of followers, both men and women, never assumed official responsibilities within the Dominican Order. Office represses the spirit; freedom from office gives it life.

13. St. Zita of Lucca (d. 1272) is an example of a saint coopted by the mendicants. See Vauchez, *La Sainteté*, p. 246.

Status and charisma thus offered medieval women two alternate routes to social influence, social visibility, among the saints and in secular life, too. Concerning status, this further observation can be made. Much more than the males, medieval women were crucially dependent upon the family to gain access to power and property with which to influence society.[14] Either they inherited office directly as queens or princesses, or, as regents for their frequently absent husbands or sons, they gained it through close relationship with powerful families. Finally, through their rights of inheritance over family property, they acquired the wealth that allowed them to found or endow religious communities and, as abbesses, to take a prominent role in their management. On the other hand, women fared rather poorly under social systems where families had no exalted functions—in republican regimes, for example, where offices were elective and not linked to family membership. It would be possible to write the political history of medieval city-states, for example, Florence or Venice, and scarcely mention women.

A further, important conclusion follows from this argument. If women depended upon the family for status, wealth, office, and power, so their position within the family and their public role in society were intimately connected. If the first weakened, so also would the second.

Female saints who gained recognition by status and those who did so by charisma do not show the same distributions across the Middle Ages. In the earliest period, the age of persecutions, women were numerous among the martyrs. It would be easy to attribute their prominence to the persecutions themselves; opportunities for the exercise of heroic virtue abounded. But more profoundly, the importance of women among the martyrs reflects the highly mystical, charismatic flavor of religious life in the early Christian communities. The martyrs, of course, appear to us through clouds of legend, and it is hard to gain a sense of their personalities and char-

14. J. McNamara and S. Wemple, "The Power of Women through the Family in Medieval Europe: 500–1100," *Feminist Studies,* 2 (1973), pp. 126–41; reprinted in *Clio's Consciousness Raised: New Perspectives on the History of Women,* ed. M. Hartman and L. Banner (New York, 1974), pp. 103–18. The authors make the point that weak central government and the strength of great local families enhanced the status of women in the "first feudal age" (to ca. 1050). On the prominence of women in one dynastic line, see M. C. Facinger, "A Study of Medieval Queenship in Capetian France, 987–1237," *Studies in Medieval and Renaissance History* (1968), pp. 3–48.

acter. In regard to female martyrs, the capital text is surely the passion of the two women of Carthage, Perpetua and Felicity, martyred
in 202 or 203. In a big segment of their Life (chapters 3 to 10), Perpetua relates in the first person the story of her trial and passion, and
concludes with an apocalyptic vision of heaven.[15] The Life over-
flows with allusions to her emotions and inner experiences. Perpetua is a young matron, aged 22, with a baby at her breast; she
fears for her baby's fate, yet still invites martyrdom. In one of her
visions she is turned into a man: "I am stripped and I am made
male."[16] This, not so much out of modesty; she wishes more powerfully to wrestle with the devil. In her last agony, she asks for a hair-
pin. She wants to set her hair, lest she appear sad and unkempt at
this moment of supreme satisfaction and ecstatic joy. Felicity, her
slave girl, is pregnant when arrested and delivers her baby in prison.
The husbands of the women are nowhere identified. Scholars have
discerned in the Life strong influences of the Montanist heresy, an
eschatological movement originating in Asia Minor, which counted
among its early leaders two women prophets, Priscilla and
Maximilla.[17] In the Montanist vision, all Christians, even the humble
and the unlearned, even women and slaves, could prophesy under
the promptings of the Holy Spirit. Charismatic women fitted, and
helped form, the religious style of the age.

The peace of the Church in 313, the stabilization of ecclesiastical
structure and discipline, and perhaps too the decline of urban communities and an urban culture in the western provinces of the
empire, stilled the voice of feminine prophets and mystics within the
Latin Church. These changes did not reduce the number of female
saints, only changed their character. The great female saints of the
early Middle Ages—St. Radegund of Gaul, St. Brigid of Ireland, St.
Lioba of England and Germany—were abbesses, queens, wonder-
workers, but none of them was truly a mystic.[18] In the early

15. "Passio Perpetuae et Felicitatis," in The Acts of the Christian Martyrs, ed. and
trans. H. Musurillo (Oxford, 1972), pp. 106–31.

16. Ibid., p. 118 "et expoliata sum et facta sum masculus."

17. W. Le Saint, "Montanism," New Catholic Encyclopedia, vol. 9 (1967), pp.
1078–79.

18. On Lioba, see Rudolf, monk of Fulda, "Life of Saint Leoba," in The Anglo-Saxon
Missionaries in Germany, ed. and trans. C. H. Talbot (New York, 1954), pp. 205–26.
On Radegund, see Baudonivia, "De vita s. Radegundis Liber II," in Passiones vitaeque
sanctorum aevi Merovingici, Monumenta Germaniae Historica [henceforth, MGH],

medieval world, office rather than charisma distinguished the female saints. Out of 54 sainted abbesses, 37, nearly 70 percent, lived before 751; so also did nearly one-half the queens. Thereafter, holy queens retained importance chiefly in central Europe—in Germany, Hungary, and Poland.[19]

Our count of women saints confirms their prominence in the early Middle Ages, but also marks a deterioration in their status from the Carolingian age on. Women saints, as we have mentioned, marshal their fewest number in the middle of the Middle Ages, from about 1000 to 1150.

Why did holy queens and abbesses fade from the ranks of the blessed in the central Middle Ages? One reason often given for their deteriorating status is the changes wrought by the Gregorian Reform, in particular the removal of women from centers of authority within the Church.[20] The frequency of clerical marriages in the pre-reform Church gave to women, if not ecclesiastical office, then at least proximity to it. In a Lombard charter dated 724, the wife of a priest is even called *presvitera*, "priestess."[21] Marozia, the lady senator of Rome, ruler of the city from 928 to 932, was the concubine of one pope and the mother of another.[22] Her career would have been inconceivable in the absence of clerical marriage or concubinage. The reformers were intent on placing distance between the now-celibate clergy and women. One casualty of their policies was the double monastery, including both nuns and monks, common in the early Middle Ages and especially in England.[23] Usually, the feminine com-

ed. B. Krusch and W. Levison, *Scriptores rerum Merovingicarum*, vol. 2, (Leipzig, 1920), pp. 377–95. One of several versions of the life of St. Brigid, and probably the oldest, is in *Vitae sanctorum Hiberniae ex codice olim salmanticensi nunc bruxellensi*, ed. W. W. Heist, Subsidia Hagiographica, 28 (Brussels, 1966), pp. 1–37.

19. For example, Elizabeth of Thuringia (d. 1231) or Margaret of Hungary (d. 1271). See Vauchez, *Sainteté*, pp. 427–48.

20. The effects of the reform movements on female religious is treated extensively in P. Schmitz, *Histoire de l'ordre de saint Benoit*, 7 vols. (Paris, 1942–56). The entire seventh volume is given over to *les moniales*. On the relation of the reform to numbers of female saints, see also J. Schulenburg in the article cited in note 4.

21. *Codice diplomatico longobardo*, ed. L. Schiaparelli, Fonti per la Storia d'Italia, 62–64 (Rome, 1929) I, 122, no. 34, October 724: "Romualdo prete cum coniuge mea presbitera nomine Ratperga . . ."

22. The career of Marozia and of other members of the House of Theophylact is primarily based on the account of Liutprand of Cremona, *Antapodosis* II, 48, in *Works*, trans. F. A. Wright (London, 1930), 1, pp. 92–93.

23. Schmitz, *L'ordre de saint Benoit*, vol. 7, pp. 45–52. Schmitz believes that all English convents were double houses in the early Middle Ages. See also M. Bateson,

ponent had dominated these co-residential institutions. But this close association of the sexes was anathema to the reformers.

The reform, in sum, unquestionably restricted the functions of women within the Church and so also their access to sainthood—or at least one style of sainthood. Still, it would seem an exaggeration to attribute the declining number of women saints solely to the Gregorian movement. In fact the number of women saints was falling well before the Gregorian epoch. Women, it would appear, fell victim to a more profound and powerful social movement. I would argue that the declining number of holy queens and abbesses reflects their deteriorating position within the elite family of medieval Europe, their weakening grasp over its resources. In the second part of this essay, I will examine the changing status of women within elite households across the medieval centuries.

WOMEN AND THE FAMILY

How can we evaluate the position of medieval women within the family? We shall utilize three indicators: the place and role of women within the kinship systems of the Middle Ages; the function of women in passing on property down the generations; and the contributions of women in the production and management of wealth. All these topics are large and complicated, and all have attracted much study in recent years.[24] The following remarks will summarize what seems to be the thrust of current research.

_____

Origin and Early History of Double Monasteries (Royal Historical Society Transactions, n.s. 13; London, 1899); L. Eckenstein, Women under Monasticism: Chapters on Saint-lore and Convent Life between A.D. 500 and A.D. 1500 (Cambridge, 1896); F. Hilpisch, Die Doppelklöster: Entstehung und Organisation (Münster, 1928); M. de Fantette, Les religieuses à l'âge classique du droit canon: Recherches sur les structures juridiques des branches féminines des ordres (Paris, 1967).

24. Famille et parenté dans l'Occident médiéval; Actes du colloque de Paris (1974), ed. G. Duby and J. LeGoff, Collection de l'Ecole française de Rome, 22 (Rome, 1977). On the character of the early medieval family, see the review article by R. Fossier, "Les structures de la famille en occident au moyen-âge," XVe Congrès International des Sciences Historiques, Rapports II (Bucharest, 1980), pp. 115–32. See also K. Schmid, "Heirat, Familienfolge, Geschlechterbewusstsein," in Il matrimonio nella società altomedievale: Settimane di Studio del Centro Italiano sull' Alto Medioevo (Spoleto, 1977), pp. 103–37; G. Duby, "Structures de parenté et noblesse dans la France du nord au 11e et 12e siècles" (1967), reprinted in his Hommes et structures du Moyen Age (Paris, 1973), pp. 267–85. An English translation by C. Postan appears

In describing the kinship system of the early Middle Ages, we can take as a convenient point of departure a treatise written about 1063 by the Italian reformer and saint Peter Damian.[25] It is entitled "On the Degrees of Kinship"; Damian wrote it at the request of the Florentines. They were confused—many persons in the early Middle Ages must have been—about the methods of calculating degrees of kinship and why it all mattered. They sought enlightenment from jurists at Ravenna, and Damian was in essence replying to what he thought to be their erroneous opinions.

Jurists and theologians of the period had in fact several models of kinship from which to choose. In the ancient world, Roman law had measured the degrees of kinship by counting backward from Ego to the common ancestor, and then forward again to the targeted relative.[26] The Romans had defined the degrees, within which marriages were prohibited, as a narrow four. In the early Middle Ages, a new method of reckoning degrees of kinship emerged, called Germanic and later accepted as canonical. This method struck forth in a direct path from Ego to the targeted relative and counted the lines of descent that had to be crossed or touched to reach the target. And a council at Rome, held in the year 721, defined the degrees within which marriage was prohibited as seven.[27] The new boundaries and the new methods of calculating kinship expanded the kin group to enormous, truly unrealistic dimensions. How many people in early medieval society could trace their ascendants back seven generations, as the system required? Realistically then, Pope Gregory II in 726, and several councils after him, affirmed that a vague sense of kinship,

---

in G. Duby, *The Chivalrous Society* (London, 1977), pp. 134-48. Finally, see D. Herlihy and C. Klapisch-Zuber, *Les Toscans et leurs familles: Une étude du catasto florentin de 1427* (Paris, 1978), pp. 525–51.

25. "De parentelae gradibus, ad Ioannem episcopum caesenatensem et d. d. archidiaconum ravennatem," *Patrologia Latina*, ed. J. P. Migne (Paris, 1853), 145, cols. 191–208. For Damian's sources, see the study by J. J. Ryan, *Saint Peter Damian and His Canonical Sources* (Toronto, 1956).

26. On degrees of kinship, see most recently C.R. Bouchard, "Consanguinity and Noble Marriages in the Tenth and Eleventh Centuries," *Speculum*, 56 (1981), pp. 268–87, with a chart on p. 270. For measurement of consanguinity from Roman times, the basic study is A. Esmein, *Le mariage en droit canonique*, 2nd ed., ed. R. Genestal (Paris, 1929), I, pp. 371–93.

27. For the council of Rome in 721, see J. D. Mansi, *Sacrorum conciliorum nova et amplissima collectio* (Venice, 1758–98), 12, pp. 262–67.

a suspicion of relationship, was sufficient to define a kinship group and to prohibit marriage within its bounds.[28]

To set the stage for his disquisition on kinship, Damian first sought to justify why blood relationship should matter at all in determining eligibility for marriage. Here, he makes much use of earlier writers— St. Augustine, Isidore of Seville, Burchard of Worms—but he still describes ideas and a system very much alive in the eleventh century.

All human beings, he reminds his readers, are descendants of the same first parents, Adam and Eve, and all are therefore members of the same descent group, a *genus cognationis*. Human beings, unlike animals, have only a single pair of first parents; this should remind all human beings that they are in fact brothers or sisters, members of the same clan. But in fact, over time, the lines of descent—*progenies*, in Peter's technical terminology—grow apart. As the distance among them increases, so their mutual love cools and dies. This distancing of the strands stemming from a common source, this extinction of love, threatens social peace. The descent groups could easily turn to war, against their now-estranged neighbors. Here, marriage and affinity perform their essential services to society. "When blood relationship," he writes, "along with the terms that designate it, expire, the law of marriage takes up the function, and reestablishes the rights of ancient love among new men."[29] Marriage is thus much more than the casual union of two persons.

Rather, it ties together two clans; it restores affection between two hitherto alienated lines of descent. It reintegrates human solidarity, which time and divergence of family lines relentlessly pull asunder. On marriage and its integrating, reconciling powers, social harmony crucially depends.

Now, if members of the same clan were allowed to marry, this would obviously defeat the sublime purposes of exogenous marriage. Members of the same group are already morally obligated to love one another, by reason of their common blood. They have no further need of cohesion; they have much need to seek through exogenous marriages the reestablishment of "ancient love," as Damian says, "among new men."

28. "Dicimus, quod oportuerat quidem, quandiu se agnoscunt affinitate propinquos, ad hujus copulae non accedere societatem," letter of Gregory II, *Monumenta Germaniae Historica, Epistolarium,* vol. 3, p. 275, dated 726.
29. "De gradibus," col. 193.

Damian expresses a further, and for our purposes, a crucial principle. The right to inherit from a person is conclusive proof of kinship relation with him or her, but the same right to inherit totally excludes the right to marry. He explains: "One right excludes the other, so that the woman from whom one could inherit cannot be taken as a legitimate spouse, even as the women whom one can legally marry can have no title of inheritance [over her husband's property]."[30] The kin group which Damian describes thus possessed the following characteristics: it was Ego-focused, in sense that all lines stretch out, and are measured from, the place which Ego holds among the lines of descent. This means that the descent group, or *genus*, in Damian's language, was redefined every new generation, as its focus settled upon a new person, a new Ego. It did not accumulate members over time. Its limits were precisely defined, however they be measured, whether over four or seven degrees. It was obviously cognatic or bilineal, as the strands of relationship ran indifferently through men and women. It assumed that women too, as authentic kins, enjoyed rights of inheritance over the property the kin group carried with it over time.

Damian's model fits well with the little that we know of kinship organization in the early Middle Ages. Given the imperfection of genealogical memory, it would then have been very difficult to distinguish patrilineal from matrilineal relationships stretching far backward into time. Pope Gregory II thought that proof of kinship ties required only a vague sense of relationship; how could he have demanded more?

Then too, the sexual practices of the early medieval elites were singularly loose, even promiscuous, both for men and for women.[31] Polygyny or sexual promiscuity in any form has the result of obscuring the line of descent through males—patrilineal linkages, in sum—and of emphasizing the importance of descent through females. Here, we cite only two of many possible examples. King Hugh of Italy (926–947) allegedly ignored his queen and consorted with three concubines, who were popularly nicknamed after pagan goddesses, Venus, Juno, and Semele. He sired children on all of them. Or did he? "As the king was not the only man who enjoyed

---

30. *Ibid.*, col. 194: "Quod quibus est jus haereditatis, est et affinitas generis."
31. On polygyny among the Merovingians, see most recently Wemple, *Women in Frankish Society.*

their favours," our source, Liutprand of Cremona, relates, "the children of all three are of uncertain parentage."[32] (He wrote *parentage*, but he meant paternity.) As late as the eleventh century, Emperor Henry IV for long refused to accept a legal wife, but kept two or three concubines simultaneously. If he discerned among his courtiers an attractive wife or daughter, he attempted promptly to seduce her; if his suit failed, he sometimes resorted to violent abduction. Women who came to court with petitions he also seduced. When he tired of them, he discarded them and gave them in marriage to his servants. Once, he persuaded a courtier to undertake the seduction of his queen, in order to disgrace her. His plot failed, but clearly he believed that success was in the realm of possibility. He tolerated the rape of his own sister.[33] The account we have of the mores of his court and courtiers, from Bruno of Saxony, is admittedly biased. But if their behavior in any way resembled what Bruno describes, it would have been hard to trace with confidence patrilineal relationships at Henry's court. In this social environment, women, and relationships to women, were the surest indicators of close kin.

The importance of women, in indicating to Ego who his certain relatives were, further affected, it would appear, our second indicator, the role of women in passing property down the generations, through inheritance customs and marriage settlements.[34] As Damian asserts, women as full-fledged members of the *genus* must have a right to inherit. To be sure, the various legal traditions of the early Middle Ages defined that right in particular ways. But even in the worst case—such as the provisions of the famous Salic law—women were postponed in regard to brothers, not totally excluded, from the inheritance of real property; and all the traditions gave them a right to inherit movables. By the eighth century, when our

32. Liutprand of Cremona, *Antapodosis*, vol. 5, p. 32; *The Works of Liutprand of Cremona*, trans. F.A. Wright, X (London, 1930), p. 199.

33. *Brunos Buch von Sachsenkrieg*, ed. H.-E. Lohman (Leipzig, 1937), p. 195. "Binas vel ternas simul concubinas habebat, nec his contentus, cuiuscumque filiam vel uxorem iuvenem et formosam audierat, si seduci non poterat, sibi violenter adduci praecipiebat."

34. The inheritance customs in the barbarian laws are reviewed in McNamara and Wemple, "The Power of Women," cited in note 14 above, although the authors tend to confuse postponement with exclusion from the inheritance. K. F. Drew, "The Law of the Family in the Germanic Barbarian Kingdoms: A Synthesis," *Studies in Medieval Culture* (Houston, 1977).

oldest charters survive, women commonly appear as holders of inherited land.[35]

Marriage settlements, the second great channel through which the old directed wealth to the young, also favored women. In A.D. 98 Tacitus, in his famous description of the Germans, observed that among these barbarians, the groom brought the dowry to the bride, not the bride to the groom, as was the Roman practice.[36] This system of reverse dowry or of bridewealth became, as far as we can judge, the universal practice in early medieval Europe, even in areas, such as the Mediterranean lands, where Roman traditions remained strong.[37] It is interesting to note that the marriage goods Tacitus described—oxen, a horse and bridle, a shield and spear—were clearly intended, as he himself remarked, for male use, though given to the bride. The descent group used an affine, the daughter-in-law, as a kind of trustee, offering assurance that these resources would flow to the certain benefit of the clan, even its male descendants. The system survived intact into the early Middle Ages. "The dowry," reads a charter from St. Gall in 758, "which my father gave to my mother, and I have given to my wife."[38]

In sum, from even this brief consideration of early medieval inheritance and marriage settlements, there emerges a special relationship between women and property.[39] Their control over wealth equipped them to be founders of monasteries and benefactors of religion, and famed throughout their communities.

Women in early medieval society had a special role not only in the conveyance of wealth down the generations, but also in its production and management—our third indicator of their status. At humble social levels, still according to Tacitus, women performed the princi-

35. Many examples appear in the *Codice diplomatico longobardo*, ed. Schiaparelli, no. 18, 27 November 714: a married couple donates "omnem facultatem nostram quam possidemus vel quam ex parentum successionibus seu ex regio." On women as property owners, see my study "Land, Family and Women in Continental Europe, 701–1200," *Traditio* ,18 (1962), pp. 89–120.

36. *Taciti De origine et situ Germanorum*, ed. G. Forni, with commentary by F. Galli (Rome, 1964), cap. 18. p. 114: "Dotem non uxor marito, sed uxori maritus offert."

37. D. O. Hughes, "From Brideprice to Dowry in Mediterranean Europe," *Journal of Family History* , 3 (1978), pp. 262–96.

38. *Urkundenbuch der Abtei Sanct Gallen*, ed. H. Wartmann (Zurich, 1863–82), vol. I, no. 26 (year 758).

39. On women in barbarian law see Wemple, *Women in Frankish Society*, pp. 27–50; G. Merschberger, *Die Rechtsstellung der germanischen Frau* (Leipzig, 1937).

pal agricultural labors, while the free adult male was either away at war or at home in indolence.[40] Women seem to have exerted a virtual monopoly over the processes of cloth production. The large estates of the period typically contained a *gyneceum*, a workshop which, as its name suggests, was staffed by women engaged in making cloth. Even the dyeing of cloth seems to have been a specifically feminine skill.[41] The life of the ninth-century German saint, Liutberg, depicts a servant in an aristocratic household, as *"multorum muliebrium operum artifex"* (skilled in many feminine labors). Among them was the *"ars texturae"* (the art of weaving); she also kept a vat in her room filled with burning coals, in order to dye cloth with diverse colors.[42] St. Severus of Ravenna, according to his ninth-century life (he lived in the fifth), was so humble that he labored with his wife and daughter, "with whom he did women's works ... he was accustomed to weave wool after the manner of women."[43]

Among the arts considered appropriate, at least for elite women, were reading and writing. The eighth-century nuns Herlindis and Renildis were trained in "reading, singing, chanting psalms ... also writing and painting." They copied and decorated the four gospels, a psalter, and "many other texts."[44] They were "perfect workers" "in skills of every kind, which are usually done by women"; among the skills mentioned are weaving, sewing, and embroidery.[45] Even lay noblewomen seem often to have been literate. The lady Gisila read

40. *De origine et situ Germanorum*, cap. 15, p. 107: "delegata domus et penatium et agrorum cura feminis senibusque et infirmissimo cuique ex familia"; *ibid.*, cap. 25, p. 132: "cetera domus officia uxor ac liberi exsequuntur."

41. On the dyeing of cloth as woman's work among the Irish, see Ch. Plummer, *Vitae sanctorum Hiberniae* (Oxford,1910), p. ci.

42. *Vita Liutbirgae virginis: Das Leben der Liutbirg*, ed. O. Menzel, *MGH*, Deutsches Mittelalter, 3 (Leipzig, 1939), p. 13: "propter diversorum tincturam colorum."

43. *ASS I Februarii, Vita auctore Luidolpho prebytero*, p. 88: "cum quibus [Vincentia uxore et Innocentia filia] opera muliebria, victum quaeritans, operabatur. Nam lanam ... more feminarum, texere solebat."

44. *ASS III Martii*, p. 384: "erant beatissimae Virgines erudiendae ... id est, in legendo, modulatione cantus, psallendo, necnon quod nostris temporibus valde mirum est etiam scribendo atque pingendo." *Ibid.*, p. 386: "Quatuor Evangelistarum scripta ... honorifico opere conscripserunt. Nihilominus Psalmorum libellum, ... aliasque quamplures Scripturas."

45. *Ibid.*, p. 384: "Simili modo, in universi operis arte, quod manibus foeminarum diversis modis et varia compositione fieri solet, honestissime fuerant instructae, videlicet nendo et texendo, creando ac suendo, in auro quoque ac margaretis in serico componendis, miris in modis extiterant perfectae opifices."

her psalter so often that it angered her husband, Count Eppo, who threw the book into the fire.[46] The association of women with special skills, *muliebria opera*, which men did not understand—with dyeing, brewing, milking cows and churning butter, and of course with cooking—may have suggested that they were proficient in occult arts as well, with magic and witchcraft. Witchcraft too was, after all, a *muliebre opus*.

Aristocratic women also played a prominent role in administration, in marshaling and managing resources. A curious passage out of Irish historiography tells of the three orders of the saints of Ireland. The oldest order flourished in Ireland soon after the time of St. Patrick and consisted of 350 bishops, renowned for their chastity and sanctity. "They did not," says the passage, "spurn the company of women, or their administration."[47] What service did women perform for these chaste bishops? Perhaps continental sources can offer some illumination. Under the Carolingians, the stewards, the managers of the royal estates, presented their accounts to the queen, at least during the absences of her husband, which were likely to be frequent and prolonged. The queen also guarded the royal treasure, and seems to have had chief responsibility for distributing the yearly gifts to the knights at court, the equivalent of their salaries.[48] Women, in sum, maintained a stable, continuous administration of household and estates. Their services freed elite males for their preferred activities, high politics and war.

Women in the early Middle Ages thus played a major role in the display of kin connections; they were also stations in the flow of wealth down the generations; they were supervisors, managers, producers. Their services won them high visibility in society and a strong voice in the disposition of resources. Did not their celestial prominence, which our count of saints reveals, have a terrestrial base? Status on earth helped assure to some women status in heaven.

46. *ASS, I Aprilis*, p. 666: "Comes Eppo ... librum unde illa sola solebat Psalmos decurrere, ad culinam detulit atque in ignem projecit."

47. The passage appears in several collections of saints' lives. See *Vitae*, ed. Heist, pp. 81–83.

48. The queen fulfilled this function in the Carolingian palace, as described by Hincmar of Reims, "De ordine palatii" (written in 882, but utilizing earlier materials), *Capitularia regum francorum*, ed. A. Boretius, *MGH*, Legum Sectio II (Hanover, 1883), pp. 517–30.

From about the year 1000, a new type of kinship system made its appearance in Western Europe, specifically among the elite classes.[49] This was the patrilineal lineage. It did not so much replace, as it was superimposed upon, the earlier *genus*. But it differed from the older descent group in certain crucial ways. It was ancestor-focused, not Ego-focused, in the sense that it traced its line of descent back to a particular ancestor. Like all ancestor-focused descent groups, it was likely to grow larger with each generation. Members were never lost, as with Ego-focused groups, which were redefined every generation. Its solidarity with the past came early to be proclaimed through adoption of a family name, a coat of arms, mottoes, and sometimes even a mythology. And it was patrilineal or agnatic. Daughters, and their children, were excluded from the lineage. To be sure, cognate relationships were not ignored. They remained an essential consideration in negotiating marriages, in calculating degrees of kinship, and determining the eligibility for marriage of possible partners. But in most areas of social life, they took on only secondary importance. The elite family became a solidarity of males, linked one to the others by agnate bindings.

No longer a central signpost indicating kin, women further lost their functions as principal conduits in the flow of wealth down the generations. The patrilineal family now managed its resources primarily for the benefit of sons. Daughters lost their traditional claim to an equal share with their brothers in their parents' property. The terms of marriage also turned against them. The true dowry returned in much of Europe, and even where other types of marriage settlements prevailed, the bride, and her family, lost the strong negotiating position they had held in former times. The bride, or her family, was forced to assume the principal share of the "burdens of matrimony," the costs involved in creating a new household.[50]

Many changes—cultural, social, economic—contributed to this transformation. On the cultural level, a prerequisite to this definition of the elite family in patrilineal terms was the success, always limited

49. As well as the literature cited in note 20 above, see G. Duby, *Medieval Marriage: Two Models from Twelfth-Century France*, trans. E. Forster, p. 10, on the gradual spreading among all levels of aristocratic society of a lineage-oriented family structure.

50. On the changing terms of marriage, see my own study, "The Medieval Marriage Market," *Medieval and Renaissance Studies*, 6 (1976), pp. 3–27, reprinted in *The Social History of Italy and Western Europe, 700–1500* (London, 1978), no. 14.

but still substantial, of the Church's long campaign against extramarital sexual liaisons. As long as the European elites, women as well as men, strayed from strict monogamy, any effort to define the family as a fellowship of agnates would be frustrated. Already in the ninth century, the Church seems to have enjoyed some success in setting stricter controls over sexual behavior.[51] The Gregorian reform of the eleventh century, and the centralized Church emerging out of it, imposed tighter ethical standards and a much closer scrutiny on the European elites. Lapses may have been frequent, but monogamy became established as the unquestioned rule of western marriage.

The Church's now-effective insistence on monogamous marriage was a precondition for this realignment of the elite family, but does not alone explain why realignment occurred. Simultaneously, the mode of life that these families adopted, or perhaps better, their strategies for survival, were also changing. Elite families always looked in two directions for economic support, to their landed properties and to the profits of war. But opportunities for pillage were diminishing in the post-Carolingian epoch, save along the frontiers or in the distant East. At the same time, their own growth in numbers threatened their other economic base, their landed patrimonies. The elites in response tried to preserve the integrity of their holdings, upon which their status now principally depended. Above all, they sought to prevent their division among numerous heirs. The defense of the patrimony required, in other words, that the claims of younger sons and of all daughters to shares in the inheritance be limited. Younger sons were typically required to delay marriage or to eschew it altogether. It is understandable that they filled the armies of adventurers, who from the eleventh century poured into frontier areas, including the Holy Land, where they hoped to make or repair their fortunes. Daughters did not have even this option. To some girls, their fathers and brothers provided the dowries they now needed to contract respectable marriages. Other daughters with paltry dowries had to marry well beneath their station or enter the religious life, with or without an authentic vocation.

Nor did the economic and urban revival of the eleventh century improve the social position of women. The relationship of women

51. See the comments of Wemple in "The Ascent of Monogamy," *Women in Frankish Society*, pp. 75–96.

to production was especially complicated, and seems to have differed considerably across different trades and across geographic regions.[52] Women retained prominence in some skills, such as brewing or spinning. They early acquired importance in silk manufacture—a new and growing industry in the late Middle Ages. On the whole, however, the following principle seems to have prevailed. Where the work involved high levels of family participation, the contribution of women remained substantial. Where guilds dominated the productive processes, women played a diminished role. Although there were exceptions, guilds tended to exclude women. In the medieval economy as well as in politics, the family chiefly promoted the active engagement of women; but that support tended to weaken in an urban context.

Women, for example, dominated the processes of cloth manufacture in the early Middle Ages, including such skilled arts as dyeing and finishing cloth. Males took over these activities in the cloth towns. The diminished role of women in the production of wealth reduced the economic contribution they could make to their households, whether of origin or of marriage. Their families of origin were prone to look upon them as burdens and were eager to settle their future, to give them to a husband or to the religious life, usually at young ages, and under unfavorable terms.[53]

So also, at the highest echelons of society, among princes and barons, the growing role in government of trained clerks and professional officials, of staffs and bureaus, impinged upon and narrowed the traditional place of elite women in administration. In large part, though never entirely, they lost to male officials the administrative functions that had been a chief support of their status in the early medieval household.[54]

52. For a positive assessment of women in the work force, see E. Power, *Medieval Women*, ed. M. M. Postan (London, New York, Melbourne, 1975), especially pp. 53–75, "The Working Woman in Town and Country."

53. The role of women within urban industries was also a function of the nature of the industry. Women seem to have been of scant importance in the manufactures of woolens, but played a significant role in the silk industry, perhaps because they were more dextrous than males in embroidery.

54. They retained some importance as administrators. The fifteenth century French poetess Christine de Pisan made the point that the daughters of barons must be taught how to read, as they will often have to administer the family's estates in the absence of the husband. See D. Herlihy, "Women in Medieval Society" (Houston: Smith Lecture, 1972), p. 12.

By most social indicators, women, especially elite women, were losing status, power, and visibility as the Middle Ages progressed. By many indicators, but not by all. Women possessed, as we have argued, an alternate route to social influence and visibility: through personal charisma. Indeed, the exclusion of women from office seems often to have invited them and freed them to nurture their interior powers. Catherine of Siena here offers a superb example of the late-medieval, charismatic woman. Of humble origins, she held no high office, whether in Church or state. In one of her impassioned dialogues with God, she protested that her sex prevented her from fulfilling the commissions He had laid upon her. "My sex, you know," she reminded Him in familiar language, "is here an obstacle for many reasons, whether because men disparage it or because of modesty, for it is not good that a woman consort with men."[55] But God rejects her reasoning in an extraordinary passage: "Isn't it I who have created the human race, and divided it into male and female? I dispense where I want the grace of my spirit. In my eyes there is neither male nor female nor rich nor poor. All are equal, for I can work my will through all equally."[56] Joan of Arc would be another example of this common, late-medieval type. She too held no office and enjoyed no status. Her voices alone gave her unique authority and led her to extraordinary accomplishment.

Women dominated what might be called the charismatic sectors of late-medieval society. They figured prominently among the late-medieval mystics: Margery Kempe, Julian of Norwich, Catherine of Siena, Catherine of Genoa, and many others.[57] Their cultivation of the interior spirit led many of them beyond the bounds of orthodoxy. They were numerous, for example, in the heresy of the Free Spirit, which taught that office, structures, rules meant nothing; all that mattered was God's spirit within, which conveyed full and perfect freedom.[58] Even witches might be considered part of this charismatic

55. Raimondo da Capua, *Vita*, libro 11, cap. 1 (ed. Tinagli), p. 169.
56. *Ibid.*
57. *The Book of Margery Kempe*, ed. W. B. Bowdon (London, 1936; repr. New York, 1944); Julian of Norwich, *Revelations of Divine Love*, trans. J. Walsh (New York, 1962); *Catherine of Siena as Seen in Her Letters*, trans. V. D. Scudder (London, 1926); Catherine of Genoa, *Treatise on Purgatory and the Dialogue*, trans. C. Balfour and H. D. Irvine (London, 1946).
58. R. Lerner, *The Heresy of the Free Spirit in the Later Middle Ages* (Berkeley, Los Angeles, and London, 1972).

sector; witchcraft, like mystical movements in orthodoxy, like heresy, swelled in strength in the late Middle Ages. The structure of late-medieval society may have restricted the access of women to property and office, but it could not silence or repress them.

Did women then have a Renaissance? Did they enjoy higher social status and more favorable social treatment at the end of the Middle Ages than at the beginning? The negative response, which feminist historiography has given to these questions, carries much conviction. Women did indeed lose over the course of the Middle Ages many functions, which had distinguished them and supported them in the early centuries. They came to play a reduced role in the identification of Ego's closest kin. They were no longer the important stations in the flow of property down the generations, the trustees who assured that the property devolved upon the surest members of the clan. Their importance in economic production at the lower social levels, and in administration and management at the highest, also diminished. To judge from office and authority, women were pushed to marginal positions in the structure of medieval society. Although these changes seem indisputable, yet the response they support, that women did not have a Renaissance, is not entirely satisfactory. It ignores entirely the alternate route to personal fulfillment and social leadership, that through charisma. It cannot make sense of a Catherine of Siena or a Joan of Arc. And these are figures whom no interpretation of the experiences of medieval women can leave isolated, accidental, uncomprehended.

In the traditional interpretation, the Renaissance represented a triumph of individualism over the collective restraints of traditional, medieval society. Catherine of Siena, Joan of Arc, and many other charismatic women of the epoch were individualists in the full meaning of the word, trusting in their interior voices, critical of the male-dominated establishment and the manner it was leading society. Charismatic women appear with extraordinary frequency in the late-medieval world. In at least one sector of social and cultural life, women had a Renaissance.

3

THE NATURAL HISTORY OF MEDIEVAL WOMEN

✦ ✦ ✦

Versed in reconstructing all dimensions of past human experience, many modern social historians have become especially interested in women. Partly inspired by the contemporary feminist movement (whose advocates have correctly pointed out that the history of roughly half of humanity has been systematically slighted), these historians also recognize that in the natural and social history of any society, women have unique and critical functions. They carry the new generation to term, sustain children in early life, and usually introduce the young to the society and culture of which they will be a part. Women begin the processes through which human cultures strive to achieve what their individual members cannot—indefinite life, immortality.

Few historians are willing to accept the claims of sociobiologists, who find culture already programmed in genes and who subordinate cultural history to natural history. But most would agree that human societies and civilizations cannot be properly evaluated or appreciated without considering the basic biological experiences of their members. These crucial events—including the duration of life itself under various social and historical conditions, as well as the timing of nursing and weaning, sexual maturity, marriage and mating, reproduction, menopause, and aging—are often by no means parallel experiences for both men and women and can have radically different consequences for each sex.

The biological experiences of women throughout the Middle Ages are interesting because of the length of this particular period: we can observe a thousand years of women's careers and the contours of their lives. Data concerning the Middle Ages are notoriously intractable—difficult to find, difficult to interpret. But medieval scholars advanced some general comments on the biology of women, and a few of these ideas have come down to us; even some precious statistical information that illuminates how women fared in the real world. Finally, some biographies, chiefly of saints and queens, support our rudimentary knowledge of women's situations. All these sources have manifest gaps, but taken together, they present coherent pictures of medieval women. Although medievalists are often obliged to be jugglers and prestidigitators, they are not without pins or beans with which to play.

In the Middle Ages, life expectancies apparently varied sharply, in accordance with epidemiological conditions. For unclear reasons, western Europe was practically free of epidemics from the sixth to the fourteenth century, when the infamous Black Death of 1348–1349 introduced an epoch of recurrent and devastating plagues. From the thirteenth century on, we know the birth and death dates of many medieval nobles and townspeople, predominantly male, and can venture some estimates. In the plague-free years of the thirteenth century, people could expect to live between 35 and 40 years. In the stricken generations including and immediately following the Black Death life expectancies fell to only 17 or 18 years. It thereafter slowly lengthened and averaged about 30 years during the fifteenth century.

Life expectancies for women shifted up or down in phase with this general movement. But simultaneously, a small, significant change was taking place. Women were beginning to survive better than men; they were acquiring an advantage in longevity that, in the Western world, they have not since relinquished.

Medieval natural philosophers concluded that women's chances for life were improving. The biologists of the ancient world—of whom the foremost was Aristotle—had affirmed that, saving unusual circumstances, males of all species live longer than females (hard work or excessive sexual indulgence might frustrate nature's intent and artificially shorten the male life span). Males represented the perfection of the human species; females were an imperfection of nature albeit a happy one, in view of their essential contribution to propagation. The defective females passed through all stages of life quicker than the male. They reached sexual maturity sooner, aged earlier, and were the first to die. The ancient biologists thought that specific humors determined a person's temperament and believed that women's temperaments, dominated by cold and dry humors, hurried them toward the cold and dry state of death.

In the twelfth century, when a renaissance of learning began in western Europe, scholars reexamined the biological writings of Aristotle and other classics. Initially, medieval natural scientists repeated without elaboration the ancients' opinion that men, as perfect representations of the species, live longer than women. Then, in the thirteenth century, the foremost biologist of the age, Saint Albertus Magnus (Albert the Great) who died in 1280, treated the question of the relative longevity of the sexes in a novel fashion. In Albertus's view, the Philosopher, Aristotle, was indeed correct. Men live longer than women *naturaliter*, "according to the natural order." But women live longer than men *per accidens*, "by accident," by which Albertus apparently meant under the distinctive conditions of his period. He gives three reasons for women's longer life expectancy: sexual intercourse is less demanding on women than on men; menstruation flushes impurities from women's bodies; and women "work less, and for that reason are not so much consumed." We can question what Albertus meant by the judgment that the demands of sexual intercourse or the purgative functions of menstruation were accidental, but his observation that the burdens of labor lowered men's natural life expectancies is worth remembering.

Subsequently, other medieval authors also concluded that women live longer than men. Some even occasionally pointed out that women must be the superior sex because they live longer and thus fulfil nature's intent better than males. Learned opinion shifted and the ancient belief in the greater life expectancy of males was slowly abandoned.

This change in scholarly attitudes corresponded with an actual improvement in life expectancies for women. From the opening centuries of the Christian Era, we have tens of thousands of funeral inscriptions, from visible standing monuments and from tomb stones uncovered by archaeologists' excavations. These epigraphs give age at death and allow a rough calculation of the duration of life according to sex. The evidence seems to confirm Aristotle's opinion that at their death, men in these populations of the late ancient era were four to seven years older than women. However, there may be a bias in the data; presumably, the young wife who died prematurely was more likely to earn a memorial than the aged and forgotten widow. But we are certain that women were in short supply in ancient society, either through systematic infanticide of girls or through shorter life expectancies. The biological experience of the women—or baby girls—of classical antiquity was not especially happy.

Unfortunately, we have no comparable epigraphic evidence from medieval populations. The earliest surviving relevant data are sporadic surveys made by the great European monasteries, which wanted clear records of the rents they could expect from their lands. We have between fifteen and twenty of these studies, dating from the ninth century on and enumerating populations settled on particular estates or manors. The largest census was taken by the monastery of Saint Germain-des-Près in Paris and covers lands that are now mainly Parisian suburbs. Monasterial surveys of the early medieval world characteristically show more men than women, with ratios as high as 130 men per 100 women. Women continued to be in short supply.

Of course, the monasteries may have counted males more carefully. Still, much indirect evidence suggests that women were both few and highly valued in early medieval society. The barbarian legal codes, passed down orally and finally redacted between the fifth and ninth centuries as Christianity spread and introduced literacy, characteristically imposed a fine, usually called a *Wergeld*, on anyone who caused a person's injury or death. The fines protecting women were usually as high as, and sometimes higher than, those protecting men, and women of childbearing age sometimes enjoyed special value. Moreover, in marriage arrangements, the groom brought the dowry to the bride. The male or his family assumed the principal costs of setting up the new household. This reverse dowry suggests that grooms had to compete for relatively few brides.

About 965, an Arab geographer, Ibrahim ibn-Iakub, described Slavic marriage customs, which, in many respects, were typical of all barbarian Europe. Ibrahim reported that the "marital price" required of grooms was so high that "if a man has two or three daughters, they are as riches to him; if, however, boys are born to him, this becomes for him a cause of poverty." Nearly the same complaint would be widely heard again in Europe during the late Middle Ages (1350–1500), but the sexual references would be exactly reversed.

From the eleventh or twelfth century, the relative number of women in medieval society, and presumably their life expectancies, rose. A rough estimate of life expectancies for the urban and rural population of Pistoia in Italy in 1427 is 29.8 years for women; 28.4 years for men. The shift is most apparent among the high nobility and in the towns. In Bologna in 1395, there were only 95.6 men for every 100 women; in fifteenth-century Nuremberg, there were 83.8 men per 100 women. Even in cities where the sex ratio favored men—as in Florence in 1427—women grew more numerous in the progression up the scale of ages and held an absolute majority among the elderly. Although many older women may have migrated to the city, women probably also survived better under conditions of urban life.

There are several reasons for women's improving chances of survival during the central Middle Ages (1000–1350). The establishment of strong governments and a stable political order lowered the level and reduced the incidence of violence. New ideals of chivalry restricted—although they by no means completely ended—women's active participation in warfare as fighters or as victims. Women fare better under peaceful conditions, when they do not run the constant risk of attack, rape, or abduction. But the most decisive changes were economic. Primitive agricultural economies, with their low production levels, used predominantly the labor of women, children, and the aged. In a famous description written in A.D. 98, the Roman historian Tacitus observed that among the barbarian Germans, women and children maintained the household economy, while adult males gave themselves over to war and indolence. This pattern probably was preserved well into the Middle Ages. But intensive cultivation requires heavy field work, which women cannot readily perform; peasant women in the late Middle Ages worked hard on their farms, but they were no longer alone.

Finally, the new urban economy offered little employment for women. They spun at home, prayed in convents, and labored as household servants, but they did not constitute a significant part of the urban labor force. Families considered their daughters burdens, unable to earn their keep. Girls were also burdens to prospective husbands, and so the terms of marriage turned against women. The reverse dowry all but disappeared, and the girl or her family had to meet the principal costs of marriage. Throughout the late Middle Ages, the social position of women visibly deteriorated, but so also did the social demands and pressures laid upon them. For women, less participation in economic life and diminishing social importance meant better chances of biological survival.

The other principal biological events in women's lives, menarche and menopause, are difficult to examine historically. Medieval medical writers, who abounded from the eleventh century on, commonly placed menarche at between twelve and fifteen years of age and menopause at fifty. But we have no way of knowing whether they were recording their own observations or merely echoing the ancient authorities. Both Roman law and canon law of the medieval Church set the age of puberty and of binding marriage at twelve years for girls and fourteen years for boys. Saint Augustine, who lived from 354 to 430, contracted to marry a girl "two years below the marriageable age"; presumably, she was ten. "I liked her," he reports in his *Confessions*, "and was prepared to wait." He was then thirty years old. Had his conversion to celibacy not intervened, the girl would have been married at age twelve or soon after, to a groom twenty years older. The pattern seems typical of Roman marriages within the privileged orders.

The medieval canonical requirement that girls be at least twelve years old at the consummation of their marriage was a lower bound. There are many indications that girls at menarche were closer to age fifteen than to age twelve. In the law of the seventh-century Visigoths, a girl was not considered capable of bearing children until age fifteen. In a manorial survey of the early ninth century, from the church of Saint Victor of Marseilles, girls are called "marriageable" only from age fifteen. The customs of Anjou in 1246 similarly give age fifteen as the date of presumed maturity for women.

Still, the traditional estimate of age twelve for menarche was not entirely unrealistic. To judge from marriage patterns, which we can discern from the fourteenth and fifteenth centuries on, rich urban girls tended to be very young at first marriage—younger than those of lower social station and younger even than peasant women. Chaucer's wife of Bath, a middle-class, urban woman, was first married at age twelve, and many urban women were already mothers by age fifteen. Social factors were important here: the rich were apparently eager to settle the future of their daughters as early as possible. But the evidence also hints that menarche came sooner among rich women, and amenorrhea (abnormal absence or suppression of the menses) was presumably less common among them. In consequence, rich women in marriage tended to be consistently more prolific than the poor.

Some dietitians argue that girls must achieve a certain critical amount of body fat to trigger menarche and also to sustain menstruation. The better diet and ease of living that rich Roman girls and their medieval counterparts enjoyed gave them low ages of menarche, close to the thirteenth year anticipated in Roman and canon law. Girls in the countryside and among the poor classes were probably at menarche closer to age fifteen—the year most commonly encountered in the barbarian codes, manorial surveys, and customary laws. Perhaps these same groups also experienced relatively early menopause. The laws of the Visigoths assume that a woman would no longer be fertile after age forty. Apart from what we have gleaned from legal sources, we can say little with certainty about these principal events in the female life cycle.

To add flesh and features to our portrait of women, we can rapidly review the lives of three real people—a peasant, a queen, and a bourgeois. Our peasant is a woman named Alpaix. She was eventually canonized in the late nineteenth century, and even during the Middle Ages, her sanctity was so well recognized that, unlike most peasant women, she attracted a biographer.

Alpaix was born about 1155 in a village near Sens in northern France. Her biographer says that her father, a poor man, "earned his bread by the sweat of his face," by laboriously tilling the soil. Alpaix was the eldest child with several younger brothers. From an early age, she had to assist her father in the heavy work of cultivating the fields. As he drove his two oxen at the head of the plow, she marched alongside, goading the animals to more strenuous effort. When so ordered, she carried manure and sheep dung on her slight shoulders to the fields and gardens. Her young frame could not easily bear the weight, and her father, who seems to have felt no particular sympathy for her, lashed the burdens to her back. Besides her other chores, she had to lead the cattle and sheep to pasture and guard them as they grazed.

All this she did willingly, even on Sundays and festivals, when other peasant girls gave themselves over to dancing and "frivolous things." But then, at the age of twelve, she could no longer sustain the charges laid upon her. According to her biographer, "the tender maiden could no longer bear such heavy labors. Rather, her entire insides were broken and torn from the magnitude of unrelieved work. Drawing deep sighs from the depths of her heart, with the color of her lovely face all marred, she finally gave external, visible signs of her internal suffering. What more can be said? Gripped by unyielding weakness, she remained for an entire year recumbent on her hard and bitter bed, made of straw, without mattress and sheets … ." Ugly lesions appeared on her skin, and her body exuded such a repulsive odor that her family isolated her in a hut. For her sustenance, they delivered black bread daily to her door. But because she could no longer contribute to the household, her brothers demanded that no food be wasted upon her. Their heartless proposal implies that the favorable social position of the peasant woman was indeed linked to her labors.

After a year of excruciating pain, Alpaix was visited in a vision by the Virgin Mary, who cured her of her sores and smell. But Alpaix never recovered the use of her limbs and remained bedridden the rest of her life. She took no food apart from Communion, and died in 1211. Before the eyes of this ignorant, invalid peasant girl, spectacular visions paraded; she was allowed to contemplate the splendid court of heaven and terrifying scenes of hell. Her powerful visions gave her a reputation for sanctity, and pilgrims began to find their way to her bedside. Eventually a biographer arrived and preserved for modern historians an account of a girl's hard childhood in the medieval countryside.

Our medieval queen was also acquainted with holiness; she is Blanche of Castile, mother of Louis IX, or Saint Louis, king of France. She was born on March 4, 1188, in Palencia, Spain, the third daughter of King Alphonso VIII and the granddaughter, through her mother, of Eleanor of Aquitaine, who had been, in succession, queen of France and of England. Blanche was taken to France, where on May 23, 1200, not long after her twelfth birthday, she married the French heir apparent, who would later reign as Louis VIII (1223–1226). The marriage was not consummated until 1205, when Blanche was sixteen years old. The delay probably indicates, not her own retarded menarche, but the youth of her husband, only a few months older than she.

According to differing sources, Blanche's marriage, which ended when Louis died in 1226, gave her either eleven or twelve children. Blanche's deliveries included one set of twins, born dead in 1215. The spacing of her children suggests that Blanche initially tried to nurse her babies, although the king's disposition and his absences on royal business may also have affected the rhythms of her births. Thus, three and a half years elapsed between the birth of her second baby, Philip (born September 9, 1209), and her next delivery on January 26, 1213, when the dead twins were born. No period of nursing followed here, and her next child, the future Louis IX, was born only fifteen months later. Another lengthy interval of two and a half years followed until the next child, presumably because Louis was being nursed by his mother. Thereafter, births in rapid succession (five or six of them in the eight years from 1219 to 1227) suggest that Blanche—now maturing and occupied with children, household, and the affairs of state—no longer suckled her babies but instead relied on wet nurses. Several tracts on nursing have survived from the thirteenth century, and the assumption in all of them is that the nurse was not likely to be the child's mother.

Blanche's career illustrates the powerful position that women could still attain among Europe's high nobility in the thirteenth century. Of course, given the shortage of males, many noble girls did not marry. Most of those who remained single were forced into the religious life and all but excluded from lay society. A woman lucky enough to marry, often did so very young, produced babies in rapid succession, did not nurse her own children, and was likely to be relieved of the risks and burdens of childbearing by her husband's early death. Women frequently figured prominently as administrators and regents for their often absent, or short-lived, husbands and sons. At this elevated social level, a widow with children was not likely to remarry; rather, she would dedicate herself to defending and advancing her children's interest.

Blanche herself was effectively regent of France during the minority of her son Louis (1226–1234), and regent again during his absence on the ill-fated Egyptian crusade (1252). She dominated her son and tyrannized her daughter-in-law; she even tried to prevent the royal couple from chatting together before retiring for the night. Surviving her husband by twenty-eight years, Blanche died at the age of sixty-four in November 1254.

The woman who for us perhaps best represents the medieval bourgeois is Alessandra, daughter of Bardo dei Bardi. She was born in Florence in 1414. We know a good deal about her because a Florentine book dealer named Vespasiano da Bisticci wrote the story of her life. His work, probably the oldest surviving biography of a European woman who was neither a princess nor a saint, tells us, for example, that Alessandra grew to be the tallest young woman in Florence, delighted ambassadors by her grace in promenading and in dancing, learned to read, and could do excellent needlework. She was engaged to be married at age fourteen, but for unknown reasons, the marriage was delayed until 1432, when she was eighteen years old. She was close to the average age of first marriage (17.8 years) for Florentine women in 1427. We can make refined estimates because in that year, a large census was taken of the city. Alessandra's husband, Lorenzo, was the son of Palla di Nofri degli Strozzi, who in 1427 was Florence's richest citizen. Then twenty-seven years old, Lorenzo was young by Florentine standards. The average age of first marriage for males in 1427 was 29.9 years. As Lorenzo was the first-born son in Palla's family, he was probably permitted to marry somewhat earlier. His new wife quickly produced three children in four years—an indication that she was not nursing her own babies.

Disasters then struck Alessandra's family. In 1434, her father, an opponent of the Medici family, was exiled. He was sixty-six years old at the time; Alessandra was twenty. This long generational distance of forty-six years between father and child seems typical of Florentine households. Alessandra's unmarried sisters, left without dowries, were desperate. "What will become of us?" they protested to their departing father. "In whose care will you leave us?" Amid the continuing tumult of Florentine politics, Alessandra's husband,

Lorenzo, was similarly exiled in 1438, freeing her, at the age of twenty-four, of the risk of further pregnancies. In 1427, the average age of mothers at the birth of their middle children was twenty-six, the fathers' average age was forty.

Lorenzo eked out a living as a tutor in the town of Gubbio, but in 1451 he was assassinated by a disgruntled student. He was forty-six at the time. Alessandra, now widowed, had to raise her children alone. Her biographer presents her as a model of dedication and sober deportment for young widows, of whom there were many in Florentine society. He mentions one other, Caterina degli Alberti, who was married at fifteen, bore two children over the next twenty-three months, lost her husband, and remained a widow for the following sixty years. Alessandra herself remained a widow for seventeen years, and died in 1468, at the age of fifty-four.

The bourgeois woman, like the lady of the landed nobility, was very young at first marriage, and her groom was even older than among the nobles. She, too, bore her babies in rapid succession, did not herself nurse them, and through the death of her older husband, was more likely than the noblewoman to be free of the dangers of continual pregnancies. As a child bride married to a mature man, she probably had little influence on her husband and his generation. But as a young mother destined to have intimate and usually extended contact with her children, she could be a respected and influential figure for the young. Married women occupied a strategic position. As intermediaries between the distant generations of fathers and their children, they could readily shape the tastes and values of the young and thus profoundly influence the culture of the city. And widow-hood seems to have suited women well. In Florence in 1427, more than half the adult population of women were widows.

Both the biological and social experiences of women changed substantially during the long medieval centuries. In the overwhelm-ingly rural world of the early Middle Ages, women enjoyed a high social value and entered marriage under favorable terms. But the bases of their preferment seem to have been the taxing physical labor they performed and the substantial contribution they made to the peasant household. With the growth and transformation of the medieval economy—and in particular the rise of towns from the twelfth century on—women's participation in the domestic economy grew restricted. Daughters no longer made a father rich and the terms under which they entered marriage turned against them. But this partial exemption of women from hard labor conferred some benefits: "They work less," observed Albertus Magnus, "and for that reason are not so much consumed." Women in modern Western history still enjoy some of the advantages and bear some of the penalties bequeathed to them by medieval society. We have yet to see what will happen to these advantages and penalties, in our own, rapidly changing times.

4

WOMEN'S WORK IN THE TOWNS OF TRADITIONAL EUROPE

✦ ✦ ✦

"*L'esprit de monopole, qui a présidé à la confection de ces statuts, a été poussé jusqu'à exclure les femmes des métiers les plus convenables à leur sexe, tels que la broderie, qu'elles ne peuvent exercer pour leur propre compte … *" Turgot, on the ancient guild statutes of France, 1776

The participation of women in the urban economies of pre-industrial Europe underwent a profound transformation between the thirteenth and the fifteenth centuries. In the thirteenth century, urban women appear frequently as independent artisans in many crafts and trades. By the late fifteenth century, their participation in the urban work force greatly diminished. Either they no longer worked at all, or the labor they performed had become subordinated to that of male masters and employers. This reduced role of women workers remained characteristic of the urban economies up until the eighteenth century and even beyond.

CITIES, CA. 1300

Paris under Philip the Fair

The city that best illustrates women's participation in the work force in the central Middle Ages is Paris. In ca. 1300, during the reign of Philip IV the Fair, this great northern metropolis, with a population probably surpassing 200,000, was Europe's largest city.[1] Paris also possesses exceptional sources for the history of labor. About 1270, the provost of Parisian merchants, Etienne Boileau, copied into one great collection the statutes of the city guilds.[2] There have also survived from the years 1292 to 1313 seven tax rolls (tailles), surveys of the urban population; four of them are published and readily accessible.[3] They have been used in the past for the study of the Paris work force, but never with a systematic consideration of the specific role of women.[4] Rigorously structured, the tailles invite computer processing. I shall use here the earliest and largest of the tailles, dated 1292 with 14,517 persons entered (excluding institutions and groups), and the latest and smallest, dated 1313, with 6,324 entries. A later, regrettably much smaller set of three Parisian tailles, dated 1421, 1423 and 1438, gives a rough indication as to how the employment of women at Paris changed across the late Middle Ages.[5]

The assessors in the earlier tailles call the entries "hearths" (foca), but it is clear that they did not rigorously use the hearth as the unit of assessment.[6] Persons almost certainly living together—masters and servants or apprentices, parents and children, even husbands and wives—are at times separately assessed. For example, in 1313 Morise the Breton bears an assessment of 70 sous, and his wife Jaqueline is charged separately with 48 sous.[7] And of course, the unstable totals of foca across the separate surveys show that many hearths were omitted.

1. The population of Paris under Philip the Fair has been much discussed and disputed, but I favor the high estimate supported by R. Cazelles, "La population de Paris devant la Peste Noire," in Academie des Inscriptions et Belles Lettres: Comptes Rendus (1966), pp. 539–554, as opposed to P. Dollinger, "Le chiffre de population de Paris au XIVe siecle: 210,000 ou 80,000 habitants," Revue Historique, 216 (1956), pp. 35–44.
2. Le livre des métiers d'Etienne Boileau, ed. R. De Lespinasse, F. Bonnardot (Paris 1870).
3. H. Géraud, Paris sous Philippe le Bel d'après les documents originaux, Paris, 1837, edited the taille of 1292. For the later tailles, see Le livre de la taille de Paris, l'an 1296, ed. K. Michaelsson, Acta Universitatis Gotoburgensis, 67, 3 (Göteborg, 1958), and Le livre de la taille de Paris, l'an de grace 1313, ed. K. Michaelsson, Acta Universitatis Gotoburgensis, 57 (Göteborg, 1951).
4. Besides Géraud, Paris, see G. Fagniez, Etudes sur l'industrie et la classe industrielle à Paris (Paris, 1879), who occasionally provides a count of women in various crafts, but not consistently.
5. Les contribuables parisiens à la fin de la guerre de cent ans: les rôles d'impôt de 1421, 1423 et 1438, ed. J. Favier, Génève 1970 (Hautes études médiévales et modernes, 11).
6. See Le livre de la taille (1313), p. 9, "usque huc lxxviii foca".
7. Ibid., p. 202.

The number of recorded taxpayers falls by more than one half between 1292 and 1313, though the tax imposed remains virtually the same (12,222/11/0 *livres* in 1292, 13,284/11/2 *livres* in 1313). Clearly the assessors had come to concentrate their efforts on ensnaring the rich.

Women make up 15 percent of the assessed taxpayers in 1292 and 11 percent in 1313. It is hard to know how many of these women were widows (almost 200 in 1292 were servants, presumably young and unmarried). The presence of large numbers of women of unstated marital status supports this observation: the assessors did not identify women primarily in relationship to their fathers or husbands, living or dead. They regarded thousands of women, whether single, married, or widowed, as financially independent and hence liable to taxes.

Of the 2238 women taxpayers who appear in the taille of 1292, 883 (39 percent) show an occupational name. The number of occupations represented is an extraordinary 172. In the smaller survey of 1313, of the 735 women who appear within it, 347 (47 percent) are identified by occupation, and the different occupations there represented number a still astonishing 130.

Were these occupational names borne by women in the Parisian tax lists in fact family names? Or did they represent the employment of a deceased husband which the widow did not in fact exercise?[8] But family names remained rare at Paris at the time of Philip the Fair, and the occupational name carried by a woman is always in the feminine gender—not to be expected in a true family name. Moreover, the assessors did not consistently identify widows by the names of their deceased husbands. Why would they identify them by their husbands' occupations? Parisian women, we must conclude, really did practice the employments attributed to them.

The women of Paris are represented in most principal economic sectors. As drapers, money changers, jewelers and mercers, they appear among the richest professions. The wealthiest woman in the survey of 1313 was a dame Isabeau, a *drapière* or cloth merchant from the village of Tremblay, probably Tremblay in Normandy; she

---

8. See K. Wesoly, "Der weibliche Bevölkerungsanteil in spätmittelalterlichen und frühneuzeitlichen Städten und die Betätigung von Frauen im zünftigen Handwerk (insbesondere am Mittel- und Oberrhein," *Zeitschrift für die Geschichte des Oberrheins*, 128, n. s. 89 (1980), p. 117, for the argument that women in German hearth lists carried the names of occupations they did not exercise.

bore an assessment of 75 *livres*.[9] There are even women moneyers or mint workers.[10] They are copyists and artists. There are women tavern keepers, firewood dealers, even masons, shoemakers, girdle makers, millers, smiths, shield makers and archers. Like males, women trained apprentices who were not necessarily other women. Thus, in 1292 a "valet" named Oudet works in the household of Aveline, a milliner.[11] A lady juggler and dancer are present among the taxpayers of 1292.

Few occupations seem to have been exclusively male. Those which involved either distant travel or heavy hauling such as sailors and porters appear without women. Women were also excluded from some licensed professions, such as those of notary or lawyer. However, in these fields even male practitioners were surprisingly few.

Although women show a wide distribution across the occupations, they also show a marked tendency to specialize in particular trades. Table 1 shows the fifteen most numerous professions for women at Paris in 1292 and 1313.

Not surprisingly, household servants were overwhelmingly female (they were also omitted in the survey of 1313). Women were important in the preparation or sale of food. There are five women "fryers" *(fritières)*, five millers, five sellers of milk, four soup makers, four sellers of oil, three brewers, three sellers of cheese, two wine dealers, and several types of bakers (nine *pastaières,* three *oublaières)* in the taille of 1292. But somewhat surprisingly, professional cooks *(cuisiniers* or *keus)* were usually men—11 out of 12 in 1313.

Women were prominent as *regratières,* peddlers who at Paris sold foodstuffs and salt. They were also many among the peddlers of rags and old-clothes *(fripières).* Women washed the clothes of the city, although eight male *lavandiers* also appear in the taille of 1292.

Women are also very prominent in the care of the sick and the prescription of medicine. There are eight lady doctors at Paris in 1292. There were also two *ventrières* or midwives. Three other women with the title of *mestresse* may have been doctors. Not counted here among the doctors, as she was not head of her households, is a Jewess named Sarre or Sarah, a *mirgesse* and an apparent refugee from England. She lived with her husband Vivant, not him-

9. *Le livre de la taille (1313),* p. 202.
10. See *Le livre de la taille (1297),* p. 428, Jehanne la moussete, and p. 430, Eremborc, both listed among the moneyers.
11. H. Géraud, *Paris,* p. 95.

Table 1
The Fifteen Largest Feminine Occupations in the Paris Tailles.

1292		1313	
Household servants	197	Tavern keeper	23
Peddlar	50	Peddlar	20
Dress maker	46	Hostel keeper	18
Laundress	38	Barber	13
Beguine (religious)	29	Dress Maker	11
Hairdresser	22	Laundress	10
Silk thread worker	20	Silk spinner	10
Silk worker	14	Candle maker	10
Barber	13	Mercer	9
Nurse	12	Silk thread worker	7
Hostel keeper	12	Wool worker	7
Fishmonger	11	Linen worker	7
Wax worker	10	Hairdresser	7
Candle maker	10	Wax worker	7
Old clothes dealer, weaver, milliner, pastry maker, baker	9	Poultry dealer, firewood dealer, goldsmith	5

Key: baker = fournière, candle maker = chandelière, dress maker = cousturière, firewood dealer = buchière, fishmonger = poissonière, goldsmith = orfevresse, household servant = chamberière, hair dresser = coiffrière, hostel keeper = hostelière, laundress = lavandière, linen worker = linière, mercer = mercière, milliner = chapelière, nurse = nourrice, old clothes dealer = fripière, pastry maker = pastaière, peddlar = regratière, poultry dealer = poullaière, silk thread worker = crespinière, silk worker = ouvrière de soie, wax worker = cirière, weaver = tesserande, wool worker = lanière.
Source: Géraud, *Paris* and *Taille (1313)*, Michaelsson ed. (see note 3).

self a doctor. Barbers too performed medical services, such as blood letting or the setting of bones; 13 were women in both 1292 and 1313. The many nurses (twelve *nourrices* in 1292) in the tax lists were all female. Spice dealers were also pharmacists; two were women in 1292 and two again in 1313. Finally, women administered the women's bathhouses at Paris (there were three *estuveresses* in 1313) where adult males were not supposed to enter.

Notable among the industries that engaged women in significant numbers was the sale of wax and candle making. Woman candle and wax dealers *(cirières)* outnumber the males ten to eight in 1292, and they are well represented (ten women, 67 men) among the candle makers *(chandelières)*.

An industry dominated by women was the making of silk cloth. There is only one male spinner of silk to be found in 1292; the named women *filleresses de soie* are eight. The great corpus of guild statutes gathered by Etienne Boileau about 1270 identifies five silk guilds, the membership of which seems to have been chiefly female.[12] Probably, the numerous women simply called "weavers" in 1313 were working in silk. These feminine silk guilds show the same structure as the predominantly male guilds. Their statutes mention *preudes fames,* or "good women", charged with enforcing regulations. Spinners could not employ more than three girl apprentices, and for not fewer than seven years. The girls could then become mistresses of the trade in their own right.

As the chief spinners and weavers of silk, women were very visible in the making of luxury fabrics and clothes. They embroidered cloths (eight *broderesses* in 1292) and made lace (six *lacières),* purses (four *boursières),* pillow cases and altar cloths (twenty *crespinères),* and ribbons, coifs and hats.

Why were women so important in the working of silk? One reason may be that most silk products, purses, coifs, ribbons, and the like, were made specifically for women. It is, however, also likely that their smaller fingers and greater manual dexterity gave them an advantage over men in spinning and weaving the fine silk threads. They were surely also more adept in lace making and embroidery than men.

Gold thread was often used in embroidery, and this probably explains the appearance of women as goldsmiths (there were *six orfevresses* in 1292).

Women were very visible too in the production of another fabric: linen. The guild statutes, while mentioning only male *liniers,* assume that both apprentices and workers in a linen shop will be female.[13] There were eight *linières* registered at Paris in 1292 (eleven males), and four linen weavers *(telières).* While males may

12. The statutes are in R. De Lespinasse, F. Bonnardot, *Le livre des métiers,* p. 68, "Fileresses de soye a grans fusseaux;" p. 70, "Fileresses de soye a petits fuseaux;" p. 74, "Ouvrieres de tissuz de soie;" p. 83, "Tisserandes de soies;" p. 207, "Chapeliers et chapelieres d'orfois." The text of these last statutes makes it apparent that the membership was chiefly female. It mentions, for example, the employment of only female workers or apprentices.

13. R. De Lespinasse, F. Bonnardot, Le livre des métiers, p. 118: "Nos liniers de Paris ne puet ne doit avoir que i. aprentice ... la quale aprentice il ne puent ne doivent prendre a mainz de vi anz de service ... "; "Li linniers de Paris prent tant d'ouvrières comme il voudront ... "

have sold the finished cloth, the workers who produced it were chiefly women. Flax was a garden crop and probably grown chiefly in the suburbs. Since immemorial time, gardens were the preserve of women. It is further worth noting that at Paris these *ouvrières* in silk and linen seem to have worked in their masters' shops or houses and not their own.

Parisian women at the time of Philip the Fair thus appear in significant numbers in a wide variety of crafts and trades. However, these same records offer some slight evidence that women's prominence in the city economy was already beginning to fade.

Their representation seems surprisingly low in one of the most important urban industries, the manufacture of woollens. There were 73 male weavers at Paris in 1292 and only nine female, and these latter may have been working in silk or linen. In 1313 the comparable figures for weavers are 63 males and only four females. Among dyers, the sexual division is even more unbalanced. There were 15 male dyers and one female in 1292; 25 males and one woman in 1313. Women doubtlessly spun the wool into yarn, but there are only six spinners *(filandières)* identified at Paris in 1292, and we cannot be certain that they were spinning wool, rather than flax or silk. It almost appears as if the spinning of wool, though widely done by Parisian women, was not considered a primary profession worth naming in the surveys.

Then too, women consistently appear in the two surveys poorer than males in the same professions. In 1313, for example, women across all named employments carry only 66 percent of the assessment borne by men (277.8 deniers for women, 423.5 deniers for men).

Moreover, between 1292 and 1313, the representation of women among the independent taxpayers falls from 15 to 11 percent. This also implies that their economic weight was diminishing, though it may only reflect the assessors' concentration on catching the wealthy. Finally, women in 1292 constituted 13 percent of all Parisians showing an occupational title (883 out of 6,759) but only 8 percent (347 out of 4,494 in 1313). Even if we exclude servants from the earlier count (they are not included in 1313), a decline is still visible; among all taxpayers showing an occupation (excluding servants) women represent 10 percent in 1292, 8 percent in 1313.

In spite of these hints of slippage in women's presence in the crafts and trades, the principal conclusion stands: the Parisian economy at the time of Philip the Fair remained remarkably open to women. Was this characteristic of other towns in other regions of Europe at about 1300?

Germany, Spain, Italy

In Germany, the Rhine city of Cologne was an important center of silk manufactures; like Paris, it even contained guilds, four as compared with the five in Paris, that were exclusively feminine in membership. There were the yarn makers, the gold spinners, the silk spinners, and the silk weavers.[14]

Toulouse in Languedoc claims a rich series of guild statutes, dated between 1270 and 1322.[15] Women were active participants in five guilds: as weavers, finishers, candle makers, merchants of wax, and dealers in small weight merchandises (in effect, pedlars) which probably included old clothes. The statutes of the finishers and weavers, dated 1279, imply that all spinning was done by women.[16] Women at Toulouse were still engaged in weaving wool cloth and in dyeing it.[17]

Barcelona in Catalonia was late in acquiring a wool industry, but it does appear as if women helped in its establishment. A report presented to the King James II of Aragon in 1304 observes that the new industry was attracting to the city "from other lands numerous masters, both men

14. The fundamental study of women workers in medieval Cologne is M. Wensky, *Die Stellung der Frau in der stadtkölnischen Wirtschaft im Spätmittelalter,* Quellen und Darstellungen zur Hansischen Geschichte, (Bonn, 1980). She largely agrees with the classic statement by Karl Bucher, published in 1882, that German women in the late medieval towns participated in all the trades that their strength allowed. For a review of Wensky's data but with differing interpretations, see M. C. Howell, *Women, Production, and Patriarchy in Late Medieval Cities* (Chicago-London 1986), pp. 124–158. For further discussion of women's work and its restricted range in early modern Germany, see M. E. Wiesner, *Working Women in Reformation Germany* (New Brunswick, N.J., 1986).

15. *Early Guild Records of Toulouse,* ed. Sister M.A. Mulholland, B. M. V. New York.

16. *Ibid.,* p. 5: " ... quod aliqua filandaria lane non recipiat ab aliquo homine vel femina lanam causa filandi ..."

17. *Ibid., p.* 6: " ... omnes textores et omnes alii homines et femine huius ville Tholose possunt et liceat eis facere pannum ... "; and p. 5: " ... si aliquis tincturerius vel tinctureria ... ".

and women".[18] In the first half of the fourteenth century at Barcelona, "women not only worked at the loom, but they were able to own their own shops, giving work to their employees and apprentices".[19]

Italy was a land not particularly favorable to women artisans or entrepreneurs. Lombard law subjected them to perpetual male tutelage; they could not independently enter into contractual obligations. Moreover, the republican constitutions of the Italian city states excluded women from political society. The Italian urban woman could not look, as could women in the north and even in Iberia, to the women members of princely dynasties for examples of feminine influence and, occasionally, power. The exclusively male world of Italian urban politics reinforced male dominance in economic life as well.

Nonetheless, even in Italy, women appear more economically active in ca. 1300 than they would be in later centuries. Robert Davidsohn, for example, that punctilious historian of Florence, was impressed by the participation of girls and women in both the silk and woolen industries at about 1300. He wrote: "In the textile trade women appear to have been occupied in very great numbers since early times, to the extent that all the apprenticeship contracts I have noted concerning the branches of silk and wool weaving involve girls, up to the first third of the fourteenth century".[20]

The earliest notarial chartularies of Florence do contain numerous references to women weavers. In 1288, for example, as seen in her will, a woman named Donata, an immigrant from Castellonchio in the countryside, supports herself by weaving cloths; after her death, her loom is to be sold and the proceeds given to the poor.[21] In 1299, another woman weaver, named Tessa, the wife of a shoemaker, accepts

18. C. Carrère, *Barcelone: centre économique à l'époque des difficultés, 1380–1462* (Paris and The Hague, 1967), p. 431. For further comment on this "carta del *battle*" with recent bibliography, see *El trabajo de las mujeres en la Edad Media Hispana*, ed. A. Munoz Fernandez, C. Segura Graino (Madrid, 1988), p. 260.

19. ???

20. *Forschungen zur Geschichte von Florenz, I, Regesten zur Geschichte des Handels, des Gewerbes und des Zunftwesens* (Berlin, 1901), p. 222: "Im Textilgewerbe scheinen Frauen seit früher Zeit in sehr starkem Maasse beschäftigt gewesen zu sein, derart sogar, dass alle von uns bemerkten Lehrverträge aus den Zweigen der Seiden-und Wollenweberei bis zum ersten Drittel des 14 Jahrhunderts sich auf Mädchen beziehen."

21. See D. Herlihy and C. Klapisch-Zuber, *Les Toscans et leurs familles. Une étude du catasto florentin de 1427* (Paris, 1978), p. 582.

two brothers, ages 18 and 17 respectively, as apprentices, in order to learn the art of weaving. They will remain with her for six years, and she will provide them support as stipulated in the contract.[22]

On the other hand, the guild statutes of Italian towns indicate that the labor force engaged in cloth production was mixed and seemingly tipping toward males. The communal statutes of Bologna, dated 1288, mention "dyers, cleaners, shearers, finishers, weavers, burlers, stretchers of cloth, male combers and female combers, beaters, male spinners and female spinners, washers of wool".[23] The only two occupations cited in the feminine gender are combers and spinners. Even the washers are treated as males.

Florentine statutes, dated 1296, of dealers in old clothes and workers in linen *(rigattieri e linaioli)*, mention women vendors of clothes and workers in linen; they are subject to the guild's authority and must post surety for their honest behavior. They were not, however, formally matriculated and were not fullfledged members of the guild.[24] A man who married the daughter or sister of a master could be matriculated for a lower fee into the guild, but this favor probably allowed guild members to pay a reduced dowry for their daughters' marriages. On the other hand, the guild statutes of the Florentine wool dealers *(lanaiuoli)*, dated 1317 to 1319, continue to refer to weavers as both male and female.[25]

Finally, a Tuscan poet named Francesco da Barberino in the first half of the fourteenth century wrote a long didactic poem on proper behavior for women.[26] In the fifteenth part of the poem, he warns against the temptations and sins involved in the typical occupations

22. *Ibid.,* p. 573.
23. *Statuti di Bologna dell'anno 1288,* ed. G. Fasoli, P. Sella, Studi e testi, 85 (Città del Vaticano, 1939), II, p. 208, "tintores, battarii, tonditores, cimatores, tessarii, delapolatores, tiratores pannorum, petenatores et petenatrices, verghezatores, filatores et filattrices, lavoratores lane."
24. *Statuti dell'arte dei rigattieri e linaioli di Firenze (1296–1340),* ed. F. Sartini, Fonti e studi sulle corporazioni artigiane del Medio Evo (Florence, 1940), p. 9: "venditores et venditrices pannorum."
25. *Statuto dell'arte della lana di Firenze (1377-1319),* ed. A. M. Enriques Agnoletti, Fonti e studi sulle corporazioni artigiane del Medio Evo, Fonti, I (Florence, 1940), p. 143: "quod nullus eorum (lanificum) det ... aliquam telam alicui textori vel textrici ad tesendum."
26. The poem has been several times edited; a recent and good edition is Francesco Da Barberino, *Del reggimento e costume di donne,* ed. G. E. Sansone (Turin, 1957). For comment, see G. B. Festa, *Un galateo femminile del trecento* (Bari, 1910), pp. 155–160, on occupations.

the women held. The occupations he mentions are those of barber, baker, seller of fruits and vegetables *(treccola),* seller of eggs or chickens *(pollaiuola),* or cheese *(caciaiuola),* beggar *(accattatrice,* literally a woman who receives) innkeeper or cook, hawker of charms, mercer, and uncloistered religious *(conversa).* The mention of the barber's art and the allusion to sorcery recall the medieval woman's ancient association with the medical or magical treatment of ills. Women appear in his list in the familiar role as innkeepers, offering travelers lodging and food (they are not to provide, Francesco insists, additional comforts). The larger number of the named occupations involve sales of food or clothing.

This rapid and partial survey of urban horizons in ca. 1300 supports the conclusion that the urban economy was everywhere relatively open to women. Though represented in a great variety of occupations, women were particularly important in the manufacture of silks and linens (while retaining a reduced presence in wool work, apart from spinning and washing); in making dresses, hats, gloves and purses; in selling new and used clothing; in hawking fruits and vegetables; in the keeping of inns and the preparation of food; in candle making; in nursing, in empiric medicine and in magic.

How did the participation of women in the urban economies change across the late Middle Ages?

CITIES IN THE FIFTEENTH CENTURY

Paris

In 1421, King Charles VII of France and Henry IV of England (Charles' heir by the treaty of Troyes of 1420) imposed a tax in marcs on the city of Paris; two of three accounts, comprising nine out of sixteenth urban parishes have survived, listing 1394 household heads. In 1423 the king imposed a loan, with assessments stated in francs, on the whole city, but only 502 household heads were registered. In 1438, Charles VII, who had recently retaken Paris from the English, collected another *aide* from the city; the full account has survived, though the number of household heads included is a again small, 578. In 1970, Jean Favier edited all three rolls and provided a critical introduction.[27] Though short, these fifteenth-century surveys are complex documents, showing numerous emendations. (In the following analysis, I count only those households to which the editor Favier assigns a number; many of these same households are subsequently listed as exempt). The names of occupations also shifted. The generic title *marchant* has become much more common (133 appearances) in the later than in the earlier surveys. Men bearing the title *maistre* without further specification of profession or trade proliferate in the late surveys (195 appearances in 1421–38, 197 in the much larger combined surveys of 1292 and 1313).

In regard to male occupations, the great contrast that these tailles present with the earlier surveys is the marked increase in notaries, lawyers, officials and soldiers—occupations from which women were traditionally excluded.

The partial taille of 1421 lists 1187 men and 143 women; that of 1423, 475 men and 27 women; and that of 1438, 544 men and 34 women.

The appearance of women as household heads at Paris falls from 15 percent in 1292 to 11 percent in 1313 to 8.5 percent in 1421-38. In 1421-38 only 20 percent of the women (41 out of 204) show an occupation, as opposed to 41 percent in the combined surveys of 1292 and 1313 (1229 out of 2973 women household heads). The proportion of visibly employed women household heads thus drops by one half. The number of occupations shown by women declines by 92 percent from those displayed in 1282 and 1313 (from 212 in the earlier combined surveys to only 19 in 1421-38). The proportion of men showing an occupation actually increases from the earlier to the later surveys, from 56 percent in 1292-1313 to 64 percent in 1421-38 (1416 out of 2206 male household heads).

However, many of the men (197) in the later surveys bear only the title "maistre" without further specification of the art they exercise. The number of occupations displayed by males in these small, later surveys is 124—a decline of 64 percent from the 366 professions that males showed in the earlier two surveys. Still, the drop is far less than the 92 percent registered by women.

Women in Paris in the early fifteenth century were still important as innkeepers and food preparers. They were retailers, especially of

27. *Les contribuables parisiens.*

Table 2
Women Showing Occupations in the Parisian Tailles. 1421–38.

Occuptn	Ttl	Women	Occuptn	Ttl	Women
Merchant	125	8	Maker of amices	2	1
Mercer	42	7	Purse maker	1	1
Draper	46	4	Butcher	33	1
Spice dlr	87	3	Silk worker	1	1
Innkeeper	64	2	Tapestry worker	5	1
Hostel kpr	16	2	Patinière	1	1
Baker	64	2	Hay dealer	1	1
Barber	10	2	Used clothes dlr	9	1
Maker of hutches	5	1	Glove maker	3	1
			Candle maker	13	1

Source: Favier, 1970. Maker of hutches = huchière, used clothes dealer = fripière, candle maker = chandelière. The one "patinière" who appears may have been a "polisher".

food products and clothing. They worked in wax. Although female weavers, dyers, seamstresses and goldsmiths have altogether vanished, women retained at least a presence in the silk industry and in making (probably out of silk) purses and gloves. Women doctors have vanished too, but women kept at least a small place in the related arts of barber and spice dealer.

Incontrovertibly, women's place in the economic life of Paris diminished markedly over the century and more that separates the two sets of censuses. In 1313, women showing an occupation accounted for 8 percent of all household heads showing an occupation; that figure falls to 2.8 percent in the fifteenth century.

Other records, less comprehensive than the surveys but distributed over a longer span of time, also indicate that feminine participation in economic life was diminishing. In 1351 King Jean of France issued a series of ordinances, meant to control the inflation of wages that was coming in the wake of the Black Death. In describing the textile trades, Jean uses masculine forms exclusively to identify weavers, dyers, cloth makers, and fullers.[28] He uses only feminine forms for spinners and burlers. In Jean's perspective, the central operations of cloth making were now done predominantly by men.

At Paris, the statutes of the guild of pastry bakers, dated 1397, forbade women of any sort from baking communion wafers, or from

28. *Histoire générale de Paris. Les métiers,* ed. R. De Lespinasse (Paris, 1886–1897), I, p. 41. The professions named are "tixarrens de draps", "tainturiers", "faisers de toilles", "foulons", "filleresses", and "pigneresses."

going about the city selling any product of the art.[29] And no woman pastry baker without a husband who was also a baker could take an apprentice [30]. The Parisian statutes occasionally show outright discrimination against women workers. For example, women enjoyed a traditional visibility among the barbers, as they did in all the quasi medical professions. But the statutes of the barbers, dated 1438, contains the following provision:

> Also, that no male or female barber, of whatever condition he may be, may or ought to allow to be hired in the said trade any woman or girl or to support her in his house or shop, unless that she be the wife or daughter of a master of the said trade, and of good life and reputation .[31]

In sum, at Paris only the wife or daughter of a barber could aspire to become a barber, but males as yet faced no such restriction. By 1450, the five women's guilds at Paris were reorganized and absorbed into predominantly male corporations.[32]

In 1488, the statutes of weavers and drapers of the small Norman town of Gruchet-le-Valesse seem to exclude women, except the wives and daughters of masters, even from spinning:

> Also, no woman, who is not the wife of a master or their [sic] daughters can do anything of the said art under pain of three sous nine deniers of penalty, except that they may burl [espincher] the cloth and that only.[33]

England, Flanders, Germany

At Bristol in England in 1461, the town government forbade weavers to employ their wives, daughters or maids at the loom.[34] This is one of the few texts that states a reason for the restriction: "Lest the king's people likely to do the king's service should lack employment".

29. *Ibid.,* II, p. 371: "Item, que femme quelle qu'elle soit ny puisse faire pain a chanter n'a celebrer en eglise: aussi ne puisse porter aval la ville vendre aucune chose dudit mestier."

30. *Ibid.*: "Item, que feme oubloyere senz mary oubloyer ne put prendre apprentiz audit mestier de l'oubloyere."

31. *Ibid.,* III, p. 654: "Item, que nul barbier ou barbiere, de quelque condition qu'il soit, ne pourra ne devra souffrir besongner dudit mestier aucune femme ou fille, ne tenir en son hostel ou ouvrouer, sinon qu'elle soit femme ou fille de mastre dudit mestier et de bonne vie et renommee".

32. E. Ennen, *Frauen im Mittelalter* (Munich, 1986), p. 162.

33. L. Chaumet, *La corporation des tisserands,* in *Le textile en Normandie: Etudes diverses,* Société libre d'émulation de la Seine-Maritime (Rouen, 1975) , p. 110.

34. Cited in A. F. Green, *Town Life in the Fifteenth Century,* 2 vols. (New York and London, 1895), II, p. 96, n. 1.

Obviously, in the view of the city fathers, the king's people were exclusively males.

At Ghent in Flanders in 1374, the wives of fullers or women of any sort were forbidden to wash any type of clothes.[35]

The status of women workers in late-medieval German towns has attracted much recent attention. The point of departure of this research is the thesis put forward by Karl Bucher in 1883.[36] Bucher argued that for reason of wars and plagues women outnumbered men in the German towns, and that they were admitted into every kind of work that their strength allowed them to perform.

The recent research revises both these conclusions. Women often did outnumber men in commercial towns (at Cologne or Nuremberg, for example, at least in certain years). But men outnumbered women in industrial towns, especially those with many workers in wool or metals. Women's participation in the work force was limited and small. Cologne with four feminine guilds was exceptional; only Nuremberg and Basel in Switzerland had single guilds of women members[37]. Women did not freely enter into every occupation. The occupational names that widows often inherited from their husbands do not prove that they continued to work at their husbands' trades. They were rather concentrated in household service, food sales and petty retailing. They tended to form the lowest, least trained and least paid level of the urban work force.

> For girls [concludes Peter Ketsch], at least in the late Middle Ages, it was no way usual to learn a trade. General government regulations, that admit young men and women in equal measure into training, should not be overvalued, for they derive in part from a time in which girls certainly could not learn a trade.[38]

Finally, guild and government regulations from many towns imposed mounting restrictions upon women, both religious and lay. In 1421 at

35. *Recueil de documents relatifs à l'histoire de l'industrie drapière en Flandre,* ed. G. Espinas, H. Pirenne (Brussels, 1906–) I, p. 171. "20. Item, que nulle femme de foulon n'autre quelle que soit, puis hores en avant, ne puist laver piece ne drap quelconque, sous 5 s. d'amende."

36. There are good introductions to the literature in C. Howell, *Women, production,* pp. 1–6; and E. Ennen, *Frauen,* pp. 134–163.

37. *Ibid.,* p. 162.

38. P. Ketsch, *Frauen in Mittelalter. Quellen und Materialen,* ed. A. Kuhn, I, *Frauenarbeit im Mittelalter, Frauenbild und Frauenrechte in Kirche und Gesellschaft* (Düsseldorf, 1983–4), I, p. 117.

Cologne, as the result of a dispute between linen weavers and beguines, the government allowed the beguines to operate only six looms; in 1437, the number was reduced to three. By the second half of the fifteenth century, it forbade all kinds of textile work in religious houses.[39] In 1330 the aldermen of Strasbourg allowed women weavers of linen or of silk to work independently, but if they wove wool or cotton or employed helpers, then they were to be subject to the male weavers.[40] In the biggest of the textile industries, that of wool, women at Strasbourg as indeed in many towns were reduced to helpers and auxiliaries.

The status of the wives, widows and daughters of the male masters attracted much attention in the regulations. At Lüneburg, the widow of a shoemaker could continue his practice for one year, but if she had no children or only daughters, then she had to sell her franchise.[41] But almost everywhere, some privileges were extended to widows and daughters. A man who married a master's daughter could usually enter the guild with a reduced fee and other exemptions. This doubtlessly served the masters by facilitating the marriages of their daughters and reducing the required dowries. Widows too could usually continue the trade. But almost everywhere, they could not take on apprentices, unless they married another master. The regulation allowed widows to support themselves but not to compete effectively or for long with the male masters. Peter Ketsch sums up the situation in German lands:

> Without doubt with the closing of the guilds in the late Middle Ages the tendency grew stronger to force women completely out of the crafts and to disqualify them.[42]

Iberia

As Mediterranean communities, the Iberian Christian states presented women with many of the same cultural obstacles to independence as they faced in Italy. The high value placed on feminine virginity before marriage imposed a close supervision upon young

39. M. Wensky, Die Stellung der Frau, pp. 38–40.
40. P. Ketsch, Frauen, I, p. 1979. If they weave "wollenen Tuch oder Baumwolltuch oder Stulhltuch oder Knechte beschäftigen, mit der Webern dienen."
41. E. Ennen, Frauen, p. 137.
42. P. Ketsch, Frauen, I, p. 117: "Ohne Zweifel verstärkt sich jedoch mit dem Abschliessen der Zünfte im ausgehenden Mittelalter die Tendenz, die Frauen gänzlich aus den Handwerken zu verdrängen und sie zu deisqualifizieren." For discrimination against women workers in German lands in the early modern period, see E. Wiesner, Working Women.

girls and limited their freedom of movement within society. But there were also compensating factors.[43] The Visigothic law prevalent in Iberia was perhaps the most liberal of all the Germanic codes for women; it allowed them to enter contractual agreements without male supervision, assured them an equal share with their brothers in the paternal inheritance, and granted them a portion too of their husbands' acquisitions during their years of marriage. The *reconquista* took males away from home for lengthy periods, conferred important administrative functions on women, and assured that many women would inherit lands and offices from males who died in the fighting. Iberian history and Iberian literature give many examples of resourceful and vigorous women, ruling states, even directing armies. Finally, the efforts to resettle lands recently taken from the Moors led the Christian kings to grant generous terms to new settlers—to both men and women.[44]

Barcelona, a big city of about 35,000 in ca. 1400, included many women in its work force but also confronted them with declining opportunities as the fifteenth century progressed. Women *custureras,* dressmakers or seamstresses, were active in the city.[45] As widely across Europe, women seem to have been especially employed in working linen. On 2 March 1448, the confraternity of linen and cotton weavers required that candidates for the mastership pass an examination and pay a fee. The fee was set at ten sous for men and five for women. Like the men, the women who passed the examination and paid the fee became masters, could open a shop and, if they wished, become a member of the confraternity, a *confraressa de la dita confraria.* Further regulations in 1456 set the apprenticeship period at three and one half years, and raised the fee for admission to the mastership at 10 sous for women, 30 for men, and 60 for foreigners. The low fee for women may mean they earned less as masters, but otherwise the statutes were not visibly discriminatory. In linen and cotton manufacture, they were indispensable.

43. For a collection of studies of women and work, largely concerned with the late Middle Ages in Spain, see *El trabajo.*

44. H. Dillard, *Daughters of the Reconquest: Women in Castilian Town Society, 1100–1300* (Cambridge, 1984).

45. C. Carrère, *Barcelone,* pp. 371-374. The textile trades at Barcelona are also discussed by the "Equip Broida" in *El trabajo,* pp. 260–273; it discerns "una marginacion femenina a principios del siglo XV" most pronounced in the wool industry.

The situation is very different in regard to the wool trades at Barcelona. Although women masters had helped establish the industry at Barcelona at about 1300, by the fifteenth century their participation seems limited to the poorly remunerated, low skilled work of spinning. In weaving, dyeing, fulling and finishing the cloth, they appear in the statutes and chartularies neither as masters, nor as apprentice , nor even as workers. "Outside of spinning", Claude Carrère, the historian of Barcelona's economy, concludes, "the textile trades seem to have been almost uniquely male".[46] Even the widows of masters were by then harshly treated. An ordinance of 1402 prohibited the widow of a weaver from taking over his shop, unless she had a son of 12 years to succeed him.[47]

Seville, the Andalusian port in the southwest corner of the Iberian peninsula, was about 1400 a moderate-sized town of some 13,000 inhabitants. A *padron* (survey) of 1384 names 2457 household heads, more than 100 of them women, and 55 of these show an occupation.[48] Women's occupations trace a now familiar pattern. They are retailers of many kinds of food: barley *(cebadera)*, honey *(melera)*, milk *(lechera)*, bread *(panadera)*, fish *(pescadera)*, fruit *(frutera)* and spices *(especiera)*. They are potters *(ollera)*, ribbon or lace makers *(cordonera)*, apparently brokers *(corredera)*, and pedlars *(buhonera)*. But they are also still actively engaged in cloth making, as drapers *(lencera)*, tenters *(tendera)*, and weavers *(texedera—*three, as opposed to 38 male *tejedores)*. The contemporary guild statutes also refer to weavers as both men and women.[49] Would it be fair to attribute this large participation of women in Seville's labor force in 1384 at least partially to its diminished population, recently wracked by plagues, and to the labor shortage that must have accompanied it? The urban economy becomes visibly less favorable to women as the fifteenth century progresses. Surviving surveys from late in the century show us women engaged in textile work, but almost all of them are spinners. In 1484 a Guiomar Rodriguez declares "that she has no work except the distaff with which to earn

46. C. Carrère, *Barcelone*, p. 484, n. 1: " ... en dehors de la filature, les métiers du textile semblent avoir été presque uniquement masculins."

47. *Ibid.*, p. 476.

48. The occupations of 1384 are discussed in J. Gonzalez, *"La poblacion de Sevilla a fines del siglo xiv,"* Hispania (1975), pp. 49–74.

49. See A. Collantes De Teran Sanchez, *Sevilla en la baja Edad media: la ciudad y sus hombres* (Seville, 1977), pp. 311–330 for what follows.

her bread".[50] In the survey of the neighborhood of San Lorenzo of 1500, there are 52 women with distaffs and two more with spinning wheels, but only two with looms, and these latter may have been weaving linen or silk. A compensating factor was the establishment from the early fifteenth century of silk working in the city, an art traditionally open to women. The statutes of the *sederos* excuse from examination the girls and "honest women" who work at the trade at home. On the other hand, the statutes of the other textile trades were following the now common policies of imposing tests and high entrance fees on those who would open a shop.[51] These tough requirements went against the interests of women, who always commanded fewer resources than men.

Italy

The towns of late-medieval Italy possess the largest and most detailed town surveys of any European region, but the picture they present of urban working women is consistently bleak. One such survey, dated 1395, survives from the university town of Bologna. It lists all household members, and it gives their ages and occupations though not an estimate of wealth. Some few women appear with occupations. Madonna Zohana, age 80, "who spins", lives with her daughter Bartolomea, age 60; here are two old women surviving in the city by the work of their hands.[52] Another old lady named Fiore, age 60, is a *revendetrixe,* a retailer of rags and old clothing. Margherita, age 40, who is not given the title *donna* and may therefore not be married, is a spinner of linen. Four other women spinners of linen are her near neighbors. They are the widow donna Mina Pifari, age 50, who lives with her daughter age 11; donna Francesca, age 40, apparently a widow with a family of two girls, ages 15 and 14, and two boys, ages 5 and 3; and another widow named Armelina, age 45. Armelina presides over a large family of five persons. Two boys, age 16 and 12, are learning how to make keys; their younger brother is age 3; and her two daughters are also young, age 9 and 6 respectively. Three unmarried girls, presumably

50. *Ibid.,* p. 323: "que no tyene fasienda saluo la rueca con que gana de comer."
51. *Ibid.*
52. *Documenti sulla popolazione di Bologna alla fine del trecento,* ed. P. Montanari, Fonti per la storia di Bologna, 1 (Bologna, 1966), p. 64.

young though their ages are not explicitly stated, are *fanti,* servants. Another unmarried girl is a *famula,* also a servant. One older woman, addressed as a *donna* and presumably *a* widow, serves *as a massaia, a* housekeeper. These fourteen or fifteen women are the only ones in the survey who show an occupation and no one of their jobs seems notably prestigious or remunerative.

This and other surveys frequently name both widows, and their late husbands' occupations. At Bologna, for example, the occupations once filled by the deceased husbands were those of baker *(fornaro),* gardener *(ortolano),* mercer *(merzero),* tailor *(sarto),* armorer *(armaiolo),* shoemaker *(chalçolaro),* hose or girdle maker *(challegaro),* and the like. It is possible, but not provable, that these widows continued their husbands' work. Women participated minimally in the Bolognese work force, and then only in such specialized work as the spinning of linen.

If women workers are few at Bologna, women beggars are many, some married, most widowed or single. The laborer Iohannes of Padua and his wife Guaxia, of unstated ages, are both of them described as "poor and beggars".[53] Ser Iohannes de Fregano—his title indicated that he was once a notary—and his wife Nobilis, are both "poor, sick, who beg and live from charities".[54] Two poor women, probably widows, donna Fiore, age 70, and donna Pina, age 80, called "her companion", apparently share together their common poverty.[55] Donna Antonia, age 70, is widowed and poor; donna Iacoma, poor. Zohanna, age 100, is "poor"; Benvegnuda, age 50, is "widowed and poor". Iacopa, of no stated age, is "widowed, poor and begging"; Donella, "widow, a wretched little woman, begging"; donna Iohanna, also "widow, poor and begging". This survey of 1395 is rare in registering another type of woman: the prostitute. Donna Iacoba, who lives with her widowed mother Taliola, earns the admiration of the census takers; she is described as "best in the superlative".[56] Apparently her charms earned her some prosperity, as she employs a servant. Her neighbor is a Paulus de Regio, "poor and a beggar"; his wife Agnesina from Germany is "a prostitute or

53. *Ibid.,* p. 98, "pauperes et metici."
54. *Ibid.,* p. 96: "pauperes, infirmi, qui mendicant et de elemosina vivunt."
55. *Ibid.,* p. 64.
56. *Ibid.,* p. 96: "dona Jacoba eius filia optima in superlativo."

nearly".[57] Georgius from Venice works in the wool trade, and his wife Lucia is "a declared prostitute".[58] But donna Caterina of Parma who seems to live alone, is "maxima meretrix", "the biggest prostitute". A donna Iacoba, also from Parma, is "a tacit prostitute". Donna Paula of Florence is called a "public prostitute"; she lives with her husband Iacobus, identified as her "concubitus", presumably her pimp.[59]

A donna Margherita is described somewhat ambiguously as "a not perfect slave"; she lives with her husband, Guilielmus of Verona, and Bartolomeus their son.[60] The entire group is characterized as "poor". The prostitute wife and mother is listed first among the household members; presumably she earned what few resources the family possessed.

Prostitutes form the largest feminine profession at Bologna in 1395. It is surely significant that many of them are immigrants— from Germany, Venice, Parma and Florence. Either prostitutes were prone to travel, or women who traveled were prone to prostitution.

The biggest of all late-medieval surveys is the Florentine Catasto redacted in 1427–30; it included not only the city of Florence but all the regions—cities and countrysides—then subject to its authority.[61] In the entire Catasto, some 7063 women appear as household heads (out of 60,705). As the number of occupations they show is so small, we consider here all these Tuscan women, not only Florentines and not only city dwellers. Finally and unfortunately, the Catasto tells us nothing explicitly about prostitution.

The visible participation of women household heads in the productive life of the Tuscan community was exiguous. Out of the 7,063 female household heads, only 270, less than one half of one percent of the total, claim an occupation. To be sure, many other women were doubtlessly employed in households and farms who cannot be identified in these records. Nonetheless, the visible economy was a male bastion.

57. *Ibid.*, p. 96: "dona Agnesina de Alamania putana vel quasi."
58. *Ibid.*, p. 96: "dona Lucia eius uxor rufana expressa."
59. *Ibid.*, p. 97: "dona Paula de Florencia putana publica, Iacobus eius maritus suus concubitus."
60. *Ibid.*, p. 97: "dona Margarita sclava non perfecta."
61. On the catasto, see D. Herlihy, C. Klapisch-Zuber, *Les Toscans.*

Few in number, the occupations that Tuscan women held in 1427 are also humble, by reason of the wealth or dignity they generated. The largest feminine occupation was service in the employment of private families (103 women), of the government (8) or of the Church (2). The richest women are engaged in Tuscany's biggest industry, the making of woolens, but they are only two. In this, the central source of Tuscan wealth, women chiefly participated in the low-skilled occupations of spinners, carders and washers. There are women weavers (13), but other sources suggest that they worked chiefly in silk and linen rather than in wool (12 are identified as silk weavers). And these were still small industries in 1427. One Florentine carnival song presents us women out in search of weavers, who are males.[62] Women beggars are also many in Tuscany (22), as at Bologna. Religious women too are numerous; they represent, after the servants, the biggest group (59 *pinzochere,* 41 *commesse).* The other occupations that women held are those of hose makers, mercers, furriers, seamstresses, food dealers, and innkeepers, but in trivial numbers.

Verona in the Veneto has preserved a series of *estimi* from 1423. Here we use the partially surviving *estimo* of 1423 and the declarations from the same parishes out of the survey of 1502. Again because the number of women showing occupations is so small, we combine the surveys.

Women at Verona across the fifteenth century also formed a minuscule part of the officially recognized labor force. Still, the cluster of weavers (14) is notable, and there are also eight spinners. Both groups probably worked in silk rather than in wool, as probably did also the otherwise unspecified "workers" (2). The growth of the silk industry was to confer substantial benefits on women, who worked better at several of its processes (spinning, weaving, embroidery) than did men. But its great age lay in the future.

The small participation of women in the Italian labor force parallels their virtual exclusion from (or at least subordination within) the urban guilds. I know of no guilds in Italy that were exclusively female. At Florence, matriculation lists of the guild of silk mer-

---

62. *Canti carnascialeschi del Rinascimento,* ed. by C. S. Singleton (Bari, 1936), p. 107: "Donne, che tessitor cerchando andate ... "

chants, the Por Santa Maria, begin as early as 1225; the lists over the centuries show not a single feminine name.[63]

CONSIDERATIONS

Women's participation in urban economic enterprises was reduced dramatically across the late Middle Ages. In the thirteenth and early fourteenth centuries, women retained high visibility in a great variety of urban employments. They dominated some industries, such as the making of silk and linen cloths; in many other industries, they worked alongside men without apparent discrimination.

The closing period of the Middle Ages, the fourteenth and fifteenth centuries, was a violent age of deep crises and difficult recovery; it also saw the end of this easy partnership between men and women in the urban economies. Guilds and governments, especially in the fifteenth century, imposed severe restrictions on women's work. These restrictions amounted at times to the full exclusion of women from prestigious and well-paying jobs.

In the thirteenth century, as at Paris, the high visibility of independent women taxpayers and artisans meant that they were not subject to the discipline of a household unit of production. Many women did not work under the supervision and primarily for the benefit of a male head of household. Indeed, it is even questionable whether the term, "domestic mode of production", can appropriately be applied to the Paris economy under Philip the Fair. Households were clearly not alike in their economic activities; not all of them were self-contained units of production. Rather, some (surely the larger and wealthier) took in journeymen, apprentices, helpers and servants, whom other households (surely the smaller and poorer) supplied. Not all and perhaps not most Parisians, men or women, worked in their own homes.

The full subordination of women's work to household work and to the male household chief awaited the late Middle Ages; it was directly linked to the establishment of guild monopolies and the exclusion of women from the master ships. Women's work thus

63. The matriculation lists are preserved in the Manoscritti deposit of the Florentine state Archives. I have prepared a machine readable edition of them from 1225 to 1430.

looks quite different at the end of the Middle Ages from what it had been in the thirteenth century.

The factors driving this evolution are hard to isolate and still harder to weigh. But four factors merit thought and attention: urbanization, capitalization, the saturated markets of the medieval economy, and monopolization.

Urbanization

In the rural economy of the early Middle Ages, the sexual division of labor assigned the heavy tasks of plow agriculture to the males, and left domestic chores chiefly to the women. The making of cloth and clothing was a principal domestic chore, and women dominated it almost totally. The growth of population in the central Middle Ages induced many persons to leave the old-settled, now crowded regions and to seek out new occupations in the towns. But in the growing towns, men needed to ply a trade in order to earn a living, and understandably they penetrated into many domains which were formerly the preserves of women. Urbanization also brought with it the specialization and professionalization of productive activities. Artisans had to sell their products in order to live, and markets were becoming intensely competitive. The artisans had to satisfy a discriminating demand for quality products at affordable prices. Now, men could develop these specialized skills more easily than women. In coming from the countryside, women were not entirely freed, as were the men, from their former duties. In the towns, women now as before delivered and nursed the children; took care of the sick in the household; cooked and cleaned. While they could combine these domestic tasks with some market-oriented work such as spinning, they had not the time and the freedom to develop real expertise in most crafts. The men in the urban households became the professional artisans, and the women served as their helpers and assistants.

On the other hand, we ought not exaggerate the specific influences of the urban environment on the sexual divisions of labor. In classical antiquity, cloth making was carried on largely within cities, and women then dominated the craft, even the making of woolens. Moreover, the working of silks and linens remained salient exceptions to the principle, that urban conditions favored the masculinization of all productive processes.

Capitalization

Still another factor is the difficulty experienced by women in marshaling capital. Women, as in the Paris tailles, consistently appear poorer than the men in the same occupation by a substantial margin—about one third. The growth of the cloth industry was significantly stimulated by technological changes—by the development of large and complex horizontal looms; by the application of water power in fulling; by the use of a larger range of dyes and mordants. Technological change in turn required capital infusion. Women, part-time workers in an urban context, neither accumulated, nor attracted nor controlled capital to the same extent as men. Their comparative deprivation also undermined the influence they could exert within occupations and professions.

Saturated Markets

Robert Davidsohn implies that the prominence of women weavers in apprenticeship contracts at Florence persists through the first third of the fourteenth century. At about the same time—from the late 1320s—the major Florentine guilds were restricting the matriculation of members who were not the descendants or close relatives of active or former masters.[64] If the Florentine case is typical—and it appears to be—then the closing of the most remunerative urban employments to outsiders (including women) anticipated by two decades the onslaught of the Black Death and the great depopulations of the late Middle Ages.

It would appear that the master tradesman working in the crowded Europe of the early fourteenth century were facing saturated markets for their products. Diminished opportunities pressed them into a defensive posture; they sought to restrict entrance to their own sons and thus limit the numbers of masters and the competition they offered.

The Black Death itself and the fall of population, in creating a shortage of workers, seem to have blunted these policies for a while. On the other hand, the disasters of the late Middle Ages hardly worked to instill in the masters a sense of security and confidence in

64. They did this principally by imposing high entrance fees but also through privileges known as *beneficium patris, beneficium avi,* and the like, exempting descendants from the full charge.

the future. When in the fifteenth century the population stabilized and began once again to grow, the old fear of competition was renewed. From the late fifteenth century, guilds, with the support or at least the consent of governments, returned with even greater commitment to the policy of restricting entrance into their ranks and access to the best-paying urban jobs. Again, outsiders and marginal workers, including women, were the chief victims of these policies.

Monopolization

In the eighteenth century, the great French physiocrat and statesman, Turgot, gave this perceptive account of the origins of guild monopolies:

> It seems that, when the towns began to free themselves from feudal servitude and to form themselves into communes, the ease of classifying the citizens by means of their occupations introduced this usage, unknown up until then. The different occupations thus became like particular communities, out of which the general community was composed ...

> The communities, once formed, redacted statutes, and, under various pretexts regarding the public good, had them validated by the authorities. The basis of these statutes is to exclude from the right of exercising the craft whoever is not a member of the community; their general spirit is to restrict as much as possible the number of masters, to render the attainment of the mastership of nearly insurmountable difficulty for everyone except the children of present masters. This is the purpose for the multiplicity of charges and of formalities of admission, the difficulties of the masterpiece (always judged arbitrarily) and, above all, the useless expense and delay of the apprenticeship and the prolonged servitude of the compagnage (status of journeyman)—institutions designed to permit the masters to enjoy for nothing the labor of the novices for many years.[65]

Turgot specifically adds, in the passage cited in this paper's heading, that this "spirit of monopoly" has excluded women too from the trades, such as embroidery, that he considers "most suitable to their sex". Turgot's chronology may be vague and his knowledge of the Middle Ages faulty, but his analysis is nonetheless perceptive.

In the present state of knowledge, it is impossible to offer a truly rigorous explanation as to why women lost visibility in the urban economies between the thirteenth and the fifteenth or sixteenth cen-

---

65. *Histoire générale de Paris. Les métiers,* ed. R. De Lespinasse, I (Paris, 1886–1897), p. 164. Turgot's words are imbedded in an ordinance issued in the name of Louis XVI abolishing guild monopolies, in February 1776.

turies. But the fact that they did so seems indisputable. The fact itself and the reasons for it attracted surprisingly little interest in the older scholarship on labor history. The current interest in the history of women has helped highlight a problem not only in women's history but in economic history too. What happened to women's participation in the labor force in European cities across the late Middle Ages, and why? We may hope that historians of the European economy will now devote to this issue the research it richly deserves.

5

MAKING SENSE OF INCEST:

Women and the Marriage Rules
of the Early Middle Ages

───── ✦ ✦ ✦ ─────

Of all social rules, the incest prohibition comes closest to representing a universal law of behavior: almost all known societies have forbidden marriages between brothers and sisters.[1] Most societies have also refused to allow other types of close relatives to contract legal marriages. Typical of those prevented from marrying are ascendants and descendants in the direct line.

In the early Middle Ages, between the third and the eighth centuries, the Christian Church, with the approval of Roman emperors and barbarian kings, extended the domain of relationships within which marriages were prohibited to extraordinary lengths.[2] No other society is known to have applied the incest taboo with such extreme rigor. The Church also came to prohibit marriages between persons related in ways other than by blood. Although this extension and redefinition of the prohibition was common to both eastern and western Christianity, in the West the Frankish councils of the eighth and ninth centuries were particularly active in elaborating the new understanding of incest.

1. For a rare example of sanctioned brother-sister marriages, together with a useful review of recent sociological and anthropological literature on incest, see K. Hopkins, "Brother-Sister Marriage in Roman Egypt," *Comparative Studies in Society and History,* 22 (1980), pp. 303-54.

2. On the development of the incest prohibition, see G. Oesterle, "L'incest," *Dictionnaire de droit canonique,* vol. 5 (1953), cols. 1297-1314; E. Mangenot, "L'inceste," *Dictionnaire de théologie catholique,* vol. 7 (1930), cols. 1539-55.

Consanguinity, or blood relationship, had been the traditional basis for identifying incestuous unions. In the early Middle Ages the Church established two new impediments to marriage: affinity, or relationship through marriage; and compaternity, or relationship linking spiritual sponsors at baptism or confirmation with those receiving the sacrament.[3] And it also greatly enlarged the network of persons to whom these new impediments applied.

To be sure, at least in regard to affinal relationships, there was some precedent for the prohibition of close marriages. According to the Old Testament Book of Leviticus, I cannot marry my stepmother (Lv 18.8) or mother-in-law (Lv 20.14), the wife of either a paternal or maternal uncle (Lv 20.20), my stepsister (Lv 18.11) or sister-in-law (Lv 18.16; 20.21), my stepdaughter (Lv 18.17) or daughter-in-law (Lv 18.15). These are all technically affines, though it seems apparent that these women are likely to be living with me in the same household and family. Leviticus seems to lay a permanent taboo against all sexual activity, present or possible, involving co-residents apart from the married couple. The purpose seems to be the suppression of sexual rivalries or jealousies which were likely to disturb the peace of the domestic group. At all events, it would be hard to extract from the prohibited marriages listed in Leviticus a general principle making close affinity a direct impediment of marriage. Indeed, the institution of the Levirate (Dt 25.5-10) requires that a widowed woman without children marry her deceased husband's brother so that he might "raise up seed for his brother." The obligation directly contradicts the prohibition of Leviticus against marriage with a sister-in-law.

The history of the incest prohibition under Roman law seems to record a progressive restriction of its range. From approximately the second century B.C. and consistently thereafter, the law forbade marriages between ascendants and descendants in the direct line, or those who entered that line through legal adoption or through marriage.[4] The male Roman citizen could marry neither his stepmother nor step-

3. On the history of spiritual kinship, see J. H. Lynch, *Godparents and Kinship in Early Medieval Europe* (Princeton, 1986), esp. "Spiritual Kinsmen and Sexual Taboos," pp. 219-57.

4. On incest in early and classical Roman law, see M. Kaser, *Das romische Privatrecht*, Handbuch der Altertumswissenschaft, 10. Abt.: Rechtsgeschichte des Altertums. 3 T. 3. Bd. 1. Abschnitt. Das altrömische, das vorklassische, und Klassische Recht; 2 vols. (München, 1954-59), I, pp. 269-70 and II, pp. 113-14.

daughter, neither a woman his father had adopted nor his daughter-in-law. The principle here seems to be that persons living under the same *patria potestas* cannot marry.

While Mosaic and Roman law offered a weak precedent for the Church's impediment from affinity, neither legal tradition, as far as I can judge, recognized anything resembling the impediment for reason of compaternity or spiritual relationship. It is important to note that these three relationships not only prohibited marriages between an individual man and an individual woman, but also between their close kin, affines, and spiritual relatives. I cannot marry my godchild, or any of her kin and affines. This principle led to certain bizarre practices in the early medieval world. The council of Estinnes in 743 forbade a parent to serve as sponsor to his or her own child at baptism or confirmation. Those who violated this rule had to separate from their spouses.[5] Strange though it appears, the establishment of this spirituai relationship dissolved, ex post facto, an otherwise valid marriage. The council of Chalons, meeting in 813, explicitly condemned those women, some of them conniving, who presented their own children before the bishop at confirmation, "so that they might be separated from their husbands."[6] The council ordered them to do penance and to remain with their husbands. Evidently, however, the ruse of establishing a spiritual relationship with their own children, and hence with their own husbands, had allowed some women to escape from unwanted marriages.

Moreover, not only marriage itself, but illicit sexual unions, created a domain of affinal relationships excluding marriage. This also invited trickery and abuse. For example, as described in a letter of Hincmar of Reims dated 860, a Frankish magnate named Regimund complained that a count, Stephen of Auvergne, had endowed his daughter and had publicly married her, but now was ignoring her; Stephen was even living with a relative of his legal bride.[7] Stephen

5. *Concilia Aevi Karolini*, Tomus II, Pars 1, ed. A. Werminghoff, *MGH, Legum Sectio* 3 (Hanover and Leipzig, 1908; repr. 1979), p. 6, Concilium liftinense, anno 743. The council also requires that a husband who served as sponsor for his stepson or stepdaughter at confirmation be separated from his wife. For other examples, see J. H. Lynch, *Godparents*, pp. 278-79.

6. *Concilia Aevi Karolini* II, p. 279. The text is also discussed in J. H. Lynch, *Godparents*, pp. 279-80.

7. *Die Briefe des Erzbischofs Hinkmar von Reims: Hincmari Archiepiscopi Remensis Epistolae,* ed. E. Perels, *MGH, Epistolae* 8. *Epistolae Karolini Aevi* Tom. VI, Fasc. 1, Teil I (Munich, 1975), no. 136 (Oct. or Nov. 860), p. 89. His confessor

justified his misbehavior in the following fashion. In his youth, a fragile time of life as everyone knows, he had had sexual relations with a young woman. When the time came for him to take a legal wife, with the consent of relatives and friends he asked for the hand of Regimund's daughter, and the two were formally betrothed. But then his conscience began to bother him, or so he alleged. He went to his confessor, who produced a book of canons. The canons stated clearly that cognates or blood relatives must never marry, nor may a man marry a woman and then another woman related to her. Now it so happened that the paramour of Stephen's youth was related to his new bride. Stephen at first did nothing, as he was frightened by the possible anger of his father-in-law and the displeasure of the emperor. Fearful of his own safety, he went ahead with the wedding. Now, however, mindful of the divine laws condemning incestuous marriages, he gave up his bride and apparently went back to his former paramour. His youthful fling thus dissolved what most observers, including the bride's father, considered a valid marriage.

The Church not only established new definitions of close and prohibited marriages but also extended the domain of relationships over which those impediments were operative. Roman law in the classical age had come to recognize two separate domains of blood relationship, the one governing inheritances and the other marriages. Blood relationship governing inheritances extended up to the full seven degrees of kinship. Marriages, however, were allowed initially from the sixth degree, then from the fifth, and finally from the fourth. This meant that first cousins were allowed to marry. In A.D. 49, Emperor Claudius permitted an uncle to marry his brother's daughter, who was only three degrees removed.[8] The emperor then promptly married his fraternal niece, Agrippina. The Mosaic law again expressed no general principle making consanguinity an impediment to marriage, and it also allowed such close unions as that of an uncle with a niece, or a nephew with his maternal aunt.

---

instructed him "quoniam, quamdiu potest adfinitatis propinquitas computari, mihi nec cuiquam Christiano cum cognata sua vel quam cognatus habuit vel cum duabus cognatis salubriter liceret coniungi".

8. The evolution is well described by Ulpian: "Inter cognatos autem ex traverso gradu olim quidam usque ad quartum gradum matrimonia contrahi non poterant, nunc autem ex tertio gradu licet uxorem ducere; si tamen fratris filia, non etiam sororis filia, aut amita, aut materna, quamvis eodem gradu sit. Hoc genere connubii primus inter Romanos usus est Cl. Caesar Agrippina filia fratris uxorem ducta" (*Patrologia Latina* 16.1234).

In sum, according to both Mosaic and Roman law, the domain of consanguinity in which marriages could not occur was narrow and not very rigorously defined. We should especially note the toleration shown to marriages between a man and his brother's daughter. One seemingly universal purpose of close marriages is the re-integration of a patrimony divided among brothers. The marriage between the paternal uncle and his niece is an efficient means of achieving this goal.

In place of this small and inconsistently defined domain, the Church applied the incest rule over a much larger set of kin, affines, and spiritual relatives. In 342, the emperors Constantius and Constans, doubtlessly under Christian influence, threatened with death the paternal or maternal uncle who married a niece. In 355, the same emperors declared illegitimate the offspring of a union between a man and his sister-in-law.[9] About 393, St. Ambrose warned a man named Paternus against marrying his son to his granddaughter through a daughter.[10] This uncle-niece marriage would have re-united two descent lines and presumably brought together two shares of Paternus's patrimony. Ambrose forbade the contemplated marriage on the not very compelling grounds that it would bring about a confusion of names. Uncles, moreover, should bestow only fatherly kisses on a niece.[11]

From the fifth century, the Church was also shifting from the Roman to the Germanic method of counting degrees of kinship, which considerably enlarged their scope.[12] Thus an Irish council, supposedly held under the auspices of St. Patrick in the mid-fifth century, prohibited marriages not within four degrees but four *genicula* or joints, as the Germans counted kinship according to joints of the body.[13] In the late sixth century, Gregory the Great, in a letter of dubious authenticity directed to the apostle of the English, St. Augustine, forbade marriages between first cousins, that is, through

9. *Codex Theodosianus* lib. 3, cap. 12.1-2.
10. Epistola 59, dated about 393 *(PL* 16.1234).
11. *PL* 16.1236.
12. On the difference, see E. Champeaux, " *Ius sanguinis*. Trois façons de calculer la parenté au Moyen Age," *Revue historique de droit français et étranger,* 4th ser., 12 (1933) pp. 241-90.
13. *Councils and Ecclesiastical Documents Relating to Great Britain and Ireland,* ed. A. West Haddan and W. Stubbs, 3 vols. (Oxford, 1869–78), II, p. 338: *"De consanguinitate in conjugio.* Intelligite quid Lex loquitur, non minus nec plus: quod autem observatur apud nos, ut quatuor genera dividantur, nec vidisse dicunt nec legisse."

the fourth degree by Roman count, but allowed more distant relatives to marry. He permitted, as later law would not, two brothers to marry two sisters. He condemned marriages with a stepmother or a sister-in-law. Those involved in such marriages should be warned of their perilous state, but not otherwise punished for what they had done in pagan times.[14]

The Church was moving toward still more rigorous and comprehensive definitions of the span of relationships within which marriages were prohibited. The council of Toledo, in 527, declared:

> For these things we salubriously authorize to be observed, that no one of the faithful should desire to join to himself in matrimony a woman of his blood, up to the point that he recognizes lines of affinity from the succession of generations. [15]

In 726, in a letter to St. Boniface in Germany, Pope Gregory II allowed marriages beyond the fourth degree, but his successors returned to the blanket prohibition of marriages between persons who even suspected that they were related.[16] Gregory III extended the prohibition as far as the Romans counted relationships, up to seven degrees.[17] A council of Rome in 743 in effect forbade the marriage of a man with any woman *de propria cognatione*.[18] In a letter dated 747 to Pepin, the Frankish mayor of the palace, Pope Zacharias explained that

> according to the decrees of our predecessors, the pontiffs going before us ... we say that up to the point that relationship is recognizable,

14. On the questions allegedly posed by Augustine to Gregory, see *Baedae Opera Historica,* ed. and trans. J. E. King, Loeb Classical Library, 2 vols.: *I. Ecclesiastical History, Books I-III* (Cambridge and London, 1971), 1.27 (I, p. 124).

15. *Concilios visigoticos e hispano-romanos,* ed. J. Vives, Espana cristiana, Textos, I (Barcelona and Madrid, 1963), pp. 44-45, Toledo II, anno 527, cap. 5.

16. *The Letters of St. Boniface,* ed. and trans. E. Emerton, Records of Civilization, 31 (New York, 1940; repr. 1976), p. 53, no. xviii [26], 22 Nov. 726: "We reply: strictly speaking, in so far as the parties know themselves to be related they ought not to be joined together. But since moderation is better than strictness of discipline, especially toward so uncivilized a people, they may contract marriage after the fourth degree."

17. On the elaboration of the incest prohibition in the councils of the eighth century, from as early as 721, see A. Esmein, *Le mariage en droit canonique,* 2nd ed., 2 vols. (Paris, 1929-35), II, pp. 371-92.

18. *Concilia Aevi Karolini* Tomus 1, Pars 1, ed. A. Werminghoff, *MGH, Legum Sectio* 3, 2.1, esp. to the account of Concilium Romanum, anno 743 (mense Septembris vel Octobris) (Hanover and Leipzig, 1906; repr. Hanover, 1979), p. 14: "vi. capitulo, ut consobrinam, neptem, novercam, fratris uxorem vel etiam de propriae cognationis [sic] nullus praesumat in coniugio copulari ..."

according to the rite and rule of the Roman Church, let them not be joined in marriage.[19]

New definitions of incest and enlarged domains of persons over whom these impediments reigned: this was the extraordinary marital discipline established by the Church in the early Middle Ages, most forcefully in the West. Why did the Church adopt so rigorous a policy? Contemporary explanations do not entirely satisfy. The most influential justification of the incest prohibition comes from St. Augustine. There are two loves in this world: those we owe our close kin, and those we give to our spouse and her or his relatives. The two loves need to be cultivated and ought not to be confused. If I am bound to love a woman by reason of blood relationship, then it is superfluous and redundant to love her also for sexual reasons. Incestuous love accomplishes nothing for society. Marital affection is *seminarium charitatis,* a sowing—perhaps we should say a scattering—of affection. It re-unites persons and kindreds that would otherwise remain indifferent or hostile one to the other.[20] Augustine is eloquent, but his rationalizing still does not explain why the early medieval Church pushed the incest prohibition to such extreme limits.

The common argument against the marriage of affines ran as follows. Marriage made husband and wife two in one flesh, and thus the husband became a brother to his wife's sisters. Hence, if his wife should die, he had to look beyond the circle of her sisters if he wished to remarry.[21] But was this metaphor cogent enough to determine policy?

Gregory the Great, if it truly was he, is the only contemporary I know of who advanced an argument out of nature for the incest prohibition. The marriages of first cousins, he affirms, do not produce children.[22] But even this interesting opinion does not explain why the boundaries of incestuous marriages were so broadened.

In a recent study, *The Development of the Family and Marriage in Europe,* the English anthropologist Jack Goody has hazarded an

19. From the *Codex Carolinus,* cap. 22, ed. W. Gundlach, *MGH, Epistolae* 3, *Epistolae Merowingici et Karolini Aevi* 1.8 (Berlin, 1957), p. 486.

20. *De Civitate Dei* xv.16, "De iure coniugiorum." *The City of God against the Pagans,* ed. and trans. P. Levine, Loeb Classical Library, vol. 4 (Cambridge, 1956), pp. 500-11.

21. For an example, see n. 27 below.

22. J. E. King, *Baedae Opera Historica* I.27.5, p. 124.

explanation.[23] The great virtue of Goody's book is the cross-cultural perspective he brings to the problem. He stresses the unique nature and range of the incest prohibition as it was developed in the early medieval West. Not the Mosaic law of the ancient Israelites, nor classical Roman law, nor the religious teachings of medieval Islam imposed such sweeping restraints on close marriages. All three legal traditions allowed marriages between the paternal uncle and his niece, which, as we have mentioned, was critical in preventing the dispersion of a patrimony among many descent lines. Medievalists do indeed tend to confine their attention to a narrow cultural sphere. Goody instructs us that, in looking at the incest prohibition in the West, we are viewing in cultural terms a *rara avis.*

He is, however, less convincing in his own explanation of why the western Church was so opposed to close marriages. He again links the prohibition to the efforts of families and of family lines to preserve the integrity of their properties through directing the lines of descent inward. The propertied families pursued, or hoped to pursue, what Goody calls a "strategy of heirship." They wanted, in sum, through close marriages, to produce heirs who would re-unite the divided parts of the family's holdings. But the Church had an interest in obstructing the pursuit of these goals. The incest prohibition forced members of the propertied elite into distant marriages. These exogenous unions were more difficult to arrange and less desirable, as they were likely to scatter the inheritance. Many great property owners would choose not to marry at all and, for the good of their souls, were likely to bestow their properties on the Church. The incest prohibition was thus inspired by the Church's desire to expand its own landed endowment. The Church pursued the same goal through other means as well. It insisted that owners have the right to make wills, and thus convey lands to the Church, but that legal adoption not be recognized. And the clergy was to remain celibate. All these policies contributed to the aggrandizement and preservation of Church lands. The Church, in sum, had its own strategy of heirship.

There are, however, difficulties with Goody's thesis. As he admits, no contemporary links the incest prohibition with an effort to promote bequests to the Church. Indeed, the council of Fréjus, held in

23. *The Development of the Family and Marriage in Europe* (Cambridge, 1983).

796 or 797, stipulated that if a husband and wife discover that they are in fact cognates they must immediately separate. However, and here we quote: "The children who were procreated by such a marriage are to be held legitimate and able to receive the inheritance of the dead."[24] If the incest prohibition was meant to prevent people from producing legitimate heirs, why is an exception made here?

Moreover, it is hard to believe that the decentralized Church of the early Middle Ages could have pursued a uniform, subtle, even tricky, policy of this kind. Goody does not inquire how in fact the Church of the early Middle Ages acquired property. It was quite common for great families to offer their young children as oblates to the monasteries, and almost always they would convey some property with the child. The Church, it would appear, had as good a chance of receiving property from those families with children as from those without. Many great personages of the early medieval world—queens were prominent among them—would found or endow a monastery late in life. The state of childlessness seems not to have mattered. Finally, the Church needed personnel as well as property, and it recruited its leaders primarily from the propertied classes. To interfere with the fertility of the magnates would have been to obstruct the Church's own capacity to maintain its cadres over time. The strategy envisioned by Goody, unmentioned by any contemporary source, does not make much sense.

But what then is the sense in the incest prohibition, and why did the early medieval Church stretch it so far? It may be that it gave the Church an excuse for extending its jurisdiction over marriages, which traditionally fell within the lay and secular spheres. But the early councils clearly considered marriage to be a civil matter and were not eager to rush to judgment. Hincmar of Reims affirmed that "we bishops ought not to be experts in civil judgment," by which he meant judgments regarding marriages.[25] It may be also that the incest prohibition was popular with the laity, as it offered an easy way of arranging a divorce; women, as we have seen, could get rid of their husbands simply by serving as sponsors for their own children. But such ruses officially condemned, again seem not a sufficient explanation for the vigorous campaign against incestuous marriages.

24. *Concilia Aevi Karolini*, II, pp. 192.
25. *Die Briefe des Erzbischofs Hinkmar von Reims*, p. 90.

Perhaps we can better discern the purposes of the incest prohibition if we look not at the sweeping prohibition against close marriages
but at those relatives whose marriage the canons explicitly forbid.
Thus, the council of Elvira, held sometime between 300 and 303, one
of the earliest western councils, forbade marriage with a sister-in-law
or stepdaughter.[26] The council of St. Patrick also cited a sister-in-law
as an incestuous partner.[27] The council of Agde, in 506, offered in its
sixty-first chapter a particularly complete list. I cannot marry my
brother's widow, my wife's sister, my first cousin or her descendant,
stepsister uncle's widow on both sides, or stepdaughter. Finally, the
council of Rome in 721 visited anathema on whoever married his
brother's widow, stepmother, daughter-in-law, or first cousin.[28]

We could multiply these citations, but perhaps enough has been
said to justify the following conclusions. The prohibitions were chiefly
laid upon men, although many of the councils expressly stated that
they applied to women as well. The marriage system was presumably
virilocal, that is, the new bride joined her husband's household, and
it seems appropriate that the responsibility was placed upon the male
to choose a suitable bride. The incest rules, in sum, primarily affected
the movement of women among the households.

Now, most of the women whom the canons forbid me to marry
are already present in my household. Thus, according to the Roman
canons of 721, I cannot marry my widowed stepmother, my widowed sister-in-law, or my widowed daughter-in-law. It is not
unlikely that my first cousin is also in the household. Households
formed of two married brothers were surely common. The thrust of
these rules seems to be that if I already live with a woman, whether
kin or affine, in the same household, I cannot marry her.

The incest prohibition thus helped preserve the internal peace
and stability of the domestic community. I cannot contemplate
eventual marriage with my stepmother, sister-in-law, daughter-in-
law, or stepdaughter and therefore am less inclined to initiate a sexual intrigue with any one of them. I am also less likely out of lust for
another household member to get rid of my present wife, whether

---

26. *Concilios visigoticos,* pp. 13, Elvira, anno 300-306?, cap. 66. See cap. 61 for
prohibition against marriage with the sister of a dead spouse.
27. West Haddan and Stubbs, *Councils and Ecclesiastical Documents Relating to
Great Britain and Ireland,* II, pp. 337.
28. Mangenot, "L'inceste," p. 1547, for regulations of the first council of Rome.

through murder or divorce. The death or departure of the current spouse does not free me to marry any of the above-mentioned women likely to be living in my household. According to Thomas Aquinas, one basis for the prohibition in natural law is that incestuous desires militate against "the community of life," that is, peaceful co-residency.[29]

But even this effort to exclude sexual intrigue and tensions from the domestic community does not seem a satisfactory explanation for the range of the incest prohibition. One of the women most frequently cited as one I must not marry is my wife's sister. Under a virilocal marriage system, it is not likely that she will be living in my household. Why does the Church think of marriage with her as incestuous?

In my view, we must read this prohibition in the light of the other contemporary rules concerning marriage. The Church attempted, though for long with limited success, to suppress polygyny and concubinage.[30] A curious canon of the council of Rome of 826 forbade a man to have a wife and concubine, which seems conventional enough, but also two concubines and apparently no wife.[31] I know that I cannot have one concubine; why does the council forbid me to have two? The fathers explained: they do not want two mistresses in the same household, whether wives or concubines, "since it is not beneficial to the house, and is a detriment to the soul."

This prohibition against the presence of several mistresses in the same household recalls an anecdote told by Gregory of Tours and many times repeated by modern historians. Queen Ingund, wife of the Merovingian king Chlothar I, asked her husband to find a rich spouse for her sister Aregund. Chlothar inspected the girl and found her very appealing. He reported back: "I found nothing [sic] better than myself." Accordingly, he married Aregund, without of course divorcing her sister.[32] The Church's prohibitions against both polygyny and incest seem consciously aimed at preventing unions of this

29. Cited in Mangenot, "L'inceste," p. 1549.
30. S. F. Wemple, *Women in Frankish Society: Marriage and the Cloister, 500 to 900* (Philadelphia, 1981), pp. 27-97, treats at length polygyny and concubinage in Frankish society and the Church's efforts, not truly successful before the ninth century, to suppress these practices.
31. *Concilia Aevi Karolini* Tomus 1, Pars 2, p. 582, canon. 37.
32. *Historiae Francorum, Gregorii episcopi turonensis libri historiarum X*, editionem alteram curaverunt Bruno Krusch et Wilhelm Levison, *MGH, Scriptores rerum merovingicarum*, Tomus 1, Pars I (Hanover, 1951), lib. 4. cap. 3, pp. 136-37.

kind. If Chlothar abided by the law, he could not take these two sisters to wife, either simultaneously or sequentially.

Not only the Franks, but also the great magnates of Gallo-Roman society, seem to have gathered numerous women into their households. Or so that historian of Roman vices, Salvian of Marseilles, would have us believe. Writing in the fifth century, Salvian regarded as common the rich man "who from his slaves has a crowd of concubines; polluted by the foulness of numerous wives like pigs or swine, he thinks he ought to have as many wives as he can submit to his lusts."[33]

The marriage system of early medieval Europe resembles what anthropologists call "resource polygyny." If we assume that the sexes are in approximate balance, only a few males will actually be able to recruit multiple sexual partners in a society that permits one man to have several wives. These privileged males will be the rich and the powerful. Those males with wealth and authority will claim women also. And many males among the poor and the powerless will have little or no chance of gaining a mate. Women, in consequence, will not be evenly distributed across society but will be gathered in disproportionate numbers into the households of the powerful. It further seems that women in early medieval society were valued in elite households not only for sexual services but also for their administrative contributions, for the special skills and arts that they had mastered, and for the *muliebria opera* that they performed.[34] In a curious passage from Irish hagiography, telling of the "three orders of the saints of Ireland," the first and indeed the holiest of the orders flourished from the days of St. Patrick. Some 350 chaste bishops, founders of churches, comprised it. "They did not," reads the passage, "spurn the administration of women and their company."[35]

The polygynous marriages and widespread concubinage of early medieval society favored women in several ways. Aregund did indeed find the richest and most powerful mate she could have wanted, even though he was already married to her sister. Many

33. Salvian, *De Gubernatione Dei* lib. 4:28; *Opera Omnia,* ed. E. Pauly. Corpus Scriptorum Ecclesiasticorum, 8 (Vienna, 1883), p. 73.

34. For further discussion, see D. Herlihy, *Medieval Households* (Cambridge, MA, 1985), pp. 39-40, 52-53.

35. *Vitae Sanctorum Hiberniae ex codice olim Salmanticensi nunc Bruxellensi,* ed. W. W. Heist, Subsidia Hagiographica, 28 (Brussels, 1965), p. 81.

women would come to live in privileged surroundings. But it was not in all respects "a profit to the house," in the phrase of the council of Rome. It was likely to ignite jealousies and sow tensions in the household, between wife and concubine, chief and mistresses. Still, according to Irish hagiography, the father of St. Brigid, a petty king named Dubtach, rendered both his legal wife and his concubine pregnant.[36] His concubine was bearing a future saint. A singularly tactless bishop prophesied in the wife's presence that the concubine's progeny would rule over her own child and indeed over all Ireland. The now enraged legal wife forced her reluctant husband to expel his concubine from her house.

The promiscuity of males invited promiscuity among females, no matter how closely they were guarded. According to Gregory of Tours, King Gunthram refused to believe that the child of his sister-in-law Fredegund really was the son of his deceased brother Chilperic.[37] "I think," he affirmed, "that he is the son of some member of our following." Fredegund had to swear solemnly before three bishops and three hundred great men of the realm that Chilperic really was the father.

The incest prohibition, together with the suppression of polygyny and concubinage, assured that women would circulate among households and across kindreds. It forbade parallel marriages between kindreds. If I marry a girl, then my brother can not marry her sister. He must look to another kindred to find a wife. Most decisively, the incest prohibition prevented a widow who wished to remarry from remaining within the household of her deceased husband. Whom could she take in a second marriage? Not her father-in-law, not a brother-in-law, not a stepson or son-in-law. If she wanted to remarry, then she had to move out. She had to seek to join a different household and enter a different kindred; she had to move widely across society. For males, especially poor males, the incest prohibition thus facilitated access to women and improved their chances of marrying.

Mandating a circulation of women among households, the incest prohibition had two further, profound consequences. It helped reduce abductions and with it the level of violence in early

36. *Vitae Sanctorum Hiberniae*, p. 2.
37. *Gregorii Episcopi Turonensis Libri Historiarum X* 8.9.

medieval society.[38] In assuring that a broader range of males would have access to women, it made the marriages and the households of the poor resemble those of the rich. The rich could not monopolize women, at least not ethically or legally. No longer could a barbarian chief accumulate wives and concubines under his roof while poor males looked on in envy. No longer could a rich senator purchase or maintain, as Salvian described, numerous concubines.

Was this a goal that the Church was consciously pursuing? The Church was certainly eager to suppress abductions, which the skewed distribution of women across society strongly invited. The council of Rome affirmed that multiple mistresses were harmful to the domestic community. While tying the policy closely to supposed biblical and patristic precedents, the Church seems to have been not altogether unconscious of its social consequences.

To conclude: the early Middle Ages witnessed the emergence in Europe of commensurable and comparable household units, based in part on rules that forced a circulation of women through society. Poor males had improved chances of attracting a mate, and women came to be more evenly distributed up and down the social scale. The new similarity of marriages and households, fairer access to women, and reduced levels of violence helped lay the foundations for a stable social order in the early medieval West.

38. See, for example, Hincmar of Reims's denunciation of abductions. Nothing, he claims, so provokes the wrath of God and so disturbs the peace of the realm as these crimes (Hincmari Ad regem De coercendo et exstirpando raptu viduarum puellarum ac sanctimonialium, PL 125.1017-36). He obviously considers this a major social problem of the Carolingian realm, and he appends a list of canons forbidding the abduction of women.

PART III

6

FAMILY

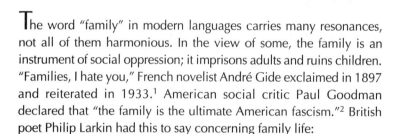

The word "family" in modern languages carries many resonances, not all of them harmonious. In the view of some, the family is an instrument of social oppression; it imprisons adults and ruins children. "Families, I hate you," French novelist André Gide exclaimed in 1897 and reiterated in 1933.[1] American social critic Paul Goodman declared that "the family is the ultimate American fascism."[2] British poet Philip Larkin had this to say concerning family life:

> Get out as early as you can
> And don't have any kids yourself[3]

But to others the family is a haven in a hostile world. To be treated "like family" in common parlance means to be loved and supported. A justice of the Rhode Island Supreme Court, in upholding an ordinance against domestic picketing in January 1990, described the home as "the one retreat to which men and women can repair to escape from the tribulations of their daily pursuits." It was, in his estimation, "the last citadel of the tired, the weary and the sick."[4]

1. A. Gide, *Nourritures terrestres,* 4, p. 1, cited in *Dictionnaire alphabétique et analogique de la langue française,* ed. P. Robert (Paris, 1966), 10, p. 830. He later explained: "Sans doute, j'écrivais un jour: 'Familles, je vous hais,' mais il s'agit d'institutions, non de personnes. Et ce n'est pas du tout la même chose"; *Journal,* 1l68, cited in *Trésor de la langue française* (Paris, 1980), 8, p. 635. See also *A History of Private Life,* gen. eds. P. Ariès and G. Duby, Vol. 4: *From the Fires of Revolution to the Great War,* ed. M. Perrot (Cambridge, Mass., 1990), p. 241.

2. P. Goodman, cited in J. Winokur, *The Portable Curmudgeon* (New York, 1987), p. 98.

3. From P. Larkin, "This be the Verse," in *High Windows* (New York, 1974), p. 30.

4. Cited in *The Providence Journal* (January 24, 1990): 1. The author of the decision was Justice T. F. Kelleher.

Here, I want to explore the distant origins of this double vision: of the family as loving and of the outer world as loveless. Put another way, I want to examine the emergence of the family in the West as a moral unit and a moral universe: a unit in the sense that it is sharply differentiated from the larger associations of kin and community, and a universe in the sense that human relations within it are very different from human relations outside its limits. The epoch of our interest, late antiquity and the Middle Ages, is admittedly remote, but it is also a formative period in the history of Western domestic culture. The writings we shall explore are legal, philosophical and theological texts. Historians of law have systematically analyzed the legal codes of antiquity and the Middle Ages bearing on the family, but their goals have been much different from my own.[5] Philosophical and theological tracts have been, in contrast, rarely scrutinized for purposes of social history; the materials in them seemed too speculative and abstract, too far removed from quotidian experience.

We must first attempt brief definitions of crucial terms. What did the ancient and medieval writers call the family? Curiously, the ancients had no exact equivalent to our modern word "family." This fault of terminology suggests that they came only slowly to conceive of the domestic community as sharply separated from the larger society.

The English word "family" is a direct borrowing from the Latin, *familia*, which also supplies a common word for family to most other modern European languages, including German and Polish. It appeared very early in the Romance languages, from at least the twelfth century; it entered English by the fifteenth and German only in the sixteenth.[6] In classical Latin, *familia* carried several meanings.[7]

5. See most recently the remarkable survey of medieval canon law bearing on sexual and marital issues by J. A. Brundage, *Love, Sex, and Christian Society in Medieval Europe* (Chicago, 1987).

6. *The Oxford English Dictionary,* 2nd edn. (Oxford, 1989), 5, p. 707, cites its use in *circa* 1400 in the sense of servants. Compare its use in Scottish dialect as a community of consumers in *Bernardus de cura rei famuliaris with Some Early Scottish Prophecies, etc.,* ed. J. R. Lumby (London, 1870), p. 4, "Fede nocht thi famel with costly victuale." The translation is of the fifteenth century. *Altfranzösisches Worterbuch,* eds. A. Tobler and E. Lormatzsch (Berlin, 1925-), 3.2 (1952), col. 1622, cites its appearance in the poems of Gilles li Muisis and in Statutes of Lille from the fourteenth century. *Deutsches Wörterbuch* (Berlin, 1940), 2, p. 289, notes an appearance (in the form *Familien*) in 1564, but it does not become common until at least a century later.

7. On the word's origins, see R. Henrion, "Des origines du mot *Familia,*" *L'Antiquité classique,* 10 (1941), pp. 37–69; 11 (1942), pp. 253–90. M. R. Leonhard, "Familia" *Paulys Realencyclopadie der classischen Altertumswissenschaft,* ed. G. Wissowa (Stuttgart, 1909), 6, cols. 1980–85.

As the ancients themselves noted, the word could refer to both persons and property.[8] Both ancient and medieval grammarians believed, correctly it seems, that the Romans had borrowed the word from a neighboring people, the Oscans. The Oscan root, *famel,* meant slave, and the word also supplied Latin with a common name for slave, *famulus.*[9] *Familia* thus originally meant a band of slaves. "Fifteen freemen make a people," wrote the second-century novelist Apuleius; "fifteen slaves make a family, and fifteen prisoners make a jail."[10] The word in its original sense thus implied an authoritarian structure and hierarchical order founded on but not limited to relations of marriage and parenthood. In a related way, the Latin word for father, *pater,* designated in its original sense not a biological parent but the holder of authority. The biological male parent was *genitor.* Authority, in sum, and not consanguinity, not even marriage, was at the core of the ancient concept of family. Even an unmarried male could be a *paterfamilias.* Moreover, in early Roman law, the father's authority, the *patria potestas,* was absolute, including even the *ius necis,* the right to put to death members of his family.

Familia long held this meaning of a band of slaves. "We are accustomed to call staffs of slaves families," the jurist Ulpian observed in the second century A.D.[11] Even when slavery waned in late antiquity and the Middle Ages, the term family continued to be used to designate servants or serfs. Pope Gregory the Great at the end of the sixth century compared the human mind to a family. Our separate thoughts are like numerous servant girls, who gossip and neglect their chores, until their mistress, reason, shushes them and sets them to their tasks, imposing order on our mental *familia.*[12] Elsewhere, Gregory applied the word to

8. See the comment by Ulpian, *Digest,* 50.16.195. *The Digest of Justinian: Latin Text Edited by Theodor Mommsen with the Aid of Paul Krueger,* trans. and ed. T. Watson (Philadelphia, 1985), 4, p. 949: "Familiae appellatio … varie accepta est: nam et in res et in personas deducitur." The *Codex Justinianus* (6.38.5) states "we discern that the name of family has the following force: parents and children and all relatives and property, freedmen also and their patrons and likewise slaves are identified by this word"; *Corpus Iuris Civilis,* ed. P. Kruger, et al., 3 vols. (Berlin, 1928), 2, p. 571.

9. Sexti Pompei Festi, *De verborum significatu quae supersunt cum Pauli Epitome,* ed. W.M. Lindsay (Leipzig, 1933), 77, pp. 11–12: "Famuli origo ab Oscis dependet, apud quos servus famel nominabatur unde et familia nostra."

10 Apuleius, *Pro se de magia liber (apologia),* ed. R. Helm (Leipzig, 1959), 47.437, "XV liberi homines populus est, totidem serui familia, totidem uincti ergastulum."

11. Ulpian, *Digest,* 50.16.195, "servitium quoque solemus appellere familias."

12. *S. Gregorii Magni Moralia in Job Libri I–X,* ed. M. Adrizen (Turnhout, 1979), 1.3, "Multam nimis familiam possidemus cum cogitationes innumeras sub mentis dominatione restringimus, ne ipsa sui multitudine animum superent."

the *coloni,* or peasants, who worked on the papal estates.[13] The staffs
of both lay and ecclesiastical officials in the Middle Ages were routinely referred to as "families." Still, in the nineteenth century, the
entire papal bureaucracy, including hundreds of functionaries from
clerks to cardinals, was known as the pontifical family.[14]

From slaves subject to a master, the word was easily extended to
all persons—wives and children, natural or adopted—who were
under the *patria potestas.* "In strict law," explained Ulpian, "we call
a family the several persons who by nature or law are placed under
the authority of a single person".[15] Even the clients or retainers of a
powerful person, though not fully subject to the *patria potestas,*
were reckoned to be part of the great man's family. The ancient family in this sense could reach colossal size. Julius Caesar, in his *Gallic
War,* related how the Helvetian chief Orgetorix, when put on trial
by his tribe, "gathered from every quarter to the place of judgment
all his family, to the number of some ten thousand men."[16]

By further extension, the word applied to groups of people possessing some organization, or at least some similarity, in their styles
of life. In classical Latin literature under the name of "family," there
appear prostitutes in a brothel; publicans or tax collectors, moneyers; military units; schools of philosophers; and, in Christian usage,
demons, monks, and the clergy generally.[17] St. Augustine of Hippo
referred to the entire Christian church as the "family of Christ" or
the "family of God."[18] The Christian author Lactantius, in his dia-

13. *Gregorii I Papae Registrum epistolarum,* 1.42 (Munich,1978), 1, p. 64, "si quis
ex familia [colonis] culpam."
14. *Dizionario di erudizione storico-ecclesiastica,* ed. G. Moroni (Venice, 1843),
23, pp. 27ff., entry under "Famiglia pontificia."
15. Ulpian, *Digest,* 50.16.195, "iure proprio familiam dicimus plures personas,
quae sunt sub unius potestate aut natura aut iure subiectae."
16. Julius Caesar, *De bello Gallico* i.4, *The Gallic War,* trans. H. J. Edwards (Cambridge, Mass., 1979), 9: "Orgetorix ad iudicium omnem suam familiam, ad hominum
milia X, undique coegit et omnes clientes obaeratosque suos ... eodem conduxit."
Edwards translates "familiam" as "retainers."
17. See numerous examples in the *Thesaurus linguae Latinae,* vol. 4, pt. 1 (Leipzig,
1892–1926), cols. 234–46. For the "familia ecclesiastica," see Gregory the Great,
Regestum Epistolarum, 1.42 (May 591) (1.67), "Si vero ex familia ecclesiastica sac-
erdotes vel levitae vel monachi vel clerici vel quilibet alii lapsi fuerint." For the sense
of descent group, compare Bede, *Historia ecclesiastica gentis Anglorum* 1.7, *Opera
historica,* trans. J. E. King, Loeb Classical Library (Cambridge, Mass., 1963), 1, p. 38,
"Cuius, inquit, familiae vel generis es?"
18. St. Augustine of Hippo, *De civitate Dei,* i.29, *The City of God against the Pagans,*
trans. G. E. McCracken (Cambridge, Mass., 1981), 1, p. 122, "Quid familia Christi
respondere debent infidelibus ... Habet itaque omnis familia summi et veri Dei."

tribe *On the Death of Persecutors*, gave the word an even larger sweep. Lactantius was condemning the cruelty of the pagan emperor Galerius. The wicked Galerius, wrote Lactantius, like the Persian kings before him, treated the entire empire *tamquam familia*, "like a family," that is, a limitless aggregation of sullen slaves all suffering under his tyrannous power.[19] This use of the word family to designate a huge community of the cowed rings strange to modern ears, but it is consistent with the term's core meaning, as an aggregation of slaves.

Did the ancients even recognize the domestic unit to be a distinct social entity separate from the outside world? They certainly had a developed sense of what was public and what was private. In the second century A.D., the moralist Aulus Gellius posed the question whether a father was obligated to give up his seat of honor to a magistrate son.[20] He replied that "in public places and functions," magisterial authority prevailed over paternal authority, and the father must defer to his magistrate son. Within the domestic sphere, however, "public honors cease and the natural honors conferred by birth are recognized." Here, the magistrate son must yield place of honor to the father. The ancients did draw a firm line between the *res publica* and the *res domestica*. In the public realm, the state commanded; in the domestic, the father. On the other hand, the father's authority could extend well beyond the co-residential unit, to slaves working elsewhere, to freedmen likely to be living elsewhere, to absent but unemancipated sons, such as those serving in the army. The ancient *familia* was therefore not coterminous with the household.

As Ulpian noted, the second principal meaning of *familia* was property. This usage seems to have represented an extension from its original meaning of "vocal" property—that is, slaves—to the master's other possessions. In the word's earliest attestation in the Roman Law

19. Lucii Caecilii De mortibus persecutorum Liber vulgo Lactantio tributus, *L. Caeli Firmiani Lactanti Opera omnia*, ed. S. Brandt and G. Laubmann (Prague, Vienna, and Leipzig, 1897), cap. 21, p. 196: "nam post deuictos Persas, quorum hic ritus, hic mos est, ut regibus suis in seruitium se addicant et reges populo suo tamquam familia utantur, hunc morem nefarius homo in Romanam terram uoluit inducere." There is an English translation of this work in Lactantius, *The Minor Works*, trans. Sister M. F. McDonald, O.P. (Washington, 1965), pp. 117–203.

20. Aulus Gellius, *Noctes Atticae* 2.2.9, ed. P. K. Marshall, 2 vols. (Oxford, 1968), 1, p. 86: "sed cum extra rem publicam in domestica re atque uita sedeatur, ambuletur, in conuiuio quoque familiari discumbatur, tum inter filium magistratum et patrem priuatim publicos honores cessare, naturales et genumos exepiri."

of the Twelve Tables (fifth century B.C.), it carries the sense of "inheritance." The Justinian code in the sixth century A.D. affirms that in certain instances "the word family should be understood as property, because it designates slaves and other things in a person's patrimony."[21] This understanding also persisted in medieval usage. The Venerable Bede, in his *Ecclesiastical History of the English People* in the early eighth century, used *familia* in the sense of peasant farm or peasant inheritance.[22] This meaning may have been reinforced with the revival of Roman legal studies in the West from the twelfth century. A fourteenth-century Italian author, Paolo da Certaldo, used the Italian word *famiglia* with the sense of patrimony. "In order that the *famiglia* may grow," he counseled his readers, "it is desirable to save and to put aside in just measure as much as you can."[23]

Among the master's possessions, the *domus,* house or domicile, held a special importance, and *domus,* too, is often used in classical Latin to identify the domestic unit.[24] A girl in marrying, wrote Aulus Gellius, leaves the *domus* of her parents in order to join the *familia* of her husband.[25] St. Augustine instructed in a sermon: "The residents of a house are called a house … [We here call] a house not walls and rooms, but the residents themselves."[26] But *domus,* like *familia,* had many derivative meanings and could be applied to much larger groups than the domestic unit. The seventh-century Spanish encyclopedist Isidore of Seville explained: "The house is a residence of a single family, just as the city is the residence of a single people, just as the world

21. *Corpus Justinianum* 6.385.3, eds. Krueger, et al., 2, p. 571, "In aliis autem casibus nomen familiae pro substantia oportet intellegi, quia et servi et aliae res in patrimonio uniuscuiusque esse putantur."

22. See, for example, Bede, *Historia ecclesiastica* 1.15, *Opera historica,* trans. King, 1, p. 106 in relation to the Isle of Thanet "magnitudinis iuxta consuetudinem aestimationis Anglorum, familiarum sexcentarum"; compare *ibid.* 4.23, "locum unius familiae"; 2, p. 128

23. Paolo da Certaldo, *Libro di buoni costumi,* no. 142, in *Mercanti scrittori: Ricordi nella Firenze tra Medioevo e Rinascimento,* ed. V. Branca, 2nd. edn. (Milan, 1986), pp. 31–32, "E anche, perché la famigla sempre cresce, però si vuole avanzare e mettere innanzi quanto puoi con giusto modo."

24. For examples of the word's many meanings, see the entry "domus" in the *Thesaurus Linguae Latine* (Leipzig, 1909-34), 5, p. 1, cols. 1949–87.

25. Aulus Gellius, *Noctes Atticae,* 13.10.3, ed. Marshall, 2, p. 393, "Soror," inquit, "appellata est, quod quasi seorsum nascitur separaturque ab ea domo in qua nata est et in aliam familiam transgreditur."

26. Augustin Sermo 170.4, *Patrologia Latina,* ed. J. P. Migne, (Paris, 1861), 1, 38e, col. 920, "Quomodo dicitur domus habitatores domus … domum appellans non parietes et receptacula corporum, sed ipsos habitatores."

is the residence of the entire human race. 'House' is also the kindred, family or the union of man and wife. It begins from two persons, and is a Greek word."[27] It could be applied, in other words, to descent groups, tribes, and entire nations, such as the "house of Israel," that claimed to be based on blood relations. Later, in medieval usage, it would be equally applied to religious communities and to representative assemblies, such as the houses of parliament.

To identify the domestic unit, ancient and medieval writers usually combined *domus* and *familia*, as did Isidore. When, in the thirteenth century, Thomas Aquinas wished to identify the household, he used such terms as *familia domestica* or *domus vel familia*, "house or family."[28]

The laws and institutions governing the domestic community changed profoundly from early Roman times into the Middle Ages. The Roman father soon lost his powers of life and death over family members, if, indeed, he had ever really used them. In medieval law, the father could discipline for just cause his wards, including his wife, but not to the point of maiming them.[29] Even his authority over family property or its patrimony weakened. He could not consume that property arbitrarily but had to accept responsibility for the support of wife and children. We do not follow these diverse evolutions here. But, in one respect, the ancient understanding of the family survived. The family continued to be viewed as an organized and stable community, what the medieval doctors called a *multitudo ordinata*, set within another organized community, the state itself.[30]

And the family was in Aquinas's phrase a "communion of domestic persons", or a "domestic communion," that is, a community that

27. *Isidori hispalensis episcopi etymologiarum sive originum libri XX*, ed. W. M. Lindsay, 2 vols. (Oxford, 1911), 9.4.3: "Domus unius familiae habitaculum est, sicut urbs unius populi, sicut orbis domicilium totius generis humani. Est enim domus genus, familia sive coniunctio viri et uxoris. Incipit a duobus, et est nomen Graecum."
28. Thomas Aquinas, *Summa Theologica* [hereafter, ST] 2.2.2, *Opera omnia* 9 (Rome, 1897), p. 81, "Pater autem et dominus, qui praesunt familiae domesticae"; *ibid.*, 2.2.47, *Opera omnia* 8 (Rome, 1895), p. 359, "oeconomica, quae est de his quae pertinent ad bonum commune domus vel familiae."
29. See, for example, Aquinas, ST 2.2.2, *Opera omnia*, 9, p. 81: "Pater autem et dominus, qui praesunt familiae domesticae, quae est imperfecta communitas, habent imperfectam potestatem coercendi secundum leviores poenas, quae non inferunt irreparabile nocumentum. Et huiusmodi est verberatio."
30. Aquinas, ST 3.8.1 2nd 2., *Opera omnia* 11 (Rome, 1903), p. 127: "aliqua multitudo ordinata, est pars alterius multitudinis. Et ideo paterfamilias qui est caput multitudinis domesticae, habet super se rectorem civitatis."

acquired and shared the resources, especially food and shelter, needed to sustain the lives of its members.[31]

The progressive weakening of paternal authority allowed for, and perhaps even made necessary, the strengthening of another form of bonding that gave cohesion to the household: domestic affection. The ancient writers often mention, even if they are slow to emphasize, love within the household, the *amor* or *amicitia, caritas* or *dilectio* shared by family members. Cicero in the first century B.C. alluded to that special *caritas* joining parents and children, which cannot be destroyed except by heinous crime.[32] Emperor Caligula in the first century A.D. is said to have imposed a special oath on his soldiers and functionaries. Those taking the oath swore not to hold themselves and their children dearer than Caligula and his sisters.[33] Clearly, for Caligula, the love of parents for children was the supreme measure of devotion.

Even more than their pagan predecessors, Christian writers in the late imperial period commented extensively on love, in its social as well as religious dimensions. *Caritas* bonded together individuals and communities, marriages and households. In his Commentary on Genesis, Augustine raises the question why Adam obeyed Eve's bidding to eat the forbidden fruit.[34] He was not yet prompted by lust, which in the state of innocence did not rule his members; he was not maneuvering to seduce her. And he was much too intelligent to believe the Devil's ruse, that the shared and eaten fruit would change him and his mate into gods. He obeyed her simply because

31. Aquinas, ST 1.2.105, *Opera omnia* 7, (Rome, 1892), p. 271.

32. Cicero, *Laelius de amicitia*, 8.27, *De senectute, De amicitia, De divinatione*, trans. W. A. Falconer, (Cambridge, Mass., 1964), p. 138: "Quod in homine multo est evidentius, primum ex ea caritate quae est inter natos et parentes, quae dirimi nisi detestabili scelere non potest."

33. Suetonius, Caligula, *De vita Caesarum*, 4.15.3, *Suetonius*, J. C. Rolfe, trans. (Cambridge, Mass., 1970), 1, p. 424: "He caused the names of his sisters to be included in all oaths: 'And I will not hold myself and my children dearer than I do Gaius and his sisters.' "

34. Augustine,*De genesi ad litteram*, 11.42, ed. J. Zycha, (Prague, Vienna, and Leipzig, 1894), p. 378: "[Adam] noluit eam contristare ... non quidem carnis uictus concupiscentia, quam nondum senserat in resistente lege membrorum legi mentis suae, sed amicali quadam beniuolentia, qua plerumque fit, ut offenditur deus, ne homo ex amico fiat inimicus." See also *De civitate Dei*, 14.11, *The City of God against the Pagans*, trans. P. Levine (Cambridge, Mass., 1966), 4, p. 330. Adam obeyed for reason of friendship, "sociale necessitudine." There is an English translation, *The Literal Meaning of Genesis*, trans. J. H. Taylor, S.J., (New York, 1982).

he loved her and wished to please her. He acted, in Augustine's phrase, out of loving good will. Many, Augustine reflected, like Adam, offend God in order to please their friend. *Amicitia* in marriage, in Augustine's view, was present from the Creation.

Even earlier, around 230 A.D., Tertullian detected in families a "common spirit," although he was limiting his observations exclusively to his fellow Christians.[35] These families share emotional experiences; they feel, in his words, "common hope, fear, joy, pain and suffering." Emotional communion linked together, in his phrase, "brothers and fellow slaves," by which he seems to have meant family members who served one another. In a discourse written for his wife, he stated that between him and her there was "no difference of soul or body."

In more general terms, "love," Augustine affirmed, "ties men together in a knot of unity.[36] "Many souls," he wrote elsewhere, "are made one soul through loving."[37] In a famous passage out of the *City of God,* he stated that "two loves have made two cities," the one Jerusalem, the other Babylon, the one oriented toward Heaven, the other toward Earth, both embracing all humanity and active throughout history.[38] In patristic thought, *caritas* in the community functions as an essential cohesive force, much as *potestas* or power had served in pagan conceptions of society.

But *caritas* could work mischief, too, as Adam's fall confirmed. Christians were supposed to love everyone, but were they required

---

35. Tertullian, *De paenitentia,* 10.4, J. C. Ph. Borleffs, ed. (Turnhout, 1954), 1, p. 237: "Inter fratres atque conservos, ubi communis spes, metus, gaudium, dolor, passio, quia communis spiritus de communi domino et patre, quid tu hos aliud quam te opinaris." Elsewhere, Tertullian used "fratres et conservos" to refer to himself and his wife; *Ad uxorem* 2.7, ed. A. Kroymann (Turnhout, 1954), II, p. 393, "quale iugum fidelium duorum unius spei, unius uoti, unius disciplinae, eiusdem servitutis! Ambo fratres, ambo conserui, nulla spiritus carnisue discretio."

36. Augustine, *De doctrina Christiana,* Proemium, 6, ed. J. Martin, in *Aurelii Augustini Opera,* 4.1 (Turnhout, 1962), p. 4: "Deinde ipsa caritas, quae sibi homines inuicem nodo unitatis adstringit, non haberet aditum refundendorum et quasi miscendorum sibimet animorum, si homines per homines nihil discerent."

37. Augustine, *In Iohannis ... evangelium tractatus CXXIV,* ed. R . Willems, O.S.B., (Turnhout, 1984), p. 348, "multae animae per charitatem una anima est et multa corda unum cor." There is an English translation, *Lectures or Tractates on the Gospel according to John,* trans. M. Dods, D.D. , 2 vols. (Edinburgh, 1873).

38. Augustine, *De civitate Dei,* 14.28, *The City of God,* trans. Levine, p. 4, "Fecerunt itaque civitates duas amores duo." See also in his Commentary on the Psalms 64.2, *Patrologia Latina,* ed. Migne, col. 223, "Duas istas civitates faciunt duo amores: Jerusalem facit amor Dei; Babyloniam facit amor seculi."

to love everyone equally? Could they love some persons more, others less? The theologian who launched a tradition of speculation on degrees of affection was Origen of Alexandria, active in the early third century, one of the most original minds of the early church. Origen wrote extensive commentaries on the books of the Old and New Testaments and made fundamental contributions to the methods of biblical exegesis. Our interests here are in a commentary and two homilies he devoted to the Old Testament Canticle of Canticles, or Song of Songs. This erotic text perplexed ascetically minded Christian exegetes as it had Jewish commentators before them. Origen's commentary and homilies do not survive in the original Greek, but they are extant in Latin translations, by Jerome and by Rufinus, respectively.[39] Authors of the high Middle Ages commonly attributed these works to Ambrose of Milan, and this association with one of the four Latin fathers gave them added authority.

The crucial passage was Canticle 2.4, in which the maiden says of her king-lover, "he has ordered me in love." Inspired by this statement, Origen affirms that "saints" or the "perfect" would not love everyone equally but in ordered degrees. Love was, to be sure, a universal human experience. "Without doubt," he stated, "all men love something, and there is no one who arrives at an age when he can love who does not love."[40] But we do not and should not love all equally. First and foremost, we are to love God. After God, we love in order our parents, our children, and our "domestics," by which Origen seems to mean both co-residential relatives and servants. Finally, we love our neighbors—those outside our homes.[41]

39. The standard edition of the commentary and the two homilies is Origen, *Homilien zu Samuel I zum Hohelied und an den Propheten: Kommentar zu Hohelied in Rufus und Hieronymus Uebersetzungen*, ed. W. A. Baehrens (Leipzig, 1925). The two homilies, which seem to have circulated more widely than the commentary, are printed in Latin with a French translation in Origen, *Homélies sur le Cantique des Cantiques: Introduction, traduction et notes* by Dom O. Rousseau, O.S.B., 2nd edn. (Paris, 1966). There is an English translation of these works in Origen, *The Song of Songs: Commentary and Homilies*, trans. R. P. Lawson (Westminster, Md., and London, 1957).

40. Cant. Cantic. Liber 3, *Homilien*, edn. Baehrens, p. 186, "Omnes homines amant sine dubio aliquid et nullus est qui ad id aetatis venerit, ut amare iam possit et non aliquid amet."

41. Origenes in Cant. Cantic. Homilia 2.8, *Homilien*, edn. Baehrens, p. 52, "Ut autem post Deum etiam inter nos ordo ponatur, primum mandatum, ut 'diligamus' parentes, secundum ut filios, tertium ut domesticos nostros."

Origen assigned no formal place to love of self, and he did not in this ranking mention love of spouse or siblings. In another passage, however, he proposed a parallel order of affection in regard to women: we should love first our mothers, who also deserve the highest reverence; then our sisters but not with the same honor; then wives in a special fashion; and then all other women, both relatives and neighbors, according to their merit, but always chastely.[42] Origen, in sum, was not rigid or rigidly consistent in the order or orders he proposed. But, quite clearly, in the force field of affection, the persons presumably living with us—parents, children, and domestics—were at the center. Fondness, on the other hand, fades with distance.

Biblical commentators and theologians of late antiquity received Origen's notion of an *ordo caritatis* with enthusiasm.[43] Augustine provided a dynamic version of the same model.[44] Love, Augustine explained, is like a fire that first consumes the objects close to it, then those more distant. Your brother is closest to you, and he is first to be warmed by your love. Then love should be extended to neighbors, and then to strangers who do not wish you ill. "Go beyond even these," he urged his readers, "reach the point that you love even enemies."[45] Love for those closest to us is thus a school of sentiment, from which all other loves are learned.

Moreover, this notion of an *ordo caritatis* explained several discomfiting passages in the New Testament, in which the founder of Christianity apparently condemns familial affections. In Matthew 10.37, Jesus asserted, "He that loveth father or mother more than me is not worthy of me, and he that loveth son or daughter more than

42. *Ibid.*, pp. 188–89: "Et maiore quidem cum honorificentia matri deferenda dilectio est, sequenti vero gradu cum quadam nihilominus reverentia etiam sororibus. Proprio vero quodam a sequestrato ab his more caritas coniugibus exhibenda. Post has vero personas pro meritis etiam et causis uniquique in omni, ut supradiximus, castitate deferenda dilectio est. Secundum haec vero etiam de patre vel fratre atque aliis propinquis observabimus."

43. See H. Pétré, *Caritas: Etude sur le vocabulaire latin de la charité chrétienne* (Louvain, 1948).

44. Most particularly in Augustine, *In epistolam Iohannis ad Parthos tractatus decem* 8.10, translated as *Commentaire de la première épître de S. Jean*, trans. P. Agaësse, S. J. (Paris, 1961), p. 346. See J. Gallay, *La Charité fraternelle selon les "Tractatus in Primam Johannis" de St. Augustin* (Lyon, 1953).

45. Augustine, *In epistolam Iohannis* 8.10, "Transcende et ipsos; perveni, ut diligas inimicos." Earlier, he stated, "Qui usque ad inimicos pervenit, non transilit fratres" (Who reaches enemies does not skip over brothers).

me is not worthy of me."[46] Still stronger are his words in Luke 14.26: "If any man come to me and hate not his father, and mother, and wife, and children, and brethren, and sisters, yea, and his own life also, he cannot be my disciple."[47] These passages, concluded the commentators, were not a condemnation of familial love or of self-love but rather of disordered love. The good person should love parents, wife, and children, and even himself, but only after God.

The ancient sages, in sum, both pagan and Christian, recognized in the household a community of especially strong affection. Moreover, they saw within it a place of psychological solace or refreshment. Cicero contrasted the relaxation and enjoyment deriving from domestic activities with the vexing labors of public life.[48] Augustine went so far as to compare the *requies temporalis,* "which you find when you enter your home," with the *requies sempiterna,* the "eternal rest," to be expected in the house of God.[49] He seems to make of the home a terrestrial analog to Heaven.

Much has been written in recent years about the loving or affective family as a modern, even a recent formation, about the coldness, indifference, or insensitivity that allegedly characterized domestic ties in the distant past.[50] But what, then, are we to make of these sentimental passages, of many others that could be cited, from ancient authors? Unmistakably, these authors assume that persons

46. The Vulgate text of Matt. 10. 37 is, "Qui amat patrem et matrem super me, non est me dignus; qui amat filium aut filiam super me, non est me dignus."

47. Luc. 14.26: "Si quis venit ad me, et non odit patrem et matrem et uxorem et filios et fratres et sorores adhuc autem et animam suam non potest meus esse discipulus."

48. M. *Tulli Ciceronis epistulae,* Vol. 2, *Epistulae ad Atticum,* ed. L. C. Pursen (Oxford, 1958), 9.10.3, "et, ut verum loquar, aetas iam a diuturnis laboribus devexa ad otium domesticarum se rerum delectatione mollivit."

49. Augustine, *In epistolam Iohannis tractatus decem,* 10.9: "Domum tuam intras propter requiem temporalem, domum Dei intras propter requiem sempiternam. Si ergo in domo tua, ne quid peruersum satagis, in domo Dei ubi salus proposita est et requies sine fine, debes pati quantum in te est, si quid forte peruersum videris?"

50. On the alleged "sentimentalizing," see E. Shorter, *The Making of the Modern Family* (New York, 1975). On the "affective" family, see also L. Stone, *The Family, Sex and Marriage in England 1500–1800* (New York, 1977). A recent statement of this view may be found in P. Ariès, "Introduction," *A History of Private Life,* gen. eds. P. Ariès and G. Duby, Vol.3: *The Passions of the Renaissance,* ed. R. Chartier (Cambridge, Mass., 1989), p. 8: "Ultimately [in the eighteenth century] the family became the focus of private life ... It became something it had never been: a refuge, to which people fled in order to escape the scrutiny of outsiders; an emotional center; and a place where, for better or for worse, children were the focus of attention." For the most recent of many criticisms of Ariès's thesis on the supposed failure in the past to recognize children as children, see S. Shahar, *Childhood in the Middle Ages* (London, 1990).

who live together will normally love together, and that this love is the first to be learned and the last to be relinquished.

I ought not to imply that a modern set of familial sentiments emerged fully formed out of ancient Mediterranean waters. As suggested by the lack of a single name to identify it, the co-residential unit still did not show clear boundaries with or against the larger society. Augustine, for example, in his Commentary on John, was very vague in distinguishing the circles of *fratres, proximi, ignoti,* and *inimici*; in this instance, he made no mention at all of the family or domestic unit. There is little sense of polarity, still less of hostility, between the domestic and the public realms. Only the intensity, not the nature of affection, changes as one moves beyond the domestic circle. Neighbors and strangers are not viewed as heartless and menacing, only as persons whom we are justified in loving less.

Medieval commentators and theologians were equally attracted by Origen's seminal concept of the *ordo caritatis*.[51] In the twelfth century, in one of the earliest systematic works of medieval theology, Hugh of St. Victor proposed a simple ranking: one loved God above all, then one's self, then "others."[52] This would be a standard ordering. If the high ranking given one's self seems odd to us, it was because the salvation of one's soul outranked every other value; one could not sin, for example, to aid a neighbor. Hugh's student Richard of St. Victor, writing some time between 1152 and 1173, distinguished four degrees of what he called "violent," meaning passionate, love. His chief interest was in the psychological states of love and not its objects. He did, however, affirm that, in the domain of human relationships, conjugal love dominates all other affective ties. It unites the married couple in "chains of peace" and makes their union "pleasing and joyous."[53]

51. P. Rousselot, *Pour l'histoire du problème de l'amour au Moyen Age* (Münster, 1908). Rousselot found a distinction in the medieval authors between "physical" (that is, natural) and "ecstatic" (mystical) love. His chief interest was in the latter.

52. Hugh of St. Victor, Summa Sententiarum Tract. 4.2., cap. 7, *Patrologia Latina,* 176, col. 126, "Et in hoc etiam potest ordo charitatis considerari; quia Deum prae omnibus diligere debemus … post ipsum nos ipsos, tertio loco alios." This tract is traditionally attributed to Hugh.

53. Richard of St. Victor, *Epître à Severin sur la charité, par Ives; Les Quatre degrés de la violente charité: Texte critique avec introduction, traduction et notes,* ed. G. Dumeige (Paris, 1955), p. 145, "Mutuus namque intumi amoris affectus inter fedeatos pacis vincula adstringit, et indissolubilem illam perpetuandam que societate gratam et jocundam reddit"; this passage is from the "De IV gradibus violentae caritatis." Accord-

For our purposes, the most influential of all twelfth-century commentators on love and its objects was Master Peter Lombard, bishop
of Paris. Probably between 1155 and 1160, he published the *Four
Books of Sentences*, which was destined to become the standard
textbook of medieval Christian theology.[54] Subsequently, too, it
attracted numerous commentaries.[55] The *Sentences* include an
entire chapter entitled "The Order of Loving, What Should Come
before and What After."[56] Peter first examined the opinion of the
ancients as to the proper ranking. His own conclusion is the following: "From the foregoing it is clearly to be concluded that a distinction is to be made in loving, so that we love different persons with a
differing, not equal, affection; above all we love God, ourselves in
second place, in third our parents, then our children and siblings,
then domestics, finally enemies."[57] The Master's dependence on
pseudo-Ambrose, really Origen, is clear, but he also departed from
him in one striking way. Origen had made clear distinctions
between neighbors, whom we must love "with our whole heart,"
and enemies whom we only have to love and not hate.[58] Master
Peter, on the other hand, called all those beyond the domestic circle *inimici*, "enemies." We must still love these unfriendly outsiders,
but his words strongly imply that they do not love us.

Lombard's assumption, that all beyond the domestic circle were
enemies, bothered his commentators. For example, in 1245, Albert
the Great argued, "Between the domestic and the enemy, there are
many degrees of love, as for in-laws, fellow citizens, godparents,

ing to Dumeige, Bernard of Clairvaux is more likely than Richard to have been the
author of the letter to Severinus. Other twelfth-century theologians who commented
extensively on love were William of St.-Thierry and Peter of Blois, but their interests
tended to be again in the psychological stages of love and not its different objects. See
also G. Dumeige, *Richard de Saint-Victor et l'idée chrétienne de l'amour* (Paris, 1952).

54. *Magistri Petri Lombardi Sententiae in IV Libris distinctae* (Rome, 1981).

55. For an inventory, see F. Stegmüller, *Repertorium commentariorum in Sententias
Petri Lombardi*, 2 vols. (Würzburg, 1947).

56. "De ordine diligendi, quid prius, quid posterius"; *Sententiae*, 2.174.

57. *Ibid.*: "Ecce ex praemissis aperte insinuatur quae in affectu charitatis distinctio
sit habenda; ut differenti affectu, non pari, homines diligamus, et ante omnia Deum;
secundo nosipsos, tertio parentes, inde filios et fratres, post domesticos, demum inimicos diligamus. Sed inquunt illi, quae de ordine dilectionis supra dicuntur, esse ref-
erenda ad operum exhibitionem, quae differenter proximis exhibenda sunt. Primo
parentibus, inde filiis, post domesticos, demum inimicos."

58. Origen, *Homélies*, trans. Rousseau, p. 94: "nec dicit 'diligite inimicos vestros'
ut vosmetipsos, sed tantum: 'diligite inimicos vestros.' Sufficit eis quod eos 'diligimus'
et odio non habemus."

and the like."[59] In his view, Master Peter must have been using the term "domestics" in a metaphorical sense to signify the entire church. By this strained interpretation, the *inimici* become not all those outside our households but all those outside the church. But was this really the Master's intent?

Thomas Aquinas, in his own Commentary on the Sentences and in his *Summa Theologica*, seems not to discuss the question whether all persons outside the household can be called enemies.[60] But he did have much to say about the "order of loving" and devoted to it an entire "Questio" of his Summa Theologica.[61] He developed several distinctions between the love owed to one's closest relatives and the love owed to neighbors. Like many commentators before him, Thomas affirmed that domestic love is marked by greater intensity, while *caritas* cools with distance, like heat emanating from a fire.[62] Thomas further affirmed, as his predecessors seemingly had not, that love of those close to us differed in its origins from love for outsiders. Origen wrote about love among the "saints," that is, those moved by grace. Aquinas, in a manner typical of thirteenth-century scholasticism, stressed instead nature and the natural wellsprings of human behavior. In his view, our love for those joined to us by blood relationships was founded on nature and was therefore stable and durable; in contrast, our love for those unrelated to us was based on convention and was unstable and shifting.[63] Finally, the love that joins us to our closest relatives has many modes. We may count, as Thomas did not explicitly do, the

59. *B. Alberti Magni ... Opera omnia*, ed. St. C. A. Borgnet (Paris, 1894), 28, p. 547: "Inter domesticum et inimicum sunt multi gradus, scilicet affinis, concivis, compaternalis, et hujusmodi." Albert further observed that the circle of loved ones up to domestics constituted a *societas ex convictu*, a community of those eating together, a *domus* or household.

60. See *S. Thomas Aquinatis Scriptum super Sententiis*, ed. M. F. Moos, O.P. (Paris, 1956), 3, pp. 918–49, for his comment on Book 3, question 39 of the Sentences. For comment on Thomas's views, see L. B. Geiger, *Le Problème de l'amour chez saint Thomas d'Aquin* (Montreal, 1952).

61. Aquinas, *ST* 2.2.q.26, *Opera omnia* 8 (Rome, 1895), pp. 209–23.

62. Aquinas, *ST* 2.2.q.27, a.7, *Opera omnia*, 8, p. 230: "Ergo diligere amicum est magis meritorium quam diligere inimicum ... Sed sicut idem ignis in propinquiora fortius agit quam in remotiora, ita etiam caritas ferventius diligit coniunctos quam remotos."

63. *Ibid.*, a.8, 8, p. 218: "Si autem comparemus coniunctionem ad coniunctionem, constat quod coniunctio naturalis originis est prior et immobilior: quia est secundum id quod pertinet ad substantiam; aliae autem coniunctiones sunt supervenientes, et removeri possunt ... Et ideo amicitia consanguineorum est stabilior.... Amicitia tamen consanguineorum est in his quae ad naturam spectant."

ways of loving: these are the *amicitia* due to friends regarded as other selves, the sympathy from shared experiences that Tertullian noted, parental commitment to children, conjugal love, filial respect for parents, and so on. The love for neighbors, simple *amor caritatis* in Thomas's phrase, is single stranded and necessarily weak.

Thomas did not here draw explicit distinctions between co-residential and non-residential kin, but elsewhere he showed a clear picture of the *domus* as the constituent element of society. "It is manifest," he wrote, "that the *domus* holds an intermediate position between the individual and the city or the kingdom; for just as a single person is part of the *domus*, so each *domus* is part of the city of kingdom."[64] The *domus* is in turn based on three sets of relationships: lord to servant, husband to wife, father to child, all of which Thomas explored.[65]

Thomas further attempted to determine the order of loving among household members, although his efforts sometimes seem exercises in futility. Do parents love their children more or less than children love their parents? Parents love their children more, he concluded, for two reasons. Parents have greater certainty of who their children are than children have of who their parents are. And parents are conscious of their children for a longer time than children are conscious of their parents, and time strengthens love.

Are parents or spouses loved the more? By "reason of the good" they have wrought, parents merit greater affection, as we owe them our being. But, "by reason of the tie," spouses are more loved, as the conjugal pair are two in one flesh; to love one's spouse is therefore equivalent to loving one's self. Parents, however, deserve the greater honor. Is the father or the mother to be loved more? Thomas seems uncertain here, as personal qualities enter so strongly. However, other things being equal, fathers are to be loved more, since, in the ancient and scholastic view of procreation, mothers supplied the active element in conception. Quaint though his arguments may be, Thomas

64. Aquinas, *ST* 2.2.50.3, *Opera omnia*, 8, p. 376: "Manifestum est autem quod domus medio modo se habet inter unam singularem personam et civitatem vel regnum: nam sicut una singularis persona est pars domus, ita una domus est pars civitatis vel regni."
65. Aquinas, *ST* 1.2.105.4, *Opera omnia*, 7, p. 271: "Sic igitur in domestica communione sunt tres combinationes: scilicet domini ad servum, viri ad uxorem, patris ad filium."

clearly thought of the household as a community of affection. Moreover, the love within it is intense, natural, complex, and lasting.

If Thomas presented a rather static and detached model of society and family, his approach may mirror the relatively stable state of medieval society in the placid thirteenth century. In contrast, over the fourteenth and fifteenth centuries, plagues, famines, wars, and social unrest shook the equilibrium of the medieval world and undermined the serene outlook of its thinkers. The greatest sages in that disturbed epoch tried not so much to construct abstract models of the natural order as to offer moral guidance to perplexed individuals living amid tumultuous surroundings. One theologian sensitive to moral issues was Antoninus, archbishop of Florence in the middle fifteenth century, shepherd to a large, rich, and troubled flock of merchants, bankers, and artisans. In his own *Summa Theologica*, Antoninus included a chapter called "De amore" (On love). In it, he examined love of God, love of self, love of children, and love of wife. Antoninus saw no need to exhort his readers to love children or spouse. Rather, he warned them repeatedly against excessive attachment to offspring, husband, or wife. Here is his denunciation of parents:

> Oh how many are the parents, who because of disordered love for their children, earn damnation! Oh how many are they, who serve their children like idols! ... [Making] idols of their children, they accumulate wealth by fair means or foul in order to leave them wealthy, and they are unconcerned about going to hell.[66]

Antoninus also condemned the tyranny of parents who prevent their children from entering the religious life. He gave expression to a longstanding ecclesiastical suspicion of parental power.

There was danger, too, in conjugal love; it was not that spouses lacked affection but, in Antoninus's view, they often loved not wisely but too well. He cited from Augustine the salutary example of Adam who, at Eve's request, ate the forbidden fruit "lest he displease

---

66. Aquinas, *ST* tit. 5, cap. 2, "De amore," 1, p. 432: "O quot sunt parentes, qui propter inordinatum amorem ad filios, damnationem incurrunt! O quot sunt, qui eis quasi idolis inserviunt! Et nota, quod idolotatria habuit initium ab inordinato amore parentum in filios, et e converso. Nam Ninus, qui aedificavit Ninivem, mortuo Bello patre suo, ... Sic multi faciunt de filiis idola. Nam, ut dimittant eos divites, congregant per fas et nefas, nec curant ire ad infernum."

and sadden his companion."[67] The church gave no blanket endorsement to familial sentiments.

Did these speculations of schoolmen reflect deeper changes in late medieval society? We can look for evidence of shifting attitudes toward the family to movements of popular piety. A cult of paramount interest here is that of St. Joseph, the foster father of Christ. Late ancient and early medieval piety had largely ignored Joseph. In contrast, in the late Middle Ages, he attracted considerable attention, even in lay and vernacular poetry. In the fourteenth century, French poet Eustache Deschamps composed a ballad in praise of Joseph. The poem observes that Joseph had guarded his wife and child "in great fear" and "never in this world had a holiday."[68] Eustache says to fathers everywhere

You who serve wife and infants
Ever have Joseph in your remembrance.[69]

Closely related to the veneration of Joseph is the cult of the Holy Family. The words *Sancta Familia* seem totally absent in the voluminous devotional literature antedating the fourteenth century. Artistic representations of the Holy Family also seem to date only from the fourteenth century. Eustache Deschamps reported that he had seen in many churches representations of the flight into Egypt.[70]

How can we explain the growing veneration of these domestic images, of the solicitous father and the small family forced to flee into a foreign land? Could it have been that many small families in the late Middle Ages felt themselves isolated and harassed, beleaguered by plague, famines, wars, and social uncertainties? The Holy Family according to its legend survived amid hostile and dangerous surroundings. For families facing similar uncertainties, perhaps its image offered a model of behavior and a promise of help.

In the late Middle Ages, this sense of an order in loving found expression in secular as well as religious writings. Lay people are, to

67. *Ibid.*: "non quia credidit se per hoc similem Deo futurum, sed ne displiceret et contristaret sociam ductus non amore concupiscentiae, quae adhuc non erat in eo, sed amore sociali, quo timet quia non offendet amicum suum, ut dicit Augustinus."

68. *Oeuvres complètes de Eustache Deschamps*, ed. Le Marquis de Queux de Saint-Hilaire (Paris, 1878), 1, pp. 277–78 (no. 150): "Mère et enfant garda en grant doubtance ... Et si n'ot oncq feste en ce monde ci." The allusion to a holiday may reflect the efforts of such prominent churchmen as Jean Gerson chancellor of the University of Paris, to have Joseph honored by a major feast day in the church calendar.

69. *Ibid.*: "Vous qui servez a femme et a enfans/Aiez Joseph toudis en remembrance."

70. *Ibid.*: "En plusieurs lieux est figuré ainsi, Lez un mulet, pour leur fair plaisance."

be sure, slow to acquire voices in medieval cultural history. One place where they precociously learned to speak was Florence, capital of a new lay learning that was to culminate in humanism. In both domestic memoirs and formal treatises, Florentine writers commented extensively on the family and the sentiments associated with it. About 1360, a layman named Paolo da Certaldo included in his "Book of Good Customs" a passage on the four "greatest loves" in life. The greatest of all was love of one's own soul, followed by love for one's children, then for one's wife, and finally for one's friend. He did not mention love of God, but his ranking seems an expression in secular terms of the order proclaimed by theologians since Origen's time.[71] About 1393, an unnamed townsman of Paris instructed his wife on how she should order her affections: "You ought to be very loving and privy towards your husband above all other living creatures, moderately loving and privy towards your good and near kinsfolk in the flesh and your husband's kinfolk, and very distant with all other men."[72] The ancient concept of degrees of loving extended beyond the ranks of the erudite.

The abundant domestic literature of late medieval Florence further indicates a sharpening division between the family's inner circle and the surrounding society. Giovanni Morelli, a Florentine writing in the years from 1393 to 1403, instructed his descendants on how to counter the dangers of the world. One such danger was plague. The defensive perimeter he drew up encircles the family. The family also was to be taken to a safe locale and given the proper food. The family also had to be treated to the proper cultural diversions to maintain morale, even if they were costly. "Hold your family," Morelli recommended, "in pleasure and delight, and seek together with them the good and healthy life."[73]

Although the menace of plague threatened the family from the outer world, there were other dangers, too. The government's insa-

71. Paolo da Certaldo, *Libro di buoni costumi*, cap. 156, ed. Branca, p. 37: "I maggiori amori che sieno si sono quattro: il primo si è quello de l'anima tua, il secondo si è quello de' tuoi figli, il terzo si è quello de la tua donna, cioè della buona moglie, lo quarto si è da l'uno amico a l'altro."

72. *The Goodman of Paris (Le Ménagier de Paris): A Treatise on the Moral and Domestic Economy by a Citizen of Paris (c. 1393)*, trans. E. Power (London, 1928), p. 107.

73. G. Morelli, *Ricordi*, ed. V. Branca (Florence, 1969), pp. 213–14: "tieni in diletto e in piacere la tua famiglia e fa con loro insieme buona e sana vita."

tiable appetite for taxes and the machinations of dishonest neighbors could rain ruin on the family, if these intrusions were not countered by appropriate measures. In describing those methods, Morelli warned against trust in anyone outside the household, even seeming friends, even close relatives. "Strangers I call them," he pronounced, "since where money is involved or any property, there can be found neither relative nor friend who loves you more than he does himself."[74] He continued: "A relative or friend will remain for as long as your property and status shall last, whence he thinks to gain some profit."[75] Morelli would have agreed with Peter Lombard's blunt assessment that, beyond the domestic circle, there are only enemies.

But, if the Florentine family felt threatened by disease, taxes, and pervasive dishonesty, its members seem to have developed a stronger sense of internal cohesion and seem to have found, or hoped to find, in their companionship essential rest and refreshment. Giannozzo Alberti, the sage who dominates the third book of Leon Battista Alberti's *Four Books on the Family,* urged the young Alberti males to eschew public office and government honors. "My children," he advised, "let us remain happy with our little family."[76] He uses here the diminutive form, *famigliola,* clearly implying affection. This seems a novel usage. The Latin equivalent of the word, *familiola,* meant in classical times only a small band of slaves. Alberti means by it a dear and loving group of parents and children, clearly separated from the outer world and emotionally independent of it.

What explains the new and wide division between household and society evident in these Florentine texts? The real change, as I see it, was less in the family itself—always thought to be a community of affection—than in the apprehension of external society as hostile and demanding. Governments were becoming better organized, more powerful, and, through their taxes and policies, more

74. Morelli, *Ricordi,* p. 173, "Istrani gli chiamo, perché dove giuoca pecunia o alcuno bene proprio, né parente né amico si truova che voglia meglio a te che a sé, disposta la buona coscienza da parte."
75. *Ibid.:* "Peró che tanto basta il parente e l'amico quanto ti basterà l'avere e lo stato dove e' penserà trarre utilità."
76. L. B. Alberti, *Opera omnia,* ed. C. Grayson (Bari, 1960), 1, p. 182: "Figliuoli miei, stiamoci in sul piano, e diamo opera d'essere buoni e giusti massai. Stiànci lieti colla famigliuola nostra, godiànci quelli beni ci largisce la fortuna faccendone parte alli amici nostri, ché assai si truova onorato chi vive senza vizio e senza disonestà."

intrusive than ever into the domestic realm. The family itself was coming to rely more and more for its support on cash transactions. Contractual obligations and cash connections now linked households within the larger society. But loan oft loses friend, and so might every other type of monetary transaction.

The unnamed citizen of Paris told of a couple who drew up a nuptial agreement, stipulating their separate rights and duties.[77] One day, the husband fell into a river and called upon his wife to save him from drowning. The wife consulted the agreement and found no clause obligating her to rescue a drowning spouse. She let him sink, though others finally saved him. The moral here seems clear: contract and cash, which govern relationships in the outer world, should not do so within the family. By the end of the Middle Ages, at least in certain areas and certain classes of European society, the family had become a moral unity and a moral universe, in the sense I have defined.

Of course, the evolution of family structures and cultures continued after the Middle Ages ended. Styles of domesticity, the set of values and expectations associated with it, have changed across modern times even as lifestyles change. The tension between the family and the greater society has also waxed and waned, according to shifting patterns of politics and modes of private behavior. Many of these fluctuations in modern family history have been studied in what is now a vast literature.[78]

Nonetheless, the ancient and medieval origins of many contemporary attitudes toward the family need to be recognized. Still today, the family seems to some a prison. For them, it preserves its ancient meaning as a band of slaves; it continues to reflect the emphasis on authority written into its distant past. To others, it seems a haven, a refuge in which the furious pace of getting and spending is slackened, the burden of affairs is lightened, tensions are eased, enmities

---

77. *The Goodman of Paris*, trans. Power, p. 138.
78. The recent, collaborative *History of Private Life*, Vol. 4: *From the Fires of Revolution to the Great War*, is devoted almost entirely to the family, especially in France. Also see M. Mitterauer and R. Sieder, *The European Family*, trans. K. Osterveen and M. Hörzinger (Oxford, 1982); and *Histoire de la famille*, ed. A. Burguière, et al., Vol. 1: *Mondes lointains, mondes anciens*; Vol. 2: *Le Choc des modernités* (Paris, 1986). For relations of the family with kin and community, see P. Laslett, "Family, Kinship and Collectivity as Systems of Support in Pre-Industrial Europe: A Consideration of the 'Nuclear-Hardship' Hypothesis," *Continuity and Change*, 3 (1988), p. 153–75.

forgotten. For these as for Augustine long ago, the family is *requies*. Still others argue that the traditional family, based on monogamy and child rearing, does not meet their own emotional needs, that other forms of domestic partnerships should be accepted. They question only the universal applicability of one definition of the family, not the value of the supportive and recreative functions the small domestic community has long provided. The cult and culture of the modern family, its problems, too, have traces running deep into ancient and medieval history, which here in part I have tried to follow.

7

THE MAKING OF THE MEDIEVAL FAMILY:

Symmetry, Structure, and Sentiment

✦ ✦ ✦

In any examination of the family, it is useful initially to define what we mean by that common and yet extraordinarily resonant term.[1] Definitions, in classical Aristotelian logic, should state the genus of the entity and then its specific differences—those which distinguish it within its class. The family is obviously a society, an organized, though usually small, group of human beings. Its specific differences are in turn two. The family members live together. Living together has often meant working and producing together, but historically, the fundamental implication of coresidency seems to have been common consumption. Members of the family eat the same food at the same table. The second specifying difference is the close, we might call it primary, relationships among the members through blood or marriage. Coresidency and primary relationship through blood or marriage are thus the specifying differences which identify families within the larger community. To claim membership in the family, at least one of these conditions must be fulfilled. The family defined by the test of coresidency is the household; the family defined by primary relationship in blood and marriage is the bio-

1. For a recent bibliography on the history of family and kinship, see G. L. Soliday, ed. *History of the Family and Kinship: A Select International Bibliography* (New York, 1980). For works on the medieval family, see M. Sheehan and K. Scardellato, *Family and Marriage in Medieval Europe: A Working Bibliography* (British Columbia, 1976), which is currently being revised. The collection of essays entitled *Famille et parenté dans l'occident médiéval* (Rome, 1977), provides a fine example of recent research on medieval household structures.

logical descent group—parents and children. In our use of the term, the family is thus a coresidential unit, with a kin group at its core.

These qualities differentiate families from other social groups, but they also link them to the larger society; this fact lends to the study of families its extraordinary complexity. Coresidency implies that the household members live in a defined space; however, they rarely live in total isolation, in a spatial sense, from other households. These nearby households are of course neighbors, and the relationships among the neighboring households reverberate upon and affect the internal structure of each. The consanguinity and affinity of household members also sets them in a larger network of kin and affines, which orients them toward exterior society. These linkages through proximity, blood, and marriage make the family the building block of larger social structures. However, their presence also means that the family cannot be studied in isolation; we must constantly shift our gaze from its internal structure to its connections with the larger society, and back again.

My topic in this essay is the "making of the medieval family," by which I mean the emergence in western Europe during the Middle Ages of a distinctive type of domestic group, which seems to have differed markedly from those which populated ancient Mediterranean societies. I am not competent to compare these medieval households with families in non-Western societies, or even to judge the extent to which this medieval family might also be regarded as "modern." My limited point here is that the Middle Ages did produce a type of domestic organization, or perhaps I should say, a domestic system, which was apparently unknown, or at least not predominant, in earlier societies within the Western tradition.

What then distinguishes families in the medieval world? Three things do, in my view: a particular composition, a particular structure, and a particular set of emotional ties binding the members. The composition of households is not only particular, but is also roughly uniform in society. Medieval households can, in other words, be regarded as largely comparable and commensurable. We might also say that the array of medieval households was symmetrical, in the sense that the observer would see roughly the same form of households no matter in what direction he looked—toward urban or rural areas, or up or down the scale of wealth. In exploring the novel attributes of the medieval domestic system, these then are the three qualities we shall examine: symmetry, structure, and sentiment.

First then, when can commensurable households within a symmetrical array first be discerned? They do not seem discernible in ancient Mediterranean societies. Households differed so widely from each other that they could not be encompassed in a single system of social analysis, or utilized as a useful unit of social measurement. Two considerations support this conclusion. The first is the peculiar meaning which the classical terms for household and family usually bear. The ancients, of course, wrote extensively about households. "Economics," the science of household management, was the counterpart to "politics," the science of city government.[2] However, they seem to have defined the household in two different, although still related, ways. To the Greek educator and philosopher Xenophon, who wrote one of the earliest tracts on "economics, " the household was equivalent to its property, to the material possessions under the ownership of the household head. "The household," he writes, "looks to us to be the totality of possessions."[3] Consistent with this view, the law of household management, or economics, becomes the study of managing property, and thus approaches our own understanding of the term. In Latin too, *familia* sometimes bears this meaning: the household is the material possessions of its head, the *paterfamilias*. The more usual Latin meaning, however, is the following: The household consists of all those under the authority of its chief, under his *patria potestas*. It thus includes persons rather than possessions—the wife, unemancipated children of any age, and slaves. In the second century A.D., the Roman jurist Ulpian writes: "… in strict law, we define the family as the many persons who by nature or law are set under the authority of an individual, such as the *paterfamilias*."[4] Isidore of Seville, who died in 636 and gave to the Middle Ages its most popular encyclopedia, the *Etymologies*, states that *familia* derives from *femur*, "loin," and

2. Thus, a long disquisition on household management appears in Aristotle, *The Politics of Aristotle*, trans. E. Barker (Oxford, 1946), pp. 1–38.

3. The definition appears in Xenophon, *Oeconomicus*: see L. Strauss, *Xenophon's Socratic Discourse: An Interpretation of the Oeconomicus* (Ithaca, 1970), p. 26.

4. P. Krueger, et al., ed., *Corpus Iuris Civilis* (Berlin, 1928–29), Digest, 50.16.195, "iure proprio familiam dicimus plures personas, quae sunt sub unius potestate aut natura aut iure subiectae, ut puta paterfamilias…" An English translation is available in S.P. Scott, *The Civil Law* [incomp. cit.].

means "offspring" in the strict sense.[5] The following conclusion seems unavoidable, if still surprising: the Roman understanding of family excluded its chief, the *paterfamilias*, from membership within it. He was not subject to his own authority, as Ulpian requires, nor was he his own offspring, in Isidore's etymology. The wide gap between *pater* and *familia* may further have blocked the development among the ancients of a deep consciousness of the family as a moral unity.

Are there, perhaps, other classical terms which might have identified the coresidential domestic unit, including the father? The Romans had words for hearth, *focus*, and for household gods, *lares*, *penates*. *Focus* meant the physical hearth or, in late Latin, the fire within it, as in the modern Italian *fuoco*. It was used to connote the collectivity of households, as in the rallying cry, *pro aris et focis*, "for altars and hearths." It seems rarely to have been used as a metaphor for households, however, and it never represented a coresidential domestic unit common to all social levels.[6]

The conclusion I would draw from this use of words is the following: The model of the family in classical "economics" was the propertied, surely slave-holding household; for this reason, it could not have applied to the humble levels of society. It did not reflect the domestic arrangements of large segments of the ancient population, notably, slaves and the poor. Ancient concepts of the family were fundamentally elitist, consistent with the entire bent of classical literary culture. However, if the ancient concept of the household was inapplicable to large segments of society, it follows that ancient households were not commensurable.

Further evidence that the households of the classical Mediterranean world lacked uniformity comes from the methods adopted in taking surveys. Ancient societies did not use the household or hearth as a unit of social measurement, whether for the imposition of taxes or the recruitment of soldiers. The ancient peoples were inveterate census takers. The Bible itself records some nine cen-

5. *Isidori Hispalensis episcopi etymologiarum sive originum libri XX*, ed. W. M. Lindsay (Oxford, 1911), 9.4.4: "Nam familia est liberi ex liberis legibus suscepti, a femore ..."

6. For numerous examples of the classical use of these terms, see the *Thesaurus linguae latinae editus auctoritate et consilio academiarum quinque Germanicarum* (Leipzig, 1900–), sub verbis.

suses; King David was even reprimanded for engaging in this exercise.[7] Most Biblical censuses were taken for purposes of recruitment; thus, in one of them, men "fit for war," from 20 years of age on, were to be counted in their houses, families, and kin. However, the target of the Biblical surveys remained the individual, and not the family or the hearth. According to the Greek historian Herodotus, Amasis, king of Egypt, took a census which the Athenian lawgiver Solon later imitated.[8] Here too, adult males and their professions, not households, were the object of the census. The Romans were perhaps the most industrious of the ancient census takers. Every five years, special officers known as the censors were required to register citizens capable of bearing arms or of paying taxes; we have fragmentary results of their efforts dating from 225 B.C. The practice continued into the imperial period, apparently until the reign of Vespasian (A.D. 69–79).[9] As the empire expanded, the government took similar surveys of subject territories. However, neither in counting its subjects nor in assessing their wealth did the Romans make use of household units.

Most remarkable is the assessment system developed in the late empire (fourth and fifth centuries A.D.), known as the *capitatio iugatio*.[10] Although its exact methods remain obscure, *capitatio* involved a count of heads, presumably able-bodied workers, whereas *iugatio* was an estimate of land and productivity, with animals also somehow factored into the equation. It would seem that the results would have been much the same, and the procedures greatly simplified, if households had been taken as the basic unit. However, the Romans did not do so. Presumably, the agricultural system, with large, slave-run estates alongside single-family farms, did not yet lend itself to the use of a common unit.

7. Kings 2.24. In the descriptions of these censuses given in the Latin Vulgate edition, the word *domus* is often used, but its clear sense is kin group, not household. For example, "recensentes eos per cognationes et domos ac familias," Numbers 1.1–3.

8. "It was Amasis who made the law that every Egyptian should yearly declare his means of livelihood to the ruler of the province. Ion the Athenian got this law from Egypt and established it among his people; may they ever keep it! for it is a perfect law," *Herodotus*, trans. A. D. Godley (Cambridge, Mass., 1911) II, p. 177.

9. On the character of Roman censuses, see P. A. Brunt, *Italian Manpower, 225 H.C.–A.D. 14* (Oxford, 1971).

10. The system, much discussed, has been recently reexamined in W. Goffart, *"Caput" and Colonate: Towards a History of Late Roman Taxation* (Toronto, 1974).

Only in one sector of Roman institutions and life do households appear as commensurable units in a symmetrical array: the laying out of new settlements or colonies. Since the early Republic, the Roman government had rewarded veteran soldiers with grants of land. Grouped into colonies, the veterans worked their farms primarily with the aid of their families; they could only have owned few, if any, slaves.[11] In the late empire, barbarian contingents were settled on the land in similar fashion, on the basis of hearths or households.[12]

The appearance and spread of commensurable household units thus seems intimately related to the extension of family-based, or peasant, agriculture throughout the Empire. This close association of peasant agriculture with the use of households in tax assessments perhaps explains why the ancient censors so rarely used hearths in their work. The hearth or household could not be easily used to assess large, slave-run estates (or big ranches in the pastoral regions). In addition, ancient societies showed enormous variations in the range of wealth—from patricians owning thousands of slaves to the slaves themselves, pitiful chattel, most of whom were herded into barracks. Household units, which imply a rough equality across society, could not measure the size, wealth, and productivity of such disparate social strata. In other words, the households of ancient society, under the prevalent slave system, lacked commensurability.

If this analysis is correct, comparable and commensurable households did not fully emerge until the demise of ancient slavery, which was replaced in most areas of the former Roman Empire, and indeed beyond its borders, by an agricultural system based on a settled peasantry. As far as our sources allow us to judge, this transformation had triumphed by about A.D. 700. In England, for example, the Venerable Bede, who died in A.D. 735, routinely used *familiae* (he was doubtlessly thinking "hides") to estimate the size both of individual estates and entire.[13] Instances of a comparable usage

11. See the uses in *Livy in Fourteen Volumes*, trans. B. O. Foster (Cambridge, Mass., 1967), xxxii.29.4, in regard to five colonies founded in Italy, "trecenae familiae in singulas colonias iubebantur mitti ... "; and xxxvii.34.1, in regard to Spain, "sex milia familiarum conscribant, ... quae in eas colonias dividerentur ... "

12. See the biography of Emperor Aurelian in D. Magic, ed. and trans., *Scriptores Historiae Augustae* (Cambridge, Mass., 1961), xivii.2. Aurelian settled "familias captivas" in Tuscany and commissioned them to raise vines.

13. *Baedae opera historica*, trans. J. E. King (Cambridge, Mass., 1971), 3, 24. "Regnum australium Merciorum, qui sunt, ut dicunt, familiarum quinque mila ...æ

can be found in the contemporary continental sources. The earliest surviving surveys based on households or hearths date from the late eighth century—from Europe of the Frankish kingdom and of Charlemagne.[14] The key words are now the classical terms *familia* and *focus* and many medieval neologisms—"hide" in England, *Hufe* in Germany, *mansus* widely across Europe. Note that in this usage the term *familia* signifies a family occupying a farm sufficient for its needs, that is, a coresidential kin group which includes the household head. Medieval writers often use familia in the classical sense to connote all those, including servants, who are subject to the authority of a chief or lord. In addition to this ancient use, however, the term was slowly acquiring its new, medieval, and modern meaning.

From the Carolingian age on, hearth lists were used as a means of social measurement; this implies that the domestic system was now based on commensurable households. Two further comments seem appropriate. Of course, the households of the rich were different from those of the poor; they were generally larger and invariably included servants. However, the terms derived from humbler hearths were applied to them as well: in the ninth-century survey of the estates of Saint Germain des Prés, along with the farm of the lowly slave, the *mansus servilis*, there is counted the lord's manor house, the *mansus indominictus*.[15] The continuing vast differences between rich and poor did not break the bonds of comparability. In the cities of the late Middle Ages, as in Florence of 1427, the big and bursting patrician families, and destitute, solitary widows, still live in units which the government treats as comparable.[16] Was this simply a matter of administrative convenience? I would argue that it signals

---

1, 454. In similar fashion he reckons the size of northern Mercia as 7,000 "familiae." He mentions several times (in 3,4) that he gives these estimates "iuxta aestimationem Anglorum": *ibid.,* 3,4. In 1, 340 he writes, "Neque enim magna est, sed quasi familiarum quinque, iuxta aestimationem Anglorum."

14. For an example of the use of family farms to estimate the return from episcopal estates, see T. J. Rivers, trans., *Laws of Alamans and Bavarians* (Philadelphia, 1979), chap. 21, 22. For a full discussion of the emergence of the family farm as an assessment unit, see D. Herlihy, "The Carolingian Mansus," *Economic History Review,* 13, pp. 79–89. Reprinted in Herlihy, *Social History,* no. 4. [incomp. cit.]

15. See B. Guerard, ed., *Polyptyque de l'Abbé Irminon,* 2 vols. (Paris, 1844), the largest and richest of the Carolingian surveys.

16. D. Herlihy, and C. Klapisch-Zuber, *Les Toscans et leurs familles: Une étude du catasto florentin de 1427* (Paris, 1978), especially Chapter 17, "Le feux."

the presence of a fundamentally symmetrical array of households, based on commensurable units.

Hearth lists remained the most common form of tax assessment throughout the entire course of the Middle Ages. In the twelfth and thirteenth centuries, with the growth of towns, they were applied to urban populations as well. Even within an urban environment, households continued to serve as units of production and consumption, and this probably explains their continuing uniformity. Uniformity is necessary, of course, before we can make any general statements concerning medieval families.

How did religion contribute to the emergence of commensurable household units in the early Middle Ages? Historians have much discussed the influence of Christianity on the Roman law of marriage, and most conclude that it was surprisingly slight.[17] But one principle of Christian ethics certainly facilitated this transition, if only slowly and indirectly: all believers—men and women, rich and poor, the free and the unfree—were obligated to follow the same code of sexual morality. There could be no variant standards of behavior within the Christian community. Roman law recognized several forms of marriage or concubinage; for Christians, however, marriage was the same for all persons, no matter what their class or condition. Similarly, the Christian insistence on monogamy undermined, though again only slowly, the polygyny practiced by several barbarian peoples (or rather, the elites among them).[18] A single ethic of marriage surely aided the emergence of comparable households.

More distantly, the image of the Holy Family may have strengthened the sense that a kin group which lived and worked together formed a strongly cohesive moral unit. This sentiment is clearly present in the legend of St. Severus of Ravenna. Severus lived in the fourth century, but as a ninth-century author, a priest named Luidolphus, wrote his life, we can assume that the familial portrait he draws is typical of the author's times. Severus was a wool worker, and he labored together with his wife Vincentia and daughter Innocentia at making cloth. He was eventually called to be bishop of Ravenna, but at his

17. The literature is reviewed in J. Gaudemet, *Les transformations de la vie familiale au Bas Empire et l'influence du Christianisme* (Romanitas, 1952) pp. 58–85, and M. Humbert, *Le Remariage a Rome* (Milan, 1972).

18. On the polygynous practices of the Frankish aristocracy, see S. F. Wemple, *Women in Frankish Society. Marriage and the Cloister, 500–900* (Philadelphia, 1981), and of the Irish, see P. C. Power, *Sex and Marriage in Early Ireland* (Dublin, 1977).

death, he requested that he be buried with his wife and daughter, both of whom had predeceased him: "Since we in this world had a life in common, so let us have a common tomb."[19] Severus's family was unmistakably a moral unit, in life and in death.

The second novel quality which we attribute to the medieval family has to do with structure, by which we mean its relationship with the larger society. Lack of space precludes a consideration of neighborhood ties, though they are admittedly important, especially in an urban context.[20] We shall deal here with the place of the family within the larger network of kin and affines.

My thesis is as follows: From the central Middle Ages (approximately the twelfth and thirteenth centuries), a new kinship system, agnatic or patrilineal in basic design, came to be superimposed upon an older system, especially a cognatic or bilineal one. Not only was the new system agnatic, but it also increasingly favored the interests of a single son, usually the eldest, over other brothers. The new system was superimposed upon the old, but did not entirely obliterate it. As far as household organization and the recognition of close kin were concerned, medieval people, especially the elites, came to follow two different and in some ways inconsistent, sets of rules, in pursuit of two sets of goals. The older goal was the preservation of the bilineal descent or kin group; the newer, the promotion of the agnatic lineage within it. The overlaying of these two systems helps explain the interior structure, and even some of the tensions, of the medieval family. To be sure, we shall here be chiefly concerned with elite families. Only slowly did the new goals and rules affect the behavior of the humble. It would be foolish, however, to slight the importance of the elite model for this reason. Here, as is usually the case, poverty and deprivation affected the free play of social systems. The rich, by virtue of their resources, come closer than the destitute to achieving purposes and goals which many share.

Historians today are generally agreed that the prevailing kinship system of early medieval society, from the fall of the Roman empire to the twelfth century, was exclusively bilineal; relationships traced

19. "ut qui in hoc seculo communiter viximus, etiam communi sepultura utamur," De S. Severo episcopo Ravennae Vita … auctore Luidolpho presbytero, in *Acta sanctorum quotquot toto orbe coluntur*, I Februarii (Antwerp, 1643–), p. 89.

20. "For an example of this type of study, see C. Klapisch-Zuber, "Parenti, amici, vicini. Il territorio urbano d'una famiglia mercantile nel XV secolo," *Quaderni storici*, 33 (1976), pp. 953–82.

through women were equally important as those traced through men.[21] In describing this system, we can take as a convenient point of departure a treatise entitled "On Degrees of Kinship," which was written about 1063 by the Italian reformer and saint, Peter Damian, at the request of the Florentines.[22] They were confused (many persons in the early Middle Ages must have been) about the methods of calculating degrees of kinship and why it all mattered. Damian first seeks to justify why blood relationships should matter at all in determining eligibility for marriage. Here, although he makes much use of earlier writers (St. Augustine, Isidore of Seville, Burchard of Worms) he is still describing ideas and a system very much alive in the eleventh century.[23]

All human beings, he reminds his readers, are descendants of the same first parents, Adam and Eve, and all are therefore members of the same descent group—a *genus cognationis* in his phrase. Human beings, unlike animals, have only a single pair of first parents; this should remind us all that we are in fact brothers or sisters, members of the same kin group. Over time, however, the lines of descent (*progenies* in Peter's technical terminology) grow apart. As the distance separating them increases, their mutual love cools and expires. This dispersion of the strands stemming from common ancestors extinguishes love and undermines social peace. Descent groups then become inclined to fight against their estranged neighbors. Here, marriage performs its essential service to society. "When blood relationship," Peter explains, "along with the terms that designate it, expires, the law of marriage takes up the function, and reestablishes the rights of ancient love among new men."[24] In other words, when

---

21. See the recent review article, R. Fossier, "Les structures de la famille en occident au Moyen-Age," in *XVe Congres International des Sciences Historiques Rapports*, 2, pp. 115–32 (Bucharest,1980). See also K. Schmid, "Heirat, Familienfolge, Geschlechterbewusstsein," *Il matrimonio nella societa altomedievale*, Settimane di Studio del Centro Italiano sull'Alto-Medievo (Spoleto, 1977); see also G. Duby, "Structures de parenté et de la noblesse dans la France du nord au IIe et 12e siècles," *Miscellanea mediaevalia in memoriam Jan Frederik Niermeyer* (Groningen, 1967); reprinted in *Hommes et structures du Moyen Age. Recueil d'articles* (Paris and the Hague, 1973). A translation by C. Postan is available in *The Chivalrous Society*.

22. J. P. Migne, ed., *Patrologiae cursus completus. Series latina* (Paris, 1841–64), 145, cols. 191–208, "De parentelae gradibus, ad Johannem episcopum caesenatensem."

23. His sources are identified in J. J. Ryan, *St. Peter Damiani and His Canonical Sources* (Toronto, 1956).

24. Migne, *Patrologia Latina*, 145, col. 193.

consanguinity fails, marriage intervenes, in defense of social peace. Marriage is not simply the union of two persons; rather, it binds together two kin groups. It reunites human society, which time and the divergence of family lines relentlessly pull asunder.

Women, of course, were fullfledged members of the *genus* or kin group. Their membership, according to Peter, necessarily included a right to share in the inheritance of the property, which the descent group carried with it down the generations. As Damian explains, the right to inherit from a person is conclusive proof of kinship relation with him or her. The right to inherit and the right to marry are mutually exclusive. "One right," he states, "excludes the other, so that the woman from whom one could inherit cannot be taken as a legitimate spouse, even as the woman whom one can legally marry can have no title of inheritance [to her husband's property]."[25]

The kinship system which Damian describes thus possesses the following characteristics. It is ego-focused, in the sense that all lines stretch out and are measured from the place which the ego holds in the descent group. This means that the composition of the kindred is redefined for each new generation, as its focus settles upon a new person, a new ego. It does not continuously accumulate members over time. Its limits are set in precise degrees: four in classical Roman law, seven in medieval Germanic and canon law, and reduced to four again after the Fourth Lateran Council in 1215.[26] It is cognatic or bilineal, as the strands of relationship run through both men and women. It assumes that women, as authentic kin, also enjoy rights of inheritance. As a truly bilineal system, it does not impose patrilocal residence upon newlyweds, but allows them neolocal or even matrilocal residence.[27]

Even as Damian was writing, a new type of kinship system was making its appearance in western Europe, most forcefully among the elite classes, but, to a lesser degree, among the nonelite as well. This

25. "Quod quibus est jus haereditatis, est et affinitas generis," *ibid.*, 145, col. 194.
26. On methods of calculating degrees of kinship and their changes across the Middle Ages, see A. Esmein, *Le Mariage en droit canonique*, 2nd. edn. R. Génestal (Paris, 1929–35). See also C. R. Bouchard, "Consanguinity and Noble Marriages in the Tenth and Eleventh Centuries," *Speculum*, 56 (1981), pp. 268–87, with a tree of relationships on p. 270.
27. Among the serfs of the church of St. Victor of Marseilles, the women rather frequently remained with their families of origin after marriage—a rare occurrence in later medieval society. See D. Herlihy, "The Generation in Medieval History," *Viator* 5, pp. 346–64; reprinted in D. Herlihy, *Social History*, no. 12, pp. 14–15.

was patrilineage. As we argue, in its goals and rules, it does not so much replace, as is superimposed upon, the earlier, *cognatic* genus. However, it differs from the older descent group in certain crucial ways. It is ancestor-focused, rather than ego-focused; it traces its line of descent back to a particular ancestor. Like all ancestor-focused descent groups, it tends to grow with each generation. Members are never lost, as with ego-focused groups, which are redefined for egos of successive generations. Its solidarity with the past is proclaimed through the adoption of an agnatic family name, a coat of arms, mottoes, and sometimes even a mythology. Its agnatic character is shown in its exclusion of daughters and their offspring from the lineage. It is marked by solidarity among males, who are linked to each other by descent from a common patrilineal ancestor.

Cultural, social, and economic changes all contributed to the emergence of patrilineage. Prerequisite to its appearance was the long-delayed success, always limited but still substantial, of the Church's long campaign for monogamy, its efforts to suppress all manner of extramarital sexual liaisons. Sexual promiscuity inevitably obscures patrilineal relationships, and, as mentioned, much recent research has stressed the loose sexual behavior of early medieval elites, both men and women.[28] As long as the European elites strayed from strict monogamy, any effort to define the family as a fellowship of agnates would be frustrated. The Gregorian reform of the eleventh century which contributed to the emergence of the centralized Church carried forward with new vigor this long effort to impose the Christian ethic of marriage upon the reluctant elites. Lapses may have remained frequent, but monogamy became enforced as the unquestioned rule of western marriage.

The Church's now effective insistence on monogamous marriage was a precondition, but surely not the principal cause, of this realignment of elite families around patrilineages. The crucial factor seems to have been diminishing opportunities and resources available for the support of elite households. The establishment of stable feudal principalities, the partial pacification of European life, reduced the profits of pillage, apart from along the distant frontiers. The chief remaining resource was the landed patrimony. Elite families struggled to preserve the extent and integrity of their holdings.

28. See above, n. 18.

They forced their younger sons to delay or eschew marriage, or they sent them forth to make their fortunes. Daughters did not even enjoy this last option. Some girls were given the dowries they now needed for marriage; however, barring unusual circumstances, such as the death of all male heirs, a girl's dowry represented the extent of her claims upon the family patrimony. The position of women, central in the cognatic system of the early Middle Ages, clearly deteriorated as the lineage took on a pronounced agnatic cast.

Nonetheless, the new organization of the elite family did not replace the older bilineal system. The traditional definition of kin, though modified, continued to determine eligibility for marriage and to require that some support be given to daughters and younger sons. Families still hoped to recruit rich, powerful, and supportive affines through opportune marriages. Seeking to preserve and promote the status of the eldest son but mindful too of his siblings of both sexes, elite families often had to resolve contentious questions. The welfare of the lineage was not always the welfare of the kindred. How much help should be extended to daughters? How well should younger sons be supported? How assiduously should matrilineal relatives and affines be cultivated? These difficult questions worked often to create tensions within the household and kin group, but they also extended the options and broadened the strategies which families could adopt, as they struggled to preserve their status over time.

What kind of emotional bonds came to link members of the medieval family? To penetrate the emotional world of the medieval household is a supremely difficult task. Comments on familial ties are frequent in the abundant doctrinal literature of the times, but these are not especially helpful. Medieval writers, in the vast majority clerics, tirelessly reiterate the patristic argument that marriage was an acceptable state of life for Christians, although greatly inferior to virginity and even to widowhood. In St. Jerome's scoring, virginity was rated at 100 points, widowhood at 60, and marriage at only 30.[29] In medieval writings, there is also an unmistakable strain of hostility toward family life and the emotional demands it made on household members. Many of the great medieval saints—Francis of Assisi and Thomas Aquinas among them—entered their religious careers over

---

29. Epistulae 22.20, cited in Humbert, *Le Remariage à Rome*, p. 321.

the strident opposition of their families. Similarly, many of the great moral guides of the age, such as Catherine of Siena, warned the faithful that children, along with riches and status, distracted the committed Christian from religious sentiments and service.[30]

Jean Gerson, the prolific and eloquent chancellor of the University of Paris in the early 1400s, tells an anecdote about a rich but childless couple.[31] They prayed to God for a child and assiduously performed their religious and charitable duties. They were rewarded with the birth of a beautiful baby. However, they turned all their attention to their baby and neglected their religious obligations. They wished for their child the things of this world and forgot the things of the next. God gave them a painful lesson, Gerson relates, by reclaiming His gift, their baby, in death. He does this often, Gerson reminds us, lest familial obligations—and affections—distract us from our primary duty, to serve Him above all. The medieval Church, in sum, saw no absolute, no sovereign value in familial affections. However, these reservations show beyond doubt that, contrary to the opinions of some modern scholars, those affections could be intense.

One possible window onto the emotional world of the medieval family is religious practice, as distinct from formal doctrine and admonition. We can examine those devotions and cults which make use of family imagery or carry strong reminiscences of family life. The assumption here is that these public devotions correspond in some manner to the private attitudes and values of the participants. This approach, though clearly speculative, may also be appropriate here, in a collection of essays devoted to religion and the family. The devotions we shall consider here, briefly to be sure, are three: the cult of the Virgin Mary as interceding mother; of Jesus as adorable child; and of St. Joseph as patron and provider.

The oldest and most widespread of these devotions was directed toward Mary herself and made her a principal intermediary between the faithful and her son, very nearly the "mediatrix" of all graces, in the language of modern Marian theology. The cult gained enormous

30. See, for example, Catherine's condemnation of the "disordered love" which the "slaves of the world," and women in particular, hold for "children and husband and brothers and father and mother ..." Caterina da Siena, *Epistolario*, 3 vols, ed. D. U. Meattini (Siena, 1966), 2, p. 46 (letter written to the Contessa Benedetta Salimbeni).
31. J. Gerson, *Oeuvres complètes*, ed. P. Glorieux (Paris and New York, 1966), 7, p. 322.

popularity from the twelfth century on, even as western society was experiencing profound social changes which affected the family, as we previously mentioned. Did this devotion find any correspondence in the changing position of the wife and mother within the medieval family?

The emergence of the patrilineal family did affect the position of women. As the position of women within the elite family deteriorated, the age at which the daughter was given in marriage seems to have fallen to very young levels, even to the low and middle teens.[32] At the same time, however, the age of her prospective groom seems to have advanced in response to the cautious attitudes which elite families now cultivated in regard to the marriage of their sons. Roughly estimated, girls in the elite classes would marry at fifteen and men at thirty. Moreover, the stern discipline which the families imposed on young males, forcing them to wait long years for marriage and entry into adult careers, invited intergenerational conflict. Obstinate fathers and frustrated, rebellious sons—was there a more common, more antagonistic domestic situation in feudal society during the central Middle Age?

The new marriage pattern set the young wife between the aged and powerful father and his often alienated sons. She was thus ideally placed to serve as intermediary between the conflicting male generations. She often assumed that role in both religious and secular culture. In the legend of St. Francis, his mother removes the chains with which his father has bound him in the dungeon of their home. In the French *chansons de geste*, the hero often appeals to his mother to secure favors from his father. This role of the mother as intercessor, helping her deprived and weak children to gain concessions from a distant, powerful father—could this have affected the attitudes of the Christian faithful toward and their appreciation of Mary? To be sure, she intercedes for them with her divine son, not a

32. For evidence on age of marriage, see D. Herlihy "Generation," reprinted in D. Herlihy, *Social History*, no. 12, p. 357. As a typical example, the twelfth century nobleman Arnold d'Ardres took a wife thirteen years after he was dubbed a knight, which would have made him thirty or even older at first marriage. The question of whether this marriage pattern is more "Mediterranean" than "medieval" is much discussed but has not yet been satisfactorily resolved. See R. M. Smith, "The People of Tuscany and Their Families in the Fifteenth Century: Medieval or Mediterranean?" *Journal of Family History*, 6, no. 1, pp. 107–28. At least among the northern nobles, however, it was common for a mature groom to marry a young bride.

father. However, the services she seeks from him are not specifically filial. She approaches him as a deity, as one who has the means of helping her needy children.

The cult of the child Jesus also gained remarkable popularity in the twelfth century, initially among Cistercian and later mendicant circles. The Cistercian Aelred of Rievaulx contributes a long and passionate meditation on the child Jesus at the age of twelve.[33] He dwells in strikingly sensuous language on the boy's beauty and the joy he conveys to all who see him, talk with him, and care for him. Francis of Assisi, according to his legend, makes the first Christmas creche so that the faithful could behold with their own eyes Jesus as a humble, approachable child. Many saints (especially, but by no means exclusively, women) ask and are allowed to see the infant or child Jesus. They play with him, fondle him, hug him, and gain boundless satisfaction. Henrich Suso (d. 1366), the Dominican theologian and mystic, was once favored with a vision of Jesus appropriate for a teacher; he appeared to him "as a schoolboy of surpassing charm."[34] The life of St . Gertrude of Ostend in Belgium, who died in 1358, richly reflects these familial sentiments in religious garb as well as the Church's doubts about them. So powerful are her meditations on Jesus' infancy that "the breasts of this virgin Gertrude began to swell and fill with milk." Gertrude's attraction to childhood was not limited to Jesus' alone. "This virgin Gertrude loved babies and children, so much so that [to tempt her] the devil often transformed himself not into an angel of light but took on the form of a crying child ... ."[35]

It is no easy task to explain this cult of the Holy Child, and of childhood itself ill concealed behind it. I can only offer some tentative observations. Almost all these child-loving saints came from urban origins; clearly they sought to replicate within the religious life the emotional experiences of which they had been deprived, whether through their own vocational choices or through force of circumstances. They usually lacked the company and support of a

33. See Aelred of Rievaulx, "The Pastoral Prayer," in *The Works of Aelred of Rievaulx*, Cistercian Fathers Series, vol. 2 (Spencer, Mass., 1971).

34. "puerum scholasticum tantae venustatis," *Vita Henrici Susonis Ord. Pred., Acta Sanctorum,* 2 Januarii, p. 660.

35. "Infantes dilexit et pueros haec virgo Gheertrudis. Quapropter diabolus saepe se transfiguravit non in Angelum lucis, sed in formam pueri plangentis ... ." De venerabili virgine Gertrude ab Oosten beghina, *Acta Sanctorum, I Januarii,* p. 350.

natural family, but they did not renounce the emotional rewards which membership conveyed. St. Gertrude wished to nurse a baby and to soothe a crying child, even though she was a virgin, and even when the child was the devil transfigured. This implies in turn that urban households had themselves come to be oriented in significant measure toward children, to be aware of them and to delight in them. Is this surprising? The urban Renaissance from the twelfth century brought with it, and indeed required, a rebirth of schools and of formal training in the various skills and professions. Medieval townsmen had to pay attention to their offspring; and from pedagogical curiosity, awareness also grew of the special psychological traits of children. In the wake of this psychological awareness, childhood was apparently idealized as an age of life marked by innocence, openness, simplicity, and contentment. These qualities and virtues were much admired, but not easily cultivated, in bustling commercial communities. Many wearied and worried adults viewed childhood as life's happiest period and the child himself as a person worth observing and enjoying for his innocence and charm.[36]

St. Joseph, patron and provider for the Holy Family, is perhaps the key figure in our set of family-linked devotions.[37] He is a nearly ignored figure in the early Middle Ages, at least in the Latin West. However, his cult also grew in popularity across the closing Middle Ages (from the fourteenth century on), somewhat later than the other two cults we have discussed. Spiritual Franciscans, Petrus Olivi in particular, seem to have been among the first to promote his cause. In the early fifteenth century, Jean Gerson, following the lead of his mentor Pierre d'Ailly, conducted a veritable campaign across Europe in favor of Josephine devotions. Through his initiative, the Church finally granted to Joseph a major feast, on March 19. Gerson's contemporary in Italy, Bernardine of Siena, was no less active in propounding his virtues.[38]

36. For recent studies of medieval children, see D. Herlihy, "Medieval Children," in *Webb Memorial Lectures*, ed. Lackner and Philp, pp. 109-41 [incomp. cit.]; and K. Arnold, *Kind und Gesellschaft in Mittelalter und Renaissance*, Zebra collection, series B, vol. 2. (Paderborn and Munich, 1980).

37. The history of Josephine devotions is well surveyed in J. Seitz, *Die Verehrung des hl. Joseph in ihrer geschichtlichen Entwicklung bis zum Konzil von Trient dargestellt* (Freiburg, 1908).

38. "De sancto Ioseph sponso beatae Virginis," in Bernardino da Siena, *Opera omnia*, ed. Pp. Collegii S. Bonaventurae (Florence, 1950-), 7. On Joseph's particular gifts, see J. Seitz, *Die Verehrung des hl. Joseph*, pp. 253–261.

Those virtues had to be many, these theologians concluded, although the Testament tells us little about Joseph. He must have been cleansed of original sin, through baptism of desire, in the womb of his mother. Before meeting Mary he could not have been previously married, as the apocrypha wrongly state. As the spouse of an immaculate wife, he must have maintained virginity and chastity all his life. However, he must also have been freed from the promptings of concupiscence; he could never have looked with stirrings of lust upon his pure wife, although she was surpassingly beautiful. He was young too, not an old man, as he is often portrayed by mistaken artists. How else could he have provided for and protected his young wife and infant son in the arduous flight into Egypt, and during the long years of exile there? Bernardine, the eloquent preacher, plays on the care, the exertions, and the wakeful hours which this solicitous father spent in support of his poor and menaced family.[39] Finally, both Gerson and Bernardine agree that Joseph must have been bodily assumed, like Mary, into heaven. Bernardine's arguments are particularly telling here. The family had passed through many troubles and much sorrow upon earth, although they were sustained by the *charitas* they held for each other. Having endured so much together in this world, they can expect to be reunited in glory in the next, in body as well as spirit, still bound by their mutual *charitas*.

The cult of Joseph, patron and provider, thus blends imperceptibly into the cult of the Holy Family. The Holy Family itself was viewed as a trinity, which in some ways replicated on earth the Blessed Trinity in heaven. One of Gerson's short poems reads: "O veneranda trinitas Jesus, Joseph et Maria, quam coniunxit divinitas, Charitatis concordia!" ("Oh, venerable trinity Jesus, Joseph and Mary, which divinity has joined, the concord of love!")[40] Note that he names Joseph before Mary. *Concordia charitatis*: here we have the cultural and emotional ideal to which medieval families were invited to aspire.

Why did these great churchmen so assidually promote Josephine devotions during the troubled period of the late Middle Ages? Perhaps this was the reason: The great plagues, famines, and wars, the

39. "Considera etiam cum quanta compassione in itineribus, quae fecerunt, parvulum Iesum ex labore lassatum, cum grandiusculus, in suo gremio requiescere faciebat!" Bernardino da Siena, *Opera Omnia*, 7, p. 26. He also praises his "sedulam administrationem" (p. 24) and the fact that "pro eis et cum eis labores atque peregrinationem die noctuque sustinens."
40. Cited in Seitz, *Die Verehrung des hl. Joseph*, p. 259.

economic troubles and social upheavals, threatened the welfare and even the survival of households. However, the wise and dedicated household head might partially ward off these evils, even as Joseph rescued Jesus and Mary from the clutches of Herod. Joseph was a shield against adversity, especially those adversities which menaced the family. With reason then, Gerson believed that devotion to Joseph was especially suited for those entering the married state, those assuming the grave responsibilities of directing a household. The cult of Joseph, protector of the family, thus seemed appropriate in an age when families were threatened.

In the long course of the Middle Ages, families thus acquired a certain uniformity as comparable units of production and consumption in countryside and town. They developed a distinctive set of relationships with the larger networks of kin and affines. Within families, strong emotional bonds were also taking form, based on particular conceptions of domestic roles, of the functions, and contributions to the common life of father, mother, and children. The emotional world of the medieval household is an elusive subject, but one of surpassing importance. In this rapid survey of religious cults and devotions rich in family imagery, we have tried to capture its traces.

8

THE FAMILY AND RELIGIOUS IDEOLOGIES
IN MEDIEVAL EUROPE

———— ✦ ✦ ✦ ————

The histories of medieval religion and of the family intersect at so
many points that we need a clear analytical framework with which
to guide our discussion. To begin with, the objects of our inquiry are
the medieval Christian religion and the Christian family. Space and
the author's competence preclude an examination of family and
religion in Byzantium, in Islam, or in medieval Jewry, in spite of the
interest of recent work in these areas.[1] Nor can I consider in any
depth the currently debated issue of what was the true domain of
Christianity in medieval society.[2] Was it limited to a tiny elite of
clergy and literate laymen, while the unlettered masses followed a
folk religion with its origins lost in Indo-European antiquity? We
assume here that the Christian religion, and its variants in the form

1. See S. D. Goitein, *A Mediterranean Society: The Jewish Communities of the
Arab World as Portrayed by the Documents of the Cairo Genize*, 4 vols., 3: *The
Family* (Berkeley, 1967-). Initial orientation into the Byzantine family can be gained
from E. Patlagean, *Structure sociale, famille, Chrétienté à Byzance* (London, 1981).
Not recent, but recently reprinted, is W. R. Smith, *Kinship and Marriage in Early
Arabia* (New York, 1979). The book was originally published in 1903.
2. The argument that official Christianity did not penetrate beyond the clerical and
a tiny lay elite has been most vigorously advanced by J. Delumeau, *Catholicism
between Luther and Voltaire: A New View of the Counter Reformation* (Philadelphia,
1977) and J. Delumeau, G. Gaudet-Drillat, S. Jannssen-Peigné, and C. Tragnan, *Un
chemin d'histoire: chrétienté et christianisation* (Paris,1981), to cite only two of
Delumeau's many publications. J. Le Goff and J.-C. Schmitt have also maintained
that the unlettered masses of medieval society followed a kind of folk religion, with
roots stretching far back into the European past. For the latter, see J. C. Schmitt.
[incomp. cit.]

of heresies, governed marriage and family life in the Middle Ages. There is no evidence, as far as I can judge, that folk religion ever challenged the precepts regarding marriage proposed by the established Church, or ever reached the status of recognition and fear as a formal heresy.

As our analytical framework, I shall use the distinction common in the social sciences between performance and structure. Performance is action and event, or. in a historical context. the record of events. Structure is everything that makes possible, supports or affects action and event. It includes a community's natural surroundings, from stable lands to unstable weather. The characteristics of the community itself—its size; distribution of members across space, and by sex and age: their health—are similarly parts of structure. So also are its laws, customs, attitudes, values and ideologies. Structures of course are themselves changing constructs, and occasionally they echo and reinforce events, sometimes absorbing and transforming them into laws, customs and rituals. But they alter only slowly, and their relative immobility gives them high visibility in the historical record. The analysis of structure does not allow us to organize our observations into causes and effects; but it does make more understandable the complex happenings of history.

In this article, I seek to filter out one element of the structure of the medieval world, religion, and to examine how it interacted with performance, specifically marriages and domestic organization. Are there discernible some reciprocal influences between religious life and domestic life in the Middle Ages?

We look first at medieval religion, and then at the medieval family.

RELIGION

What did the fathers and doctors of the ancient and medieval Church think about the family?[3] The answer must be, not a great deal, in both meanings of the phrase. Not really until the twelfth century did the

3. For orientation in the literature, particularly in regard to the development of canon law, see J. Gaudemet, *Sociétés et Mariage. Recherches institutionelles, 4,* "Bibliographie internationale d'histoire du mariage" (prepared with the collaboration of M. Zimmermann) (Strasbourg, 1980), pp. 454-77. On the formation of the early Christian ideas on marriage, see among recent publications J. Cottiaux, *La sacralisation du mariage de le Genèse aux incises Matthéennes* (Paris, 1982), and E. Fuchs,

Church develop a comprehensive canon law, and an accompanying theology, of marriage. Before then, secular law, Roman legislation or the barbarian codes, had directed the behavior even of Christians in regard to marital and domestic issues. It is striking to observe that the sixth-century *Corpus Iuris Civilis* of the Emperor Justinian still permits divorce, as Roman law had always done; this Christian emperor was governing a Christian state, and yet he did not feel compelled to revise the traditional law of marriage.[4] The Church limited its interventions in marital matters to questions of sin and of penitence. Its appeal did not reach beyond the private consciences of Christians.

ATTITUDES AND ETHICS

This long-standing indifference to most questions of marital and family life surely reflects the dominant ascetic temperament of the patristic and early medieval Church. Questions of contract, of dowry and bridewealth, of inheritance—these were secular issues, and the true kingdom of God was not of this world. Then too, the Christian fathers looked upon the state of matrimony as distinctly inferior to virginity and even to widowhood. St. Jerome scores the relative value of these three states: virginity rates 100 points, widowhood 60, and wedlock only 30. "I praise weddings, I praise marriage," he writes, "but because for me they produce virgins."[5] The

---

Sexual Desire and Love: Origins and History of the Christian Ethic of Sexuality and Marriage, trans. M. Daigle (Cambridge, New York, 1983).

4. On the slow and late extension of the Church's jurisdiction over marriage, see A. Esmein, *Le mariage en droit canonique.* Essays in History, Economics and Social Science, 7, 2 vols. (New York, 1968), I, pp. 3ff. As late as the ninth century, Hincmar of Reims apologizes for speaking out on a marriage issue, "concerning a civil judgment, of which we bishops are not supposed to be experts," from *Hincmari archiepiscopi remensis epistolae. Die Briefe des Erzbishofs Hinkmar von Reims.* Monumenta Germaniae Historica, Epistolae 8, Teil 1 (Munich, 1975), pp. 90: "In quibus nihil de civili iudicio, cuius cognitores non debemus esse episcopi, ponere, sed quae ecclesiasticae diffinitioni noscuntur competere, quantum occurrit memorare, breviter studui adnotare." On the issue of divorce, see F. Delpini, *Indissolubilità matrimoniale e divorzio dal I al XII secolo* (Milan, 1979).

5. "Laudo nuptias, laudo coniugium, sed quia mihi virgines generant," from M. Humbert, *Le remariage à Rome: étude d'histoire juridique et sociale* (Milan, 1905), p. 321. On the origins of the Christian valuation of virginity, see K. Deschner, *Das Kreuz mit der Kirche: Eine Sexualgeschichte des Christentums.* 2d ed. (Düsseldorf,1974), pp. 48, 61, "Die Heraufkunft der Askese." J. McNamara, *A New Song: Celibate Women in the First Three Christian Centuries. Women and History,* 6–7

fathers saw little value in those two traditional functions of house-holds—production and reproduction.

Production implied involvement in material things. Reproduction, in the patristic view of the world, was, strictly speaking, not needed.

In lauding virginity over marriage, the fathers had to face an embarrassing rebuttal. If all Christians adopted the preferred state of virginity, would not the Church quickly disappear? Augustine, for one, feigns indifference. This would be altogether a good thing; it would indicate that the roster of predestined saints had been filled, and the number of fallen angels replaced; like stars falling from the heavens, it would portend that history was nearing its term. "The coming of Christ," he affirms, "is not served by the begetting of children."[6]

The fathers saw no need for the further expansion of the human race, but they still insisted that every act of sexual intercourse between married persons be open to procreation. Here again, Augustine was the chief formulator of what would become the offi-cial norm. John T. Noonan, in his valuable history of contraception in Catholic thought and discipline, believes that Augustine was here reacting against the Manicheanism of his youth[7]. The Manichees, opposed to the multiplication of material bodies, minions of the god of darkness, allegedly considered contraception a meritorious act. Whatever the accuracy of this view, the Catholic Church has retained to this day an essentially Augustinian view of the uses of sex within marriage.

In giving low prestige to procreation, the Christian fathers reflect a cultural attitude which was common among pagans too. This was the sense that the world was already excessively crowded with people, and could contain no more.[8] Christians too need rear few

---

(New York, 1983), analyses the particular appeal of this attitude for women. J. Bugge, Virginitas: *An Essay in the History of a Medieval Ideal* (The Hague, 1975), traces the later history of this ideal.

6. From the tract Contra Jovinianum. See Augustine, *Treatises on Marriage and Other Subjects*, trans. C. T. Wilcox and others. *The Fathers of the Church*, A New Translation, 27 (New York, 1955), pp. 159. On Augustine's theology of marriage, see E. Schmitt, *Le mariage chrétien dans l'oeuvre de saint Augustine: Une théologie bap-tismale de la vie conjugale* (Paris, 1938). On patristic attitudes on procreation and the rearing of children, see my further comments in D. Herlihy, "Medieval Children," in *The Walter Prescott Webb Memorial Lectures. Essays on Medieval Civilization* (Austin, London, 1978), pp. 109–142. [ch. 11, below.]

7. See his *Contraception* (Cambridge, 1965).

8. See, for example, the words of the North-African writer Tertullian, *Opera, II: Opera monastica. Corpus christianorum, series latina, 2* (Turnholt, 1954), p. 827:

children, but they must train them conscientiously. Parents and teachers must suppress the promptings of concupiscence within the growing child through harsh discipline. The patristic (and especially Augustinian) theory of concupiscence assured the survival under Christian auspices of that cruel principle of ancient schooling: "No progress without pain."[9]

Moreover, there is within the Christian tradition a strain of suspicion concerning family ties. The claims of kin might compete with the claims of God. "He who loves father or mother more than me," Jesus warns, "is not worthy of me; and he who loves son or daughter more than me is not worthy of me" (Matthew 1 1.37-38). Numerous medieval saints enter the religious life over the adamant opposition of their families. St. Francis defies his father before the bishop of Assisi, strips off his clothes, and hands them back. He will no longer address Pietro Bernardone as father; only God in heaven deserves that title. The mother and brothers of Thomas Aquinas kidnap him, hold him prisoner in a castle for two years, and send a "lusty girl" to tempt him, so that he will lay aside the habit of the Dominican Order. Catherine of Siena warns her correspondents, particularly women, against excessive attachment to husband and children.[10] These are the things of this life, not the things of God.

"Everywhere there are buildings, everywhere people, everywhere communities, everywhere life."

9. See, for example, in *The Confessions of St. Augustine*. A New Translation by R. Warner (New York, 1963), p. 45, the story how he and some friends stole pears for which they had no need. " ... I became evil for nothing, with no reason for wrongdoing except the wrongdoing itself. The evil was foul, and I loved it: I loved destroying myself; I loved my sin—not the thing for which I had committed the sin, but the sin itself." See also ibid., p. 26 for his views on pedagogy: "O God, my God, what misery did I experience in my boyhood ... if I failed to work hard at my studies, I was beaten. This kind of discipline was considered very good by our ancestors, and many people before us, who had gone through this way of life, had already organized wearisome courses of study along which we were compelled to go; the trouble was multiplied and so was the sorrow upon the sons of Adam." See H. I. Marrou, *A History of Education in Antiquity*. Trans. by G. Lamb (New York, 1956, 1981), pp. 158–59, for comments on this "brutality of discipline."

10. *Le lettere di S. Caterina da Siena ridotte a miglior lezione*, 6 vols., ed. P. Misciatelli. (Siena, 1913–21), II, p. 102, to madonna Laudomia donna di Carlo degli Strozzi da Firenze. Catherine warns against excessive attachment to "o figliuoli o marito o alcuna creatura." Laudomia should regard them as "cose prestate."

UNIFORMITY AND PERMANENCE

And yet, in spite of indifference and even wariness toward the family, its needs and its claims, the patristic and early medieval Church did develop some general principles of great significance in the future. The fathers affirmed that sexual morality had to be the same for both sexes, and for all nationalities and social classes, "because," as Paul says, "with God there is no respect of person" (Romans 2.11). "Una lex de mulieribus et viris," says Jerome, "there is one law for women and for men."[11] Moreover, the union of husband and wife was both privileged and permanent. Jesus himself cites with approval the text from Genesis: "Wherefore a man shall leave father and mother, and shall cleave to his wife: and they shall be two in one flesh" (Matthew 19.5). Paul develops an extended analogy between the conjugal union and the relationship of Christ to the Church (Ephesians 5.21-33). Drawing inspiration from all these texts, Augustine attributes three "goods" to marriage, *fides, proles, sacramentum,* fidelity, offspring, and permanent union.[12] Marriage had to be indissoluble, even as the union of Christ and the Church. This Augustinian analogy—husband is to wife as Christ is to Church—becomes the basis for the Church's rejection of divorce. The union of Christ and the Church, and its earthly analogue, the marriage of husband and wife, were perforce indissoluble.[13] Consistent with his view of marriage, Paul advocates a kind of ethical reciprocity among all household members. Roman law, by its famous doctrine of the *patria potestas,* had made the father a despot over the family. Paul rather emphasizes the father's obligations. He is ethically bound to love his wife as his own body, and he ought not nag his children. Paul draws domestic relations between husband and wife, parents and children, masters and slaves, fully into the domain of Christian con-

11. Cited and discussed in J. Gaudemet, "Les transformations de la vie familiale au Bas Empire et l'influence du Christianisme," in *Romanitas: Revista de Cultura Romana,* 5 (1952), p. 62. See also A. Esmein, *Le mariage en droit canonique,* I, p. 91.

12. Augustine, *De genesi ad litteram libri xii,* ed. J. Zycha, Corpus scriptorum ecclesiasticorum latinorum 28, (Vienna, 1894), p. 275: "hoc autem tripartitum est: fides, proles, sacramentum."

13. A. Esmein, *Le mariage en droit canonique,* I, p. 5, stresses this analogy as the basis for the Church's opposition to divorce. See also G. Torti, *La stabilità del vincolo nuziale in Sant' Agostino e in San Tommaso* (Parma, 1979).

sciousness and conscience. The household becomes a domain of intense moral relationships.

INCEST

A final area in which Christian teachings exerted a profound influence was eligibility for marriage. The Church accepted the requirements of Roman law concerning age of marriage (twelve completed years for girls and fourteen for boys) and sexual maturity and potency. But it greatly expanded the incest prohibitions characteristic not only of Roman but also of ancient Jewish law. Roman law had allowed first cousins to marry, who were related by four degrees of kinship in the Roman count. The early medieval western Church extends the prohibition to the full seven degrees. Already the Council of Toledo in 527 and later the Council of Rome in 721 declared that if a man and a woman even suspected that they were related by blood, they could not marry.[14] The Church was comparably rigorous in prohibiting the marriage of affines. Finally, the spiritual relationship assumed by the sponsor toward the recipient at baptism or confirmation also precluded their marriage.

Jack Goody's recent study of family and marriage in medieval Europe examines as one of its principal themes the incest prohibition of the western Church[15]. The great service of this book is that Goody, from his knowledge of many cultures, is able to show historians that the medieval western incest prohibition is extraordinarily broad, perhaps unique in human experience. He also tries to explain why the Church was so opposed to close marriages. In his view, great lay property owners sought to pursue an "heirship strategy" based on close marriages to prevent the dispersion of their landed holdings.

14. For the council of Toledo, see, *Concilios Visigóticos e hispano-romanos*, ed. J. Vives, España cristiana, Textos, 1. (Barcelona, 1963), 11, chap. 5. "Nam et haec salubriter praecavanda sancimus, ne quis fidelium propinquam sanguinis sui, usquequo adfinitatis liniamenta generis successione cognoscit, in matrimonio sibi desideret copulari ..." For the Roman provision, see *Monumenta Germaniae Historica. Epistolarum Tomus II: Merowingici et Karolini Aevi, 1* 2nd ed. (Berlin, 1957), III, p. 485. "Nos ... iuxta praedeccssorum et antecessorum pontificum decreta ... dicimus, ut, cum usque sese generalio cognoverit, iuxta ritum et normam christianitatis Romanorum non copulentur coniugiis."

15. J. Goody, *The Development of the Family and Marriage in Europe* (Cambridge, 1983).

The incest prohibition obstructed this strategy. Prohibited from marrying blood relatives, great property owners would often not marry at all. Childless and heirless persons were more likely than others to bequeath their properties to the Church. The incest prohibition is thus linked with the Church's desire to increase its landed endowment.

The argument is ingenious, but not in the final analysis convincing. It would be difficult to show from the thousands of surviving donations to churches that the donors were childless in any significant number. No contemporary hints at or alludes to this rather devious strategy. The Church needed personnel as well as property, and its leaders were drawn from the same class of wealthy property owners from whom donations might be expected. Would the Church have wished them childless, and its own pool of potential leaders reduced? Moreover, when an offspring entered the religious life, he or she almost always brought property to the Church, as a kind of spiritual dowry. It is not at all certain that the strategy Goody describes would have had the results he attributes to it. I shall make further comments on the incest prohibition (and suggest a reason why the Church may have favored it) later in this essay.

MODELS

The body of ecclesiastical teachings concerning marriage formed the legal and religious model of marriage during the Middle Ages. The word "model" has been much used in the recent literature, at times, in my mind, inappropriately. Georges Duby, for example, identifies two models of marriage in twelfth-century France[16]. One was based on the Church's rule of monogamy and its prohibition of divorce and remarriage, bigamy and incest. The second, associated with the lay aristocracy, allowed divorce and remarriage, and incestuous unions, whenever the good of the lineage required such actions. The "modern marriage" which Duby believes took shape in northern France by the thirteenth century was a fusion of and compromise between these two formerly competitive models.

Duby's studies provide a vivid and valuable picture of marriages within the northern French aristocracy in the twelfth century, but his

16. See, e.g., G. Duby, *Medieval Marriage* (Baltimore, 1978).

analysis seems to confuse two quite different kinds of models. These can be either prescriptive or descriptive. A prescriptive model is a set of rules or recommendations, which may or may not be respected. The apostolic exhortation, *Familiaris consortio*, which Pope John Paul II issued in 1980, presents a model of this sort, but it could hardly be called a description of modern marriage. A descriptive model, on the other hand, is a generalized portrayal of actual behavior, and is commonly utilized in the social sciences. Now, the ecclesiastical model of medieval marriage, described by Duby, is incontrovertibly prescriptive. But the lay model is just as surely descriptive, as it is constructed out of chronicle accounts of elite behavior. Nowhere is it suggested that the French lay aristocracy was bent on establishing norms for others to follow. Duby treats the two types of model as the same, and this clouds his analysis. To say that the two fused seems only to mean that behavior eventually influenced the norms that governed it, as it often does.

FAMILIES

How did these teachings affect this history of the medieval family? We must first, as best we can, recapitulate that history. There are three areas of domestic life in which changes across the Middle Ages seem especially pronounced. The first touches upon the internal structure of families and households. In the slave-holding societies of antiquity, households differed so greatly across society that they were never treated, whether by policy makers or by social theorists, as commensurable units. From about the year 700, medieval households display much greater uniformity. The domestic living arrangements of the medieval rich, in other words, show more similarities with than differences from the homes of the poor. The second major innovation in the history of the western medieval family is the emergence, from about the year 1000, of a new type of kin organization. The dominant kin group of early medieval society, often called in the literature by its German name *Sippe*, had been cognate or bilineal, which is to say, blood relationships were traced equally through men and through women. From approximately the eleventh century, initially on elite social levels, a new type of kin grouping, the agnate lineage or the patrilineage, achieves visibility. In the patrilineage, blood relationships are traced exclusively through males. The curiosity here is that the new agnate lineage does not really replace, but is superimposed upon, the older, cognate group. The competition between these two rival definitions of kin and family is a marked characteristic of domestic life in the central and late Middle Ages. The third area of change involves the distinctive roles which medieval culture comes to assign to family members—to wives, children, and husbands and also the set of emotional rewards by which the culture encouraged good performance.

COMMENSURABILITY OF HOUSEHOLDS

Many factors doubtlessly contributed to the emergence in the early Middle Ages of commensurable households. Chief among them was the decline of ancient slavery. By about 700, in place of the great villas worked by gangs of slaves, the small peasant property, worked by families, overlay the European countryside. The emergence of commensurable households is thus intimately connected with the crisis of ancient slavery, and the rise of the new peasant economy of the Middle Ages.

But religion contributed too, particularly in its insistence that rich and poor, the free and the unfree, follow the same sexual morality. To be sure, the patristic assumption that in sexual matters there was but one law for all triumphed only slowly. Apparently not until the twelfth century did Pope Hadrian IV (1152-1159) explicitly declare that the marriages of serfs were as valid as any other. So also, the Church's insistence on monogamy encountered tenacious opposition among the European elites, as several scholars have shown. But unquestionably, the Church's teachings acted as a powerful leveling, standardizing and stabilizing influence.

The success, even if limited, of this rule of monogamy, and the associated opposition to other forms of sexual liaison, had this subtle, but I think profound social repercussion. Women came to be distributed more evenly across society. Males who controlled wealth and power could not use these resources to accumulate

17. See, e.g., S. F. Wemple, *Women in Frankish Society* (Philadelphia, 1981), p. 380.

women as well. Males of the lower social order now had improved
chances of attracting a mate. The incest prohibition should have had
a comparable effect. It prevented privileged households from claiming or retaining more than their fair share of women. Gregory of
Tours tells of a Merovingian queen named Aregund, who asked her
husband Chlothar to find a rich and powerful husband for her sister
Ingund. Upon viewing the beautiful young woman, Chlothar
decided that the most suitable husband was himself; he therefore
married her, bigamously. The Church's rule of monogamy, if effective, would have prevented this union; the incest prohibition would
have blocked him from ever marrying Ingund, even after Aregund 's
death. He cannot have his pick of women.

   The incest prohibition meant that after the death of her husband, the
widow cannot marry any male already in her household—not her
father-in-law, not a brother in-law, not a step-father, or step-brother. If
she wishes to marry again, she must move out of her former household. The incest prohibition thus forced a circulation of women
through society, and made them accessible to a larger group of males.
The households of the great and powerful cannot monopolize women.

   Would not this enhanced accessibility of women have reduced
incidents of rape and abduction, commonplace events in the social
history of the early Middle Ages? And would this not act as a pacifying, stabilizing influence in society? The result too was an assimi-
lation of family forms at all social levels.

LINEAGES

The second major change we have identified is the coming of the
agnate lineage.[18] It differs in several crucial ways from the older
cognatic kin group, the *genus* or *cognatio* in contemporary terms,
the *Sippe* in much modern scholarship. The *cognatio* was ego-

---

18. The change in the structure of noble families from the early to the central Middle Ages was emphasized for Germany by Karl Schmid in the late 1950s. His most
important studies have been reprinted in K. Schmid, *Gebetsgedenken und adliges
Selbstverständnis im Mittelalter. Ausgewählte Beiträge; Festgabe zu seinem sechzig-
sten Geburtstag* (Sigmaringen, 1983). An English translation of a summary of his principal thesis is available in *The Medieval Nobility: Studies on the Ruling Classes of
France and Germany from the Sixth to the Twelfth Century. Europe in the Middle
Ages. Selected Studies, 14*, ed. T. Reuter (Amsterdam, 1979) pp. 38–42.

focused, as anthropologists would say, in the sense that lines of relationship were viewed as radiating forth from the living individual. The boundaries of the *cognatio* changed with every generation, as its center came to rest on a new ego. The lineage was, in contrast, ancestor-focused, as it characteristically traced its descent in the male line back to a historic, or sometimes mythical, founder. It was a solidarity of males linking the living and the dead. It displayed that solidarity through the use of a family name, which sometimes recalled the revered ancestor himself, sometimes the castle or estate associated with him. It showed it also through the adoption of a coat of arms, a written genealogy, and sometimes even a mythology. The daughter passed out of the lineage at marriage, and all her descendants after her; they became members of their father's line.

The role of religion in the appearance of the agnatic lineage is again secondary but still significant. The chief motivation for this redefinition of the kin group seems to have been the desire of elite families to limit claims upon their resources, particularly their landed patrimonies. The chief losers in this effort were daughters and, in lesser measure, younger sons. The claims of daughters were limited to the dowries they now needed to contract an honorable marriage; those without suitable dowries had little choice but to enter the religious life. Younger sons were often forced to delay marriages; rather than remain inactive at home, many chose to wander widely over Europe in search of fortune. The common strategy was that the family's resources should be mobilized primarily in support of a single heir, usually the eldest son, who could best maintain the prestige and power of the lineage.

However, no agnatic or patrilineal identification of principal kin can operate under conditions of sexual promiscuity. And the reasons for this seem clear. The promiscuity of males tends to invite promiscuity among females. The legal wife might resent the entry of another wife or concubine into her home, and seek revenge through infidelity. And extramarital liaisons will inevitably obscure the line of descent through males. Instances of uncertain paternity are common in early medieval sources. According to Gregory of Tours, the Merovingian king Gunthram refuses to believe that the son of Fredegundis, who was married to his deceased brother Chilperic, was truly his brother's. "I think," he broods, "that he is the son of one of our retinue [*leudi*]."

To prove the child's paternity, Fredegundis must summon the great persons of the Frankish realm—three bishops and 300 *optimati* and before this august assembly she swears that Chilperic really was the boy's father. "And thus," Gregory tells us, "the suspicion of the king was removed." But could he be absolutely certain?

In the tenth century King Hugh of Italy allegedly ignored his queen and consorted with three concubines, who were popularly nick-named after pagan goddesses, Venus, Juno and Semele. He sired children on all of them. Or did he? "As the king was not the only man who enjoyed their favors," our source Liutprand of Cremona, relates, "the children of all three are of uncertain parentage." He writes parentage, but he means paternity.

In sum, prerequisite to the appearance of the patrilineage was the Church's success in imposing the rule of monogamy and in repressing sexual promiscuity, among both men and women. At the same time, the Church did not allow the patrilineage to overwhelm and replace the old *cognatio*. As Duby again has illustrated, the great laymen wanted to arrange the marriages of their offspring in the interest of the lineage, and their designs often ran up against the incest prohibition.[19] And the old rules continued to determine degrees of kinship and eligibility for marriage. The Church liberalized the rules a little when, at the Fourth Lateran Council in 1215, it reduced the degrees in which marriage was prohibited from an unrealistic several to four. But it still maintained that relationships through women were no less important than those through men, in determining who might marry.

The Church also restricted the authority of the chiefs of lineages over their own offspring. Pope Alexander III in the twelfth century is credited—or criticized—with establishing in the canon law the principle that only the mutual consent of bride and groom, expressed through words of present tense, *verba de presenti*, was required in a valid marriage. To contract a valid marriage, serfs did not need the permission of their masters. Serfs who married without that permission contracted, in the technical language, an illicit, but not an invalid marriage. They could be punished; even so, they remained validly married. Curiously, even the blessing of the Church was not a prerequisite to a valid marriage. But most important, the principle

19. G. Duby, *The Knight, the Lady, and the Priest* (New York, 1983).

precluded even parents from exerting control over the marriages of their children. The necessary and sufficient condition for a valid marriage was the consent of otherwise eligible partners: nothing less and nothing more. This principle prevented an unrestricted patriarchy from dominating medieval society. Religion made possible the emergence of the patrilineage, but also limited its triumph.

The exclusion of daughters and younger sons from a full share in the family's resources inevitably induced tensions within the medieval household. Medieval heresies, which were waxing strong even as the patrilineage took form, perhaps reflect those tensions in the antagonism they often manifest toward marriage. Most notorious though not alone in their opposition toward marriage were the Albigensians or *Cathari*, who in the twelfth century mounted a powerful challenge to orthodoxy in southern France and northern Spain. "For the common opinion of all *Cathari*," a former heretic declared, "is that physical marriage has always been a mortal sin, and that in the future no one will be punished more severely because of adultery or incest than for legitimate matrimony. So also among them no one is more gravely punished than for this".[20] For many of the heresies, the principle held: In *matrimonio non est salus*. And the heresies had particular appeal to women. St. Dominic, for example, established his order's first convent for women at Prouille, where the *Cathari* were many. He wished to counter the success of the heretics, who had been rearing and teaching poor and probably unmarriageable noble girls, and teaching them how to read. Presumably, the heretics told the girls that the marriages they could not have were sinful anyway, and that the parents who treated them so shabbily were the devil's minions. Ironically, proof of the parents' sinful ways was the girls themselves. The system of medieval marriages was not without its committed enemies.

FEELINGS

We enter now into the emotional life of the medieval family, indisputably the most elusive of subjects. According to various early modern or modern historians, medieval people were wanting in an

---

20. Cited in D. Herlihy, "Alienation in Medieval Culture and Society," in F. Johnson, ed., *Alienation* (New York, 1971), p. 134.

appreciation of childhood, and medieval families were not "affec-tive" (Ozment, 1983; Stone, 1977; deMause, 1974:174). Suppos-edly, sensitivity to childhood and familial affection first appear either in Reformation Europe or in the seventeenth century, or in compara-tively recent times. But these views seem based on false assumptions concerning the emotional life, or lack thereof, of the medieval fam-ily. As Barbara Hanawalt has recently argued,[21] the families with which these authors people the Middle Ages are made of straw. Weinstein and Bell's study of the life course of 864 medieval and early modern saints draws the same conclusion: "The widely held modern view that a concept of childhood did not emerge until the early modern period is emphatically contradicted by our reading of the evidence on saints, where we find a clear sense of what it was to be a child."[22] Their study also shows the exceptional value of saints' lives in assessing the domestic emotions of the Middle Ages.

In the history of emotions, medieval religion serves both as a mir-ror and a model. In other words, medieval spiritual writers, particu-larly the authors of saints' lives, make constant appeal, by analogy, to domestic acts and emotions. These familial images, I argue, must respond to the emotional climate of real medieval households. Doubtlessly, too, the familial images they employ were meant to influence domestic conduct. The faithful should both empathize with, and imitate, the behavior of the saints. Structure, in this case religious structure, directs behavior.

We look first at marriage itself. Mystical marriages are common-place in the pious literature, and they usually unite a female saint with Christ. Some of them, such as the life of Angela of Foligno in Italy, who died in 1309, go beyond formalities of marriage to unabashedly sexual allusions to embraces and kisses.[23] One of the most revealing images of marriage comes from the life of St. Hermann of Steinfeld near Cologne, who died about 1240; his biography is written by a contemporary who knew his subject well.[24] Hermann marries the Vir-gin Mary. One day, two angels escort Mary to him; she is described as

21. B. Hanawalt, *Ties That Bound* (Oxford, 1986), xvii.

22. D. Weinstein and R. M. Bell, *Saints and Society* (Chicago, 1982), p. 10.

23. The life of Catherine of Alexandria provides the apparent model for these mystical marriages, but many medieval women saints imitate her, including Catherine of Siena.

24. *ASS*, (Paris, 1863–1910), I *Aprilis*, p. 692: cited in D. Herlihy, *Medieval House-holds* (Cambridge, 1985), pp. 119, 209.

a young girl of ineffable beauty and royal bearing. "It is fitting," says one of her angelic sponsors, "that this brilliant virgin be married to you." The angel took his right hand and joined it to the hand of the virgin, and with these words he married them. "Behold," the angel said, "I give you as wife this virgin, even as she had been married to Joseph. And you shall take the name of the husband even as you take the bride." Hermann thus replaces Joseph as Mary's spouse, and assumes his name as well.

The domestic life of this mystically married pair was blissful. In fact, even before the formal wedding, they cultivated a supportive relationship. "We often heard that it happened to him," his biographer writes, "that in a recess of the monastery, as he was occupied in prayer and meditation, he would hear the voice of his holy and dearest friend standing across from him ... he would go to her, and sitting together in some place, Blessed Mary would ask him in detail upon his affairs and he would answer; and he in turn would ask of her, whatever he wanted. In such conversations he passed in contentment the nighttime hours. With such a consoler, he bore defeats of any kind; he was warmed by the consoling breasts of such a mother; by such a teacher, through her instruction, he learned of many doubtful and uncertain things." Encouragement, advice, consolation, instruction, and dearest friendship—this is what Hermann Joseph gained from Mary, his *amica* and his bride. Surely this spiritual marriage celebrates and idealizes earthly marriage too.

The image of the mother is as common as that of the bride or wife in the religious literature. She is the intercessor *par exellence*; she aids, whenever summoned, her poor banished children. As Bynum shows,[25] medieval religious writers applied the figure of mother even to the person of Jesus. I have argued elsewhere that within the real world of the Middle Ages women often fulfilled that function, intervening between aged fathers and their often alienated sons.[26] The strategies adopted by the lineage imposed late marriages on men, if they were allowed to marry at all, and early marriages on women. The young wife thus typically found herself set between conflicting male generations. She was ideally placed to soothe the tensions and quarrels that divided them. The mother of Francis of

25. C. Bynum, *Jesus as Mother* ((Berkeley, 1982).
26. D. Herlihy, *Medieval Households* (Cambridge, 1985), pp. 120–23.

Assisi frees him from the chains, with which his angered father has bound him in the dungeon of their home.

But perhaps a more instructive role, which women saints assume, is that of teacher. From the thirteenth century, as several scholars have observed, women saints multiply to the point of dominating the ranks of the blessed.[27] Often they attract a following, a spiritual family, whom they instruct in matters of holy wisdom. The best known of these spiritual families is the "joyous brigade" that accompanied Catherine of Siena. But many holy women exercise a similar spiritual leadership. "Who can count," writes the biographer of Margaret of Cortona, who died in 1297, "the number of Spaniards, Apulians, Romans and others, who came to her, that they might be instructed by salutary admonitions". Christ himself confers on her the office and title of *mater peccatorum*, the mother of sinners, in recognition of her achievements. Does this role assumed by numerous women saints of the late Middle Ages find no parallel within real families? Here too, the comparative youth of mothers, which allowed them longer and closer contact with their children than aged fathers could enjoy, may have equipped them to serve as prime conveyors of religious and cultural values. Anthropologists tell us that one avenue to prestige and power in any society is the possession of knowledge, including and perhaps especially sacred knowledge. If this analogy has any value, women may not have been repressed and passive persons within the late-medieval household. They had more functions, and more important functions, than we have recognized.

The cult of the child Jesus enjoys great popularity, at least from the twelfth century. Did it not conceal beneath it a cult of childhood? The infant or child Jesus visits many saints, both men and women. One of the most charming of these visitations involves St. Ida of Louvain in modern Belgium, who died in 1300. Mary, and her cousin St. Elizabeth, bring the blessed infant to Ida, and Ida is honored with the chore of giving the infant a bath.[28]

> Taking him, she squeezes him hard with hugs and kisses, as his mother blessed above all things stands by ... On the other side was the mother of

27. See, e.g., R. Kieckhefer, *Unquiet Souls* (Chicago, 1984).

28. *ASS,* II *Aprilis,* p. 166; D. Herlihy, *Medieval Households,* pp. 127, 211. On the linkage between representations of the Christ child and sentiments toward childhood, see F. Bonney, "Enfance Divine et Enfance Humaine." in *L'enfant au Moyen-Age* (Littérature et Civilisation). Colloque organisé en 1979 per le CUERMA, Aix-en-Provence (Paris, 1980), p. 123.

[John] the Lord's precursor, Elizabeth. She drew a bath to wash the child. with tubs already prepared. Together with the venerable Ida, she lowered the child ever so carefully into the warm water. When he was sitting, this the most chosen of all children, after the manner of playing infants. clapped with both hands in the water, and in childlike fashion stirred and splashed the water. He thus soaked his surroundings, and as the waters splashed here and there, he made all parts of his little body wet, before the ladies could wash him ... After the bath, she again lifted the baby from the water, wrapped him again in his swaddling cloths, enfolded him on her breast, playing intently with him as mothers do. How she wonderfully exalted in her saving God, cannot be described or imagined.

The male author of this life had clearly observed babies in the bath, and noted the delight which real mothers took in washing their infants.

These familial images would have been totally ineffective, had they not reflected authentic domestic experiences and emotions. But in one particular area the medieval Church apparently did not make a conscious effort not only to reflect but to shape a particular domestic role. It is strange that after the thirteenth century—the age of Francis, Dominic and Louis of France—there are virtually no prominent male saints, and none who might serve as an example to married men and heads of households. Patriarchy did not rule the ranks of the blessed, at least not in the late Middle Ages. In what seems a reaction to the dearth of saints, several prominent church-men set about promoting the cult of St. Joseph.

Joseph had been nearly a forgotten saint in the early medieval world. The *Patrologia Latina* of J. P. Migne, containing over 200 volumes of religious tracts antedating 1216, provides an index of saints mentioned in the prolix writings. Joseph appears not at all. And he rarely figures in the visions recorded in saints' lives. When he makes a showing, he is usually presented as old and ineffectual. In the life of St. Hermann of Steinfeld. previously quoted, he loses his wife and even his name to Hermann. He seems unable or unwilling to preserve his rights.

But from the late fourteenth century, figures such as Jean Gerson, chancellor of the University of Paris, and Bernardine of Siena in Italy, undertake an active campaign in favor of Joseph, demanding for him a major feastday, urging Josephine devotions upon the faithful.[29]

29. See especially the collection of devotional poems called the "Josephina," in J. Gerson, *Oeuvres complètes. Introduction, texte et notes*, 10 vols., ed. Mgr. Glorieux. (Paris, 1960–73), IV.

They systematically rework his image. Joseph, they argue, could not have been, as traditionally presented, an ineffectual old man. He had to be young and vigorous when he married Mary. How else could he have protected and supported the Holy Family during their seven years of exile in Egypt? He was the *seculus administrator*, the attentive head of the holy household and promoter of its fortunes. These doctors claim that Joseph, like Mary, was assumed bodily into heaven. It was appropriate that the Holy Family. which endured so much together on earth, should be reunited in body as well as spirit, in their heavenly home. Joseph is the head of the Holy Family, and as such holds under his loving authority Jesus himself and his immaculate mother. Ruling the rulers, Joseph, the doctors claim, deserves recognition as lord of the world.

Evidence, such as the choice of proper names. indicates that the cult of Joseph was slow to evoke a spontaneous response from the faithful, and not until the sixteenth and seventeenth century did he achieve the stature which Gerson and Bernardine sought to attain for him. In Florence, for example, the name Giuseppe, commonly borne today in Italy, was absolutely rare before 1500.[30]

Why were these ecclesiastical leaders so interested in promoting the cult of Joseph? It is tempting to argue that they were seeking to counter certain trends in late-medieval piety. In his massive study of sanctity in the medieval West, the French scholar Andre Vauchez speaks of a "feminization" of sainthood and of sanctity across the late Middle Ages.[31] Now, the Church was traditionally uneasy about women assuming the functions of prophets and priests. St. Paul instructed women to be silent in the churches, and some early Christian sects, which accepted women prophets, became branded as heresies. Perhaps there was a fear, as there seems to be today, that the admission of women would eventually compromise the prestige of such offices and provoke a flight of males. At all events, the late-medieval doctors seem intent on developing Joseph as a counterpoise to Mary and a correction to the lack of contemporary male saints.

The promotion of Joseph thus seems connected with the history of piety, and doubtlessly also with the history of the family. This age of plague, famine, war and death placed many households in

30. Among 30,000 names of Florentine officeholders I have collected from the middle fourteenth century to 1530, Joseph does not appear at all before 1500.
31. A. Aauchez, *La Saintété en Occident* (Rome, 1981).

jeopardy and required of their chiefs the sedulous administration which Bernardine admires in Joseph. As Gerson affirmed, this world is Egypt.[32] Harrassed fathers needed a patron. a powerful in heaven who knew and understood the difficulties they confronted, and, as lord of the world, could come to their assistance. If nothing more, the image of Joseph, the conscientious, wise and loving father, shows us what great churchmen thought to be appropriate deportment, for real fathers in a troubled world.

The history of medieval religion is thus intimately connected with the history of the family. The rule of monogamy and the prohibition of incest fostered the spread of commensurable household units within society, achieved a more even distribution of women across social levels, and helped pacify and stabilize social relations. The same ethic made possible the emergence of the patrilineage in the central Middle Ages, but also restricted the power of fathers within it. And religious cults both mirrored and modeled domestic roles and emotions. The connections between religious history and domestic history are thus many, even if they cannot be entirely untwined from the web of social interactions. Perhaps no other motives so powerfully affected the behavior of medieval people than family interests and religious commitments. And in affecting people, the medieval Church, and the medieval family, inevitably affected each other.

32. J. Gerson, *Oeuvres complètes*, V, p. 97: "... nos heu retinet tenebrosa/Torquet et Aegyptus."

9

SANTA CATERINA AND SAN BERNARDINO
Their Teachings on the Family

━━━━ ✦ ✦ ✦ ━━━━

Santa Caterina and San Bernardino: the writings of these two great saints, whose memories we celebrate today, must be read from several perspectives. Both of them were eminent theologians, doctors of the Catholic faith. They earned this recognition in different ways. Caterina, as far as I can judge, is the first Christian mystic to divide her hours between ecstatic conversations with God, and sweeping the floor, washing dishes, and performing the other chores which families traditionally impose upon their daughters. God Himself, according to her biographer Raimondo da Capua, once cut short her ecstasy, and ordered her to go to eat with her family, to reenter the world, and take stock of its needs.[1] Her mystical marriage with Christ, which she celebrated probably in 1367, meant no divorce from earthly society. On the contrary, it prepared her for her mission to the world. Caterina became, as Raimondo affirms in an elaborate pun, a *catena*, a chain, binding the whole earth to the heavenly kingdom, in love, peace and joy.[2]

Bernardino was a saint of a different sort. He did not shift his gaze repeatedly from heaven above to the world below. There is no report in his biographies of impassioned conversations with God. His chief

---

1. *S. Caterina da Siena.Vita scritta dal B. Ramondo da Capua, confessore della santa*, trans. P. G. Tinagli O.P. (Siena, 1934) (I Classici Cristiani, nn. 47–49), II, 1, 174. "Vai: è l'ora di desinare, e i tuoi vogliono andare a tavola: vai! Stai con loro, e poi ritorna da me."

2. *Ibid., Prologo*, p. 37.

attention was given to the conduct of his contemporaries, and to its social as well as religious implications. Bernardino radically transformed the art of preaching in Italy, in both its content and its style. In content, he showed no reticence in describing and condemning the moral failings of his contemporaries. Ignorance, Bernardino affirmed, was no excuse for immoral behavior; all lay Christians had to be informed concerning the ethical content of their creed. They should know too the temporal, social damage which sins engendered, and the advantages which righteous living conveyed. In style, he cultivated a direct, simple, colloquial, but also colorful method of preaching. "Before the time of [God's] servant Bernardino," one of his biographers relates, "preachers did not propound the word of God plainly and without confusion; they seemed rather to read a speech or to recite an oration in rhetorical style ... ."[3]

Bernardino taught, to be sure, a hard doctrine, particularly in sexual matters. According to a later preacher, Beato Michel da Carcano, Bernardino was the first "a revelare le iniquità del santo coniugio."[4] And yet he enjoyed enormous popularity. Thousands flocked to hear him, and he responded, as say his several biographers, with intense dedication to preaching over a long life. This surely was his secret: he directed his words not to scholars, not even to the learned, but to troubled congregations, lay people chiefly, who needed moral guidance in a tumultuous age.

Though both these saints were actively involved in secular affairs, their theological styles differed markedly. Caterina wrote, or rather dictated, much, but she imparted her most powerful lessons through passive example. When she wished to show that good Christians ought not to frequent baths, she went herself, at her mother's urgings, to the baths, but she allowed her body to be scaled by the hot water.[5] She once asked God that the souls of all the damned be released from Hell, and that she alone be allowed to take their place. God would then acquire more saints to praise Him, and Cate-

---

3. *Vie inédite de S. Bernardin de Sienne, par un frère mineur, son contemporain, Analecta Bollandiana* , 25 (1906), p. 310: "Neque enim tunc temporis ante servum Bernardinum predicatores plene et sine strepitu proponebant verbum Dei, verum magis legere quendam viderentur sermonem aut aliquam orationem oratoris ordine recitare ..."

4. See the comments by M. Sticco, *Il pensiero di S. Bernardino da Siena* (Milano 1924), p. 142.

5. *S. Caterina da Siena.Vita*, I, 7, p. 109.

rina, though under torment, could take satisfaction in the salvation of all her fellow humans.[6] She took upon her own frail body, and bore her entire life, the pains which her father Giacomo would otherwise have suffered in Purgatory.[7] These and similar tales, which fill her legend, were a principal source of her reputation for sanctity and her success as a Christian teacher. Bernardino, on the other hand, relied upon a strong voice, large piazzas, and great crowds. Caterina's reliance on passive example reflect her own femininity? And was Bernardino's aggressive proclamation of the Christian message a specifically masculine response to the challenge he confronted: the need to reach masses of people, and to reach them quickly? We cannot examine further these contrasting styles, but we still can wonder: in the last analysis, whose voice carried the farther?

The writings of these two great saints must be read from several perspectives. They were both of them masters of the young Italian language, which they used with unprecedented vigor, clarity and color. Here too, the audience which they addressed surely influenced their styles. Caterina was herself a *popolana*.[8] She sought to and did influence the mighty of the earth, but always in the interest of her humblest brethren. Bernardino was of patrician origins; he did not want to preach for fear that he could not master the traditional rhetorical style. But the young Franciscan soon recognized this crucial fact: the old canons of rhetoric did not allow the forceful and effective proclamation of the Christian message. He chose to speak directly, plainly. He reported what he saw, and said what he believed. He filled the piazzas.

The writings of these saints must be read from several perspectives. Finally, their works are important sources of social history, revealing the powerful forces which tore at late-medieval society, and the fears and passions that animated the people of the age. In this paper, we shall view the writings of Caterina and Bernardino, and the writings about them, primarily from this last perspective, as sources of social history. Specifically, we shall consider what they had to say concerning a basic social institution, which was much troubled in their times: the family. To appreciate their teachings on the family requires, however, that we initially consider the objective state of

6. *Ibid., Prologo,* 41: "Sarebbe meglio per me che tutti si salvassero ed io sola, salva sempre la tua carità, sostenessi le pene dell'inferno."
7. *Ibid.,* II, 8, pp. 298–99.
8. *Ibid.,* I, 1, p. 51.

Tuscan or Italian society across the combined duration of their lives, from 1347 to 1444, or thereabouts. The wondrously fertile Tuscan archives have yielded an abundant harvest of data, illuminating demographic, economic and cultural trends in this disturbed century, most of which directly affected births, marriages, deaths and the character of the Tuscan household. This review of certain salient characteristics of the late-medieval Tuscan family will allow us to listen with greater understanding to what our two saints said about it.

Over the years from the middle fourteenth to the middle fifteenth century, the dominant factor in Tuscan social history was a radical decline in the size of population. Many contemporaries affirmed this, but until recently historians tended to regard their estimates of human loss as gross exaggerations. They could not, for example, believe the claim of the Sienese chronicler Agnolo di Tura, that the Great Pestilence of 1348 carried away 52,000 of Siena's population.[9] Today, archival data, even when they do not fully confirm such estimates, at the least bring them within the realm of the plausible.

Before the onslaught of the great plague in 1348, the city of Florence contained probably 120,000 inhabitants. In 1427, it counted fewer than 40,000. Its population thereafter stabilized at low levels, and shows no signs of renewed expansion until after 1480.[10] Many other Tuscan cities Pistoia, Prato, San Gimignano suffered losses of a comparable magnitude; about two-thirds of their numbers disappeared from the early fourteenth to the early fifteenth centuries.[11]

At Siena, the plague seems to have been even more devastating than elsewhere. According to the recent and reasonable estimates of William M. Bowsky, the population of the city and its suburbs, the *Masse*, was certainly more than 52,000 and was probably closer to 70,000, in the early fourteenth century.[12] The Black Death of 1348,

9. *Cronache senesi*, ed. A. Lisini and F. Iacometti (Bologna 1931-37) (*Rerum Italicarum Scriptores*, n.e. XV, pt. 6), p. 54. For an example of the scepticism expressed toward such figures, see G. Pardi, "La popolazione di Siena e del territorio attraverso i secoli, " *Bullettino Senese di Storia Patria* [henceforth *BSSP*], 30 (1923), p. 102.
10. The data are taken from D. Herlihy and C. Klapisch-Zuber, *Les Toscans et leurs familles: Une étude du Catasto florentin de 1427* (Paris, 1978), pp. 173-88.
11. See D. Herlihy, *Medieval and Renaissance Pistoia. The Social History of an Italian Town* (New Haven, 1967); and the several studies of E. Fiumi, *Storia economica e sociale di San Gimignano* (Florence, 1961) and *Demografia, movimento urbanistico e classi sociali in Prato dall'età comunale ai tempi moderni* (Florence, 1968).
12. W. M. Bowsky, "The Impact of the Black Death upon Sienese Government and Society," *Speculum*, 39 (1964), p. 134.

if it did not take the 52,000 Agnolo di Tura reported, probably carried off one-half the urban population. Agnolo buried with his own hands five of his children. And this was only the first of numerous disasters to flay Siena and its countryside. The plague struck again in 1363, 1374, 1383, 1400, 1410-11, and 1421. Famines visited Siena and its countryside with almost equal frequency: 1368, 1370 and 1374 were all of them years of hunger. Wars too added to the havoc; even in periods of supposed peace, companies of mercenaries lived violently off the land. In 1370, invading Florentines allegedly burned more then 2000 houses in the Sienese *contado*.[13] All social order seemed to be collapsing. "A tanto venne," a Sienese chronicler observed under the year 1368, "che in Siena e nel contado si uccideva e rubava ogni persona."[14] "Bandits closed the roads," a biographer of Bernardino noted, "pirates blocked the seas."[15]

These disasters deeply influenced the personal careers and experiences of both Caterina and Bernardino. During the plague of 1374, Caterina worked several miracles; she cured of infection Matteo di Cenni, rector of the hospital, the Casa di Santa Maria della Misericordia di Siena. She cured too her later biographer, Raimondo da Capua.[16] But she also lost in the same plague her sister Lisa and at least seven nephews or nieces.[17] "Sono io forse Iddio," she protested to someone asking for a miracle, "da poter liberare i mortali dalla morte?"[18]

In 1440 the plague wiped out nearly the entire staff of Siena's principal hospital of Santa Maria della Scala. It carried off 22 friars, 18 sisters, 9 priests, 5 clerics, 7 pharmacists, 36 young assistants and 60 servants, in all 157 persons.[19] Hardly anyone remained to care for the sick, whose numbers had been swollen by the many pilgrims, stricken

13. *Cronaca senese di Donato di Neri e di suo figlio Neri*, in *Cronache senesi*, ed. Lisini and Iacometti, p. 637.

14. *Ibid.*

15. *Vita post corporis translationem composita, Acta Sanctorum* [henceforth *ASS*] *V Maii*, 263 A: "Erant itinera latronibus clausa, maria obsessa praedonibus."

16. *S. Caterina da Siena. Vita*, II, 8, pp. 332–45.

17. Their burials are recorded in the *Necrologi di San Domenico in Camporeggio*, ed. H. Laurent O.P. and F. Valli (Florence, 1937) (Fontes Vitae S. Caterinae senensis historici, I). See the family tree constructed by F. Grottanelli, in S. Caterina Da Siena, *Epistolario*, ed. U. Meattini (Siena, 1966), II, pp. 296-97.

18. *S. Caterina da Siena. Vita*, II, 8, p. 330.

19. Stated in the "Vie de S. Bernardin de Sienne par Léonard Benvoglienti," *Analecta Bollandiana*, 21 (1902), p. 68.

on their way to Rome in this jubilee year. Bernardino, then a young layman of 20, assumed responsibility for the hospital, recruited twelve helpers, and himself personally cared for the sick. The effort nearly cost him his own life, as he fell gravely ill soon after the plague abated.

Over these disastrous times, the population of Siena and its suburbs fell from perhaps 70,000 in the early fourteenth century to 18,000 in the first decade of the fifteenth century.[20] The population dwindled still further as the century progressed, to about 15,000 in the 1420's. It remained at this level across the middle decades of the fifteenth century and did not register even a modest increase until after 1460. To many observers, it must have appeared that the human race was doomed to extinction. Bernardino several times remarked that the world was growing smaller. "Because of the waste of vanities," he once concluded, "the increase of peoples has altogether ended."[21] And elsewhere "E per questo e popoli mancano e la sodomia moltiplica."[22]

This steep decline in human numbers in all the Tuscan cities was not, however, smooth and continuous. Rather, the high mortalities in the plague outbreaks stimulated, through processes we cannot examine here, sharp increases in the number of births, in the immediately succeeding years.[23] The community thus quickly but always partially recovered from its horrendous losses. The phenomenon of highly unstable rates of death and birth had important social repercussions. In particular, it accelerated the replacement of individuals within the community. Former members departed and new ones joined the community even more rapidly than the decline in total numbers might suggest. This rapid turnover in turn undermined the stability of every social bonds, with a child, sibling, spouse, with parent, relative or friend. "Tutte le cose che noi possediamo," wrote Caterina, "e la vita e la sanità, moglie e figliuoli … tutte le possediamo come cose prestate … non come cose nostre."[24] And else-

20. The latter estimate is based on the number of baptisms recorded at Siena in the early fifteenth century. See Pardi, *La popolazione*, p. 108.

21. *Opera omnia*, II (Florence 1950), p. 82: "Quod propter superflua vanitatum cessat plurimum multiplicatio populorum."

22. Cited in Sticco, *pensiero*, p. 148.

23. For further discussion, see D. Herlihy and C. Klapisch-Zuber, *Les Toscans*, pp. 165-218; and D. Herlihy, "Deaths, Marriages, Births, and the Tuscan Economy (ca. 13001550)," in *Population Patterns in the Past*, ed. R. D. Lee (New York, San Francisco, and London 1977), pp. 135–64.

24. S. Caterina da Siena, *Epistolario*, II, p. 59.

where: "E tanto è la poca fermezza loro ... che di bisogno è, che elle siano tolte a noi, o che noi siamo tolti a loro."[25]

The violent swings in human numbers and the sharp downward movement had powerful demographic and economic effects upon Tuscans and their households. The immediate demographic impact was a radical reduction in the expectation of life; to judge from Florentine data, life expectancy from birth in the early fourteenth century ranged from 35 to 40 years.[26] In the lifetime of Caterina, it dropped to lower than 20. Caterina herself had reason to affirm: "Quant'è il tempo nostro? È quanto una punta d'aco."[27]

The high mortalities also affected the distribution of ages within the population. The plague was a notorious killer of children. "La mortalità fu in questo anno [1363]" a Sienese chronicler noted, "in Siena e generalmente per tutto, e morì fanciulli e giovani che pochi ne rimase in Siena ... ."[28] In her old age Mona Lapa, Caterina's mother, is said repeatedly to have exclaimed: "Quanti figlioli e figliole, nipoti grandi e piccoli, me sono morti."[29] Of her own 25 children, only eight certainly attained adulthood.[30] "Daily plagues grow more powerful," observed Bernardino, " ... children are not born in large numbers and those born soon die; necessarily the population grows smaller in these times ... ."[31]

But the plague, as we have mentioned, also stimulated births, although not, as Bernardino correctly noted, in sufficient numbers to offset the losses. Tuscan society swarmed with children, most of whom would not live through a full span of years. Paradoxically, however, these same communities contained substantial numbers of the very old. According to the Florentine Catasto of 1427, nearly 10 percent of the total population of some 260,000 was age 65 or older, a proportion to be expected in modern societies with high longevity and low birth rates. There seem to have been two reasons

25. *Ibid.*, II, p. 46.
26. Herlihy and Klapisch-Zuber, *Les Toscans*, p. 200.
27. S. Caterina da Siena, *Epistolario*, II, p. 97.
28. *Cronache senesi*, p. 605.
29. *S. Caterina da Siena. Vita*, p. 330.
30. Of the eight, only three seem to have had children of their own. See the Albero della famiglia Benincasa in Epistolario, II, pp. 296-97.
31. *Opera*, II, p. 83. "Ex his omnibus clarius palpari potest quod cum quotidie invalescant pestes ... nec propter vanitates filii in multitudine generentur atque iam nati subito moriantur, quod necesse est minui gentes, sicut his temporibus ... manifeste apparet."

for this large proportion of the very old. Even in 1427, the upper levels of the age pyramid reflected the much larger population of earlier years. Then too, Tuscans who lived through one major outbreak
of plague seem to have enjoyed a good chance of surviving the
next. It was not unusual to live to advanced old age even in the
midst of these devastating epidemics. Bernardino himself reached
age 64, and Mona Lapa survived until age 89.

The skewed distribution of the age pyramid, with disproportion-
ately large numbers of the very young and the very old, had an
important economic effect. It aggravated what demographers call
the "dependency ratio," the balance in the population between the
economically active adults in their prime years, and those dependents, young and old, whom they must support. A high dependency
ratio necessarily dampens economic productivity, as large resources
must be diverted to the support of non-producers, many of whom
will never return the moneys spent upon them. On a more personal
level, it increased the costs of maintaining a household. High costs
in turn discouraged men from marrying young or marrying at all. At
Florence in 1427, the average age of first marriage for males was
nearly 30 years. Bernardino himself repeatedly condemned those
bachelors who refused to marry, and who adduced as their excuse
the heavy economic burdens which marriage imposed.[32] "For
because of the large expenses … ," he explained, "many men do not
take wives, or they marry late, since the expenses consume often all
the dowries, and sometimes more … ."[33]

The great decline in human numbers, the unsettled balances of
births and deaths, also affected the composition and character of
the Tuscan family. The most startling characteristic of Tuscan families in the late fourteenth and early fifteenth centuries is that there
were so few of them, that is to say, there were comparatively few
complete families, formed around a husband, wife and children.
The great epidemics left in their wake numerous households which
we would call truncated, not containing at least one married cou-

32. S. Bernardino, *Pagine devote sull'amore coniugale*, ed. G. Lazzeri (Milan,
1924), p. 48. "Or a casa. Dice colui che mi bisogna pigliare moglie? Io non ho niuno
affanno … io non ho di molte ispese che io avrei."
33. *Opera omnia*, II, p. 82: "Nam multi propter maximas expensas quas in
uxoribus requirit vanitatum abusus, uxores vel non capiunt, vel tardius suscipiunt
eas, cum saepe quasi omnes dotes, et quandoque amplius, devorent expensae."

ple. At Florence in 1427, the most common type of household, accounting for some 20 percent of all households, included only a single person.

Widows in particular proliferated in the urban population. Girls married very young. According to Raimondo da Capua, Sienese girls were considered marriageable from age 12.[34] At Florence in 1427, the average age of first marriage for girls was 17 years, and they married grooms some 13 years older than themselves. In spite of the risks of child-bearing, the young brides had a good chance of surviving their much older husbands. "Ma gli altri sposi muoiono, e passano come il vento," wrote Caterina, in recommending to a twice-widowed woman that she now choose Christ for her husband.[35] Many young widows would not remarry. Bernardino himself strongly counseled against second marriages for women.[36] At Florence in 1427, about 25 percent of women in their 40's were living as widows, and they constituted an absolute majority of the female population from about the middle 50's.[37]

Widows crowded the society of both Caterina and Bernardino. Many of them adopted a religious life, although they continued to live in their own homes. The sorelle di Penitenza di San Domenico, whom Caterina joined, included, in the words of Raimondo da Capua, "solo vedove di età matura e di buona fama ... perché mancando esse di ogni clausura e rimanendo ognuna nella propria casa ... ."[38] Still according to Raimondo, of these women "nella città di Siena ve n'è tutt'ora un gran numero."[39] Widows of this sort figure prominently in the legend of Caterina, her own mother Lapa; Mona Tecca, whom she cared for, and who repaid her kindness with insults and abuse; Palmerina, who seethed with hatred against her; Andrea, who spread lies about her.[40] Although Bernardino himself avoided commerce with women, still he too was profoundly

---

34. *Caterina. Vita*, I, 4, p. 76. "Ho detto tutte queste cose, perchè quando la vergine consacrata a Dio pervenne all'età di 12 anni o circa quel tempo, secondo il costume del luogo, cominciò ad essere trattenuta in case, poiché in Siena non era facile vedere uscire ragazze da marito."

35. Caterina, *Epistolario*, II, p. 34.

36. L. Marri Martini, *Una predica inedita di S. Bernardino sulla viduità in rapporto alle usanze dell'epoca*, in *BSSP*, 2 (1931), pp. 210–24.

37. Herlihy and Klapisch, *Les Toscans*, p. 661.

38. *Caterina. Vita*, I, 7, p. 111.

39. *Ibid.*, I, 5, p. 90.

40. Caterina's contacts with all these women are described in *Vita*, II, 4, pp. 203–30.

influenced by older women, most of them widows. According to his biographer Maffeo Vegio, four women helped shape the piety of the saint: his widowed aunt Diana, who cared for the orphaned child at Massa between 1386 and 1391, when Bernardino was between 6 and 11 years of age; another aunt by marriage, Pia, who then assumed responsibility for his upbringing at Siena; his cousin Tobia, another widow some 30 years older than himself, whom he knew from age 17; and Bartolomea dei Tolomei, also a widow, whom he addressed as mother. How did these women affect his own religious attitudes? Surely they alerted him to the moral issues directly affecting women: the difficulties attendant upon marrying daughters, the size of dowries, the wasted expenditures on female fineries, sexual morality within and outside of marriage, the relations between husband and wife and parents and children, and widowhood itself. No previous preacher gave so much attention to these questions of direct concern to women; his lengthy treatment of these issues add to the excellence of his writings as sources of social history.

If Tuscan urban communities were crowded with widows living alone, they also contained a large number of another kind of unattached adult, bachelor males. Men, as we have mentioned, married late in Tuscan cities, 30 years was the mean age of first marriage for males at Florence in 1427, and some did not marry at all. These aging bachelors were one of Bernardino's favorite targets. He saw no possibility that a celibate male could live a virtuous life in secular society. Those males who remained single were surely, in his view, sodomites. "Guai guai a chi non toglie moglie, avendo il tempo e chagione lecita, ché non pigliandola, diventano soddomiti. Hali questa regola generale: come tu vedi uno in età compiuta, e sano nella persona, e non pigliassi moglie, hai di lui cattiva istigazione."[41]

The presence in urban society of large numbers of unattached adults fewer than 50 percent of Florentine lay persons were living with a spouse in 1427—invited all sorts of sexual disorders, which Bernardino reviews in his writings: prostitution, the seduction of married women and even nuns, and above all, sodomy.

In the Tre- and Quattrocento, demographic disasters threatened the integrity and survival of numerous Tuscan families. So also did other factors, which deserve from us a brief consideration. In eco-

41. Cited in Sticco, *pensiero*, p. 128.

nomic terms, the late Trecento seems to have been a period of contracting output. There were two principal reasons for this. The number of active adults in the community was falling even more rapidly than the total population. And the great plagues, families, and wars disrupted the normal processes of production. It required decades before the economy could adjust to the new demographic conditions. But high mortalities also accelerated the transfers of property, especially through inheritances. The plague threatened many with death and ruin, but it also strangely favored some with accumulated properties.

Shrinking output and perhaps too the prevailing instability in the distribution of wealth heightened competition among families and within families over wealth and property. A Sienese chronicler observes under the year 1373: "Parbe che in questio tempo regnasse nel mondo una pianeta la quale ebe a fare questi effetti ... E così fratelli carnali, cugini e consorti e congionti e vicini, parbe che generalmente in tutto il mondo fusse divisione ... In Siena non s'intendeano né osservava lealtà gentiliomini fra loro né con persona fuora di loro, né e' Novi tra loro, né i Dodici tra loro, né con altri fuora di loro ... e così el mondo è una tenebra."[42]

A biographer of Bernardino describes the plight of Italy on the eve of the saint's appearance: "At that time Italy, full of crimes, lay prostrate ... Everyone strove to increase his patrimonies ... In the insatiable heat of avarice they struggled to enlarge their possessions. Every person had taken his own path ... Cursing one another with venomous words, they fought with unrelenting hatreds ... So much did the madness of Guelfs and Ghibellines everywhere rage, that Italy ran red with their mutual atrocities and the blood of brothers."[43]

Blood was a common sight to the contemporaries of Caterina and Bernardino. Caterina herself repeatedly evokes images of blood in her letters. It was, to be sure, the blood of Christ to which she commonly refers. Perhaps she hoped that the healing blood of the Savior would cleanse society from the stains of fratricidal combat.

42. *Cronache senesi*, p. 652.
43. *ASS, V Maii*, 266 A. "Eo enim tempore Italia, plena flagitiis, prostrata iacebat ... Studebant singuli in augendo patrimonia ... insatiabili cupiditatis ardore ampliandis facultatibus incumbebant. Omnis quippe caro corruperat viam suam ... et venenato sibi ore maledicentes, odiis pertinacibus invicem dissidebant ... tanta rabies Guelforum et Givellinorum ubique incaluerat, ut cruente horrore mutuo ac fraterno sanguine maderet Italia."

Inevitably, ubiquitous violence and sudden death affected cultural attitudes. Many Tuscans refused to believe that an omnipotent and beneficent God ruled over the tumultuous affairs of men. According to Bernardino's biographer whom we have previously quoted, "rarely even on holy days did people gather to hear Mass." Many avoided confession, even on their death beds. In the view of such sceptics, chance alone ruled the universe. People hoped to control the play of fortune through sorcery, or take advantage of its vagaries through gambling.

Raimondo da Capua introduces us to one such doubter, named Andrea di Naddino, "uomo ricchissimo di beni terreni, ma poverissimo in fatto di beni celesti."[44] He says of him: " ... essendosi dato tutto al gioco dei dadi, era diventato un ributtante bestemmiatore di Dio e dei Santi ... in vita sua non aveva messo mai piede in chiesa." Andrea fell deathly ill in 1370, at the age of 40. It required all of Caterina's powerful interventions with God, before Andrea could be moved to make his first and final confession. Bernardino repeatedly condemns sorcery and gambling, the practice of which could only have been widespread in the society of his day.[45] The Middle Ages were not an age of serene faith, at least not in Tuscany.

This then was the troubled world which both Caterina and Bernardino contemplated, the wounds of which they hoped to heal. What did they say about the family?

Caterina's great contribution was to offer the consolations of Christian belief and of mystical experience to every member of society, of both sexes and every social rank. According to Raimondo da Capua, God Himself reassured her that all could approach Him: "Io diffondo dove voglio la grazia del mio spirito. Davanti a me non c'è maschio né femmina; né ricco né povero, ma tutti sono uguali, perché ogni cosa io posso ugualmente."[46] The answer to the strains and sorrows of life was to cultivate the life of grace. "O carissimo fratello," wrote Caterina, "in ogni stato che è uomo, può salvare l'anima sua e ricevere in sé la vita della Grazia ... Però che ogni stato è piacevole a Dio; e non è accettatore degli stati, ma del santo

---

44. *Vita,* II, 7, pp. 302-303.
45. See, for example, *Le Prediche volgari,* II: *Predicazione del 1425 in Siena,* ed. P. C. Cannarozzi O.F.M. (Florence, 1958), pp. 55-68. "Questa è la predica contro e' maliardi e incantatori."
46. *Caterina. Vita,* II, pp. 176-77.

desiderio."[47] In a striking simile which she develops in *Il Dialogo*, this mystical experience formed a bridge over the troubled waters of the world, which ran wild with currents of both pleasure and pain.[48]

Towards the family, Caterina's attitudes were, however, deeply ambivalent. Excessive attachment to the family, obedience to its wisher, could be obstacles and her brothers had tried to force her to marry, and persecuted her when she adamantly refused. Her closest ties were with her father Giacomo, who protected her against the anger of the others. To bear up under the cruel treatment of her closest kin, she used to pretend, according to Raimondo, that her father was Christ, her mother the Virgin, and her brothers and the household servants the Holy Apostles.[49] She thus performed with patience the menial household tasks imposed upon her. But neither her legend nor her letters suggest that her relations with her closest kin, with the exception of her father, were especially warm.

In her letters, she repeatedly warned her correspondents against excessive attachment to one's natural family. "Dico dunque, che per lo disordinato amore ch' e' servi del mondo hanno posto a loro medesimi, col quale amore disordinato amano ogni creatura e figliuoli e marito e fratelli e padre e madre e tutti e' diletti del mondo; perdendoli, sostengono intollerabili pene, e sono impazienti e incomportabili a loro medesimo."[50] She demands that her disciples regard even their spouses and their children as "borrowed goods," not truly their own. In particular, she condemns fathers and mothers for "facendosi Dio de' figliuoli."[51] Sometimes, she warns, God brings about the death of children, to free their parents from this worldly attachment. In this interpretation, she strikes on a theme which other teachers of the age repeated, such as the prominent French scholastic Jean Gerson.[52]

47. Caterina, *Epistolario*, II, p. 233.
48. *Il Dialogo della Divina Provvidenza ovvero Libro della Divina Dottrina*, ed. G. Cavallini (Roma, 1968), p. 348.
49. *Vita*, I, 4, p. 87: "Mi diceva di essersi messa in mente che suo padre rappresenteva Gesú Cristo, nostro Signore e Salvatore; sua madre, la gloriosa Genitrice Maria; i fratelli, poi, e gli altri di famiglia, i santi Apostoli e i discepoli."
50. Caterina, *Epistolario*, II, p. 46.
51. *Ibid.*, p. 405.
52. J. Gerson, *Oeuvres complètes*, ed. Mgr. Glorieux (Paris, 1966), VII, p. 322. Gerson tells of a rich married couple who became so attached to their beautiful baby that they neglected their religious obligations. God punished them for this by taking the child in death.

To be sure, she expects members of the family to act morally in regard to one another. But she never develops this theme and her recommendations concerning behavior within the family are always terse and vague. Married couples should exercise the sacrament in piety and reverence, according to the commandments of the Church. They should suppress all "disordinato desiderio," and act "siccome uomo ragionevole, e non come animale bruto."[53] They should avoid sexual relations on prohibited days. Caterina does allude, with appropriate horror though in opaque fashion, to unnatural sexual acts within marriage.[54] If possible, husband and wife should consider adopting the angelic life of permanent continence.

Toward his children, the father is obligated to "notricare, reggere e governare la famiglia vostra con santo timore di Dio."[55] He is responsible for the spiritual as well as the material welfare of the family. He should, for example, dress modestly and at small expense, and thus set an example for his wife and children. The wife is obligated to respect and obey her husband, and to rear her children "nelle virtù e nelli santi comandamenti dolci di Dio."[56]

Caterina was not concerned with the welfare of the natural family, with its unity and harmony, or even with the welfare of the total society. Presumably she ranked such values among the "borrowed things," which could only distract the believer from the mystical quest for God. Her solution to the instabilities and tensions of the age was simple and forthright. Spiritual peace lay in transcendental meditation, in forging enduring ties of love with God, in bathing, as she said repeatedly, in the blood of Christ. The good Christian need not contemplate nor consider the needs of society. He should rather cultivate mystical contact with the supernatural world.

Caterina was profoundly suspicious of the claims of the natural family upon its members, and yet it must also be said that her own mystical visions are saturated with reminiscences of family life. Probably in 1367, at the start of her public missions, she celebrated

53. Caterina, *Epistolario*, II, p. 406.
54. *Ibid.*, p. 235. "E terrà lo stato del matrimonio ordinato, ma ordinato sì come Sacramento ... Sarà, e viverà come uomo, e non come animale ... Questi sarà un arbore fruttifero, che produrrà e' frutti delle virtù; e sarà odorifero, perché stando nella puzza, getterà odor; e il seme che uscirà di lui, sarà buono e virtuoso." References to "puzzo" in regard to marital relations sometimes refer to unnatural acts.
55. Caterina, *Epistolario*, III, p. 573.
56. *Ibid.*, II, p. 60.

her mystical marriage with Christ. The marriage, unlike earthly marriages, gave her a stable relationship, and constant faith. The marriage feast occurred in her little room at carnival time, even as her natural family was reveling elsewhere in the house. The simultaneous occurrence of these two celebrations can hardly be accidental, and the parallel is rich in irony.[57]

Figures of marriages, conceptions, births and of nursing are common in letters. "Vedi adunque," she writes to a nun, "che nella carità di Dio concepiamo le virtù, e nella carità del prossimo si partoriscono."[58] The crucified Christ is compared to a nursing mother: "A noi ... conviene fare come fa il fanciullo, il quale volendo prendere il latte, prende la mammella della madre, e mettesela in bocca ... Perocché ci dobbiamo attaccare al petto di Cristo crocifisso, in cui è la madre della carità."[59] During her own active career, she formed a spiritual family with her disciples, who addressed her as "mamma." She guaranteed to them eternal life, even as a natural mother gives life to her children. Caterina, it appears, aimed at forming a spiritual association, which would escape the failings and instabilities of the natural family and yet would offer similar rewards: companionship; mutual support; abiding ties based upon love; and the promise of a stable, happy existence.

Bernardino was a saint of a different sort. He did not, as did Caterina, cast a hasty glance over the real world and then leap at once into the transcendental. He was interested in social realities; he wanted to know how society functioned. He observed closely and perceptively. His humanist biographer, Maffeo Vegio, catches the secret of his genius. "Let us further point out," he writes, "his knowledge of many things, and his shrewd awareness of the differing customs of peoples. For he visited all the cities of Italy, as he instructed them in the holy disciplines. He thus understood their different interests, and the different sins by which they were chiefly corrupted. With this understanding, he healed by diverse remedies, suitable for each disease ... ."[60]

57. *Caterina. Vita*, I, 12, p. 166. " ... ora che gli altri di casa tua si divertono a tavola, e fanno feste mondane, io stabilisco di celebrare con te la festa nuziale dell'anima tua ... ."

58. Caterina, *Epistolario*, II, p. 330.

59. *Ibid.*, p. 615.

60. "Adjuciamus insuper multarum rerum notitiam, summamque in discernendis variorum populorum moribus prudentiam; nam ut omnes adivit Italiae civitates,

In his examination of both virtues and vices, Bernardino was not content simply to point out the spiritual benefits they conveyed or the spiritual damage they caused. Almost always, he dwelt upon what he called the "temporal" or "corporal" repercussions of human behavior. For example, in urging sons and daughters to be obedient to their parents, he first examines the social roots of disobedience. He finds those roots in the malice of offspring, their avarice, pride or sensuality, or the failure of the parents themselves to rear their children properly.[61] He then points out seven rewards of filial obedience: a long and happy life, honorable possession of great riches, large numbers of grateful offspring of one's own, the blessing of one's parents, the grace of God, and finally, eternal glory. So also, the effects of filial disloyalty are an unhappy death, miserable poverty, an unhappy family, bad repute, the curse of one's parents, a wicked life, and eternal damnation. Bernardino includes in these lists spiritual rewards and punishments, but he does not emphasize them. Rather, he stresses that the virtuous life conveys an abundance of secular rewards.

Largely under the influence of Aristotle, medieval thinkers had affirmed that both family and the city or community were natural societies. But the disasters of the fourteenth century showed that unity and harmony within both institutions were highly fragile. Men had to strive, if they wished to obtain and protect the blessings of a harmonious social existence. Bernardino learned this lesson, and was one of the first thinkers of the Middle Ages—perhaps we should say, of the Renaissance—to do so. In this he shows unmistakable similarities with his contemporaries, the civic humanists of Florence.

In Bernardino's view of society, the chief threat to the internal peace of the community was factional conflict, which he extensively analyzes and bitterly condemns. Our interests are, however, in his treatment of the family. He strongly argues that marriage is the appropriate civic state for all adult males living in the world. With verve and much sarcasm, he compares the well-maintained household of the married couple with the apartment of the bachelor.[62] The diligent

---

sanctis eas instruens disciplinis; ita diversa ipsarum studia, diversaque quibus corrupta quamque magis essent peccata intelligebat; intelligensque diversis etiam ac quibusque suo convenientibus medicorum, medicus ipse exercitatus animarum admodum instructus." *ASS, V Maii,* 293 A.

61. *Opera Omnia,* III, pp. 306-18, Sermo XVII, "De Honore parentum."

62. *Ibid.,* II, pp. 107-108, Sermo XLVIII, "De honestate coniugatorum."

mistress of the house keeps up supplies of wheat and oil, and she protects the larder from vermin. She weaves linen and cuts clothing. She airs garments and washes them when needed. She also cares for the sick within the family, and sees that all fulfill their religious and charitable obligations. In contrast, the bachelor lives amid squalor and confusion, and neglects his religious and civic duties. And no one cares for him when he is sick. "[Unmarried males]," he concludes, "live such a poor and miserable life, that their habits may justly be regarded as those of animals rather than of men."[63]

To be sure, Bernardino is here not entirely consistent. He wants all lay males to marry, but not widowed women. But here too, he had practical as well as spiritual reasons to support his argument. The widow might have children of her own, and her entry into another household would cause confusion and disturb the domestic peace. It was better that she live alone, and not take on the responsibilities of a second family.[64]

But in spite of the civic advantages of the married state, many were refusing to marry. "Non vedi tu," he once asked, "che Siena viene meno, che in Milano, quando frate Bernardino tornò, li fu detto che venti milia fanciulle v'erano da maritare, senza le maritate e quelle che non avevano tempo; e più fanciulli che in tutta Italia?"[65] Why were the young—young men in particular—so reluctant to enter the married state? Bernardino knew of two reasons: the lure of sodomy, and the costly financial arrangements needed to make a marriage. As a youth in Siena, Bernardino had been solicited for sodomy at least twice by older males, with the promise of money. He himself wondered at the deep roots of this vice in Sienese society: "E perché in questa città so' tanto puzzolenti di tal vizio? ... O Toscana, che corna t'è questa, ch'è una confusione di noi per tutto 'l mondo."[66] He claimed that young girls could walk safely through the streets of Siena without harassment, while young boys would be subject to constant, indecent solicitations.

The expense of marrying a daughter was the second great obstacle to the making of marriages. Bernardino chiefly blamed the cost

63. *Loc. cit.:* "... talem huiusmodi miseram et miserabilem vitam ducunt, ut non hominum sed animalium mores merito dici possunt."
64. See sermon cited above, n. 36.
65. *Prediche volgari,* II, p. 107.
66. *Ibid.,* p. 103.

of "vanities," the expenditures on female fineries. In his analysis, families with several daughters to marry would elect to invest only in the prettiest. They would dress her in beautiful clothes and attract suitors with promises of high dowries. Her sisters—many of them ugly, lame, blind or deformed—they would confine to convents. These unhappy girls were, in the saint's phrase, "the scum and vomit of the world."[67]

To promote harmony within the household, Bernardino insisted that both the husband and the wife had responsibilities; there was no double standard in conjugal relations. Specifically, the husband had four chief obligations towards his wife: to instruct her, correct her, live with her and support her.[68] The wife had equally four obligations toward her husband: to fear him, serve him, obey him, and admonish him. The two mutually owed each other love, fidelity, respect, and the payment of the conjugal debt. Bernardino is explicit in his treatment of sexual practices within marriage. In particular he was outspoken in his condemnation of unnatural forms of intercourse, in which conception was consciously prevented. He gives the impression that such practices were widespread in his society. "Io ho grandissimo dubbio di voi," he once told the women of Siena, "ch'io mi credo che se ne salvino tanti pochi in quegli che sono in istato di matrimonio, che de' mille, novecento novantanove credo che sia matrimonio del diavolo."[69]

So also, children are obligated to love, fear, honor, obey, support, console and sustain their parents.[70] In return, the dutiful children are promised an abundance of temporal and spiritual blessings, as we have mentioned. If both parents and children fulfill these obligations, then they will all live in harmony and prosperity, and they will enjoy a full measure of earthly happiness.

Bernardino was, in sum, acutely aware of the troubled state of his own society. He therefore judged behavior, not only in terms of the eternal rewards or punishments it might merit, but in terms of its contributions to or detractions from harmonious social life. He was, if not truly a civic humanist, then surely a civic Christian. Eloquently

67. *Opera omnia*, II, p. 83.
68. *Ibid.*, VIII, pp. 57-59. From the tract, "De matrimonio regulato, inordinato et separato."
69. See *Pagine devote*, p. 19.
70. *Prediche volgari*, I, p. 11.

and forcefully, he pointed our the social costs of immorality, and the social rewards of virtuous living. To be sure, we cannot measure the effects of Bernardino's powerful exhortations. His biographer, Maffeo Vegio, thought they were considerable: "How much," he exclaimed, "did the care increase, which parents gave to children and the reverence, which the children returned! How greatly did mutual love and fidelity increase, between husbands and wives!"[71]

Our two saints shared a common experience, but yet they differed considerably one from the other in the styles of their thought and the content of their message. Still, it is fair to say that both of them expanded the boundaries of Christian theology and moral teaching. Caterina pressed upward, into the realm of sublime mystical speculations, and she invited even her humblest contemporaries to partake in the satisfactions of mystical experience. Bernardino rather looked deeply into the fabric of social institutions, and tried to direct actions in ways which would advance both the welfare of society and the salvation of souls. Both saints left behind a richer Christian heritage than what they had received. And today, their writings give to historians precious glimpses into the life and thought of a deeply troubled, but wondrously creative age.

71. *ASS, V Maii*, 293 F. "Quanta parentibus in filios diligentia, filiisque in parentes crevit reverentia? Quantus maritorum et uxorum in invicem amor et fides?"

10

THE FLORENTINE MERCHANT FAMILY
OF THE MIDDLE AGES

—— ✦ ✦ ✦ ——

The history of business organization in Italy during the Middle Ages—a subject to which Federigo Melis devoted so much creative energy—inevitably draws researchers into the history of the family. Through his studies of the enterprises of Francesco di Marco Datini, the merchant of Prato, Melis himself was already bridging the gulf between business life and private life, between commercial and familial organizations.

The literature on Italian merchant families, both on their domestic organization and their business functions, is today quite large.[1] In

1. Though not concerned with Italian merchants, students of the commercial culture of the Mediterranean world must now regard the work of S.D. Goitein, *A Mediterranean Society: The Jewish Communities of the Arab World as Portrayed in the Documents of the Cairo Geniza* (Berkeley and Los Angeles, 1967). For an older, still useful profile of the medieval Italian merchant, see Y. Renouard, *Les hommes d'affaires italiens du Moyen Age* (Paris, 1949). Melis' own many publications on the merchant are cited in the bibliography, *A Federigo Melis* (Università degli Studi di Firenze, Facoltà di Economia e Commercio, Istituto di Storia Economica; Florence, 1976). For Armando Sapori's reconstruction of the merchant's culture, see "La cultura del mercante medievale italiano," in *Studi di storia economica medievale* (Florence, 1940), pp. 285-325; *idem, Le marchand italien au Moyen Âge. Conférences et bibliographie*, with an introduction by L. Fèbvre (Paris, 1952). One of the first biographies of an Italian merchant, linking private life and commercial life, was R. S. Lopez, *Genova marinara nel duegento. Benedetto Zaccaria ammiraglio e mercante* (Messina and Milan, 1933); *idem*, "Familiari, procuratori e dipendenti di Benedetto Zaccaria," *Miscellanea di storia ligure in onore di Giorgio Falco* (Milan, 1962), pp. 209-50.

More recent studies of the Italian merchant family are: P. Jones, "Florentine Families and Florentine Diaries in the Fourteenth Century," *Papers of the British School at Rome*, 24 (1956), pp. 103-205. C. Bec, *Les marchands écrivains. Affaires et human-*

this paper, I hope to make a small contribution to our understanding of the relationship between family structures and business organization at Florence from the thirteenth to the fifteenth centuries.

A central problem in the history of medieval Italian households, and merchant households among them, is familial solidarity, the extent to which the liberty of the individual member was subordinated to the interests of the group and to the authority of a single chief. Writers of the Middle Ages and the Renaissance routinely praised the large, cohesive and disciplined household. None did so more eloquently than the Florentine humanist Leon Battista Alberti in I *Libri della Famiglia,* a tract finished in the middle 1430's. Giannozzo Alberti, the principal speaker in the third of the four books, affirms: "Vorrei tutti i miei albergassero sotto un medesimo tetto, a uno medesimo fuoco si scaldassono, a una medesima mensa sedesseno."[2] If the family grows too large to live in the same place, Giannozzo still recommends that all its members remain "almeno sotto un'ombra tutti d'uno volere."[3]

This was the ideal. But in the real world, this ideal had to be compromised. Cohesion and discipline, if pursued to extremes, can obstruct the family in critical functions, in rearing its children through to maturity, in equipping them, psychologically and culturally, for their future roles. The shadow of a single will may permanently infantilize the young, and leave them unprepared as adults to maintain the family interests. The task of educating offspring to both loyalty and liberty, discipline and initiative, a sense of solidarity and a habit of individualism, was particularly crucial for the merchants. The fortunes of the great mercantile families were critically depen-

isme à Florence. 1375-1430 (Paris and The Hague, 1967). J. Heers, *Le clan familial au Moyen Âge. Etude sur les structures politiques et sociales des milieux urbains* (Paris, 1974). R. A. Goldthwaite, *Private Wealth in Renaissance Florence. A Study of Four Families* (Princeton, 1968), and *idem* "The Florentine Palace as Domestic Architecture," *The American Historical Review,* 77 (1971), pp. 977-1012. Against Goldthwaite's thesis that the great lineages were breaking up into nuclear units in the late Middle Ages, see F.W. Kent, *Household and Lineage in Renaissance Florence. The Family Life of the Capponi, Ginori and Rucellai* (Princeton, 1977). P. Malanima, *I Riccardi di Firenze. Una famiglia e un patrimonio nella Toscana dei Medici* (Florence, 1977). Our own study, D. Herlihy and C. Klapisch-Zuber, *Les Toscans et leurs familles. Une étude du Catasto florentin de 1427* (Paris, 1978), also examines the structure of Florentine merchant families in relation to those found across the community.

2. *Libri della famiglia,* III, in *Opere volgari,* ed. C. Grayson (Bari, 1960), I, p. 191.
3. *Ibid.,* I, p. 234.

dent upon the cultivation of initiative, resourcefulness and independence, in each new generation.

How can the historian measure, among the families of a distant
epoch, this delicate balance between a sense of solidarity and a
habit of freedom? Many strategies are possible here. Mine will be to
track the career of the Florentine merchant from birth, to observe
what was required of him, and how those requirements affected his
relations with his kin. To be sure, in this reconstruction of the merchant's career, I consciously omit many topics: his formal education
and training, the exact nature of his technical skills, the content of
his culture. In apology I plead that on these topics there exist many
excellent studies, previously cited. We shall, moreover, concentrate
our attention upon the first half of the merchant's life, and upon certain formal events which marked its passage: emancipation from
paternal authority; matriculation into guilds; marriage; and the
assumption of leadership in business, guild and government. In
essence, we shall be studying the processes by which a new generation of merchants replaced their elders.

In tracing the careers of merchants, the Florentine archives offer
rich resources, but also visit the researcher with many frustrations.
Notarial chartularies, numerous at Florence from the late thirteenth
century, contain by the thousands acts of emancipation, business
partnerships, marriage agreements, testaments, and the like, in
which the members of the great mercantile families make frequent
if random appearances. Family memoirs and private account books,
also surviving from the late thirteenth century, similarly illuminate
the mercantile households, although always in checkered patterns.[4]

The records of the Florentine guilds offer numerous opportunities
to observe merchants: in lists of masters redacted at varying intervals; in the matriculation of new members; and in the lotteries or
drawings, called at Florence the *Tratte,* by which the guilds selected
their governing officials.[5] Surveys of members and of matriculation

4. G. M. Anselmi, F. Pezzarossa, and L. Avellini, *La "Memoria" dei mercatores.
Tendenze ideologiche, ricordanze, artigianato in versi nella Firenze del Quattrocento*
(L'Esperienza critica, I; Bologna, 1980), gives a bibliography of Florentine *ricordanze*
and similar writings.

5. At Harvard University we are currently engaged in entering into a machine-readable
file the guild Tratte in the Archivio di Stato di Firenze (henceforth, ASF), from the earliest
survivals until the end of the Republic in 1530. Dr. Roberto Barducci is aiding me in this
research. Citations from unpaginated archival registers are here given by date alone.

lists are very old at Florence. Those of the guild of Calimala, the importers of French and Flemish cloth, date from 1235. We can follow the membership in the guild of Por Santa Maria, which included the silk dealers, from 1225; the spice merchants from 1297; money changers from 1299; and wool manufacturers and merchants, in the Arte della Lana, from 1304. The records of electoral scrutinies for the major guilds survive in largerly continuous series from 1393. Late, they still retain a particular interest. In the repeated inspection of the members whose names were drawn from the electoral purses, the notaries of the guild usually state why a particular person was refused a particular office, why a *divieto*, in the technical language, was laid upon him. He may have been too young for the office, long absent from Florence, delinquent in his taxes, ill or already dead; or he, or a close relative, may have held the same or similar office within a proscribed period. Historians can learn much of the careers of thousands of Florentine citizens, through observing the comments made about them in the electoral drawings.

Public as well as private or guild records also aid us on the track of merchants. The communal government was ceaselessly surveying the citizenry, in whole or in part: it counted the number of household heads and sometimes enumerated their dependents; distributed loans and taxes among them; and determined, again through *Tratte* or drawings from specially prepared purses, who among them were eligible for particular offices.[6] From 1385, lists were also kept of those who died within the city, and a crude register of births (unfortunately, only of males) was begun in 1429 but contained the names of persons born fifty and more years earlier.[7] The *Tratte* associated with the numerous offices of the communal government carry valuable comments on the names of prospective office holders; they begin in continuous series shortly before the Ciompi uprising, from the early 1370's. Among tax surveys, the earliest full list of house-

6. The development of Florentine methods of tax assessment is surveyed in E. Conti, *I catasti agrari della Repubblica fiorentina e il catasto particellare toscano* (sec. 14-19). *La formazione della struttura agraria moderna*, vol. 3, Parte 1, sez. 1: *Le fonti*. Istituto storico italiano per il Medio Evo (Rome, 1966). The intricate system of Florentine electoral scrutinies and drawings is laid out most recently in G. Guidi, *Il governo della città-repubblica di Firenze del primo Quattrocento* (Biblioteca Storica Toscana, 20) 3 vols., (Florence, 1981), especially I, pp. 149-344.

7. The nature of these registrations of deaths and births are discussed in D. Herlihy and C. Klapisch-Zuber, *Les Toscans*, pp. 446-468 and p. 421 respectively.

hold heads within the city dates from 1352, and there exist thereafter numerous distributions of forced loans among the propertied
families of the city. In 1427, as part of a major fiscal reform, the
Commune introduced a new kind of survey and assessment of its
citizens, known as the Catasto. This famous document gives the
names and ages of all persons then resident in the Florentine
domains.[8] Detailed surveys of the city of Florence were several
times repeated over the course of the fifteenth century, and we shall
use here five such redactions, between 1427 and 1480.

Within this vast sea of documentation, from the late thirteenth
century, the reasonably active, reasonably long-lived Florentine citizen was likely to be observed scores, hundreds, even thousands of
times. Someday, with the aid of computers, it may be possible systematically to collect and link these citations, and thus to reconstruct the careers of substantial numbers of the Florentine patriciate
over the last 250 years of the Middle Ages. At present, we cannot
paint so grand a portrait. The most I offer here are comments on a
few principal events which marked the merchant's passage from
birth to maturity. And I shall draw support for my arguments from
the histories of six specific families: the Bardi, who, before the collapse of their bank in 1346 could claim to be, in the words of the
chronicler Giovanni Villani, "the greatest merchants of Italy;"[9] the
Pitti, who formed one of the richest houses in the fifteenth century
and gave Florence a famous palace;[10] the Corsini[11] and the Guic-

8. The document is analyzed and some results presented in D. Herlihy and C.
Klapisch-Zuber, *Les Toscans*; see especially chapters 1-3 for the technical character
of the survey.

9. *Cronica di Giovanni Villani*, IV (Florence, Sansone Coen, 1845), p. 92 (Book
12, chap. 55), " . . . i quali erano stati i maggiori mercanti d'Italia." The basic study
of the failure of the bank in 1346, now dated in parts but with much valuable information, is A. Sapori, *La crisi delle compagnie mercantili dei Bardi e dei Peruzzi* (Biblioteca Storica Toscana, 3) (Florence, 1926).

10. On the palazzo of messer Luca Pitti (1395-1472), see L. Ginori Lisci, *I Palazzi
di Firenze nella storia e nell'arte*, II (Florence, 1972), pp. 707-09; P. Sanpaolesi, "Il
Palazzo Pitti e gli architetti fiorentini della discendenza brunelleschiana," *Festschrift
Ulrich Middeldorf* (Berlin, 1968), pp. 124-35; F. Morandini, "Palazzo Pitti, la sua
costruzione e i successivi ingrandimenti," *Commentari. Rivista di critica e di storia
dell'arte,* 16 (1965), pp. 35-46. The last cited study contains extensive extracts from
unpublished archival records.

11. On the genealogy of the Corsini, see L. Passerini, *Genealogia e storia della
famiglia Corsini* (Florence, 1858). Here as in his other genealogies, Passerini tends to
be sketchy concerning the early history of the house and to omit those who died young.
On the Guicciardini, see most recently Goldthwaite, *Private Wealth*, pp. 109-56.

ciardini, houses which also possessed substantial commercial interests; and the Machiavelli, Velluti and Dati—commercial families too, if perhaps not the equals in the magnitude of their affairs to the others previously mentioned.

We select these families principally because the documentary references to them are particularly numerous. Members of the Velluti, Pitti, Dati, Corsini and Machiavelli households produced among the oldest and richest family memoirs.[12] Moreover, all these families lived in close proximity to one another in the quarter of Santo Spirito, the part of the city which extended along the Arno's left bank. Proximity of residence means that members of these households often appear side by side in the same archival source—a considerable advantage for the researcher who is trying to plumb vast depths of documentation.

After birth, the offspring of a mercantile family at Florence, and of other families too, was likely again to be noticed in a public document (apart from tax surveys) when he was emancipated from his father's authority.[13] According to the Roman law which Florence respected, the father's power over his children, his *patria potestas*, lasted as long as the father survived. Even when physically mature, unemancipated sons and daughters could not enter into binding contracts, or acquire or dispense property, without their father's consent. The act of emancipation, performed before a judge and notary, was thus a rite of passage, by which the son or daughter assumed the privileges and powers, and also the responsibilities, of adult status.

Although the emancipation of daughters was fairly common, we shall limit our attention here to sons. Florentine fathers, when they freed their sons, almost invariably endowed them with property. The gift of property to an emancipated son was called, like the comparable settlement upon daughters, a *dos, dote* or dowry. The amounts

12. Donato Velluti, *La cronica domestica scritta fra il 1367 e il 1370*, con le addizioni di Paolo Velluti scritte fra il 1555 ed il 1560, ed. I. Del Lungo and G. Volpe (Florence, 1914); Buonaccorso Pitti, *Cronaca, con annotazione*, ed. A. Bacchi della Lega (Bologna, 1905); Gregorio Dati, *Il libro segreto (1384-1434)*, ed. G. Gargiolli (Scelta di curiosità inedite o rare, 102; Bologna, 1960); *libro di ricordanze dei Corsini* (1362-1457), ed. A. Petrucci (Istituto Storico Italiano per il Medio Evo; Fonti per la Storia d'Italia, 100; Rome, 1965); Bernardo Machiavelli, *Libro di ricordi*, ed. C. Olschki (Florence, 1954).

13. On emancipation, see T. Kuehn, *Emancipation in Late Medieval Florence* (New Brunswick, N.J., 1982).

of wealth conveyed were often substantial. In 1382 Matteo Corsini, when he emancipated his eldest son Piero, gave to the boy—he was only 16—two farms, which Piero later sold for the considerable sum of 1600 gold florins.[14] When in 1468 messer Giovanni Pitti emancipated his two sons, he gave both of them agricultural lands and, in addition, the sums of 1200 and 1300 florins respectively.[15] Emancipation, with an accompanying *dota,* thus conferred upon the son not only the juridical capacity, but the material means that he needed to function independently in society.

To be sure, some acts of emancipation appear to have changed little or nothing in the lives of those who were party to them. Boccaccio Velluti was emancipated and endowed by his father Alessandro in 1433, when he was 16 years of age.[16] But he continued to live in his father's house and he is still found there, 25 years later, in 1458, when his father, now over 90, prepared his tax declaration.[17] The forty-year old Boccaccio, still unmarried, avers to the tax officials that he is "sanza aviamento," without means of making a living in the world. Soon after the death of his aged father, which occurred probably in 1460, Boccaccio finally married. As he was an only son, all hope of continuing this strand within the Velluti lineage rested with him. In 1469 he still protests to the tax assessors that he is "sanza aviamento e guadagno alchuno."[18] Clearly, his emancipation at the age of 16 changed little in his undistinguished career.

Giovanni di Niccolò Guicciardini apparently emancipated his son Iacopo twice, once in 1450, when the boy was 16 years of age, and again in 1471, when he was 38.[19] The occasion for the second emancipation may have been the son's marriage, which occurred probably in 1469. But why was a second emancipation necessary?

14. *Il libro di ricordanze dei Corsini,* pp. 66-67.

15. ASF, Repubblica, Notificazioni delle emancipazioni, [hereinafter Rep., not. emanc.] reg. 8, f. 200, September 30, 1468. Alfonso receives "per parte della dota" 1200 florins; and Giovanni 1300 florins. He also emancipated Bastiano, but the amount of his *dota* is not stated.

16. ASF, Rep., Not. emanc., reg. 2, f. 70, February 19, 1433.

17. ASF, Catasto, reg. 788, f. 703.

18. ASF, Catasto, reg. 906, f. 77. Boccaccio is 53 years old, his wife Margherita 28, and they have two sons, ages 9 and 6, and two daughters, ages 3 and less than a year, declared to be "sanza dota."

19. ASF, Rep., Not. emanc., reg. 5, f. 154, April 27, 1450; *ibid.,* reg. 9, f. 90 November 29, 1471. Kuehn, *Emancipation,* p. 71, notes the frequency of such long term duplications in the acts.

Acts of emancipation did not always profoundly affect the status, nor impress the memories, of the participants.

Table 1

Professions of Fathers Who Emancipated
Sons at Florence by Frequency of Appearance, 1422-1500.

The unit counted here is the emancipated child. A father who emancipated two or more children, separately or together, is thus counted several times. Only the fifteen professions with the greater frequency of appearance are given.

Profession	Fathers	Sons
Notary	157	107
"Citizen and Merchant"	79	0
Shoemaker	63	8
Spice Merchant	55	3
"Worker of the Soil"	53	2
Wool Merchant	45	2
Baker	42	3
Weaver	41	5
Trader in Used Cloth	39	1
Dominus (Knight or Lawyer)	36	135
Medical Doctor	34	14
Carpenter	32	1
Linen Merchant	30	1
Butcher	29	1
Miller	25	0

Source: ASF, Rep. Not. Emanc., reg. 113.

Did the various professional groups emancipate their sons at approximately the same ages? To respond to this question we shall look at the recorded emancipations in the deposit "Repubblica," from 1422, when they first survive, until 1500.[20] The sample of emancipations studied here includes more than 4600 acts which freed from paternal authority some 5100 males and exactly 335 females. Slightly more than 80 percent of these recorded emancipations involved residents of Florence; the remaining 20 percent were inhabitants of the countryside, subject cities such as Pisa, and, rarely, foreign towns such as Venice.

In about one out of four instances, the registers give the occupation of the father and sometimes that of the emancipated son. Table

20. For a statistical analysis of emancipations in the Mercanzia and Repubblica archives from 1355 to 1534, see Kuehn, *Emancipation*, pp. 76-106. Kuehn does not, however, analyze the emancipations by professional categories.

1 shows the fifteen occupations, which the fathers profess most frequently. For purposes of comparison, the Table also gives the number of sons who pursue these same professions.

Among the fathers who emancipated their children, those who call themselves *civis et mercator florentinus*, "Florentine citizen and merchant," appear with notable frequency. Only notaries are encountered in the registers more often than the *mercatores,* but notaries also formed the largest single professional group within the city of Florence, at least in 1427.[21] There is, to be sure, a lingering imprecision in the meaning of the title, *civis et mercator* and those who bore it could in fact be members of any of the seven major guilds. Not only the notaries, but members of the other liberal professions—lawyers and medical doctors—frequently emancipated their sons, many of whom were destined to follow in their fathers' careers. We might also note that among the emancipated sons priests too are frequently observed (18 appearances). These men entered into confidential relations with their clients and often acted as their agents; they clearly could not remain under another's authority. Nonetheless, there is an important difference between the behavior here of notaries, lawyers and the like, and the merchants. The members of the liberal professions often delayed the emancipation of their sons until the latter had finished their formal training and already bore a professional title, *ser* or *messer.* Even among the artisans, the usual practice was to postpone emancipation until the son had finished his formal apprenticeship and was already engaged in a trade. In contrast, among the merchants, no emancipated son as yet bears the title *mercator.* The sons of merchants were thus emancipated at very young ages, well before they had finished their training and acquired a mastery of mercantile skills.

For 439 emancipated sons, between the years 1422 and 1500, the registers give ages.[22] Table 2 shows the average ages of emancipated sons, according to their fathers' professions.

The average age at emancipation, for all groups in society was 20,09 years, but of all groups in society, the merchants freed their offspring at the youngest ages. The sons of notaries had usually

21. On the distribution of professions, see D. Herlihy and C. Klapisch-Zuber, *Les Toscans,* p. 297.
22. Usually in the form, "greater than N. years." The ages here are treated statistically as equal to N. years.

Table 2

Ages of Sons at Emancipation, 1422-1500

	By Father's Profession		By Son's Profession	
Profession	Number	Avg. Age	Number	Avg. Age
Merchant	22	15.50	—	—
Retail merchant	8	15.75	—	—
Dyer	5	18.00	—	—
Spice Merchant	10	19.20	1	24.00
Leather Merchant (*galligarius*)	5	19.80	—	—
"Worker of the Soil"	9	20.11	—	—
Silk Merchant	7	22.57	—	—
Notary	11	23.45	6	21.83
Baker	8	27.63	—	—

Source: Same as Table 1.

passed their twenty-third birthday when they were freed, and the sons of bakers their twenty-seventh. In contrast, most sons of merchants were endowed with the power and the property to make their way in the world before they had attained age 16. Of all occupational groups, the mature merchants were the first to divest themselves of power and patrimony in favor of the young.

Was this early emancipation of sons characteristic of Florentine merchants only in the fifteenth century? Our sources, while not allowing rigorous tests, rather suggest that it was an abiding principle in the governance of the mercantile household. In the fourteenth century, for example, Matteo di Niccolò Corsini, a merchant who had spent 17 years in England and other foreign lands, emancipated his six sons at the following ages: Piero in 1382, at age 16; Niccolò in 1383, at age 10; Lodovico in the same year, at age 9; Giovanni in 1388, at 12 years; Bartolomeo, also in 1388, at age 9; and Neri, before he had reached his eighth birthday. [23] To be sure, the prevailing levels of mortality affected ages of emancipation. Frequent epidemics, and a shortened span of life in the population at large, allowed the young to enter adult careers at lower ages.[24] While the usual age at emancipation surely fluctuated over time, the conclusion stands: of all groups in society, the merchants were the first to

23. *Il libro di ricordanze dei Corsini, passim.*
24. See the comments of Herlihy and Klapisch-Zuber, *Les Toscans,* pp. 198-204.

dismantle the formal authority of the father, and to break his exclusive control over the family's resources.

Closely related with the emancipation and endowment of the merchant's son was his matriculation into a guild. In spite of the many excellent studies devoted to the Florentine guilds, much obscurity surrounds the timing and the significance of the act of enrollment.[25] Why, for example, was Giuliano di Ruberto Corsini matriculated twice in the guild of Por Santa Maria—once in 1480 and again some 26 years later, in 1506? Perhaps his tender years at his first matriculation—he was then age 3—left him with no clear recollection of that important event[26]. But why was Luigi di Piero Guicciardini also matriculated twice in the guild of money changers, in 1416, when he was 9 years old, and again in 1421, when he had reached the age of 14?[27] There was no discernible change in his status over the five years separating the two matriculations, and we can suggest no reason why the act was repeated.

Many events or occasions prompted the Florentines to matriculate themselves or their sons into guilds. Buonaccorso di Neri Pitti, author of a well-known set of memoirs, matriculated in the wool guild in 1429, when he was 76 years old.[28] The oddity here is that Buonaccorso had been a successful wool merchant for most of his adult life, and had even served several times as consul of the guild, since at least 1405.[29] The guild statutes consistently require that officers be duly matriculated members, but clearly this provision was not always respected. What persuaded Buonaccorso to enroll or re-enroll in the guild at the very close of his career? Facing death, he may have wished to gain for his soul the spiritual benefits, which the prayers and Masses of the brothers earned for the members, both living and deceased. Then too, facing death, he doubtlessly wished to set his temporal affairs in order. At the time he matriculated himself, he also enrolled all the male members of his family—his five sons,

---

25. See, for example, R. Morelli, *La seta fiorentina nel cinquecento* (Milan, 1976), pp. 2-4, on incomplete matriculation lists in the guild of Por Santa Maria.

26. ASF, Manoscritti, reg. 543, IV, ff. 48 (1480) and 154 (1506).

27. Luigi di Piero di messer Luigi Guicciardini was born on May 25, 1407, according to ASF, Tratte, reg. 443 b, f. 33. See further ASF, Manoscritti, reg. 544, ff. 1044 and 1058.

28. ASF, Manoscritti, reg. 539, May 18, 1429. He claims the "beneficium fratris;" the brother had been a member in 1373.

29. ASF, Tratte, reg. 147, January 1, 1405, mentions him as "capitudo lane."

Luca, Ruberto, Francesco, Neri and Luigi, who ranged in age from 12 to 35; and three grandsons, children of Luca, who were age 4, 7 and 11 respectively. Surely he hoped that the guild would protect his progeny and advance their careers, when Buonaccorso was no longer present to help them.

Some Florentines delayed matriculation until the death of their fathers, which often deprived them and their families of representation in the councils and among the members of the guild. Piero di messer Donato Velluti died late in 1424 or early in 1425. Within months of their father's death, four of his sons enrolled in the guild of money changers: Donato at age 38, Smeraldo at age 36, Guido at age 23, and Tommaso at age 21.[30] Still other Florentines enrolled only when they wished to make substantial investments in the commerce or trade under the guild's jurisdiction. Matteo di Niccolò Corsini joined the wool guild in 1366, at age 44, a few years before he became a partner in a wool shop at Florence.[31] Luca Pitti, son of Buonaccorso and builder of the Pitti palace, matriculated in the guild of money changers in 1419, when he was 24 years of age; in the wool guild in 1429, when he was 34; and in the guild of Por Santa Maria in 1441, at age 46. His choice of guilds seems to have followed the shifts in his business interests, which brought him in middle life into the silk trade.[32]

However, for most Florentines who aspired to be merchants, matriculation in at least one guild came at very young ages. Like formal emancipation, enrollment in a guild was a rite of passage, the young man's professional debut, his introduction into the society of merchants, with whom he would interact probably for the remainder of his life. The act of matriculation was often closely associated with emancipation, which it might either shortly precede or follow. Messer Giovanni Guicciardini enrolled his son Niccolò, then 7 years old, into the guild of money changers on April 4, 1421; and two months later, on June 26, into the guild of

30. ASF, Manoscritti, reg. 544, f. 1013, which notes also that the father is dead. Donato and Smeraldo in 1407 had matriculated in the wool guild, *ibid.* reg. 539, October 24, 1407.

31. ASF, Manoscritti, reg. 539, February 2, 1366. According to the *Ricordanze dei Corsini*, p. 39, he was a partner in a wool shop with Filippo Manente.

32. ASF, Manoscritti, reg. 539, May 18, 1429, Luca matriculates with brothers Ruberto, Francesco, Neri and Luigi. *Ibid.* reg. 543, II, f. 131, for Por Santa Maria, and reg. 544, f. 995, April 2, 1419, for Cambio.

Calimala. His father emancipated the boy the following March, when Niccolò had already passed his eighth birthday.[33] Messer Giovanni followed a reverse sequence in regard to his second son, Francesco. He first emancipated Francesco, age 12, in 1433, and then enrolled him among the merchants of Calimala, in December of the same year.[34]

The matriculation of these boy merchants was, to be sure, more often than not an empty gesture. Some never practiced the trade which their fathers had chosen for them, or any trade at all. Giovanni di Francesco Guicciardini, son of the Francesco mentioned above, was enrolled among the money changers in 1465 at age 13. But in 1480, at age 29, the tax assessors noted concerning him: "non fa né, sa fare mestiere."[35] On the other hand, many of these youngsters participated actively in the affairs of the guild, from surprisingly young ages. They, or their fathers for them, entered their names into the electoral purses. Drawings from the purses could yield, as candidates for consul the names of boys not much older than 10. Bartolomeo di Bertoldo Corsini, for example, had his name entered into the electoral purse of the wool guild in 1477, when he was 7 years of age and was scrutinized for the office of consul in 1482, at age 12.[36] The guild of money changers also considered him for consul at age 16.[37] The minimum age required for the consular office was 30 years. Why then were these boys, or their fathers, zealous to have their names included in the electoral purses? Repeated scrutinies of these flagrantly ineligible youths at least made them known to their older confrères, and gave them contacts and reputation, upon which their ultimate success might easily depend.

Emancipated, endowed, and enrolled in a guild often before their fifteenth year, did these boy merchants really participate in the com-

33. ASF, Manoscritti, reg. 544, f. 1002 and reg. 539, June 26, 1421. In both instances the boy is granted the beneficium patris; ASF, Rep., Not. Emanc., reg. 1 fol. 11, March 24, 1422.

34. ASF, Rep., Not. Emanc., reg. 2, f. 73; Manoscritti, reg. 544, f. 1010, August 17, 1425. Francesco was matriculated into the Calimala on December 5, 1433, Manoscritti, reg. 539, on that date, and apparently a second time into the Cambio, ibid., reg. 544, f. 1038, October 8, 1443.

35. ASF, Manoscritti, reg. 544, f. 1063, matriculated with "beneficium patris." ASF, Catasto, reg. 994, f. 367, Giovanni unmarried at the age of 29.

36. ASF, Mercanzia, reg. 87, December 17, 1482, with a note that his name was in the purse of 1477.

37. ASF, Mercanzia, reg. 87, August 19, 1486, but he is declared to be a minor.

mercial life of the city? In 1375, Gregorio di Stagio Dati was taken from school, where he was studying the abacus, and placed in the shop of silk merchants. He was then age 13. Later, when he composed his memoirs, he used a Latin phrase, with evident Biblical associations, to describe these early experiences: *inveni gratiam apud eos,* "I found favor among them."[38] Giannozzo Manetti, later to gain fame as a humanist, ended his formal education in letters and the abacus at age 10, at which time his father placed him at a banker's table. Within a few days, the gifted ten-year old was given responsibility for the *conto di cassa* presumably the cash accounts, and then the *scritture,* the complex books of the enterprise.[39] These child accountants thus served the economy, even as they gained the experience and, we should add, the physical maturity needed to make their grand assault upon fortune.

There can be little doubt that the merchant families actively sought to instill habits of self-reliance and independence in their young, and saw advantages in separating them, at least for a time, from close contact with their immediate relatives. "If you have a son," Paolo da Certaldo advises his readers in the early fourteenth century, "who is not doing well in your bosom or in your country, you should at once place him with a merchant, who will dispatch him to another land, or send him to a close friend. He will lose the customs of his own land and will adopt new customs, and perhaps he will reform, and will do better. You have no other choice since, if he remains with you, he will not change at all."[40] Paolo had no illusions about the power of parents to form their offspring in the image they preferred.

Another Florentine author, Giovanni Morelli, writing in the early 1400's, similarly praises the benefits of long sojourns in a foreign land, away from family, friends and fellow citizens. If you can spend two or three years abroad, he advises his young readers, "you will

38. Dati, *Il libro segreto,* p. 14.
39. *Vita di Giannozzo di Bernardo Manetti tratta da quella scritta da Naldo Naldi, Philippi Villani Liber de civitatis Florentiae famosis civibus ... et de Florentinorum litteratura principes fere synchroni scriptores,* ed. G.C. Galletti (Florence, 1847), p. 131: "Giannozzo di Bernardo Manetti nacque a di 5 di Giugno nel 1396, e dal padre, secondo il costume de' più de' Fiorentini, fu di pochissima età, doppo avergli fatto imparare i primi elementi, posto ad imparare l'abbaco; e di poi d'età di 10 anni messo al banco, in brevi giorni li fu dato il conto di cassa e di più le scritture."
40. Paolo Da Certaldo, *Il libro di buoni costumi, documento di vita trecentesca,* ed. A. Schiaffini (Florence, 1945), p. 121.

become more expert and experienced in all things, and have more understanding; you will learn how to communicate with other men; your reputation will grow and also your estate."[41]

Considerations of property and its management also prompted the merchants to emancipate and endow even very young sons. As the Florentine Catasto of 1427 shows, citizens after the approximate age of 55 tended to become poorer as they grew older, and merchants seem particularly vulnerable to declining fortunes in their later years.[42] There were several reasons for this. Old age deprived the merchant of vigor and income. The system of forced loans and taxes within the city, probably in an effort to stimulate births, allowed the father generous deductions for his dependent children, and favored young families with numerous progeny. It consequently saddled with heavy burdens unmarried youths and still more the aged, whose children had grown and departed. The mature merchant, well before his own death, was also obligated to transfer large portions of his accumulated wealth, as dowries to his daughters and as gifts to his emancipated sons. For if the endowment of sons was a burden to the aging, it was also, as we shall see, a manoeuvre which could protect the wealth of the family as it followed down the generations.

Matteo di Niccolò Corsini, one of the merchant authors who spent long years abroad, left an encumbered inheritance when he died at Florence in 1402, at age 79. In 1411 his heirs still had not satisfied the government's claims against it, for delinquent taxes.[43] Gregorio di Stagio Dati pursued a long and apparently successful career as a silk merchant, served as Standard Bearer of Justice, and was seven times consul of his guild. In his memoirs, he describes in mournful numbers his financial situation in 1433, when he was 71 years old.[44] In 1432 and 1433, the comment *in speculo,* "in the mirror," that is, in tax arrears, flags his name in the electoral lists.[45] Messer Luca di Buonaccorso Pitti, who, with his great palace, gave Florence an unprecedented display of private magnificence, also ended his life—he died at age 77— under a fiscal cloud. In 1480,

41. Giovanni di Pagolo Morelli, *Ricordi,* ed. V. Branca (Florence, 1969), p. 197.
42. Herlihy and Klapisch-Zuber, *Les Toscans,* p. 508.
43. ASF, Tratte, reg. 150, June 1, 1411, Niccolò di Matteo Corsini, is declared to be "pro patre in speculo."
44. Dati, *Il libro segreto,* p. 113.
45. ASF, Manoscritti, reg. 155, January 1, 1432 and January 1, 1433.

eight years after his death, one of his heirs declares, "the inheritance of messer Luca my father has many burdens of debts and bequests."[46] Many other examples could be given of merchants who, as they aged, slipped into fiscal arrears.

Under these conditions, the emancipation and endowment of the young shielded substantial portions of the family's wealth from claims for overdue taxes, unpaid debts and other ruinous obligations. The endowed son retained the option of renouncing his share in his father's remaining inheritance, in its debts as well as its assets. The career of Bertoldo di Bartolomeo Corsini, born in 1439, provides an example of one variant of this strategy. Bertoldo was the eldest of four brothers, all of whom resided in the same household. In 1480, he had been for seven years under court order to pay 1200 large florins to a former business partner, Giovanni Rucellai. Bertoldo, however, in the words of a tax declaration of that year, "transferred his property to his nephews and declared himself bankrupt."[47] His brothers, who prepared the informative tax declaration, affirmed that if they, or presumably their children, had to pay Bertoldo's debt, it would have meant the ruin of the household.

Early emancipations and endowment of sons thus distributed liabilities and assets as entrepreneurs would have preferred: the debilitated aged retained the debts, and the energetic young gained the capital. In 1433, Gregorio Dati, age 71, emancipated and endowed his last born son Antonio, age 9, and enrolled him in the guild of silk merchants.[48] That one so close to death—Gregorio died two years later—should have emancipated one so young might seem inexplicable, but Gregorio was, as mentioned, already in tax arrears, already facing government action against the property he retained. In 1481, Tommaso di Bertoldo Corsini, then 74 years of age, emancipated in a single act three sons, aged 26, 27 and 19 years respectively.[49] As might have been suspected, the aged Tommaso was

---

46. ASF, Catasto, reg. 996, f. 295. Six sons shared Luca's inheritance. See also ASF, Rep., Not. emanc. reg. 286, December 17, 1489, the wife of his son Spinetto asks for the return of the dowry since "dictus Spinettus eius vir vergat ad inopiam."

47 ASF, Catasto, reg. 996, f. 197.

48. ASF, Rep., Not. emanc., reg. 2, f. 88.

49. ASF, Rep., Not. emanc., reg. 10, f. 183, June 7, 1481. The sons are Bertoldo, Castello and Domenico.

similarly in tax arrears, and through this act presumably sought to save his property for his sons.[50]

Florentine tax officials viewed with understandable scepticism these acts of emancipation, and at times refused to accept the division of a father's patrimony through the endowment of his sons.[51] Although the tactic was not always successful, still it illustrates a fundamental strategy of merchants: the young should be supplied with capital, to help them maintain or repair the family fortune.

Emancipation, endowment, enrollment in a guild and entry into a business firm, did not, however, guarantee for the young merchant success and fortune. Rather, he now entered upon a spirited competition, which often required that he spend years away from his close family and from his fatherland, roaming through the markets and courts of Europe. Totto di Boninsegna Machiavelli, according to a statement filed in 1458 by his nephew Bernardo, the future father of the famed Niccolò, spent 34 years, trading in Flanders and in England.[52] Many, perhaps even most, would fail in this effort, and return home with empty hands, if they returned at all. The winners in this often ruthless competition gained substantial rewards: the chance to marry; the opportunity to enter as full partners into the family bank or company; and the invitation to serve as influential members in the councils and offices of guild and government.

Marriage was a reward for the successful, but the great families did not limit that reward to only a single son. Luca Pitti married probably at age 22, very young for a Florentine male.[53] Luca's marriage did not prevent his younger brother Ruberto from marrying, even before the death of their father.[54] Enjoying spectacular pros-

50. ASF, Mercanzia, reg. 87, April 4, 1481, in drawing for the consulate of the wool guild, Tommaso is found to be "in speculo."

51. The complex legal questions raised by emancipation and the conveyance of a *praemium* to the emancipated child are discussed at length in Kuehn, *Emancipation*, pp. 101-16.

52. ASF, Catasto, reg. 788, f. 710. "Perché e potrebbe essere che Totto di Boninsegna Machiavelli il qual'è tra in Fiandra e in Inghilterra a fare mercantie circa d'anni 34 nel detto tempo si potrebbe avere fatti molti e debitori e creditori de' quali dicto Bernardo non à certezza e però non li da ..."

53. In the Catasto declaration of 1427, ASF, Catasto, reg. 66, f. 154, Luca says that he is 35 1/2 years old, but according to ASF, Tratte, reg. 39, f. 23, he was born on June 1, 1395. He is married to a woman of 24, with a child of 9 years of age.

54. ASF, Catasto, eg. 66, f. 154. Ruberto declares his age as 29 1/2 years, but he was only 25; his birthday was April 25, 1402 according to Tratte, reg. 39, f. 35. He is married to a woman age 18. It was quite common for Florentine males to declare

perity, the Pitti show no inclination to limit their own numbers. Six of Luca's own sons married. As he explained in a petition to the government in 1461, the needs of a numerous progeny and his desire to house them all together in appropriate comfort led him to begin the construction of his great palace.[55] Among the merchants, marriage was a goal to which all sons could aspire. But it still required of them a substantial measure of economic success.

A second reward offered to the successful young merchant was admission to full partnership in the family bank. It is a commonplace in economic history that the great Tuscan banks and business companies of the Middle Ages were family-based enterprises. In 1342, for example, the members of the house of Bardi appeared before a notary, to swear to preserve peace with their traditional enemies, the Buondelmonti.[56] The Bardi who took the oath, whether in person or by proxy, numbered 120 adult males. The first-named among the conjurors and the titular head of the house, messer Ridolfo di Bartolo, was at the same time head of the Bardi bank.[57] But the number of partners in the Bardi bank in 1310 was only 16, and only 10 of these were related to the Bardi in the male line. One of the most active partners was a Machiavelli.[58] The number of partners, and the proportions of Bardi among them, did not change substantially, through the bank's frequent reorganizations, during the first half of the fourteenth century. Of the 315 factors listed by Sapori, only nine can be identified as members of the family. Numerous Bardi were doubtlessly depositors in the bank, but otherwise the great majority of the house took no active role in the management of the enterprise which bore their name. The Bardi bank was a family business only in a loose sense. It was governed by a small and highly selected group of businessmen. There was no assurance that the sons of partners would become partners in their

themselves older than they were in fact. See Herlihy and Klapisch-Zuber, *Les Toscans*, p. 359.

55. ASF, Catasto, reg. 906, f. 49. "Una chasa per mio abitare e una chasa nuova la quale chasa ha murata per muro medesimamente per mio abbitare per la mia famiglia e chosì tre altre chasette le quali tengho ... per mio abitare."

56. ASF, Balìe, reg. 1, f. 1, September 18, 1342.

57. The bank is named the "societas Bardorum de Florentia que appellatur societas domini Rodulfi de Bardis et sociorum." See ASF, Notarile, reg. B 1951, f. 33, May 2, 1334.

58. Sapori, *La crisi*, studies the various reorganizations of the bank and gives lists of partners; see p. 249 for Gherardo di Boninsegna Machiavelli.

turn. The directorship passed from Iacopo, its chief in ca. 1300, to his brother, ser Lapo di messer Iacopo, and then to his nephew, son of another brother, Doffo di Bartolo, who later calls himself messer Ridolfo.[59] Doffo or messer Ridolfo ruled the bank for more than 40 years, and after his death, in a reorganization of 1357, the directorship passed to another nephew, Filippo di Bartolo di messer Iacopo.[60] Leadership within the bank thus easily shifted among the family's component branches.

Success for the young merchant further brought with it the occasion, and the duty, to serve in the various offices of guild and government. The authors of the family memoirs often note with pride how many offices they, or an honored relative, had held. Between 1387 and 1435, by our rough count, Gregorio Dati served the commune in various capacities more than sixty times. Like marriage and a partnership in a successful business, the frequent tenure of office, the prestige it conveyed within the community, were both reward and symbol of a successful career.

Our records also illuminate the dismal fate of the many who lost in the race for fortune. Some could not support a wife and children, or even maintain a residence at Florence. In 1480, for example, Antonio di Geri Bardi, age 54 and still unmarried, declared to the tax assessors that he was "sanza alchuno esercizio."[61] He resided with a brother, age 44 and also a bachelor, who lived "sanza stare a bottega." A lame and unmarried sister, age 50, completed the wretched household. Although they filed their return in the city, they apparently resided in Castellina in Chianti, where their father, similarly impoverished, was living in 1430.[62] Vannozzo di Simone Bardi, married but living with a bachelor brother, similarly could no longer afford to live in Florence.[63] In 1480 the tax assessors said of his son Iacopo, then age 22: "Nonne sta a botegha, istà in villa chon su padre e sua madre per non potere istare a Firenze per debito gravido ch'à suo padre."[64] Every generation, several impoverished branches of the great Florentine houses were forced to retreat to the

59. Sapori, La crisi, p. 244. He appears as a knight from 1322.
60. Ibid., p. 262.
61. ASF, Catasto, reg. 992, f. 7.
62. ASF, Catasto, reg. 393, f. 285. Geri di Geri Bardi lives "dentro alle mura della Chastellina di Chianti."
63. ASF, Catasto, reg. 785, f. 416 (1458).
64. ASF, Catasto, reg. 993, f. 316.

countryside—often to those same rural areas whence, years before, their ancestors had emerged to challenge the city.

What does this consideration of mercantile careers tell us of the character and solidarity of the merchant family? We must, it appears, consider the solidarity of the great houses on several levels. Juridically and economically, the merchant families allowed their offspring, from an early age, a maximum of independence. Historians have often assumed that fathers and adult sons, or the sons alone, sharing a common patrimony, comprised the earliest commercial companies in Tuscany.[65] But these arrangements, if they ever existed—and they are distinctly hard to detect, even in our earliest sources—must at once have displayed critical disadvantages. It was difficult to maintain the shadow of a single will over merchants, whose affairs took them to the far corners of the world. Even the effort to do so would obstruct the merchant in a basic purpose of his art, in his quest for unforseeable, but not unexpected, opportunities. To delay decisive action, to await permission from a far-off father, might mean, for a young merchant, to miss the main chance of his life.

The family of merchants also needed to maintain clear lines of ownership, authority and responsibility over the vital capital which supported its activities. A father or brother could not accept unlimited responsibility for the actions of sons or brothers who might be hundreds of miles from Florence. When the mercantile family came to include two or more adult males—whether a father and sons, or the sons of a deceased father—these natural partners tended rather quickly to divide the common patrimony, whether through emancipations and endowments, or the division among heirs. True, the father and his sons, or the sons alone, then frequently reintegrated the patrimony, in whole or in part, through notarized agreements. But the notarized stipulations, unlike the play of inheritances, spelled out clearly who owned what shares in, who could expect what profits from, and who could exercise authority over, the common enterprise. The Tuscan commercial company, even in the thirteenth century, was not a natural association of persons and capital; it was, like Burckhardt's conception of the Renaissance state, a work of art.

The economic and juridic structure of the great mercantile house was thus based on marked individualism—on the juridical auton-

65. A thesis most recently defended by Goldthwaite, *Private Wealth*.

omy of the individual and the separate ownership of the family's resources. On the other hand, on a moral and cultural level, the family sought to develop a strong sense of collective identity, which would contain the very individualism it elsewhere allowed. Toward that end, it adopted several strategies. Within the city, the numerous branches of the great houses tended to live in close proximity to one another, in the same ward or even on the same street.[66] The Bardi, for example, the largest of all Florentine houses in 1427 as it probably had been since the early fourteenth century, lived chiefly in the quarter of Santo Spirito, ward of Scala, and on the street which even today bears their name, the Via dei Bardi. The desire to live near to one's relatives inspired messer Luca Pitti, as we have mentioned, to build his palace, which would be big enough to lodge the families of six married sons, some of whom were as prolific as Luca. The community of the Pitti, established in Luca's "great house," gives excellent illustration to the principles embodied in the governance of a large *domus*. All of Luca's six sons were emancipated, all separately endowed, most seem to have pursued their separate economic interests, and all eventually married. They were not at all partners or participants in a common economic enterprise. But they all lived together, manifesting and surely themselves sensing the solidarity of the lineage of Luca Pitti.

These strategies affected the histories and the structures of the great Florentine houses in distinctive ways. The policy of permitting several sons to marry gave the lineage the power to grow in size with extraordinary rapidity. The Bardi, for example, though magnate in status, formed a comparatively new consorteria at Florence. The founder of the family's fortunes appears to have been Ricco di Bardo or Riccus Bardi, who is mentioned in the records of the guild of Calimala from 1235 to 1254.[67] Ricco had at least seven sons, most of whom were similarly prolific.[68] By 1342, only three or four generations after Ricco, the house of Bardi included more than 120 adult male members, and was most likely, as we have mentioned, the largest consortena in the city.

66. C. Klapisch-Zuber, "Parenti, amici, vicini. Il territorio urbano d'una famiglia mercantile nel XV secolo," *Quaderni Storici*, 33 (1976), pp. 953-82.
67. ASF, Manoscritti, reg. 544, f. 491, lists him among the merchants of Calimala, and f. 498 names him as consul in 1245 and 1254.
68. They are named in ASF, Notarile, reg. B 1950, f. 102, January 1, 1314, copy of will dated 1278.

In allowing many sons to marry, in giving no decisive advantage to a first-born son or to any single son, the great houses maintained no clear distinction between senior and cadet branches. Messer Luca di Buonaccorso, the richest Pitti of his day, was the eldest son, but his father Buonaccorso was the fourth of nine sons. His grandfather Neri was the fifth of six sons.[69] The fortunes of these mercantile houses were critically dependent upon early recognition of their most talented members. The mercantile family was organized not for the cautious defense of inherited positions, but for the constant renewal of their fortunes, through the energies of their young, in the markets of the world.

In sum, among the merchants of Florence, both individuals and families sought to achieve related but distinct aims. The goal of the merchant's son was the early and active pursuit of fortune. The goal of his family was to guard the traditions which inspired him, and to protect and aid him on his way. The solidarity of the mercantile houses was real, but was also designed to support and not to suppress the freedom and initiative of their members.

69. *Cronica di Buonaccorso*, pp. 12 and 13.

11

MEDIEVAL CHILDREN

✦ ✦ ✦

In a fourteenth-century French poem, one of numerous surviving depictions of the danse macabre, the grim choreographer invites a baby to join his somber revels. "Ah, ah, ah," protests the infant, "I do not know how to speak; I am a baby, and my tongue is mute. Yesterday I was born, and today I must depart. I do no more than come and go."[1]

Many, perhaps most, children in most traditional societies did no more than come and go. And most never acquired, or were given, a voice which might have recorded and preserved their impressions concerning themselves, their parents, and the world they had recently discovered. Of all social groups which formed the societies of the past, children, seldom seen and rarely heard in the documents, remain for historians the most elusive, the most obscure.

The difficulties of interviewing the mute have doubtlessly obstructed and delayed a systematic investigation of the history of childhood. But today, at least, historians are aware of the commonplace assumption of psychologists, that childhood plays a critical role in the formation of the adult personality. Perhaps they are awakening to an even older wisdom, the recognition that society, in the way it rears its children shapes itself. "Childhood is the foundation of life," wrote Philippe of Navarre, the thirteenth-century lawyer and chronicler, "and on good foundations one can raise great and good

1. "A, a, a, je ne scey parler;/Enfant suis, j'ay la langue mue/Hier naquis, huy m'en fault aller/Je ne faiz qu'entree et yssue" J. Gerson, "La Danse Macabre," in *Oeuvres complètes,* ed. P. Glorieux (Paris and New York, 1966), 7, p. 298.

buildings."[2] This medieval man already sensed that the foundations of childhood help shape and support the structures of civilization.

Today, the literature devoted to the history of children in various places and epochs may be described, rather like children themselves, as small but growing daily. It remains, however difficult to discern within that literature, a clear consensus, and acceptable hypothesis, concerning the broad trends of children's history, even within Western societies. To be sure, there is frequent allusion within these recent publications to a particular interpretation which, for want of a better name, we shall call the "theory of discovered childhood." The principal formulator of this interpretation, at least in its most recent form, has been the French social historian Philippe Ariès. In a book published in 1960, called in its English translation *Centuries of Childhood*, Ariès entitled the second chapter "the discovery of childhood."[3] In it he affirmed that the Middle Ages of Western history did not recognize childhood as a distinct phase in life. Medieval people allegedly viewed and treated their children as imperfectly formed adults. Once the infant was weaned, medieval parents supposedly made no concessions to its special and changing psychological needs and took little satisfaction in the distinctive traits of the young personality. The corollary to this assumption is that, at some point in the development of Western society and civilization, the young years of life were at last discovered: childhood needed a Columbus.

Proclamations of the alleged discovery of childhood have become commonplace in the growing literature, but wide differences in interpretation still separate the authors. When, for example, was childhood first recognized? On this important question, Ariès himself is indefinite, even evasive, and seems to place the discovery over three or four hundred years, from the fifteenth to eighteenth centuries.[4] A recent collection of essays, edited by Lloyd de Mause

2. "... car enfance est li fondemenz de vie, et sor bons fondemenz puet on bastir granz edifiz et bons," *Les quatre âges de l'homme: Traité moral de Philippe de Navarre*, ed. M. de Fréville (Paris, 1888), p. 27.

3. *L'enfant et la vie familiale sous l'ancien régime* (1st ed., Paris, 1960; 2nd ed., Paris, 1973), pp. 24–41 of the first edition from the chapter entitled "La découverte de l'enfance." The work is translated as *Centuries of Childhood: A Social History of Family Life,* trans. R. Boldick (New York, 1962).

4. *L'enfante et la vie familiale,* p. 460. G. Boas, *The Cult of Childhood* (London, 1966), p. 21, finds "the beginnings of the cult of childhood in the scepticism of the

and published in 1974 under the title *The History of Childhood*, proposes several candidates, in several periods, for the honor of having first explored childhood in the Western world. M. J. Tucker, writing on English children between the years 1399 and 1603, begins his chapter with the now orthodox affirmation: "The medieval idea that children were not terribly important persists into the fifteenth century."[5] In the conclusion of the chapter, adopting the interpretation of Ivy Pinchbek and Margaret Hewitt, he declares: "A new consciousness of childhood was beginning."[6] Later in the same volume, Priscilla Robertson selects Jean Jacques Rousseau as the first advertiser of childhood: "Special credit must go to Rousseau for calling attention to the needs of children. For the first time in history, he made a large group of people believe that childhood was worth the attention of adults, encouraging an interest in the process of growing up rather than just the product."[7]

The editor of a collection of studies, Lloyd de Mause, presents still another view of the emerging consciousness of childhood.[8] A devout believer in the idea of continuous and irreversible progress, de Mause traces the evolution in child-parent or child-mother relations through six styles of behavior, or psychogenic modes as he calls them: the infanticidal in the ancient world; abandonment in the Middle Ages; the ambivalent, intrusive, and socialization modes across the succeeding centuries; and now, at the term of this evolution, the helping mode. The helping mode "involves the proposition that the child knows better than the parent what it needs at each stage of its life."[9] Parents who help the child attain what he wants will render him "gentle, sincere, never depressed, never imitative or group-oriented, strong-willed, and unintimidated by authority."[10] According to de Mause, the full discovery of childhood and the full

---

sixteenth century." Boas does not seem to be aware of Ariès' earlier publication on the history of childhood.

5. "The Child as Beginning and End: Fifteenth and Sixteenth Century English Childhood," in *The History of Childhood,* ed. L. de Mause (New York, 1974), p. 229.

6. *Ibid.,* p. 252; and I. Pinchbek and M. Hewitt, *Children in English Society* (London, 1969), 1, p. 41.

7. *History of Childhood,* ed. de Mause, p. 407.

8. *Ibid.,* pp. 1–74. See also his reply to criticism of his views in idem, "The Formation of the American Personality through Psychospeciation," *Journal of Psychohistory* , 4 (1976), pp. 1–30.

9. *History of Childhood,* ed. de Mause, p. 52.

10. *Ibid.,* p. 54.

recognition across society of its special nature and distinctive needs are only now occurring.

If historians of the modern world do not agree concerning the date of childhood's discovery, their colleagues, working in more remote periods, show signs of restiveness with Ariès' postulate, that medieval people did not distinguish children from adults. A number of scholars—Christian Bec, Christiane Klapisch, Richard Goldthwaite, among others—have noted among the pedagogues, humanists, and even artists of fifteenth-century Italy a new orientation toward children, a new awareness of their problems, and an appreciation of their qualities.[11] The fat and frolicksome babies, the *putti*, who cavort through many solemn paintings of the Italian Renaissance, leave little doubt that the artists of the epoch knew how to depict, and they or their patrons liked to contemplate, children. A still more radical departure from Ariès' views was proposed, in 1968, by the French medievalist Pierre Riché. Riché accepted Ariès' phrase, the "discovery of childhood," but radically changed his chronology.[12] The initial explorers of childhood were, for Riché, the monastic pedagogues active in Western Europe between the sixth and eighth centuries. Their sensitivity toward the psychology of children allegedly transformed the harsh educational methods of classical antiquity and developed a new pedagogy which was finely attuned to the personality of the child-monk. Thus, over an extended period of time, from the early Middle Ages until the present, one or another author would have us believe that a consciousness of childhood was at last emerging.

The lessons that I would draw from this confusion of learned opinions are the following. Historians would be well advised to avoid such categoric and dubious claims, that people in certain

---

11. C. Bec, *Les marchands écrivains: Affaires et humanisme à Florence, 1376–1434* (Paris and The Hague, 1967), pp. 286–299; C. Klapisch, "L'enfance en Toscane au début du XVe siècle," *Annales de démographie historique,* 1973, pp. 99–127; R. Goldthwaite, "The Florentine Palace as Domestic Architecture," *American Historical Review,* 77 (1972), pp. 1009–1010. For further criticism of Ariès' use of medieval iconographical evidence, see I. Forsyth, "Children in Early Medieval Art: Ninth through Twelfth Centuries," *Journal of Psychohistory ,* 4 (1976), pp. 31–70.

12. P. Riché, "Découverte de l'enfant," in *De l'éducation antique à l'éducation chevaleresque,* Questions d'histoire (Paris, 1968), p. 30. Compare his remarks in his earlier, large work *Education et culture dans l'Occident barbare, VIe–VIIIe siècles,* Patristica sorbonensia, 4 (Paris, 1962), p. 505: "Les moines ont-ils redécouvert la nature enfantine et toutes ses richesses? Disons plutôt qu'ils ont suivi les enseignements du Christ et non la tradition romaine."

periods failed to distinguish children from adults, that childhood really did lie beyond the pale of collective consciousness. Attitudes toward children have certainly shifted, as has the willingness on the part of society to invest substantially in their welfare or education. But to describe these changes, we need terms more refined than metaphors of ignorance and discovery. I would propose that we seek to evaluate, and on occasion even to measure, the psychological and economic investment which families and societies in the past were willing to make in their children. However, we ought also to recognize that alternative and even competitive sets of child-related values can coexist in the same society, perhaps even in the same household. Different social groups and classes expect different things from their children; so do different epochs, in accordance with prevailing economic, social, and demographic conditions. In examining the ways in which children were regarded and reared in the past, we should not expect either rigorous consistency across society or lineal progress over time.

In the current, lively efforts to reconstruct the history of children in Western civilization, the long period of the Middle Ages has a special importance. The medieval child represents a kind of primordial form, an "eo-pais," a "dawn-child" as it were, against whom Western children of subsequent epochs must be measured if we are to appreciate the changes they have experienced. To be sure, the difficulties of observing medieval children cannot be discounted. Medieval documentation is usually sparse, often inconsistent, and always difficult. The halls of medieval history, running across one thousand years, are filled with lights and shadows. The shadows are particularly murky when they enclose those who "do no more than come and go." We can hope to catch only fleeting glimpses of medieval children in their rush through, or out of, life. On the other hand, even glimpses may be enough to dispel some large misconceptions concerning medieval children and to aid us toward a sound reconstruction of the history of children in the Western world.

In surveying medieval children, it is first necessary to consider the two prior traditions which largely shaped the medieval appraisal of the very young—the classical and the barbarian. It is important also to reflect upon the influence exerted upon child rearing by a special component of the ancient Mediterranean heritage: the Christian church.

Classical society, or at least the elites within it, cultivated an impressive array of intellectual traditions, which were founded upon literacy and preserved over time through intensive, and expensive, educational methods. Classical civilization would be inconceivable in the absence of professional teachers, formal instruction, and numerous schools and academies. But as social historians of antiquity now emphasize, the resources that supported ancient society were in truth, scant. "The classical Mediterranean has always been a world on the edge of starvation," one historian has recently written, with much justice if perhaps some exaggeration.[13] Scarce resources and the high costs of rearing children helped form certain distinctive policies regarding the young. The nations which comprised the Roman Empire, with the exception only of Jews, refused to support deformed, unpromising, or supernumerary babies.[14] In Roman practice, for example, the newborn baby was at once laid before the feet of him who held the *patria potestas* over it, usually the natural father. Through a ritual gesture called *susceptio,* the holder of paternal authority might raise up the infant and receive it into his family and household. But he could also reject the baby and order its exposure. Infanticide, or the exposure of infants, was a common and accepted social practice in classical society, shocking perhaps to modern sensibilities but rational for these ancient peoples who were seeking to achieve goals with limited means.

Here however is a paradox. Widespread infanticide in ancient society does not imply disinterest in or neglect of those children elected for survival. On the contrary, to assure a good return on the precious means invested in them, they were subject to close and often cruel attention and to frequent beatings. St. Augustine in his *Confessions* tells how his father, Patricius, even his pious mother, Monica, urged him to high performance at school, "that I might get on in the world and excel in the handling of words, to gain honor

13. P. Brown, *The World of Late Antiquity, A.D. 150–750,* History of European Civilization Library, ed. G. Barraclough (London, 1971), p. 12.
14. See R. Etienne, "Ancient Medical Conscience and the Life of Children," *Journal of Psychohistory,* 4 (1976), pp. 131–161, translated from the French article which appeared in the *Annales de démographie historique,* 1973: "… the right to commit infanticide was one of the attributes of *patria potestas*" (p. 134). See also the old but informative work of L. Lallemand, *Histoire des enfants abandonnés et délaissés: Etudes sur la protection de l'enfance* (Paris, 1885), pp. 31–71. Philo the Jew seems to have been the earliest ancient writer who explicitly condemned the practice of infanticide (see *History of Childhood,* ed. de Mause, p. 28).

among men and deceitful riches."[15] "If I proved idle in learning," he says of his teachers, "I was soundly beaten. For this procedure seemed wise to our ancestors; and many, passing the same way in the days past, had built a sorrowful road, by which we too must go, with multiplication of grief and toil upon the sons of Adam."[16] The memories which the men of antiquity preserved of their childhood were understandably bleak. "Who would not shudder," Augustine exclaims in the *City of God*, "if he were given the choice of eternal death or life again as a child? Who would not choose to die?"[17]

The barbarian child grew up under quite different circumstances. Moreover, barbarian practices of child rearing seem to have been particularly influential in the society of early medieval Europe, between the fifth and eleventh centuries. This is not surprising. Early in the Middle Ages, the cities which had dominated society and culture in antiquity lost importance, the literate social elites of classical society all but disappeared, and their educational institutions and ideals went down amid the debacle of the Western empire. On the other hand, barbarian practices were easily preserved within, and congenial to, the semibarbarized society of the early medieval West.

In a tract called *Germania*, written in A.D. 98, the Roman historian Tacitus has described for us the customs of the barbarian Germans, including their treatment of children. Tacitus, to be sure, likes to contrast barbarian virtues with Roman vices and doubtlessly exaggerates in his depictions of both, but his words are nonetheless worth our attention. The Germans, he claims, did not, like the Romans, kill their supernumerary children.[18] Rather, the barbarians rejoiced in a numerous progeny. Moreover, the barbarian mother, unlike her Roman counterpart, nursed her own baby and did not hand it over for feeding to servants or a hired nurse. On the other hand, Tacitus notes, the barbarian parents paid little attention to

15. *Confessionum libri tredecim*, ed. P. Knoell and M. Skutella (Leipzig, 1934), 1, p. 9; *Confessions of St. Augustine*, trans. F. J. Sheed (London, 1944), p. 8.

16. *Ibid.*

17. "Quis autem non exhorreat, et mori eligat, si ei proponatur, aut mors perpetienda, aut rursus infantia?" in *De civitate Dei*, ed. B. Dombart (Leipzig, 1909), 21, p. 14. In the judgment of George Boas, "in general the Ancients had a low opinion of children if the appraised them at all" (*Cult of Childhood*, p. 12).

18. *De Germania*, ed. C. Halm (Leipzig, 1911), chap. 19: "To limit the number of children or to put any of the later children to death is considered a crime, and with them good customs are of more avail than good laws elsewhere." The translation is taken from *Medieval Culture and Society*, ed. D. Herlihy (New York, 1968), p. 29.

their growing children. "In every household," he writes, "the children grow up naked and unkempt ..."[19] "The lord and slave," he
continues, "are in no way to be distinguished by the delicacy of
their bringing up. They live among the same flocks, they lie on the
same ground ..." Barbarian culture did not depend for its survival on
the costly instruction of the young in complex skills and learned traditions; barbarian parents had no need to invest heavily in their children, either psychologically or materially. The cheap costs of child
rearing precluded the adoption of infanticide as standard social policy but also reduced the attention which the growing child received
from its parents only. Only on the threshold of adulthood did the
free German male re-establish close contacts with adult society. He
typically joined the following of a mature warrior, accompanied
him into battle, observed him, and gained some instruction in the
arts of war, which, like the arts of rhetoric in the classical world,
were the key to his social advance.

A casual attitude toward children seems embodied in the laws of
the barbarian peoples—Franks, Lombards, Visigoths, Anglo-Saxons
and others—which were redacted into Latin largely between the
sixth and the ninth centuries. The barbarian laws typically assigned
to each member of society a sum of money—a fine, or wergeld—
which would have to be paid to the relatives if he or she was injured
or killed. The size of the wergeld thus provides a crude measure of
social status or importance. One of the barbarian codes, the Visigothic, dating from the middle seventh century, gives a particularly
detailed and instructive table of values which shows how the worth
of a person varied according to age, sex, and status.[20] A free male
baby, in the first year of life, was assigned a wergeld of 60 solidi.
Between age 1 and age 9, his social worth increased at a average
rate of only 3.75 solidi per year, thus attaining the value of 90 solidi
in the tenth year of life. Between ages 10 and 15, the rate of increase
accelerated to 10 solidi per year; and between ages 15 and 20 it
grew still more, to 30 solidi per year. In other words, the social
worth of the free Visigothic male increased very slowly in the early
years of childhood, accelerated in early adolescence, and grew
most substantially in the years preceding full maturity. Considered

19. *Germania,* chap. 20: *Medieval Culture and Society,* ed. Herlihy, p. 29.
20. *Leges visigothorum,* ed. K. Zeumer, Legum Sectio I, Legum nationum
germanicarum, 1 (Hanover and Leipzig, 1902), pp. 336–337.

mature at age 20, he enjoyed a wergeld of 300 solidi—five time the worth of the newborn male infant—and this he retained until age 50. In old age, his social worth declined, to 200 solidi between ages 50 and 65 and to 100 solidi from age 65 to death. The old man, beyond age 65, was worth the same as a child of ten years.

The contrast between the worth of the child and the worth of the adult is particularly striking in regard to women. Among the Visigoths, a female under age 15 was assigned only one-half the wergeld enjoyed by males—only 30 during her first year of life. Her social worth, however, increased enormously when she entered the years of childbearing, between ages 15 and 40 in the Visigothic codes. Her wergeld then leaped to 250 solidi, nearly equal to the 300 solidi assigned to the male and eight times the value of the newborn baby girl. The sterile years of old age brought a reduction of the fine, first to 200 solidi, which she retained to age 60, and then to 100 solidi. In old age, she was assigned the same worth as the male.

The contrasts in the social worth of the female child and the female adult are also sharp in the laws of the Salian and Ripuarian Franks. The wergeld of the free woman was tripled during her years of childbearing, when she was also considered worth three times the free male.[21]

The low values assigned to children in these barbarian codes is puzzling. Did the lawgivers not realize that the supply of adults, including the especially valued childbearing women, was critically dependent on the protection of children? This obvious truth seemingly escaped the notice of the barbarian lawgivers; children, and their relation to society, did not loom large in their consciousness.

Apart from laws, one other source offers some insight into the treatment of children in the early Middle Ages: surveys of the population settled on particular estates and manors. These sporadic surveys have survived from the Carolingian period of medieval history, the late eighth and ninth centuries. The largest of them, redacted in the first quarter of the ninth century, lists nearly 2,000 families settled on the lands of the abbey of Saint-Germain-des-Prés near Paris.[22] The

21. *Lex ribuaria*, ed. F. Beyerle and R. Büchner, Legum Sectio I, Legum nationum germanicarum, III, 2 (Hanover, 1954), p. 78, "De homicidiis mulierum." *Pactus Legis salicae*, ed. K. A. Eckhardt, Legum Sectio I, Legum nationum germanicarum, IV, 1 (Hanover, 1962), p. 92.

22. *Polyptyque de l'Abbé Irminon*, ed. B. Guérard, 2 vols. (Paris, 1844). With the aid of Mr. Larry Poos, I have prepared a machine-readable edition of the survey, and the figures cited in this article are derived from a computer-assisted analysis of the document.

survey gives no exact ages, but of 8,457 persons included in it, 3,327 are explicitly identified as *infantes,* or children. Another 3,924 may be certainly regarded as adults, as they appear in the survey with a spouse or with offspring. Some 1,206 other persons cannot be classified by age; they are offspring not expressly called *infantes* or persons of uncertain age or status within the households.

The proportion of known children within the population is very low—only 85 children for every 100 adults. Even if all those of uncertain age are considered *infantes,* the ratio then becomes 116 children for every 100 adults. This peasant population was either singularly barren or it was not bothering to report all its children. Moreover, the sexual composition of the population across these age categories is perplexing. Among the known adults, men and women appear in nearly equal numbers.[23] But among the known children, there are 143 boys for every 100 girls—a male-to-female ratio of nearly three to two. Among those of uncertain age, the sex ratio is even higher. The high sex ratio among the known children may indicate widespread female infanticide, but if this were so, we should expect to find a similarly skewed ratio among the known adults.[24] The death of numerous baby girls inevitably would affect over time the proportions of adult women in this presumably closed population. But the proportions of males and females among the known adults are reasonably balanced. The more likely explanation is that the monastic surveyors, or the peasants who reported to them, were negligent in counting children and were particularly deficient in reporting the presence of little girls in the households. As the barbarian legal codes suggest, children, and especially girls, became of substantial interest to society, and presumably to their families, only as they aged.

The low monetary worth assigned to the very young, and the shadowy presence of children in the statistical documents of the

23. Among those of uncertain age status, the sex ratio is even higher—384.3 or 957 men and 249 women.

24. For a different interpretation of these high sex ratios among the children in this survey, see E. R. Coleman, "Infanticide in the Early Middle Ages," in *Women in Medieval Society,* ed. S. M. Stuard (Philadelphia, 1976), pp. 47–70. The serfs of the monastery of Farfa in central Italy, who were listed in a survey dated ca. 820, similarly show a high sex ratio among children, 136.1. The sex ratio for the entire population is 118.1. This survey of 244 households is published in *Il Chronicon farfense di Gregorio di Catino,* ed. U. Balzani, Fonti per la storia d'Italia, 33–34 (Rome, 1903), 1, pp. 261–275. The figures were calculated by Richard Ring, who will soon publish an extended study of the families of Farfa.

early Middle Ages, should not, however, imply that parents did not love their children. Tacitus notes that the barbarian mother usually nursed her own babies. Kinship ties were strongly emphasized in barbarian society, and these were surely cemented by affection. The German epic fragment the *Song of Hildebrand* takes as its principal theme the love which should unite father and son.[25] The warrior Hildebrand flees into exile to live among the Huns, leaving "a babe at the breast in the bower of the bride." Then, after sixty years of wandering, he confronts his son as his enemy on the field of battle. He recognizes his offspring and tries to avoid combat; he offers the young warrior gold and, as the poet tells us, his love besides. But Hadubrand refuses to believe that the old warrior he faces is truly his father. The conclusion of the poem is lost, but the mood portends tragedy. The poet plays upon the irony that Hildebrand dearly loves his son but has been absent from his life for sixty years. The German warrior might have had difficulty recognizing his children, but he still felt affection for them. If classical methods of child rearing can be called cruel but closely attentive, the barbarian child grew up within an atmosphere of affectionate neglect.

The Christian church also powerfully influenced the treatment of children in many complex ways. Christianity, like Judaism before it, unequivocally condemned infanticide or the exposure of infants. To be sure, infanticide and exposure remained common social practices in Western Europe across the entire length of the Middle Ages. Church councils, penitentials, sermons, and secular legal codes yield abundant and repeated references to those crimes.[26] As late as the fifteenth century, if we are able to believe the great popular preachers of the period, the streams and cesspools of Europe echoed with the cries of abandoned babies.[27] But medieval infanticide still shows one great difference from the comparable practice in the ancient world. Our sources consistently attribute the practice to two

25. *The Hildebrandslied,* trans. F. A. Wood (Chicago, 1914), pp. 4–7. For a general treatment of the child in Old German literature, see U. Grey, *Das Bild des Kindes im Spiegel der altdeutschen Dichtung und Literatur mit textkritischer Ausgabe von Metlingers "Regiment der jungen Kinder"*, Europäische Hochschulschriften, Reihe I, Deutsche Literatur und Germanistik, 91 (Bern - Frankfurt, 1974).

26. On ecclesiastical condemnations of infanticide, see L. Godefroy, "Infanticide," *Dictionnaire de théologie catholique*, VIII, 2 (Paris, 1927), pp. 1717–1726.

27. Y. B. Brissaud, "L'infanticide à la fin du moyen âge," *Revue historique de droit français et étranger*, 50 (1972), pp. 229–256.

motivations: the shame of seduced and abandoned women, who wished to conceal illegitimate births, and poverty—the inability of the mother, and often of both parents, to support an additional mouth.[28] The killing or abandonment of babies in medieval society was the characteristic resort of the fallen, the poor, the desperate. In the ancient world, infanticide had been accepted practice, even among the social elites.

Christian teachings also informed and softened attitudes toward children. Christian scriptures held out several examples of children who enjoyed or earned God's special favor: in the Old Testament, the young Samuel and the young Daniel; in the New, the Holy Innocents and the Christ child himself. According to the evangelists, Jesus himself welcomed the company of children, and he instructed his disciples in the famous words: "Unless you become as little children, you will never enter the Kingdom of Heaven."[29]

This partiality toward children evoked many echoes among patristic and medieval writers. In a poem attributed to St. Clement of Alexandria, Christ is called the "king of children."[30] Pope Leo the Great writes in the fourth century: "Christ loves childhood, for it is the teacher of humility, the rule of innocence, the model of sweetness."[31] Christ's love for children seems to have given them occasional, unexpected prominence even in the religious wars of the epoch. Already in the Merovingian period, an account of a saint's life tells the story of Lupus, bishop of Troyes in northern France, and his efforts to defend his community against Attila the Hun.[32] An angel instructs the bishop in a dream to recruit twelve little boys,

28. The Council of Elvira, ca. 300, alludes to women who suffocate their babies in order to conceal their sins. The Council of Toledo, 589, mentions parents who kill their babies in order to escape the burden of feeding them; see Godefroy, "Infanticide," p. 1723. Some early penitentials assign lighter penances to women who kill their children because of poverty, see *Die Canones Theodori cantuariensis und ihre Überlieferungsformen*, ed. P. W. Finsterwalder (Weimer, 1929), p. 280: "Mulier paupercula si occidit filium suum homicida sit x. annos peniteat." The usual penance was twelve years.

29. Matt. 18: 1–5; see also Matt. 19: 33–37, Luke 9: 46–48.

30. "Sancte, sis dux, Rex puerorum intactorum"; cited in E. Semichon, *Histoire des enfants abandonnés depuis l'antiquité jusqu' à nos jours* (Paris, 1880), pp. 290–292.

31. Cited in Riché, *Education antique*, p. 31, from Leo's "Sermon on the Epiphany."

32. "Vita Memorii presbyteri et martyris," in *Passiones vitaeque sanctorum aevi merovingici et antiquiorum aliquot*, ed. B. Krusch, Scriptores rerum merovingicarum, 3 (Hanover, 1916), p. 102. The angel instructs the biship: "Surge, fidelissime sacerdos Christi, iube perquirere duodecim innocentes et eos baptiza …"

baptize them, and march forth from the city, singing psalms, to confront the dread chieftain. The bishop and his youthful companions are martyred, but their sacrifice saves the city. It is easy to see, in this curious incident, the same sentiments which, later in the Middle Ages, at times made Crusaders out of children.[33]

A favorable appraisal of childhood is also apparent in the monastic culture of the early Middle Ages.[34] Western monasteries from the sixth century, accepted as oblates to the monastic life children, who were hardly more than toddlers, and the leaders of the monastic movement gave much attention to the proper methods of rearing and instructing these miniature monks. In his famous rule, St. Benedict of Nursia insisted that the advice of the children be sought in important matters, "for often the Lord reveals to the young what should be done."[35] St. Colomban in the seventh century, and the Venerable Bede in the eighth, praised four qualities of the monastic child: he does not persist in anger; he does not bear a grudge; he takes no delight in the beauty of women; and he expresses what he truly believes.[36]

But alongside this positive assessment of the very young, Christian tradition supported a much harsher appraisal of the nature of the child. In Christian belief, the dire results of Adam's fall were visited upon all his descendants. All persons, when they entered the world, bore the stain of original sin and with it concupiscence, and irrepressible appetite for evil. Moreover, if God had predestined some persons to salvation and some to damnation, his judgments touched even the very young, even those who died before they knew their eternal options. The father of the Church who most forcefully and effectively explored the implications of predestination for children was again St. Augustine. Voluminous in his writings, clear in his logic, and ruthless in his conclusions, Augustine finally decided, after some early doubts, that the baby who died without baptism was damned to eternal fires.[37] There were heaven and hell and no place

33. See J. Delalande, *Les extraordinaires croisades d'enfants et de pastoreaux au Moyen Âge: Les pèlerinages d'enfants au Mont Saint-Michel* (Paris, 1962).
34. This is essentially the thesis of P. Riché, *Education et culture,* cited in n. 12 above.
35. *Ibid.,* p. 505, citing the *Regula Benedicti,* chap. 3, "Saepe juniori dominus revelat quod melius est."
36. *Ibid.* St. Columban writes, "Infans humilis est, non laesus meminit, non mulierem videns concupiscit, non aliud ore aliud corde habet."
37. A. M. Jacquin, "La prédestination d'après Saint Augustin," in *Miscellanea Agostiniana* (Rome, 1931), p. 868.

in between. "If you admit that the little one cannot enter heaven," he argued, "then you concede that he will be in everlasting fire."[38]

This cruel judgment of the great African theologian contrasts with the milder views of the Eastern fathers, who affirmed that unbaptized children suffer only the loss of the vision of God. The behavior of Augustine's God seems to mimic the posture of the Roman paterfamilias, who was similarly arbitrary and ruthless in the judgment of his own babies, who elected some for life and cast out others into the exterior darkness. And no one in his family dared question his decisions. Perhaps here as elsewhere, Augustine remains quintessentially the Roman.

Augustine was, moreover, impressed by the early dominion which evil establishes over the growing child. The suckling infant cries unreasonably for nourishment, wails and throws tantrums, and strikes with feeble but malicious blows those who care for him. "The innocence of children," Augustine concludes, "is in the helplessness of their bodies, rather than any quality of soul."[39] "Who does not know," he elsewhere asks, "with what ignorance of the truth (already manifest in babies), with what plenitude of vain desire (initially apparent in children) man enters this life? If he is allowed to live as he wishes ... he will fall into all or many kinds of crimes and atrocities."[40]

The suppression of concupiscence thus becomes a central goal of Augustine's educational philosophy and justifies hard and frequent punishments inflicted on the child. While rejecting the values of pagan antiquity, he adheres to the classical methods of education. Augustine prepared the way for retaining under Christian auspices that "sorrowful road" of schooling which he, as a child at school, had so much hated.

Medieval society thus inherited and sustained a mix of sometimes inconsistent attitudes toward children. The social historian, by playing upon one or another of these attitudes, by judiciously

38. "Ecce exposui tibi quid sit regnum, et quid sit ignis aeternus; ut quando confitearis parvulum non furutum in regno, fatearis futurum in igne aeterno" (Sermo 294, chap. 3, cited in *ibid.*, p. 912).

39. *Conf.* 1, p. 7, *Confessions,* trans. Sheed, p. 7.

40. *De civitate Dei,* 22, p. 22 "Nam quis ignorat cum quanta ignorantia ueritatis, quae iam in infantibus manifesta est, et cum quanta abundantia uanae cupiditatis, quae in pueris incipit apparere, homo veniat in hanc uitam, ita ut, si dimittatur uiuere ut uelit et facere quidquid uelit, in haec facinora et flagitia ... uel cuncta uel multa perueniat."

screening his sources, could easily color as he pleases the history of medieval children. He could compile a list of the atrocities committed against them, dwell upon their neglect, or celebrate medieval views of the child's innocence and holiness. One must, however, strive to paint a more balanced picture, and for this we obviously need some means of testing the experiences of the medieval child. The tests we shall use here are two: the social investment, the wealth and resources which medieval society was apparently willing to invest in children; and the psychological investment, the attention they claimed and received from their elders. The thesis of this essay, simply stated, is that both the social and psychological investments in children were growing substantially from approximately the eleventh and twelfth centuries, through to the end of the Middle Ages, and doubtlessly beyond.

The basic economic and social changes which affected medieval society during this period seem to have required a heightened investment in children. From about the year 1,000, the medieval community was growing in numbers and complexity. Commercial exchange intensified, and a vigorous urban life was reborn in the West. Even the shocking reduction in population size, coming with the plagues, famines, and wars of the fourteenth century, did not undo the importance of the commercial economy or of the towns and the urban classes dependent upon it. Medieval society, once a simple association of warriors, priests, and peasants, came to include such numerous and varied social types as merchants, lawyers, notaries, accountants, clerks, and artisans. A new world was born, based on the cultivation and preservation of specialized, sophisticated skills.

The emergence of specialized roles within society required in turn a social commitment to the training of children in the corresponding skills. Earlier educational reforms—notably those achieved under Charlemagne—had largely affected monks and, in less measure, clerics; they had little impact on the lay world. One novelty of the new medieval pedagogy, as it developed from the twelfth century, is the attention now given to the training of laymen. Many writers now comment on the need and value of mastering a trade from early youth. Boys, notes Philippe of Navarre, should be taught a trade "as soon as possible." "Those who early become and long remain apprentices ought to be the best masters."[41] "Men from childhood," Thomas Aquinas observes, "apply themselves to those offices and skills in which they will spend their lives ... This is altogether necessary. To the extent that something is difficult, so much the more must a man grow accustomed to it from childhood."[42]

Later in the thirteenth century, Raymond Lull, one of the most learned men of the epoch, compares society to a wheel upon which men ride ceaselessly, up and down, gaining and losing status; the force which drives the wheel is education, in particular the mastery of a marketable skill. Through the exercise of a trade, a man earns money, gains status, and ultimately enters the ranks of the rich. Frequently, however, he becomes arrogant in his new status, and he neglects to train his children in a trade. His unskilled offspring inevitably ride the wheel on its downward swing. And so the world turns. A marketable skill offers the only certain riches and the only security, and "there is no skill," Lull affirms, "which is not good."[43]

One hundred and fifty years later, the Florentine Dominican Giovanni Dominici voices exactly the same sentiments. Neither wealth nor inherited status offers security. Only a marketable skill can assure that children "will not be forced, as are many, to beg, to steal, to enter household service, or to do demeaning things."[44] Addressing a woman who belonged to one of Florence's patrician families, he still urged her to make sure that her child learned a useful trade.

41. *Les quatre ages de l'homme*, p. 10: "Après, si doit l'an as anfanz apanre tel mestier qui soit a chascun androit soi; et doit on commancier au plus tost que on puet. Car cil qui est par tems et longuement deciples doit après etre miaudres maitres de ce que l'an li avra apris ..."
42. "Liber contra doctrinam retrahentium a religione," in *Opera omnia iussu Leonis XIII P.M. edita*, LXI, pars. B-C (Rome, 1969), col. 44: "Hoc manifeste apparet, secundum quam homines a pueritia applicantur illis officiis vel artibus in quibus vitam sunt acturi; sicut qui futuri sunt clerici mox a pueritia in clericatu erudiuntur; qui futuri sunt milites opportet quod a pueritia in militaribus exerciciis nutriantur, sicut Vegetius dicit in libro De re militare; qui futuri sunt fabri fabrilem artem a pueritia discunt. ... Quinimmo necesse est ut quanto aliquid est difficilius, tanto ad illud portandum homo a pueritia consuescat."
43. *Doctrine d'enfant: Version médiéval du MS Fr 22933 de la B. N. de Paris*, ed. A. Llinares (Paris, 1969), p. 170: "Plus seure richece est enrichir son filz par aueun mestier. ... Il n'est pas mestier qui bons ne soit." For the comparison of the world with a wheel, see *ibid.*, p. 171. Raymond wrote this tract originally in Catalan, but this French translation was made soon after the original.
44. *Regola di cura familiare*, ed. D. Salvi (Florence, 1860), p. 183: "... e non saranno costretti, come son molti, di mendicare o tor quel d'altri, porsi per famigli, o fare quel che non si conviene."

Although statistics largely elude us, there can be little doubt that medieval society was making substantial investments in education from the twelfth century. Guibert of Nogent, a monk who recounted his personal memoirs in the middle twelfth century, observed that the number of professional teachers had multiplied in the course of his own lifetime.[45] The chronicler Giovanni Villani gives us some rare figures on the schools functioning at Florence in the 1330's.[46] The children, both boys and girls, who were attending the grammar schools of the city, presumably between 6 and 12 years of age, numbered between eight and ten thousand. From what we know of the population of the city, better than one out of two school-aged children were receiving formal instruction in reading. Florentine girls received no more formal instruction after grammar school, but of the boys, between 1,000 and 1,200 went on to six secondary schools, where they learned how to calculate on the abacus, in evident preparation for a business career. Another 550 to 600 attended four "large schools" where they studied "Latin and logic," the necessary preparation for entry into the universities and, eventually, for a career in law, medicine, or the Church. Florence, it might be argued, was hardly a typical medieval community. Still, the social investment that Florentines were making in the training of their children was substantial.

Another indicator of social investment in children is the number of orphanages or hospitals devoted to their care, and here the change across the Middle Ages is particularly impressive. The care

45. *Self and Society in Medieval France: The Memoirs of Abbot Guibert of Nogent*, ed. J. F. Benton (New York, 1970), p. 17. Guibert himself in his memoirs gives a long account of his childhood experiences, which are perceptively interpreted by Benton in his Introduction to the cited translation. Guibert's interest in his own childhood may well reflect this new social concern with the moral and cultural formation of children.

46. *Cronica di Giovanni Villani* (Florence, 1823), 6, pp.183–184: "Troviamo che' fanciulli che stanno ad imparare l'abbaco a algorismo in sei scuole, da mille in mille dugento. E quegli che stanno ad apprendere la grammatica e loica in quattro grandi scuole, da cinquecento-cinquanta in seicento." E. Fiumi, "Economia e vita privata dei Fiorentini nelle rilevazioni statistiche di G. Villani," *Archivio Storico Italiano,* 111 (1953), p. 207 ff., estimates that the school-age population of the city of Florence was at that time only about 9,000 persons, but his estimates of the size of the city (93,000 persons) and of the proportion of school-age children within it (10 percent) are probably low. If we estimate that Florence then contained 120,000 persons, and that the school-age children formed 16.3 percent of the total (the proportion prevailing in 1427, according to a census of the city taken that year), their numbers would have been about 15,000.

of the abandoned or orphaned child was a traditional obligation of Christian charity, but it did not lead to the foundation and support of specialized orphanages until late in the Middle Ages. The oldest European orphanage of which we have notice was founded at Milan in 787, but we know nothing at all concerning its subsequent history or that of other orphanages sporadically mentioned in the early sources.[47] The great hospital orders of the medieval Church, which sprang up from the twelfth century, cared for orphans and foundlings, but none initially chose that charity as its special mission.[48]

The history of hospitals in the city of Florence gives striking illustration of a new concern for abandoned babies which emerged in Europe during the last two centuries of the Middle Ages. In his detailed description of his native city, written in the 1330's, Villani boasts that Florence contained thirty hospitals with more than a thousand beds.[49] But the beds were intended for the "poor and infirm," and he mentions no special hospital for foundlings. A century later, probably in the 1420's, another chronicler, Gregorio Dati, in clear imitation of Villani, composed another description of the marvels of Florence. By then the city contained no fewer than three hospitals which received foundlings and supported them until an age when the girls could marry and the boys could be instructed in a trade.[50] This charity was, in Dati's phrase, "an estimable thing," and the moneys expended by the hospitals were, he claims, worth a city.

47. On the history of orphanages in the Middle Ages, see F. Romita, *Evoluzione storica dell' assistenza all' infanzia abbandonata* (Rome, 1965).

48. One of the most important of the new orders was that of the Holy Spirit, founded at Montpellier in 1178; see P. Brune, *Histoire de l'Ordre Hospitalier du Saint Esprit* (Paris, 1892).

49. *Cronica*, 6, p.185.

50. *"L'Istoria di Firenze" di Gregorio Dati dal 1380 al 1405 illustrata e pubblicata secondo il Codice inedito stradiniano*, ed. L. Pratesi (Norcia, 1905), p. 119: "V'è ancora più Ospedali i quali ricettano i fanciulli nati celatamente, de' quali l'uno è di Santa Maria della Scala; l'altro è quello di San Gallo, e quello che è in sulla Piazza de' Servi titolato Spedale Nuovo; e questi tali danno ricetto a ogni fanciullo o fanciulla e tutti gli mandano a balia e nutriscono, e quando le femmine sono grandi tutte le maritano e i maschi pongono ad arte, che è una cosa stimabile. La spesa che i detti Spedali hanno l'anno e qualunque di questi sarebbe in se una città ..." The date when Dati wrote is uncertain, but it must be later than 1421, when the Hospital of the Innocenti, to which his Spedale Nuovo surely refers, was founded at Florence. On the question of abandoned children at Florence, see the recent study by R. C. Trexler, "The Foundlings of Florence, 1395–1455," *History of Childhood Quarterly* 1 (1973), pp. 259–284.

At Rome, the history of the hospital of Santo Spirito in Sassia shows a comparable, growing sensitivity to the needs of foundlings in the late Middle Ages. The hospital, administered by the Order of the Holy Spirit, had been founded at Rome in 1201, with the blessing and support of Pope Innocent III. From its thirteenth-century rule, Santo Spirito indiscriminately accepted pilgrims, the poor, the sick and crippled, and foundlings.[51] After a period of disruption and decadence in the fourteenth and early fifteenth centuries, the hospital was reformed, and, from about 1450, it devoted its principal resources to the care of foundlings.[52] At the same time, a legend grew up concerning the hospital's early benefactor, Pope Innocent III: Instructed by a dream, Innocent one day ordered fishermen to cast their nets into the Tiber. The men hauled in from the waters the bodies of 87 drowned babies and, after a second effort, 340 more. The shocked pope thereupon endowed the hospital of Santo Spirito and commissioned it to receive the unwanted babies of Rome. The legend is today celebrated in fifteenth-century frescoes which adorn the still-standing hospital of Santo Spirito. The story is without historical foundation, but it illuminates the novel sentiments toward foundlings which came to prevail at Rome, not in the thirteenth but in the fifteenth century.

Even a rapid survey of the foundling hospitals of Europe shows a similar pattern. Bologna seems not to have had an orphanage until 1459, and Pavia not until 1449.[53] At Paris, the first specialized hospital for children, Saint-Esprit en Grèves, was founded in 1363, but according to its charter it was supposed to receive only orphans of legitimate birth. Care of foundlings, it was feared, might encourage sexual license among adults.[54] But the hospital in practice seems to

51. *La carità cristiana in Roma,* ed. V. Monachino, with the collaboration of M. da Alatri and I. da Villa Padierna, Roma Cristiana, 10 (Bologna, 1968), p. 142. The rule dates from 1228–1250, and its most recent edition is by O. De Angelis, *Regula sive statuta hospitalis sancti spiritus: La più antica regola hospitaliera di Santo Spirito in Saxia* (Rome, 1954).

52. *Carità cristiana,* p. 142, which also recounts the legend of the hospital's founding by Innocent III.

53. U. Rubbi and C. Zucchini, "L'ospizio esposti e l'asilo di maternità, in *Sette secoli di vita ospitaliera in Bologna* (Bologna, 1960), pp. 401–417; C. Biglieri, "L'Ospedale degli Esposti di Pavia," *Studi di Storia Ospitaliera* , 3 (1965), pp. 139–156.

54. Semichon, *Enfants abandonnés,* p. 80; Lallemand, *Enfants abandonnés,* p. 121. A royal letter patent of 1445 reads as follows: "Moult de gens feroient moins de difficultés de eux abandonner à pécher quand ils verroient qu'ills n'auroient pas la charge première ni la sollicitude de leurs enfants ..."

have accepted abandoned babies, and several similar institutions were established in French cities in the fifteenth century.[55]

This new concern for the survival of children, even foundlings, seems readily explicable. Amid the ravages of epidemics, the sheer numbers of orphans must have multiplied in society. Moreover, the plagues carried off the very young in disproportionate numbers.[56] Parents feared for the survival of their lineages and their communities. About 1400, the French philosopher Jean Gerson denounced the inordinate concern for the survival of children which he detected among his contemporaries.[57] The frequent creation of foundling hospitals and orphanages indicates that society as a whole shared this concern and was willing to invest in the survival of its young, even orphans and foundlings.

The medieval social investment in children thus seems to have grown from the twelfth century and to have passed through two phases: the first one, beginning from the twelfth century, largely involved a commitment, on the part of the urban communities, to the child's education and training; the second, from the late fourteenth century, reflected a concern for the child's survival and health under difficult hygienic conditions.

This social investment also presumes an equivalent psychological investment, as well as a heightened attention paid to the child and his development. This is evident, for example, in the rich tradition of pedagogical literature intended for a lay audience, which again dates from the twelfth century. One of the earliest authors to provide a comprehensive regimen of child care was Vincent of Beauvais, who died in 1264.[58] Drawing on the learning of the

55. On the care of abandoned children in France in the late Middle Ages, see Lallemand, *Enfants abandonnés*, pp. 120–130. For England, see R. M. Clay, *The Medieval Hospitals of England* (London, 1909), esp. pp. 25–34. "Homes for Women and Children."

56. This seems to have been characteristic of the plagues which struck the city of Florence during the late Middle Ages. See the analysis of age-specific mortalities at Florence in D. Herlihy and C. Klapisch, *Les Toscans et leurs familles: Une étude du Catasto florentin de 1427* (Paris, 1978).

57. *Oeuvres complètes*, ed. Glorieux, 7, p. 322: "Vrai est que ce qui seult aggrever fort la douleur et la tristesse d'aulcuns, especialement des nobles gens, est quant par la mort de leurs enfants leur lignie fault et deschiet, et que nulz heritiers ne leur succedent en droite ligne; et par ainsi leurs armes perissent et leur nom va a oubliance quant au monde."

58. *De eruditione filiorum nobilium*, ed. A. Steiner (Cambridge, Mass, 1938; repr., New York, 1970). Vincent includes the same instructions in his "Speculum doctri-

Muslim physician Avicenna, he gives advice on the delivery of the baby; its care in the first hours, days and months of life; nursing and weaning; the care of older children; and their formal education. Later in the century, Raymond Lull, in his *Doctrina pueril,* written in Catalan but soon translated into French and Latin, is similarly comprehensive, including passages not only on formal schooling but also on the care and nourishment of the child. "For every man," he explains, "must hold his child dear."[59] In the following century, a Tuscan poet, Francesco da Barberino, who evidently had read Vincent of Beauvais, incorporated his advice on the care of infants in a long, vernacular poem intended for nurses.[60] The learning of the scholars seems to have spread widely, even among the humble social classes.

These medieval pedagogues also developed a rudimentary but real psychology of children. Vincent of Beauvais recommends that the child who does not readily learn must be beaten, but he warns against the psychological damage which excessive severity may cause. "Children's minds," he explains, "break down under excessive severity of correction; they despair, and worry, and finally they hate. And this is the most injurious; where everything is feared, nothing is attempted."[61] A few teachers, such as the Italian humanists Matteo Palmieri and Maffeo Vegio, wanted to prohibit all corporal punishment at school. For them, physical discipline was "contrary to nature"; it "induced servility and sowed resentment,

---

nale," published in the third volume of the *Biblioteca mundi Vincentii Burgundii* (Douai, 1624). On Vincent's educational philosophy, see A. L. Gabriel, *The Educational Ideas of Vincent of Beauvais,* Texts and Studies in the History of Medieval Education, ed. A. L. Gabriel and J. N. Garvin, 4 (Notre Dame, Ind., 1956). Vincent's remarks on the physical care of the infant are in his "De arte medicina," Liber 12 of the Speculum doctrinale, *Biblioteca mundi,* 3, pp. 1088–1093. For a recent survey of medieval medical literature relating to children, see L. Demaitre, "The Idea of Childhood and Child Care in Medical Writings of the Middle Ages," *The Journal of Psychohistory ,* 4 (1977), pp. 461–490.

59. *Doctrine d'enfant,* p. 203: "De la maniere su laquele home doit nourir son fuiz." Raymond stresses the need for close but affectionate attention to the child: "Amable fiuz, tout home doit chier tenir son enfant ..." (p. 204).

60. In the thirteenth book, addressed to nurses, of his *Reggimento e costumi di donna,* ed. G. E. Sansone, Collezione di "Filologia romanza," 2 (Turin, 1957). On Francesco's sources, see G. B. Festa, *Un galateo femminile italiano del Trecento,* Biblioteca di cultura moderna, 36 (Bari, 1910).

61. "Ingenia tamen puerorum nimia emendationis severitate deficiunt: nam et desperant, et dolent, et novissime oderunt; et quod maxime nocet, dum omnia timentur, nihil conantur" (*Biblioteca mundi,* 3, p. 487).

which in later years might make the student hate the teacher and forget his lesson."[62]

The teacher—and on this all writers agree—should be temperate in the use of force, and he should also observe the child, in order to identify his talents and capacities. For not all children are alike, and natural differences must be recognized and developed. Raymond Lull affirms that nature is more capable of rearing the child than the child's mother.[63] The Florentine Giovanni Dominici stresses the necessity of choosing the proper profession for the child. Society, he notes, requires all sorts of occupations and skills, ranging from farmers to carpenters, to bankers, merchants, priests, and "a thousand others."[64] The aptitudes and inclinations of the young had to be acutely observed, "since nature aids art, and a skill chosen against nature will not be learned well." The young man who wishes to become a wool merchant will make a poor barber. God in his infinite wisdom has distributed all needed talents among all the members of the body social. If all young persons developed and exercised the particular talent which they possess, then, in Dominici's view, "lands would be well governed, commerce would be justly conducted, and the arts would progress in orderly fashion; the commonwealth would rejoice in peace and fat abundance, happy in all its affairs."[65]

To read these writers is inevitably to form the impression that medieval people, or some of them at least, were deeply concerned about children. Indeed, Jean Gerson expressly condemns his contemporaries, who, in his opinion, were excessively involved with

---

62. *Della Vita civile: Trattato di Matteo Palmieri cittadino fiorentino,* Biblioteca scelta di opere italiane antiche e moderne, 160 (Milan, 1825), p. 34: "Quegli che hanno il padre ed il maestro disposti e solleciti a fargli buoni, non mi piace abbino busse, prima, perché pare cosa non benigna, ma piuttosto contra natura, ed atta a fare gli animi servi, ed alla volta poi, cresciuti, se lo reputano ad ingiuria, onde se ne scema l'affezione del natural amore." Maffeo Vegio da Lodi, *De educatione liberorum et eorum claris moribus,* ed. Sister M. Walburg Fanning and A. S. Sullivan (Washington, D.C., 1933–1936), p. 19.

63. *Doctrine d'enfant,* p. 206: "Saches, fiuz, que plus sage est nature a norrir les enfanz que n'est ta mere."

64. *Cura familiare,* p. 182. Like Lull, Dominici affirms that education must conform to the nature of the child: "però che la natura aiuta l'arte, e arte pressa contra natura non s'impara bene."

65. *Ibid.,* p. 183: "... le terre sarebbono rette bene, le mercantanzie si farebbono iustamente, e l'arti procederebbono ordinate; goderebbe la repubblica nella pace e abondanzia grassa, felice in tutti i fatti suoi."

their children's survival and success. In order to gain for them "the honors and pomp of this world," parents, he alleges, were expending "all their care and attention; they sleep neither day nor night and often become very miserly."[66] In investing in their children, they neglected charitable works and the good of their own souls. Gerson tells of a rich married couple who wished for offspring and performed many good works, so that God would grant them a baby. God rewarded them with the birth of a beautiful infant. But the new parents began at once to consider how their baby might achieve success in this world. They gave up their pious thoughts and deeds and turned all their attention and wealth to the upbringing of their child. God, angered at their neglect of the Church and of the poor, took back what he had given; the splendid child died. God does this often, Gerson instructs us, in order to rescue parents from inordinate dedication to the welfare of their offspring. Gerson, one suspects, would be surprised to learn of the opinion of recent historians, that medieval parents cared little for their offspring.

Medieval society, increasingly dependent upon the cultivation of sophisticated skill, had to invest in a supporting pedagogy; when later threatened by child-killing plagues, it had to show concern for the survival of the very young. But the medieval involvement with children cannot be totally described in these functional terms. Even as they were developing an effective pedagogy, medieval people were re-evaluating the place of childhood among the periods of life.

One indication of a new sympathy toward childhood is the revision in theological opinion concerning the salvation of the babies who died without baptism. Up until the twelfth century, the leading theologians of the Western church—Fulgentius of Ruspe, Pope Gregory the Great, Isidore of Seville, Anselm of Canterbury—reiterated the weighty opinion of St. Augustine, that such infants were surely damned. [67] In the twelfth century, Peter Abelard and Peter Lombard, perhaps the two most influential theologians of the epoch, reversed the condemnation of unbaptized babies to eternal fires. A

66. *Oeuvres complètes*, 7, p. 322: "... pour avencier leurs prochains es honneurs et pompes de ce monde mettent toute leur cure et entente et n'en prennent repos ne nuit ne jour et en deviennent souvent tres avaricieux." The entire passage makes clear that the sense of "prochains" is "children."

67. J. Bellamy, "Baptême (Sort des enfants morts sans)," *Dictionnaire de théologie catholique*, II (1905), cols. 364–378. A. Gaudel, "Limbes," *ibid.*, IX, 1 (1926), cols. 760–762.

thorough examination of the question, however, awaited the work
of Thomas Aquinas, the first to use in a technical theological sense
the term *limbus puerorum,* the "limbo of children." The unbaptized
baby, he taught, suffered only the deprivation of the Beatific Vision.
As the poet Dante described their plight in a famous passage from
the *Divine Comedy,* they were "only insofar afflicted, that without
hope we live in desire."[68]

Aquinas' mild judgment on babies dead without baptism became
the accepted teaching of the medieval Church. Only one prominent
theologian in the late Middle Ages, Gregory of Rimini, resisted it,
and he came to be known as the *tortor puerorum,* the "torturer of
children."

No less remarkable is the emergence, from the twelfth century, of
a widespread devotion to the Child Jesus. The texts from the early
Middle Ages which treat of the Christ Child—notably the "Book on
the Origins of Mary and the Childhood of the Savior" falsely attributed to the evangelist St. Matthew—present Christ as a miniature
wonder worker, who miraculously corrects Joseph's mistakes in carpentry, tames lions, divides rivers, and even strikes dead a teacher
who dared reprimand him in class.[69] All-knowing and all-powerful,
he is the negation of the helpless, charming child. A new picture of
the Child Jesus emerges, initially under Cistercian auspices, in the
twelfth century. For example, between 1153 and 1157 the English
Cistercian Aelred of Rievaulx composed a meditation, "Jesus at the
Age of Twelve." Aelred expatiates on the joy which the presence of
the young Christ brought to this elders and companions: "... the
grace of heaven shone from that most beautiful face with such
charm as to make everyone look at it, listen to him, and be moved
to affection. See, I beg, how he is seized upon and led away by each
and every one of them. Old men kiss him, young men embrace
him, boys wait upon him ... . How do the older women complain
when he lingers a little longer with his father and companions? Each

68. *Inferno,* Canto IV; *The Divine Comedy: The Carlyle-Wicksteed Translation
Unabridged* (New York, 1950), p. 27.
69. "Liber de ortu beatae Mariae et infantia Salvatoris, a beato Matthaeo evange-
lista hebraice scriptus et a beato Ieronomo presbytero in latinum translatus," in *Evan-
gelia apocrypha,* ed. C. von Tischendorf, 2nd ed. (Leipzig, 1876), pp. 51–105. See p.
104 for the taming of the lions; p. 106 for divine aid in the carpentry shop; and p. 107
for the incident in the classroom.

of them, I think, declares in his inmost heart: 'Let him kiss me with the kiss of his mouth.'"[70]

Aelred goes on to speculate concerning the intimate details of the domestic life of the holy Child during the three days he was separated from his parents in Jerusalem: "Who provided you with food and drink? Who made up a bed for you? Who took off your shoes? Who tended your boyish limbs with oil and baths?" Passionate and sensuous, these meditations are the more remarkable as they come from a monk vowed to celibacy and asceticism.

Doubtlessly, the special characteristics of Cistercian monasticism were influential here. Like other reformed orders of the twelfth century, the Cistercians no longer admitted oblates, the boys placed in the monastery at tender ages, who grew up in the cloister with no experience of secular life.[71] The typical Cistercians—St. Bernard of Clairvaux and his brothers, for example—were raised within a natural family, and many were familiar with the emotions of family life. Grown men when they entered the monastery, they carried with them a distinct mentality—a mentality formed in the secular world and open to secular values. Many doubtlessly had considered and some had pursued other careers before electing the monastic life; they presumably had reflected upon the emotional and spiritual rewards of the married state and the state of parenthood. While fleeing from the world, they still sought in their religious experiences analogues to secular and familial emotions. In numerous commentaries on the biblical Song of Songs, they examine the love which joins bridegroom and bride and the mystical parallels to it offered in religion. In celebrating the joys of contemplating a perfect child, they find in their religious experience an analogue to the love and satisfaction which parents feel in observing their growing children.

---

70. *The Works of Aelred of Rievaulx,* vol. 1: *Treatises: The Pastoral Prayer,* Cistercian Fathers Series, 2 (Spencer, Mass., 1971), p. 9. St Bernard also urges Christians to imitate the simplicity and humility which the baby Jesus and all young children manifest; see his sermon in *Patrologia Latina,* ed. J. P. Migne (Paris, 1853), vol. 183, col. 152: "... primo omnium Christus appareat puer cum Virgine matre, ut simplicitatem et verecundiam ante omnia quaerendam nobis doceat esse. Nam et pueri simplicitas naturalis, et cognata virginibus verecundia est. Omnibus ergo nobis in conversationis nostrae initio nulla magis virtus necessaria est, quam simplicitas humilis et gravitas verecunda."

71. J.H. Lynch, "The Cistercians and Underage Novices," *Cîteaux* 23 (1973), pp. 283–297. The Carthusians, Grandmontines, and Templars also refused to accept children as novices.

The Cistercian cult of the Child Jesus suggests, in other words, that lay persons, too, were finding the contemplation of children emotionally rewarding.

In the thirteenth century, devotion to the Child Jesus spread well beyond the restricted circle of Cistercian monasticism. St. Francis of Assisi, according to the *Legenda Gregorii*, set up for the first time a Christmas crèche, so that the faithful might more easily envision the tenderness and humility of the new-born Jesus.[72] St. Francis, the most popular saint of the late Middle Ages, was thus responsible, at least in legend, for one of the most popular devotional practices still associated with Christmas. St. Anthony of Padua, who died in 1231, was observed one day in the quiet of his room embracing and kissing an angelic child. This legend, to be sure, appears more than a century after Anthony's death but gains wide popularity in the late Middle Ages.[73]

Saints of lesser renown also sought and were favored with visitations from the Christ Child. A widow of Florence, Umiliana dei Cerchi, who died in 1246, prayed that she might see "the infant Jesus as he was at three or four years of age."[74] She returned to her room one night to find a delightful child playing; simply from watching this child at play, she drew ineffable joy. A similar story, told of St. Agnes of Montepulciano, who died in 1317, ends with a bizarre twist. She too prayed for the special favor of holding and fondling the infant Jesus. One night in her convent cell, the Virgin gave her the sacred child; when Mary returned at dawn to reclaim the infant, Agnes, captivated by his charm, refused to give him back. The women argued, and their "loving and pious dispute," in the words of Agnes' biographer, aroused the convent.[75]

This cult of the Christ Child implies an idealization of childhood itself. "O sweet and sacred childhood," another Cistercian, Guerric

---

72. *St. Francis of Assisi According to Brother Thomas of Celano*, ed. H. G. Rosedale (London, 1904), p. 67: "De presepio, quod fecit in die natalis domini." The legend says of the crib and child: "Honoratur ibi simplicitas, exaltatur paupertas, humilitas commendatur ..."

73. The story is first recounted in the *Liber miraculorum*, which was written about 1370. *Acta Sanctorum, II Junii* (Antwerp, 1968), p. 729: "... vidit per fenestram amplectentem latenter quemdam puerum, in brachiis S. Antonii, pulcherrimum et jucundum: quem sanctus amplexabatur et osculabatur, indesinenter ejus faciem contemplado."

74. *Acta Sanctorum, II Aprilis* (Antwerp, 1675), p. 397: "... puerum Iesum aetate quatuor annorum vel trium ... talem quidem qualis erat tempore infantiae suae."

75. *Ibid.*, p. 797: "... caritativa concertatio et pia."

of Igny, writes of the early years of Christ, "which brought back man's true innocence, by which men of every age can return to blessed childhood and be conformed to you, not in physical weakness but in humility of heart and holiness of life."[76]

How are we to explain this celebration of "sweet and sacred childhood?": It closely resembles other religious movements which acquire extraordinary appeal from the twelfth century—the cults of poverty, of Christian simplicity, and of the apostolic life. These "movements of cultural primitivism," as George Boas might call them, point to a deepening psychological discontent with the demands of the new commercial economy. [77] The inhabitants of towns in particular, living by trade, were forced into careers of getting and spending, in constant pursuit of what Augustine had called "deceitful riches." The psychological tensions inherent in the urban professions and the dubious value of the preferred material rewards seem to have generated a nostalgic longing for alternate systems of existence, for freedom from material concerns, for the simple Christian life as it was supposedly lived in the apostolic age. Another model for an alternate existence, the exact opposite of tension-ridden urban experience, was the real or imagined life of the child, who was at once humble and content, poor and pure, joyous and giving joy.

The simple piety of childhood remained an ideal of religious reformers for the duration of the Middle Ages. At their close, both Girolamo Savonarola in the south of Europe and Desiderius Erasmus in the north urged their readers to look at pious children if they would find true models of the Christian life.[78] Erasmus, in his *Colloquies,* after a pious child tells him of his religious practices, affirms his intent of following the child's example.[79]

76. *Liturgical Sermons,* Cistercian Fathers Series, 8 (Spencer, Mass., 1970), p. 38.

77. A. O. Lovejoy and G. Boas, *Primitivism and Related Ideas in Antiquity* (New York, 1965); Boas, *Cult of Childhood* (see above, n. 4).

78. For the "cult of childhood" at Florence and the bands of young boys which aided Fra Savonarola in his reform of the city, see the informed if somewhat discursive study of R. C. Trexler, "Ritual in Florence: Adolescence and Salvation in the Renaissance," in *The Pursuit of Holiness in Late Medieval Religion: Papers from the University of Michigan Conference,* ed. C. Trinkaus and H. A. Oberman, Studies in Medieval and Renaissance Thought, 10 (Leyden, 1974), pp. 200–270. On Erasmus' admiration of the piety of childhood, see his "The Child's Piety," from the Colloquies, *Essential Works of Erasmus,* ed. W. T. H. Jackson (New York, 1965), pp. 186–197.

79. *Essential Works of Erasmus,* ed. Jackson, p. 197: "Erasmus: But without jesting, I'll try to imitate that course of life."

Moreover, the medieval cult of childhood extends beyond religious movements and informs secular attitudes as well. In the French allegorical poem of the thirteenth century, *The Romance of the Rose,* youth is presented as a young girl "not yet much more than twelve years old.[80] The poet remarks on her innocence: she "did not yet suspect the existence of evil or trickery in the world." She smiles continuously, for "a young thing is troubled by nothing except play." She is also free from adult hypocrisy. Her sweetheart, described as a young boy of the same age, kisses her when he pleases. "They were never ashamed ... ," explains the poet, "rather you might see them kissing each other like two turtle doves." Later in the Middle Ages, a Florentine citizen and merchant named Giovanni Morelli, reflecting on his own life, calls childhood "nature's most pleasant age."[81] In his *Praise of Folly,* Erasmus avers that the simplicity and unpretentiousness of childhood make it the happiest time of life. "Who does not know," Folly asks her audience, "that childhood is the happiest age and the most pleasant for all? What is there about children that makes us kiss and hug them and cuddle them as we do, so that even an enemy would help them, unless it is this charm of folly?"[82] Clearly, we have come far from Augustine's opinion, that men would prefer eternal death to life again as a child.

The history of medieval children is as complex as the history of any social group, and even more elusive. This essay has attempted to describe in broad outline the cultural attitudes which influenced the experiences of medieval children, as well as the large social trends which touched their lives. The central movements which, in this reconstruction, affected their fate were the social and economic changes widely evident across Europe from the twelfth century, most especially the rise of a commercialized economy and the proliferation of special skills within society; and the worsening health conditions of the late Middle Ages, from the second half of the fourteenth century. The growth of a commercialized economy made

80. *The Romance of the Rose by Guillaume de Lorris and Jean de Meun,* trans. Ch. Dahlberg (Princeton, 1971), pp. 47–48, lines 1259–1278.

81. *Ricordi,* ed. V. Branca (Florence, 1969), p. 498: "... ne' tempi piu dilettevoli alla natura." In fact Morelli's own childhood was singularly unhappy, through the early death of his father.

82. *Essential Works of Erasmus,* ed. Jackson, p. 369.

essential an attentive pedagogy which could provide society with adequately trained adults. And the deteriorating conditions of hygiene across the late Middle Ages heightened the concern for, and investment in, the health and survival of the very young. Paradoxically, too, the growing complexities of social life engendered not truly a discovery but an idealization of childhood: the affirmation of the sentimental belief that childhood is, as Erasmus maintains, a blessed time and the happiest moment of human existence.

We have sought to identify patterns in the complex experiences of medieval children, but we recognize that the model we propose doubtlessly remains too simple. But this much can safely be affirmed: the Middle Ages developed and sustained a broad spectrum of prejudices and beliefs regarding children, some of them destined to influence the subsequent centuries of Western history, some of them living today.

PART IV

12

BIOLOGY AND HISTORY:

Suggestions for a Dialogue

——— ✦ ✦ ✦ ———

Historians in their writings routinely speak of social groups: of
bands, tribes and nations; sects and churches; occupations and professions; political factions and social classes. There is often in their
works an implicit assumption that these groups remain stable over
time; they can therefore be regarded as fixed factors in history. Conventional historical analysis in effect confers upon such groups a
kind of immortality.

In reality, however, every human group, of whatever composition, is subject to the attrition of death and must seek to replace its
losses through recruiting new members. Ultimately, that recruitment
will be dependent on births. But rates of reproduction may differ
across a society; different subsets of the population may reproduce
or increase their numbers more successfully than others. Over time,
the most successful subsets in reproducing will gain a numerical
preponderance. Differential replacement over time will therefore
alter profoundly the internal composition of communities and
groups. No group of human beings is likely to be an exact image or
replica of its parents. Shifts in numbers across subsets of the group
are also likely to create powerful strains and tensions within the
community, as I shall illustrate later. The implicit assumption made
by many historians that human communities, groups or classes can
be regarded as abstract forces in history, stable over time, runs
counter to biological experience.

I argue in this paper that historians should be sensitive to biological experience. More specifically, in their own thinking about the human past, they ought to consider the observations and the theories of those biologists who study how living species change through differential rates of reproduction. I review here certain theories recently developed, to explain both the history of marriage and the significance of differential reproduction in human groups. Marriage and reproduction not only establish special bondings between husbands and wives and parents and children, but they also define larger groups such as kindreds. There can be little doubt that patterns of reproduction profoundly influence the entire fabric of human societies.

Changes in a living species over time through differential reproduction is otherwise known as evolution. Those subsets of the species that eventually prevail are said to be "naturally selected." Since the time of Charles Darwin (1859), a great body of theory has been developed in regard to evolution. Today, a science known as ethology studies the biological foundations of animal and human behavior.[1] The branch of ethology that looks at reproductive behavior in particular is known as sociobiology. According to current evolutionary theory, the basic motivation for human behavior is the biological imperative to reproduce. As one recent work puts it, "individuals have evolved to maximize their genetic representation in descendant generations."[2] The living being which is best fitted to its natural environment, i.e. the one possessing better adaptations than others for that particular environment, will also be the most successful in reproducing.

In technical language, an animal may be regarded as the "phenotype," the visible, physical expression of the invisible genes. The total complement of genes is the "genotype." The living being that is best fitted to its natural environment will also be the most successful in reproducing. The success of the phenotype assures that its genotype will gain greater representation in the new generation and ultimately preponderance.

1. For an introduction to human ethology, see I. Eibl-Eibesfeldt, *Human Ethology* (New York, 1989) L. L. Betzig, *Despotism and Differential Reproduction. A Darwinian View of History* (New York, 1983), p. 87.

2. See *ibid.*, p. 2 and p. 87. "If men and women are the products of natural selection, then the evolved end of their existence should be essentially, very simply, the production of children, grandchildren and other non-descendant kinsmen."

Under systems of sexual reproduction, animals must make certain investments or expend a certain effort in reproducing. They must first undertake a mating effort, that is, seek out a partner of the opposite sex; they sometimes further make a parental effort, that is, they must devote some care to their offspring to ensure their survival to reproductive capability. Characteristically, the reproductive effort required of females is greater than that demanded of males. Among mammals, for example, females must bear and nurse the offspring, while the biological contribution of the male is limited to coition. Because of the large reproductive effort required of them, females, especially among mammals, are more cautious than males in accepting a mate and more discriminating in their choices.

Evolutionary biologists distinguish two reproductive strategies, called r and K.[3] The two strategies are not, however, completely discrete but represent two ends of a behavioral continuum. Sexually reproducing animals are likely to show in their behavior some elements of both strategies. Under r-selection, the parents maximize the number of offspring produced and minimize the investment of parental care per offspring. Matings under r-selection are frequent, promiscuous and passing, with no stable bondings; neither parent makes a large investment in caring for the young. The r-strategy is characteristic of species living in disturbed and dangerous surroundings, where most offspring cannot be expected to survive and many must therefore be produced. Under K-selection, the parents produce few offspring but they make a large investment in their upbringing. K-strategies are characteristic of the higher primates, including man. In human communities, both father and mother usually make substantial investments in rearing their young.

The explanation offered for the K-strategy in humans is as follows. The juvenile stage in the growth of a human being is especially extended and particularly demanding on the mother. Hence, the female favors in her mate selection males that will aid her in the work of parenting. The males willing to make this investment thus have the better chance of reproducing and of enhancing the representation of their genotype in the new generation. But the male par-

---

3. R. A. Alexander, et al., "Sexual Dimorphisms and Breeding Systems in Pinnipeds, Ungulates, Primates, and Humans," in *Evolutionary Biology and Human Social Behavior: An Anthropological Perspective,* ed. N. A. Chagnon and W. Irons (North Scituate, Mass., 1979).

enting effort will also limit their opportunities to pursue other females. In compensation for this, the males insist that the offspring that they help to rear be certainly their own. The female, in other words, must offer assurances to the male that she has remained faithful to him.

What does this theory say about human marriage? One important conclusion is this. There probably never was a period in history when human beings were sexually promiscuous.[4] According to anthropologists, since the founding of their discipline "no communal right to reproduction has ever been observed."[5] This contradicts the assumptions of several, highly influential social theorists of the nineteenth century. In 1877, the American ethnologist Lewis Henry Morgan postulated that all human communities were in the first stages of development sexually promiscuous; all men allegedly shared all women. Frederick Engels adopted this postulate in his famous essay on the *Origins of Family, Private Property and the State* (1884). He placed at the origins of human evolution primitive communism, in which both women and material resources were shared. Only the appearance of private property led to the imposition of monogamy and the origins of the family. As the economy grew more productive, some males became richer than others. However, they wanted assurance that the children to whom they passed on their wealth were truly theirs; they therefore insisted that their wives be monogamous, and this directly led, in Engels' view, to the subordination of women to male power.

Current evolutionary theory turns Morgan and Engels on their heads. Private property did not bring about the family, but the urge to reproduce allegedly brought about private property. The accumulation of resources made the male more attractive to the female, as the resources lightened the burdens of parenting. In evolutionary theory, according to Betzig, "power, prestige, and privileged access to resources should be sought, not as ends in themselves, but as prerequisites to reproduction."[6]

Systems of K-selection do not, however, require strict monogamy on the part of males. A rich man will often possess sufficient

---

4. L. L. Betzig, *Despotism*, p. 19, who points out that a society without wives and private ownership has never appeared.

5. *Ibid.*, p. 26.

6. *Ibid.*, p. 2.

resources to support more than a single wife and their children. Systems of monogamous marriages are also regarded as sexually egalitarian, while polygyny produces sexual inequality. In a monogamous society, since one man can claim only one woman, all men have enhanced chances of attracting a mate. In a polygynous society, where some men have many wives, then normally other men will have none.

How did monogamy develop in human societies according to current theory? Monogamy may be ecologically imposed or socially imposed.[7] Ecologically imposed monogamy is associated with regions where resources are especially scarce and valuable, and population levels are very low. The cooperation of one male and one female is required to exploit and defend the resources, but the resources themselves are not abundant enough to support more than this pair and their offspring. It may be that the first human beings lived under a regimen of ecologically imposed monogamy.

But human beings very early learned the advantages of cooperation, and the theory discerns a correlation between the growth of social wealth, stratification, and the extension of polygyny.[8] The first organized human groups seem to have been bands of hunter-gatherers, which appear as far back as two million years.[9] Several interrelated families made up the bands. The males secured their mates by abducting women from other bands or by trade or purchase. Some males were more successful in acquiring wives than others; they were better hunters, fighters or traders, or their families were larger than others in the band. While in each generation some males would emerge as leaders, there was as yet no inherited office of leadership and no hierarchy of authority. Given the limited resources available, the ability of one male to claim more than a single wife was limited. The assumption is that the most successful male would have acquired two or at most three wives.

Social hierarchies became possible only with a growth in economic production, and this seems linked with the agricultural revo-

7. E. O. Wilson, *Sociobiology: The New Synthesis* (Cambridge, Mass., 1975), p. 330.
8. This is a principal thesis of P. L. Van der Berghe, *Human Family Systems. An Evolutionary View* (New York, 1979).
9. I follow the scheme laid out by F. H. Willhoite Jr., "Political Evolution and Legitimacy: The Biocultural Origins of Hierarchical Organizations," L. L. Betzig, *Human Reproductive Behavior: A Darwinian Perspective*, ed. in M. Borgerhoff Hulder and P. Turke (Cambridge and New York, 1988), pp. 193–223.

lution (8000 to 2000 B.C). Agricultural communities were physically stable, and also at first autonomous and sovereign. The heads of the largest families or lineages achieved the status of headmen and played a leading role in shaping community decisions. But their authority was personal, and the headmen still could exercise no sanctioned coercion. Nonetheless, the expanded wealth made possible by agriculture allowed the men who controlled the largest shares to claim more wives, sire more offspring, and produce larger kindreds. Large kindreds further buttressed the authority of the patriarchs at their head and contributed to their reproductive success.

The first authentically hierarchical communities appeared some 7500 years ago. Basically, several settled communities passed under the power of a single chief. The chief in turn claimed sacral authority (and often descent from the gods). He was a charismatic presence and he could now exercise sanctioned coercion. Continued population growth in certain favored areas of the world led to competition among the chiefs, to wars and conquests, and to the consolidation of the first hierarchical states.

The linkage between power and polygyny is very visible in stratified states. The close association between access to resources and access to women is called "resource polygyny." Polyandry, on the other hand, is very rare in human societies, develops under peculiar ecological circumstances (for example, in the mountain valleys of Tibet) and usually involves brothers sharing a single wife. "With few exceptions," writes Eibl-Eibesfeldt, "in the majority of cultures, successful men, those controlling the natural resources, also produced more descendents. They could afford to have more women, and the women of their subordinates also stood at their disposal."[10]

From her study of 104 human societies, Betzig discerns direct linkages between despotism, polygyny, and differential reproduction.[11] She extends her analysis backwards into history, where again, she argues, the same associations prevail. Historically, rulers have utilized their prerogatives to acquire wives, sometimes in fabulous numbers. Solomon, king of the Israelites, supposedly enjoyed 700 wives and 300 concubines. But if rulers use power to acquire women, they must exercise power also in retaining them and in

10. I. Eibl-Eibesfeldt, *Human Ethology*, p. 12.
11. L. L. Betzig, *Despotism*, p. 100.

procuring resources for them and their offspring. The males deprived of the chance of acquiring a mate are likely to attempt the seduction or abduction of the wives of the despot and the privileged; they will likely provoke disturbance and violence in the community. The rulers must restrain these unruly males, if need be by despotic means. They must also claustrate or confine their wives and concubines in harems or seraglios. Power makes possible polygyny, Betzig seems to argue, but extreme polygyny requires despotic controls over society.

Differential rates of reproduction under polygyny destablize society in other ways. The many offspring of the rich and powerful male enjoy a privileged birth, but they all cannot expect to retain those privileges in adult life. Competition among the many offspring (and their mothers) to succeed their father in his privileged status may lead to conspiracies, assassinations and civil wars. The Ottoman Turks resolved this dilemma by strangling with a silken cord all the sons of the sultan not chosen to succeed.

"Polygyny," writes Napoleon Chagnon, "is widespread in the tribal world and has probably characterized human mating and reproduction for the greater fraction of our species' history."[12] Polygyny seems also characteristic of civilized worlds as well; we encounter it in China and India, in ancient Israel and the Near East, and later in Muslim lands.[13] In China under the Chou dynasty (1100 to 222 B. C.), the wealthy not only enjoyed supplementary wives but could claim access to the wives of their subordinates. "The great majority of pre-industrial nation-states," writes Kevin MacDonald, "were in fact highly polygynous."[14]

In evolutionary theory, polygynous societies will tend to support a distinctive system of hypergamy for women (that is, women are likely to marry up in the social scale).[15] Rich families will favor sons over daughters, for the reason that sons who can acquire numerous

12. N. A. Chagnon, *"Is Reproductive Success Equal in Egalitarian Societies,"* in *Evolutionary Biology,* ed. N. A. Chagnon and W. Irons, p.375.

13. On China, see P. Ebrey , "Concubines in Sung China," *Journal of Family History,* 11 (1986), pp. 1–24. It is interesting to note that this is true only of traditional Muslim society (with its skewed distribution of wealth) but not, for instance, of modern Muslim states and countries.

14. K. B. MacDonald, "Mechanisms of Sexual Egalitarianism in Western Europe," *Ethology and Sociobiology,* 11 (1990), pp. 195–237.

15. M. Dickemann, "The Ecology of Mating Systems in Hypergynous Dowry Societies," *Social Sciences Information,* 18 (1975), pp. 163-95.

wives can produce numerous progeny and give greater representation to the family's genotype. The reproductive capabilities of women are in contrast restricted in comparison with males. While wealth and resources can vastly increase the reproductive performance of males, they can do little for females, as the bearing of children, lactation and child care limit the number of babies an individual woman can conceive and bear. A rich family anxious to propagate its genotype is therefore better advised to invest in its sons. The rich are therefore also more likely than the poor to practice female infanticide.

Poor families, on the other hand, operate under a different set of interests. With few resources, the poor male is likely not to marry at all. Poor girls, on the other hand, can still aspire to become the wives, or at least the concubines, of rich males. Poor families, anxious to propagate their genotype, are better advised to invest in their daughters rather than their sons. The successful girl not only reproduces but gains the advantage of living and bringing up her offspring in comfortable surroundings. The result of all these considerations was a system of hypergyny, upper vertical mobility for women through marriage.

But if polygyny seems the most common type of human marriage, why, when and where did monogamy and its associated sexual egalitarianism appear and prevail? Evolutionary theory suggests that this is an unusual arrangement. Males who control wealth or power should utilize it to enhance their reproductive success, and they should seek to acquire several wives. Monogamy in stratified societies seems inconsistent with the maximization of reproductive success. But this seeming conflict also delineates a problem of which, I believe, historians have not shown sufficient awareness.

Alexander and Chagnon relate the imposition of monogamy and sexual egalitarianism to the formation of large nation states.[16] Polygynous societies create large and powerful kindreds, as the patriarch has many descendants. But these kindreds also obstruct the forma-

16. R. Alexander, *Darwinism and Human Affairs* (Seattle and London, 1979), p. 258. See also N. A. Chagnon, "Is Reproductive Success Equal in Egalitarian Societies," in *Evolutionary Biology*, ed. N. A. Chagnon, and W. Irons, pp. 423–24: "There can be no doubt that there is a strong correlation between nations' becoming very large and the imposition of Ormonogamy on their citizens."

tion of larger social associations. Large states and powerful kindreds are in this view incompatible; this means in turn that large states and polygyny are incompatible as well.

This explanation has, however, one evident fault. Monogamy in European civilization is much older than the formation of large nation states, as it goes back all the way to the ancient times.

Betzig finds the reason for socially imposed monogamy in the industrial revolution.[17] Under industrialism, labor became highly specialized, and those who mastered the special skills were few and valuable. To maintain their morale and keep them working, they had to be offered enhanced remuneration. A crucial form of remuneration was the chance to marry. Under the force of modern industrialism and democracy, both despotism and its ancient concomitant polygyny fade away.

But this theory too seems to set the social imposition of sexual egalitarianism too late. What are its historic roots?

In the West, the achievement of a socially imposed monogamy seems to have come in two stages.[18] Legally required monogamy appears in several societies in the history of the early Mediterranean world, but was also restricted to a limited part of the population. The free male could have only one legal wife, but any number of slave concubines. Thus, in ancient Sumeria early in the second millennium B.C. the famous law code of Hammurabi (eighteenth century B.C.) and still more numerous letters preserved on clay reveal a marital system based on loose monogamy. The husband took only one wife, but could also claim a concubine whom his wife, if barren, might even be required to supply.[19] In ancient Greece and Rome, only free and full citizens could contract a legal marriage (and thus pass on their patrimonies to their heirs).[20] Although the prerogative of marriage was open only to a small segment of society, for them it had to be monogamous. As the Roman state extended its domain over Italy and the lands of the Mediterranean basin, it admitted ever greater numbers of its free subjects to the full rights of

17. L. L. Betzig, *Despotism*, p. 105.
18. My argument essentially follows that of K. B. MacDonald, "Mechanisms of Sexual Egalitarianism,"pp. 195-237.
19. C. J. Gadd, " Hammurabi and the End of His Dynasty," in *The Cambridge Ancient History*, II, pt. 1. 3rd ed. (Cambridge, 1973), pp. 205–08.
20. W. K. Lacey, *The Family in Classical Greece* (Ithaca, 1968).

citizens. Monogamous marriages thus became the norm of behavior for free Roman citizens across the Mediterranean basin.

However, the institution of slavery continued to compromise the legal rule of monogamy. And the number of slaves seems to have expanded greatly especially in Italy in the late Republican period. The successful Roman wars brought thousands of captives into the empire. The rich Romans maintained staffs of household slaves running into the hundreds. Among them were concubines; concubinage was a chief employment for young females.

The Roman marriage pattern, which imposed monogamy on citizens but tolerated concubinage, presents a puzzle. Bastards or illegitimate offspring rarely appear in ancient records.[21] Where are the offspring of the concubines? It may be that many freedmen (the numbers of whom were very large in ancient Rome) were in fact the offspring of slave mothers and their masters. Roman law required that freedmen continue to show deference to their former masters, and it may be that this obligation was based on blood relationships as well as legal status.

The strict imposition of monogamy awaited two developments of the late imperial period: the decline of the institution of slavery; and the triumph of the Christian church, which preached a rigorous ethos of sexual egalitarianism. "There is one law," St. Jerome insisted, "for men and for women." He might have added, for all nations and classes. The Church further (if slowly) extended this "leveling" ethos among the originally polygynous Celts (such as the Irish), Germans and Slavs. The Church further forbade divorce, and greatly expanded the definition and degrees of relationship in which marriages were prohibited. Not only consanguinity but affinity (relationship through marriage) could prevent a marriage. According to the rules laid down in the early Middle Ages, if a man and woman even suspected that they were related, they could not marry. This definition of incest was far more stringent than the comparable rules of ancient Israel or Rome, or of contemporary Islam. The motivation for this puzzles historians.[22] But one effect was this: A widowed woman could not marry a relative of her deceased husband. If she

---

21. R. Syme, "Bastards in the Roman Aristocracy," *Proceedings of the American Philosophical Society,* 104 (1960), p. 104.

22. See J. Goody, *The Development of the Family and Marriage in Europe* (Cambridge, 1983).

wished to remarry, she had to look beyond the circle of her former kin. This, I believe, forced a circulation of marriageable women in society and increased the chances that any given man would attract a mate. Monogamous marriage between unrelated partners was the only kind of marriage legally allowed in the Western Middle Ages. It is important, moreover, to note that the rules not only allowed but promoted and facilitated this form of sexual union.

Why did this happen? Can evolutionary theory make sense of this unexpected development? Ethology no longer assumes that animals will always act in ways to promote their own reproductive success. Rather, sociobiological theory now posits the concept of "inclusive fitness." Living beings act to enhance reproductive success, but in some circumstances they will recognize that a close relative carrying a similar set of genes has a better chance of reproducing than they do. They will therefore favor the reproductive chances of the relative over their own. This seemingly selfless or altruistic (but also sensible) behavior is called technically "kin selection." Usually, the "phenotype" is not concerned with the reproductive success of non-kin, but it may be willing under certain circumstances to favor their interests too. The motivation here is the presumption that the non-relatives will recognize the favor and in the future return it. This type of behavior in regard to non-kin is called "reciprocal altruism," or "reciprocity.' All human acts bearing upon reproduction may thus be placed under one of three rubrics: selfishness, kin selection or reciprocity.[23]

Now the balance of these three motivations can change under different circumstances, and under some conditions reciprocity may take on a special weight. The origins of socially imposed monogamy seems associated with small city states rather than great empires—with ancient Sumeria, and early Greece and Rome. These poleis or *civitates* initially formed the basic political units of the Greek and Roman worlds. Mediterranean geography tended to foster these small communities. Greece and Italy in particular were mountainous lands, divided by natural obstacles into many small regions. The communities that grew up in these segmented regions were initially small and for long remained intensely competitive. They also for long resisted inclusion into a single empire.

23. E. O. Wilson, *Sociobiology The New Synthesis*, p. 119 (Cambridge, Mass., 1975).

Under conditions of acute competition, it was necessary to maintain the moral commitment and physical energies of the citizens. Such conditions favored the development of democratic and republican, rather than despotic institutions. The citizens whose moral commitment was essential for the welfare of the state had to be granted some participation in it. But another, equally crucial means of maintaining commitment and morale was to offer all citizens access to marriage. Not only would they gain the satisfactions of sexual union, but the rearing of the family and the acquisition of heirs would give them a large stake in the *salus populi* in terms of personal and inclusive fitness. But only a system of monogamy could assure that all male citizens would have a reasonable chance of attracting a wife, siring a family, and passing on property to their certain descendants. In terms of evolutionary theory, under the social conditions created by the city states, reciprocity partially overrode both selfishness and altruism. The rich and powerful male was no longer allowed to use wealth and power to gain more than his fair share of free women. He had to allow even the poor citizen a chance to marry. This seems to have been the initial motivation for socially imposed monogamy.*

The final victory of monogamy awaited two developments, both occurring in the last centuries of the ancient epoch. The first was the decline of slavery, and the second was the triumph of the Christian church. The decline of slavery confronted ancient society with a critical shortage of workers. No longer able to rely upon coercion, the leaders of society had to develop a system of incentives to persuade now free or semi-free workers to work. One powerful incentive was again access to marriage and the chance to produce heirs. The new work unit in medieval agriculture in fact became the peasant family, and Europe would be effectively resettled on the basis of family farms. At the same time, the Church preached and eventually

---

*There are, however, two theoretical problems with reciprocity in human behavior. First, the difficulty of detecting and punishing cheaters makes a system of reciprocity evolutionarily unstable. Reciprocity requires social regulation of cheating. Second, the stricter the social hierarchy, the less likely it is to support a system of reciprocity. Trivers (1971) discusses both of these issues. A more parsimonious explanation for the evolution of monogamy does not rely on reciprocity. The rich and powerful male may have found, consciously or unconsciously, that under the circumstances (i.e., given the constraints of the situation) his reproductive success and the success of his kin were higher when he allowed even poor men to marry. R. L. Trivers, 1971. "The evolution of reciprocal altruism". *Quarterly Review of Biology,* 46 (1971), pp. 35–57.

imposed a rigorous ethic of sexual egalitarianism. The new principles, that even the richest male could claim only one wife, made women accessible and marriages possible for much larger numbers of even the poorest males. The move toward monogamy, launched in the early years of ancient Mediterranean civilization, was carried to completion even as that civilization ended. The new Western social system was thus founded upon this paradoxical combination of principles: sexual egalitarianism, but continuing inequality in wealth and status.

Monogamy, made a rule of European life in the early Middle Ages, conferred certain competitive advantages. "Perhaps," writes Eibl-Eibesfeldt, "this was a factor responsible for the great success of Europeans throughout the world."[24] Demographically, monogamy may have given Europe a greater capacity for growth.[25] Systems of extreme polygyny may dampen growth, as the patriarch is likely to acquire more women than he could possibly mate and to retain them even in his sterile old age. Many wives and concubines would not have, in other words, the possibility of becoming pregnant. Economically, monogamy seems essential in the imposition of a peasant economy, which in large part is based on family labor. Socially, monogamy exerted a pacifying and stabilizing influence. Europe was spared the disturbances which large numbers of mateless men are likely to provoke, and also spared the destructive competition of numerous sons fighting to succeed their patriarchal father and to claim family property (land, and so forth). To be sure, monogamy reduced, but it did not eliminate, differential reproduction in medieval society. At all times in medieval history, rich families reproduced more successfully than the poor, at least in terms of offspring postnatal survival. The superfluous sons of the wealthy, usually the younger sons, faced a real risk of losing status, of slipping down the social scale.[26] But this group seems also to have provided many of the innovators and entrepreneurs in medieval society—the knights, scholars and merchants who wandered away from home seeking to make their fortune. Their families gave them some

24. I. Eibl-Eibesfeldt, *Human Ethology.*
25. R. Clignet, *Many Wives. Many Powers* (Evanston, Ill., 1970) affirms that monogamous women bear more children than women in polygynous arrangements in the same society.
26. D. Herlihy, "Three Patterns of Social Mobility in Medieval Society," *Journal of Interdisciplinary History*, 3 (1973), pp. 623–48.

resources—not enough to enable them to live as well as their parents, but enough to support them in their entrepreneurial efforts.

It is harder to identify the specifically evolutionary repercussions of European monogamy. The most successful or resourceful male, constrained by monogamy, could not impress his genotype on the new generation quite as broadly as his polygynous predecessor. Conversely, sexual egalitarianism aided poor males in their search for a mate and in their efforts to secure representation for their genotype in the new generation. Under sexual egalitarianism, the distribution of genotypes in the new generation is likely to differ less radically from the distribution of genotypes among its parents.

I have so far tried to give an account of marriage and its development inhuman societies in the language of evolutionary theory. The great strength of the theory seems to be this. It emphasizes that human beings are powerfully motivated to pass on something from the past and present into the future. That "something" would seem to be more truly cultural than genetic. Today and throughout history, people have struggled to preserve and advance a cultural inheritance, whether that inheritance takes the form of a language, a religion, or a set of values. It would be hard to identify a force that has acted more powerfully on human groups than the aspiration for cultural survival. On the conscious level, culture seems to program people much as, in evolutionary theory, the genotype is thought to program individuals.

It seems to me that in developing an evolutionary theory useful for historians, the great need is to investigate possible linkages between genetic programming on the subconscious level and cultural programming on the conscious.[27] Perhaps there is imbedded in the human psyche some sort of translator, which effectively interprets and modifies biological impulses and transforms them into messages that human beings consciously recognize and to which they react. Certainly, the two goals—survival of a genotype and survival of a culture—are intimately related. Whether such an interpreter, linking the biological and the cultural realms, really exists, or what the full set of relationships between these realms may be, are problems for the future.

27. E. O. Wilson, *On Human Nature* (Cambridge, Mass, 1978).

13

AGE, PROPERTY, AND CAREER IN MEDIEVAL SOCIETY

——— ✦ ✦ ✦ ———

> Give not to your son ... power over yourself while you are alive, and do
> not give your estate to another ... For it is better that your children should
> ask of you, than that you look towards the hands of your children .... At
> the termination of the days of your life, and at the time of your death, dis-
> tribute your inheritance.
>
> Ecclesiasticus 33.20–24

This principle, that the aging father retains control over his property
until his death, is a fundamental rule of behavior in patriarchal
households. Retention of property assures that the productivity and
prosperity of the family will continuously benefit its elders. In spite
of their own declining powers, the old need not fear impoverishment in their final years. The promise of patriarchy has always been
security for the aged. And were not most families of medieval
Europe patriarchically organized?

But in spite of this counsel, medieval commentators on the stages
of life show a tendency to associate old age not with security and
comfort, but with want and deprivation. To be sure, they do not
always forcefully link poverty and aging. Many, particularly in the
early medieval period, treat the uncertainty of life and the fickleness
of fortune as independent ills, adding to the miseries of the human
condition. Gregory the Great, in his commentary on Job, thus states:

Aging and the Aged in Medieval Europe, ed. M. M. Sheehan, CSB. Papers in Mediaeval Studies, 11 (Toronto, 1990), pp. 143-158. © P.I.M.S., 1990.

"We cannot abide for long in the company of our possessions; either we loose them in death or they abandon us while we are still alive."[1] Bad luck can befall us, he implies, as it had befallen Job, at any moment of our earthly existence.

Then, too, medieval commentaries on aging are obscured by a shifting comprehension of what it meant to be poor. As Karl Bosl demonstrates, the term *pauper* in early medieval texts, up really to the eleventh century, implies lack of power and effectiveness more truly than lack of material possessions.[2] The antonym of *pauper* was *potens*, not *dives*.

We must wait, it seems, until the late Middle Ages to find clear and forceful assertions of a linkage between advancing years and deepening poverty. For example, Maurice of Sully, a preacher active in Paris in the twelfth century, identifies as the Lord's poor the widow, the orphan, the sick, the exile, and the destitute, but not the aged.[3] Lotario di Segni, later Pope Innocent III, in his well-known tract on human miseries, rehearses the ills of old age but does not include poverty among them.[4] He dwells on the instability of material possessions in a separate part of this lachrymose essay. In contrast, some two hundred years later, Bernardine of Siena singles out specifically the old, as those likely to require the support of Christian charity. "Old age," he says flatly, "is filled with numerous infirmities, labors, and complaints."[5] Bernardine's old person is clearly

1. *Moralium in Job* 18, ch. 19, cited in a sermon by Bernardino da Feltre, *Sermoni del beato Bernardino Tomitano da Feltre,* ed. P. C. V. da Milano, OFM Cap. (Milan, 1964), vol. 1, p. 240: "Dives enim cum rebus nostris durare non possumus, quia, aut nos illas moriendo deserimus, aut ille nos viventes quasi deserunt pereundo ... ."

2. K. Bosl, *Das Problem der Armut in der hochmittelalterlichen Gesellschaft,* Sitzungsberichte, Österreichische Akademie der Wissenschaften, philosophisch-historische Klasse 294.5 (Vienna, 1974), with references to his previous studies on the same subject. Bosl argues that this essentially feudal conception of poverty prevailed up to about 1050, then gave way over the years 1050–1300 to one very close to our own. For further studies of poverty in the Middle Ages, see *Etudes sur l'histoire de la pauvreté,* ed. M. Mollat, 2 vols. (Paris, 1974), and *Les Pauvres au moyen âge: Etude sociale* (Paris, 1978). These works do not note a specific tie between old age and poverty, and tend to treat the poor as marginal to medieval society; this view may not be entirely accurate.

3. Cited from a MS source by J. Longère, "Pauvreté et richesse chez quelques predicateurs durant la seconde moitié du XIIe siècle," in *Etudes,* ed. M. Mollat, vol. 1, p 261.

4. *De contemptu mundi, sive De miseria conditionis humane libri tres, Patrologia Latina* [hereinafter *PL.*] 217, pp. 701-746.

5. *Opera omnia,* ed. Pp. C. S. Bonaventurae, Vol. 6 (Florence, 1959), p. 58: "Senectus enim multis infirmitatibus, laboribus, et gravaminibus plena est."

not relaxing in the bosom of a large, supportive family. Underlying many of his allusions to the aged is the assumption that the old run greater risk of destitution than the young and the vigorous. And of course children have the weighty obligation to support their parents. If they fail to do so, they will be subject to a short life, or, even if they live long, they too will experience the same *paupertas magna*, as did their neglected parents. Bernardine, it should be noted, is also addressing his exhortations primarily to an urban audience.

This quick glance at the medieval moral comments on the stages of life is, of course, highly impressionistic, but perhaps it can still delineate a problem, central to the history of aging. Was there a novel linkage between growing older and growing poorer in the communities of the late Middle Ages? Did impoverishment mount a greater menace against the aged in towns than in rural settings? And if it did, why was it that the aged were failing to follow the sage counsel of Ecclesiasticus?

In this paper, we shall seek to investigate some relationships between aging and destitution within a late-medieval, urban community. The community we shall consider is Florence in the early fifteenth century. With a population of nearly 40,000, Florence was then one of the largest cities in Europe. Florence attracts for two reasons. It was a bastion of early commercial capitalism, and thus offers an opportunity to observe the influence of a commercialized or capitalistic economy on the organization of families and the treatment of the old. The Florentine government seems also to have been one of the first in Europe to register births, or some births, for purely secular purposes. Clearly, if we are to investigate the relationship between aging and impoverishment, we must know how old our subjects were. The life cycle, and its analysis, begins with birth.

Already from the late fourteenth century, the Florentine government was taking an interest in the ages of its citizens and subjects, for several reasons. One was fiscal. The government strove to collect a head tax imposed on able-bodied males between 18 and 60 years of age in the city and 14 and 70 in the countryside. It is clear, however, that in attributing ages to the entire male population, government officials had frequent recourse to rough approximations.[6] The

6. The quality of age reporting in the Florentine Catasto of 1427 is examined at length in D. Herlihy and C. Klapisch-Zuber, *Les Toscans et leurs familles. Une étude du catasto florentin de 1427* (Paris, 1978), pp. 350-392.

government, from about the same time, was also setting age qualifications for its principal offices. Thus, according to the Statutes of 1415, a citizen had to be over 30 years of age to serve in one of the three great councils of the communal government—the *Tre Maggiori* they were called. These were the eight priors, the twelve "Good Men," and the sixteen Standard-Bearers of the city's *gonfaloni* or wards. And only those over 45 years of age were eligible for the commune's highest office, that of Standard-Bearer of Justice.[7] Thirty seems also to have been the required age for all important administrative offices in city and countryside. Only *castellani*, or chiefs of castles, could be as young as 25.

To hold these offices was regarded as a high dignity. Indeed, it can be shown that many young men were prone to lie about their age, to claim to be past 30 when they were still in their 20s.[8] They were evidently eager for public honor and recognition. To counter this abuse, the government in August 1429 required that all who wished to hold office had to present proof of age. Specifically, they had to bring forth their family memoirs, in which were recorded their own births or those of their sons. All urban residents obligated to lend moneys to the government were regarded as eligible for office; they included between a quarter and a third of the urban families. Seemingly, many or most of these approximately 3,000 families were keeping written records of their births, marriages, and deaths. This is dramatic illustration of the extent of literacy within Florentine society. It also enhances the historian's confidence in the accuracy of the data these families were reporting.

After 1429, Florentine heads of households continued to present proof of age to the government, for themselves or their sons. We have registers of these *approbationes aetatum* through the fifteenth, into the sixteenth century. They give us an anchor, from which to study the lives of those males who aspired to public office in the last century of the Florentine Republic (1429–1530). The total number of prospective office holders who were registered between 1429 and 1530 is approximately 30,000. They constituted, as we have mentioned, from

7. *Statuta populi et communis Florentiae ... anno salutis MCCCCXV,* 3 vols., (Fribourg, 1778–1783), vol. 2, pp. 770–772, "De aetate dominorum et collegiorum et deveto." The election of castellans over age 25 was allowed, but other officials in the country-side had to be over 30 (ibid., vol. 2, p. 793).

8. D. Herlihy and C. Klapisch-Zuber, *Les Toscans,* pp. 359–360.

a quarter to a third of the city's male population. Florence in the fifteenth century was an oligarchy, but not a narrow one.

At what moments in his life was the Florentine citizen likely to experience financial duress? To answer this, we can take advantage of another remarkable set of documents. Florence chose its ruling officers, in both the communal government and the twenty-one guilds, through a kind of lottery.[9] The archival deposit describing the results of the lottery, and the office that recorded them, were called appropriately the *Tratte*, meaning sortitions or drawings. The process of election was complex and was frequently changed, but in crude description it worked largely as follows:[10] Special commissions periodically scrutinized the body of taxpaying citizens, and they entered on slips of paper the names of those deemed likely candidates for office. They excluded a small and shrinking number of magnates, and also political exiles, but otherwise seem to have been quite liberal in including names. For example, in spite of sporadic efforts to prevent it, they entered the names of children and even infants. The fathers of these underaged candidates seem to have thought that their sons' careers would ultimately benefit from this early exposure to the public life.

The slips were then collected into separate purses, corresponding to the various important offices of government and guild. When the time came to fill the offices, a slip containing a name would be drawn from the appropriate purse, in the presence of the outgoing officials and other dignitaries.[11] The name was then read aloud. In the technical language, the candidate was said to be *veduto*, "viewed" or considered for the relevant office. The outgoing officials and the invited dignitaries then judged whether or not the citizen should be awarded the office, *seduto* or "seated" in formal terminology. More often than not, he would be disqualified, for a variety of reasons. He might be too young, or already deceased, or ill, or absent from Florence; he or a close male relative might have held the same office in the recent past, or be already serving the commune in a post of greater dignity. One reason for exclusion has particular interest for us here. The candidate might be disqualified

9. For a description of the system, see G. Guidi, *Il governo della città-repubblica di Firenze del primo Quattrocento,* 3 vols., Biblioteca storica toscana 20 (Florence, 1981), vol. 1, pp. 149ff.

10. *Ibid.,* vol. 2, pp. 3ff.

11. *Ibid.,* vol. 1, pp. 283ff.

because he owed money to the government, whether from failure to pay his fiscal assessments or for some other reason. The delinquent citizen was said to be *in speculo,* "in the mirror." He was judged ineligible for election to any communal office, and even the slip of paper giving his name was at once ripped up. This public desecration of his name was a kind of symbolic execution, and carried great ritual significance. The government insisted that only those who supported it with their moneys could benefit from its offices and honors. All others endured a type of civic death.

Characteristically, the terms of service for Florentine office holders were very short, often only two months in duration and rarely longer than a year. The citizen as he aged was thus likely to be "viewed" for office scores of times in the course of his life, and the results of the viewing would be dutifully recorded in the registers of the Tratte office. The entries thus inform us when citizens were awarded offices, and when they were considered but excluded, and for what reasons. Exclusion for fiscal delinquency certainly indicates that the citizen had fallen upon hard financial times, and was probably bankrupt. Not only did he lose the honor and remunerations of service in public office, but his name was publicly disgraced. He lost in dignity and reputation, upon which his success as a merchant may well have depended crucially.

The computer allows us to do what the officials of the Tratte did not do, and could not have done very easily. We can match names of citizens in our file of birthdates with those found in the mirror of fiscal insolvency, and thus determine at what ages in life the Florentine citizen was likely to encounter financial duress. This should allow us to test whether there was a relationship between age and impoverishment, and what was its strength.

Since 1976, with the aid of a grant from the American National Humanities Foundation, I have been entering these birthdates and the other observations from the Tratte deposit into a machine-readable data base, which will eventually serve to reconstruct many individual careers of Florentine citizens. We are collecting these observations from the time of the earliest surviving registers (most of them date from the late fourteenth century) until the end of the Republic in 1530.[12] The

---

12. The episode of Ciompi (1378) represents a watershed in the survival of the Tratte records. Most survive in continuous series only after that date.

work has progressed with reasonable rapidity, though it remains far from finished. Still, the data base is now sufficiently large to support this preliminary inquiry into the relationships between aging and fiscal and financial insolvency in fifteenth-century Florence.

Of course, the number of citizens found to be in tax arrears is not exclusively a function of their ages and fortunes. It obviously must also reflect the financial demands of the Florentine government, and these varied with states of war and peace, victories and defeats. Then, too, in this attempt as in all attempts at life-cycle analysis, we ought to exclude from the scrutiny persons still living at the termination date of the time series, 1530. Otherwise, an "end effect," as statisticians call it, would bias the observations towards the younger years of life. The best strategy would seem to be to confine our analysis to a single age cohort that together had lived through periods of high and low fiscal demands and that no longer contained living members in 1530. The cohort we choose to study comprises those citizens who were entered into the original registrations of 1429, with additions up to 1435.

In this continuing project, we have not as yet entered into the data base all the electoral records of the Tratte archives. The elections to guild offices are now nearly complete, but a large gap remains after 1435 in the series of drawings to the so-called Tre Maggiori, the three chief councils of communal government. But these gaps in the data base are randomly distributed, and ought not distort the results of this inquiry. There are also problems, which we cannot treat at length here, in linking the names of those born with those cited as being "in the mirror." False linkages are always possible, but Florentine naming conventions tend to be relatively favorable to the researcher. The records usually give not only the name of the person, but that of his father and often the grandfather's too, as well as a family name if he has one. The record, in sum, carries with it a short genealogy. In testing for linkages across records, we admitted only those for which the Christian name, patronymic, and family name or occupation (which often substituted for a family name) were identical; places of residence cited in the records also had to correspond. By following strict procedures, we doubtlessly rejected many true matches, but at least we are reasonably certain that the accepted linkages are true.

Among the Florentine citizens living in 1429–1435, exactly 1,088 had been or would be excluded from office for failure to pay their fiscal charges. The total number of citizens living in 1429–1435 and cited in the birth registrations is 6,027. Thus, 18 percent of this elite group of Florentines were destined to endure, or at least brush with, bankruptcy at some moment of their lives. And this is a minimal estimate. As mentioned, our file does not yet include all citations for tax delinquency, and we have doubtlessly missed many true matches. The conclusion must be that the menace of financial ruin was not limited to small and marginal groups of urban society. Rather, it cast an extensive shadow even over the elite classes. For example, the richest citizen at Florence enrolled in the great survey of 1427, known as the Catasto, was messer Palla di Nofri Strozzi. His assets after deductions surpassed 100,000 gold florins. But in 1431, when "viewed" for election to the "Six of the Mercanzia," he was declared to be *in speculo*, and was cited again for fiscal delinquency in 1434.[13] In these same years, three of his sons, Lorenzo in 1431, Nofri in 1434, and Palla in 1426, were found to be delinquent, and even two of his grandsons (offspring of the deceased Francesco), Carlo and Giovanni: both were disqualified in 1434. The entire lineage seems to have been in a state of fiscal disarray. More surprising is the appearance in the dread mirror of tax arrears of the head of the Medici faction and architect of its hegemony over Florence, Cosimo di Giovanni di Bicci. The Florentine government after his death would honor him with the title *pater patriae*. But he too was several times caught in the mirror of non-payment of fiscal dues, in 1430, 1439, and 1441.[14] The fortunes of even the most prominent Florentines seem to have been remarkably insecure.

At what ages were these Florentine citizens likely to experience fiscal and financial difficulties? The total number of exclusions for reason of tax arrears, which these 1,088 citizens accumulated, is

13. Archivio di Stato di Firenze (henceforth ASF), Mercanzia, reg. 83, fol. 13, 30 August 1431; and ASF, Tratte, reg. 198, fol. 163, 29 August 1434. For his sons, see ASF, Tratte, reg. 198, fol. 91, 28 August 1431. (Lorenzo); reg. 198, fol. 166, 12 September 1434 (Nofri); and reg. 197, fol. 148, 28 April 1426 (Palla). The grandchildren appear in Tratte, reg. 198, fol. 158, 28 June 1434 (Carlo), and reg. 198, fol. 161, 29 August 1434 (Giovanni).

14. ASF, Mercanzia, reg. 83, fol. 7, 15 September 1430; reg. 84, fol. 202, 16 December 1439; reg. 84, fol. 28, 20 December 1441.

2,177. Although the electoral officials destroyed the slip of paper containing the name of the delinquent, that name could easily appear again in the drawings for a different office. We can judge the relationship between age and insolvency by comparing the group of citizens cited for tax delinquency with the entire group of potential office holders living in 1429–1435. In Table 1, the second column shows the distribution by decades of age of those citizens caught "in the mirror." It should be remembered that the same Florentine could be "viewed" and excluded several times, as each office had its separate purse. The third column shows the distribution again by decades of life of the entire group of office holders in the year 1432, the middle year of the range 1429–1435, when the earliest registrations were made. This distribution should roughly approximate the age pyramid of the potential office holders as it might be found at any time in the fifteenth century. The ratio in column four shows the relationship between the two columns, and because of multiple citations of the same person can go well above unity.

Table 1

Ages of Florentine Citizens in Tax Arrears
(Cohort Living in 1429–1435)

Age	Number of Citations (a)	Distribution in 1432 (b)	Ratio (a/b)
0–9	33	1,850	0.01
10–19	138	1,284	0.10
20–29	262	1,051	0.24
30–39	314	735	0.42
40–49	365	686	0.53
50–59	406	238	1.70
60–69	383	126	3.03
70–79	173	38	4.55
80–89	59	12	4.91
90–99	44	7	6.28

Source: For births, ASF, Tratte, regg. 39 and 1093; for those in tax arrears, ASF, Tratte, regg. 190–198 and Mercanzia, regg. 78–88.

Not surprisingly, the number of very young tax delinquents are few, for evident reasons. Most little children remained under the authority of their fathers, and had no independent fiscal responsibility. Some orphans might have been excluded for reason of age, before it was even discovered that they were also in tax arrears. The few young delinquents represent orphans who received an inheritance containing more debts than assets. Even then, they had the option of refusing the inheritance, as more damaging than profitable to their interests.

The proportions of delinquents increase rapidly in the second and third decades of life, even as the young Florentines were achieving fiscal and financial independence (as we shall see, it was not unusual for fathers to emancipate their children at young ages). The rate of increase falls from about 30 to 50 years of age. The Florentine male would normally marry about age 30, and gain use of the substantial dowry that his bride brought into his household. The children born to him did not place heavy demands on his assets over the first twenty years of his marriage. After age 50, however, the proportion of delinquents soars, and reaches stunning levels in the last decades of life. Many old Florentines must have passed their last years in permanent tax arrears, and in destitution.

This association of old age and impoverishment can be illustrated through the individual careers of many prominent Florentines. Matteo di Niccolò Corsini, a merchant who spent seventeen years abroad, left an encumbered inheritance when he died in 1402, at the age of 79. In 1411 his heirs still had not satisfied the government's claims against it for delinquent taxes.[15] Gregorio di Stagio Dati pursued a long and apparently successful career as a silk merchant, served as Standard-Bearer of Justice, and was seven times consul of his guild. In his memoirs, he describes in mournful numbers his financial situation when he was 71 years old.[16] In 1432 and 1433 the comment "in speculo" flags his name in the electoral lists.[17] Messer Luca di Buonaccorso Pitti, who, with his great palace, gave Florence a hitherto unprecedented display of private magnificence, also ended his life—he died at age 77—under a financial cloud. In 1480, eight years after his death, one of his heirs declares: "This inheritance of messer Luca, my father, has many burdens of debts and bequests."[18] He emphasizes that he is heir to only one-sixth of his father's patri-

15. ASF, Tratte, reg. 150, 1 June 1411. Niccolò's son is said to be "pro patre in speculo."

16. G. Dati, *Il libro segreto,* ed. C. Gargiolli, Scelta di curiosità letterarie inedite o rare 102 (Bologna, 1869), p. 120.

17. ASF, Tratte, reg. 155, 1 January 1432 and 1 January 1433.

18. ASF, Catasto, reg. 997, fol. 322, declaration of Iacopo di messer Luca Pitti: "Questa redità di messer Lucha mio padre à molti incharichi di debiti e di lasci ... ." He also affirms: "A me tocha la sesta parte della gravezza e non più." The inheri-

mony, clearly implying that Luca's liabilities outweighed his assets. Even the greatest Florentine merchants risked destitution in later life.

Our file of tax delinquents also allows us to ask whether there is a relationship between profession and impoverishment. Table 2 shows the average age of tax delinquents, according to the office for which they were being considered. The offices are the Tre Maggiori, the "Six of the Mercanzia," and the consuls or captains of twenty of the twenty-one recognized guilds. Consuls for the judges and notaries were separately elected, and therefore are not represented in the table.

All Florentine officeholders were required to join a guild, but many of them did not actively pursue the profession. However, we can assume that those who were chosen as captains or consuls really were active in the "art" or craft they represented.

Although we do not know the size of the guild membership, Table 2 at least suggests that tax delinquency and bankruptcy were much more frequent in those professions that operated with large amounts of capital, than in the lesser trades, which required little. Put another way, practitioners of the seven (here, six) major, capital-intensive professions were more likely to experience financial strain than the small shopkeepers and artisans.

They were also likely to experience these financial difficulties later in life than members of the minor guilds. One sharp contrast that emerges out of Table 2 is the high age of candidates excluded from the "Six of the Mercanzia," in relation to all the other communal offices. The Six were a kind of mercantile aristocracy, responsible for promoting the commercial prosperity of the city. The office was comparable in dignity to the Priorate, as the Priors were the chief governing board in the government. Yet the average age of excluded candidates for the Six was some twenty years higher than that of the rejected candidates for the priorate. This suggests that those actively involved in a mercantile career were likely to face financial duress at advanced ages; members of the urban elite less concerned with commerce faced failure at moments more randomly distributed through their lives.

The same conclusion would seem to follow from an examination of the elections to the major and minor guilds. The guild of Calimala, which included the city's greatest merchants, also shows, with the excep-

---

tance, but not the tax claims against it, is described ibid., reg. 998, fol. 415, where each of the six heirs could claim 1,067 florins and 7 *solidi a oro*.

tion of the innkeepers, the oldest age of insolvency in the entire list, 58.61 years, and the bankers at 56.60 years are not much younger. The wool merchants, who constituted the largest but not the richest of the major guilds, also have the youngest average age among the bankrupt, 49.24 years. But four of the minor guilds show even younger ages. Again there seems evident an association between the use of large sums of capital in one's profession and fiscal insolvency in later life.

Table 2

Average Age of Candidates in Tax Arrears, by Office

A. Communal Offices

Office	Number	Average Age
Six of the Mercanzia	121	55.97
16 Standard-bearers	188	43.28
12 Good Men	253	42.03
Notary	3	40.00
Standard-bearer of Justice	8	38.75
Prior	171	35.47

B. Captains of Major Guilds

Office	Number	Average Age
Merchant (Calimala)	132	58.61
Furrier	54	57.81
Banker (Cambio)	104	56.60
Silk Merchant	146	52.57
Spice Merchant	151	51.61
Wool Merchant (Lana)	269	49.24

C. Captains of Minor Guilds

Office	Number	Average Age
Innkeeper	27	59.51
Locksmith	48	56.68
Old Clothes Merchant	49	55.06
Butcher	34	53.52
Cuirass Maker	36	53.27
Iron Worker	70	53.20
Leather Worker	29	51.82
Shoemaker	22	51.45
Hosier	38	50.63
Master of Stone	19	49.31
Carpenter	21	47.66
Oil and Soap Dealer	64	47.60
Baker	29	46.17
Vintner	88	44.64

Source: Same as Table 1. Observations are limited to males living in 1429–1435 and entered into the birth registrations.

Why should this be? It would seem that patrimonies based largely on real property and those containing chiefly liquid capital imposed quite different constraints on those who would manage them, enlarge them, or at least preserve them over time. And those constraints reverberated back upon the organization of the household and the authority of its chief. The peasant property owner was under little compulsion to divide his holdings and to assign portions to his heirs well before his death. Rather, good management of the land recommended that the holdings be kept integral for as long as possible. As he aged, the peasant owner could look to the energies of his children, growing or already grown, to compensate for his own declining powers. The farm was most efficiently worked by the collective efforts of a family. The association of a large family and an integral patrimony seems especially intimate in a rural setting. If a young peasant should depart from his parents' home, he would usually join, as a hired hand, another big household; or he would quickly marry, and begin recruiting the large menage he needed to manage a farm. Large households under the authority of a single chief, and stable, integral holdings: these were the foundations of productivity and prosperity in the countryside.

To be sure, the peasant owner would likely experience some pressures to convey property to his children before his death. His daughters required dowries, and sons might wish for an independent life on their own parcels. But, at least in Tuscany, the peasant owners were able to accommodate these desires without significantly dismantling their holdings. Dowries were small in the countryside, and departing sons seem not to have taken much property with them.

Similarly, no reason of good management pushed the rentier, or the rich landlord, into dividing his patrimony well before his death. He could support even his grown children from his rents, and manage his properties with the help and counsel of his sons. He gained nothing from the early division of his estate, and the act would probably not enhance the revenues it yielded.

These factors affected the developmental cycle of rural households in regard to wealth—a subject we have examined in previous publications.[19] As can be shown from the Catasto of 1427, house-

19. D. Herlihy and C. Klapisch-Zuber, *Les Toscans*, pp. 491–494; D. Herlihy, "Mapping Households in Medieval Italy," *Catholic Historical Review*, 58 (1972) pp. 1-24.

hold heads in the countryside tend to grow richer as they grow older. The richest chiefs in rural areas are consequently the oldest, with the exception only of minor heirs who have not yet divided their inheritance. But this last type of estate represents as much the last stage in the developmental cycle of the rural patrimony as it does the first. This correlation of age and wealth establishes that a patriarchal system of property management and household organization prevailed in the countryside. Many heads of rural families could look forward to a materially untroubled senescence. They willingly followed the counsel of Ecclesiasticus and kept their patrimonies under their own control until their deaths.

Within the commercial economy—and commercial professions—of the city, the family usually did not function as a tight team of workers, and the family head early felt powerful pressures to divide his holdings, well before his final hours. There were several considerations prompting him to convey substantial portions of his patrimony to his children.

First of all, to render his capital productive, the household head had to marry his moneys to the energies of an entrepreneur, usually young, often his own son. This active partner would typically seek to multiply the moneys in distant markets—at Rome or Venice, Bruges or London. He had to be given control over as well as possession of these resources. In the world of long-distance trade, opportunities for profit were often fleeting. The young merchant could not wait for authorization from a distant, uninformed father to buy or sell, lend or borrow, save or speculate. The great Florentine commercial houses were often family based; the enterprise that sustained them was not. Rather, success in long-distance trade demanded individual effort, and favored the early emancipation of the young.

Then, too, in retaining or dispensing his resources, the urban head of family faced a difficult choice. Doubtlessly he wished to retain his wealth, to support himself in his final years. Doubtlessly too, this desire helped give to the aged a widespread reputation for avarice and stinginess.[20] But he had also to consider the interest of his lineage. By retaining control over his property, he would obstruct the marriages of his daughters and the careers of his sons. Dowries

20. On attitudes towards the aged in Tuscany, see D. Herlihy and C. Klapisch-Zuber, *Les Toscans,* pp. 606ff.

were high within the city, and marriage came early for the urban girl. When he was in his 50s, the father would usually have to decide whether to seek brilliant and expensive marriages for his daughters. He would gain thereby the prospect of grandchildren in the female line, and, perhaps even more important in this male-dominated society, enjoy the support of a *bel parentado*, an influential group of in-laws. It cost less to consign girls into convents, but this choice served only poorly the interests of the lineage.

The urban heads of households, especially those engaged in the mercantile professions, needed early to establish sons in careers as well as daughters in marriage, and this too required substantial amounts of capital. They looked to their sons to repair and restore the family's fortunes, always threatened by the need to support many heirs. Once successful as merchants, the sons marry and preserve over time the name and station of the lineage.

Another set of records in the Florentine State Archives captures this early conveyance of property from the older to the younger generations. These are the acts of formal emancipation.[21] According to the Roman law, which Florence respected, the father's power over his children, his *patria potestas*, lasted as long as the father survived. Even when physically mature, unemancipated sons and daughters could not enter into binding legal agreements, or acquire or dispense properties, without their father's agreement. In particular, the unemancipated son could not function as an independent merchant. The Florentine Archives have preserved many acts of emancipation scattered through the notarial chartularies, and two registers in two separate deposits, the Mercanzia and the Repubblica. Our consideration is here limited to the last register, which begins in 1422, and we shall end our scrutiny in 1500.

Florentine fathers, when they freed their sons, almost invariably endowed them with property. This conveyance of property to emancipated sons was called, like the comparable settlement upon daughters, a *dos, dote,* or dowry. The amounts of wealth involved were often substantial. In 1382 Matteo Corsini, when he emancipated his oldest son Piero, gave to the boy—he was only 16—two farms, which Piero later sold for the considerable sum of 1,600

21. On emancipations at Florence, see T. Kuehn, *Emancipation in Late Medieval Florence* (New Brunswick, NJ, 1982).

gold florins.[22] In 1468, when messer Giovannozzo Pitti emancipated his two sons, he gave both of them agricultural lands and, in addition, the sums of 1,200 and 1,300 florins respectively.[23] Emancipation, with an accompanying *dote*, thus conferred upon the son not only judicial capacity, but the material means that he needed to function independently in society and launch a career.

In some few of the acts, both the occupation of the father and the age of the son are stated. Table 3 shows the average age of emancipated sons according to the father's profession. Those fathers who style themselves *civis et mercator florentinus*, "Florentine citizen and merchant," appear with notable frequency. Only notaries are encountered in the registers more often than the *mercatores*, but notaries also formed the largest single occupational group within the city of Florence, at least in 1427.[24] The term, to be sure, is not precise, but seems to have identified members of all the major guilds.

Table 3
Ages of Sons at Emancipation, 1422–1500

Profession	Number	Average Age
Merchant (Mercator)	22	15.50
Retail Merchant (Rigattiere)	8	15.75
Dyer	5	18.00
Spice Dealer	10	19.20
Leather Dealer (Galligarius)	5	19.80
"Worker of the Soil"	9	20.11
Silk Merchant	7	22.57
Notary	11	23.45
Baker	8	27.63

Source: Repubblica, Emancipazioni, regg. 1–13.

The average age at emancipation, for all groups in society, was 20.09 years, but of all groups in society, the merchants freed their offspring at the youngest ages. The sons of notaries had usually passed their twenty-third birthday when they were freed, and sons of bakers

22. *Il libro di ricordanze dei Corsini (1362–1457)*, ed. A. Petrucci, Fonti per la storia d'Italia 100 (Rome, 1964), p. 67.

23. Alfonso describes his *dota* in ASF, Catasto, reg. 906, fol. 49, 1469, and Giovanni *ibid.*, fol. 385. The emancipation of both sons is registered in ASF, Repubblica, Emancipazioni, reg. 8, fol. 200.

24. For size of occupations according to the Catasto of 1427, see D. Herlihy, and C. Klapisch-Zuber, *Les Toscans*, p. 297, Table 35.

their twenty-seventh. In contrast, most sons of merchants were endowed with the power and property to make their way in the world before they had attained age 16. The same impressions follow from a consideration of the Florentine family memoirs. For example, Matteo di Niccolò Corsini, the merchant whom we previously encountered, emancipated his sons at the following ages: Piero in 1382, at age 16; Niccolò in 1383, at age 10; Lodovico in the same year, at age 9; and Neri, before he had reached his eighth birthday.[25] Of all groups in society, the merchants were the first to dismantle the formal authority of the father, and break his exclusive control over the family's resources.

One final consideration prompted the aging merchant to emancipate his sons and supply them with capital: the threat of debts and taxes. The moneys the aging chief conveyed to the young generation were effectively sheltered from the claims of his own debtors and of the communal government. The aged should retain the family's debts and liabilities, but pass on its assets to the entrepreneurial young: this was sensible strategy for a mercantile aristocracy. It held out the best hope that the status and future of the lineage would be maintained. But it also left the old generation exposed to a high risk of deprivation and misery.

These, then, are the conclusions that our study of fiscal delinquency in fifteenth-century Florence would seem to support. In Florence and doubtlessly, too, in other commercial towns of the late Middle Ages, the threat of poverty in old age was not confined to marginal groups in society. Rather, it darkened the final years of many members even of the privileged classes. And poverty in old age was not entirely a social accident, attributable to bad luck. It might better be viewed as structural, in the sense that it was brought about by the very operation of the commercial economy. The economy of the town undermined the solidarity of the family and weakened the authority of its chief. In doing this, it deprived him of the means that might have assured him a comfortable old age. Capital had to be joined to individual enterprise, and enterprise was the monopoly of the young. Resources flowed down the generations much more quickly in the town than in the countryside.[26] Urban conditions thus raised a social issue—widespread poverty among the aged—that seems not to have been a pressing problem under the patriarchal family system found in rural society and

25. *Il libro di ricordanze dei Corsini,* pp. 66–75, for the emancipations. The births of the sons are given ibid., pp. 87–95.
26. On the development cycle in relation to wealth, see above, n. 18.

in the earlier Middle Ages. Perhaps for this reason the great preachers in the late medieval towns dwelt upon the responsibility of the young to support the old—a duty they did not have to urge upon their hearers in other settings. The urban household may have lost in solidarity, but its members—particularly its older members—still had need of its traditional services. The urban old would doubtlessly have benefited, had they been able to follow the sage counsel of Ecclesiasticus. But this, the character of the urban economy and their own sense of duty towards offspring and lineage did not allow.

14

SOCIETY, COURT AND CULTURE IN SIXTEENTH-CENTURY MANTUA

✦ ✦ ✦

The splendid efflorescence of culture in the period of the Italian Renaissance has long intrigued historians. How can one explain this brilliant parade of masters who, in thought, literature, art and music, added immeasurable riches to the Western cultural inheritance? Why this society, this land, this time? To be sure, the deepest personal roots of human creativity may be closed to historical inquiry; perhaps only psychologists, perhaps geneticists, sociobiologists or theologians may ultimately explain them. Still, historians have the capability of examining the social foundations of past artistic or intellectual achievement. It is obvious that writers and artists do not live and labor in a vacuum. They consume resources; in the period of the Renaissance, masters of the arts were critically dependent upon the masters of power and property. "Those whose talents are obstructed by poverty at home," Giovanni Boccaccio once remarked, "do not easily make their mark." Writers and artists had therefore to please particular and discriminating audiences. They had to evoke within the idiom of their art and their times the delight, fear, wonder and, above all, the appreciation and gratitude of contemporaries. Societies as well as individuals inform the cultural history of an age, and societies usually acquire the kind and quality of culture they are willing to encourage and support.

In this paper, we shall limit our attention to the social history of one small Italian town—Mantua. Unexpectedly, in the light of its modest size and political mediocrity, Mantua in the sixteenth century flourished as one of the cultural capitals of Italy. Our task here will be to describe the economy of this little community, its population, society and government. We shall then apply to the experience of Mantua certain broad interpretations, which historians have formulated, in their continuing analysis of the social contributions to sixteenth-century culture.

Mantua stands in the middle of the long and level Po valley of northern Italy, some 100 miles east-south-east of Milan, and 25 miles southwest of Verona. The countryside which its princes ruled in the sixteenth century was only some 30 miles long and 20 miles wide; it was one of the smallest independent principalities in the entire peninsula.

Mantua and its region are in many ways distinctive. Standing some 70 miles from the Adriatic sea, it is only 88 feet above sea level. Water readily accumulates within and slowly drains from many lakes and marshes. The city is an inland Venice. It grew up on a slight elevation between two large and shallow lakes, fed by the Mincio river which, eight miles south of the city, empties into the Po. The very name, Mantua, may derive from a common Celtic word for mound. The surrounding lakes, streams and marshes make Mantua an ideal site for a fortress. Venetian ambassadors, who several times described the city in the sixteenth century, noted its formidable defenses. As one of them related in 1540, it was "a city well strengthened both by nature and by art."

The easily defensible site may well have attracted the earliest settlers to this mound between the lakes. We do not know who they were, but the town itself is very old. In the sixteenth century, its erudite historians claimed that Mantua had been founded a full 500 years before Romulus had laid out Rome. Modern scholars concur to this extent at least: its site was certainly inhabited in pre-Roman times, perhaps by Etruscans. Later, as a small Roman *municipium*, Mantua acquired considerable renown as the birthplace of the greatest Latin poet, P. Virgilius Maro. *Marone felix Mantua est*: Mantua is fortunate to have had Virgil. Indeed, without the luster his name casts upon the city, we would hear little of its existence in antiquity, even as we know little of its fate during the early Middle Ages. Only from the eleventh century does Mantua emerge from the shadows. It was by then one of many tiny city states, which dotted northern Italy; it professed a vague allegiance to the Holy Roman Empire, but was in fact largely self-governing. And Mantua kept its independence far longer than most of its neighbors, really until the eighteenth century. The feat was the more remarkable, as the tiny principality confronted, just beyond its immediate borders, two large and powerful territorial states—the Duchy of Milan to the west and the Republic of Venice to the north and east. Apparently, Mantua's wet, protected lands did not sufficiently whet the appetites of these mighty neighbors. Once again, its defensible site shaped the city's destinies.

After the sixteenth century, when its cultural splendor totally faded, Mantua remained in the annals of Italian history primarily as a fortress town. It formed one leg of a quadrilateral of fortress towns—a kind of iron square, the dominance of which assured military control over the lower Po valley and the Veneto. In the wars of the nineteenth century, French, Austrians, Piedmontese and others hotly contested the mastery of Mantua and its sister fortresses. The strategic importance of the town, not its slight economic or political weight, ignited the covetousness of these powers.

For if armies found Mantua difficult to approach, merchants did too: the town remained a commercial and economic backwater. Even its shallow lakes and small streams could not support a vigorous inland trade carried in large boats and barges. Moreover, the town lay far removed from the most important land highways stretching across the Po valley. Even foreign visitors to Italy in the eighteenth and nineteenth centuries, making the grand tour required in a genteel education, often missed the town. They crossed the Alps to Milan, proceeded down the Po valley through Brescia and Verona to Venice, and then turned south, to traverse Padua, Ferrara, Bologna, Florence and Siena, in the direction of Rome. Today too, the town is usually not packaged in the packaged tours, which promise the traveler Italy in two or so weeks. Now as in the past, Mantua is easily overlooked.

Ill-served by roads and even navigable waterways, Mantua never became an important market or commercial entrepôt. For this reason too, a strong mercantile tradition never took root among its citizens. The great merchant princes, who dominated society and politics at Florence, Venice, Genoa and other larger towns, while not entirely missing from Mantua, still exerted only a faint social presence, The dearth of great local merchants and the consequent scarcity of coin probably also explain the size of the Jewish community and the favored treatment which, on the whole, Jews received at Mantua. In 1588 a Venetian ambassador reported that Jews constituted a fifth of the population—about 8000 persons, within a city of approximately 40,000. He goes on to say: "[The management of] taxes and trade are left to them; they are of great usefulness and benefit to the Lord Duke, since the nobles, even if they are rich ..., do not wish to pay attention to such activities."

Never a great commercial center, Mantua still drew substantial economic benefits from its flat and fertile countryside. The numerous lakes, rivers and marshes of the region supplied the inhabitants with an abundance of fish—remarkably so, in a town 70 miles from the open sea. A guild of fishermen appears in the documents already by 1300. Fishermen achieved visibility even within the cultural life of the town. They organized, for example a traditional pageant, which they presented during the many urban festivals. Sturdy citizens carried on their backs through the streets of the town a fishing boat. There sailed within the boat twelve members of the guild, masqued to appear as Christ's apostles. Golden haloes encircled their heads. As the Apostles sailed through the city, they threw out fresh fish to the populace, and occasionally cast forth nets, as if to haul in the spectators. For were not the Apostles called to be, as the Gospels instruct us, fishers of men? This colorful pageant, often performed, never failed to delight the citizens, and elicited the comment and approval of foreign visitors.

The many rivers and streams also turned the wheels of mills, and the grinding of grain was a major enterprise. In 1540 the tax on mills yielded an extraordinary 25,000 ducats per year; this revenue was surpassed only by the salt tax, which brought to the governmental coffers some 34,000 ducats.

The importance of milling indicates too the fertility of the countryside. Mantua remained consistently throughout its history an exporter of foodstuffs, especially wheat and feed grains, to its neighbors, notably to Verona and the Veneto. Vines did less well on the flat plain; characteristically, they were trained to grow upon small trees, in a kind of arboreal marriage. The tree held up the vine, its leaves and its buds, to catch the rays of the nourishing, ripening, sweetening sun. Flax and hemp grew well on the well-watered land, and provided important raw materials to the cloth and rope industries of the town. In the early sixteenth century, the Gonzaga rulers promoted the cultivation of two new crops, which helped make the epoch one of high prosperity: rice, which flourished in marshlands too wet for other cereals; and the mulberry tree, which provided the essential food for silk worms. The manufacture of silk cloth and the sewing of garments, out of silk and other materials, seem quickly to have become the largest and most remunerative of the city's industries. "It supports," the Venetian ambassador reported in 1540, "a large number of poor."

But perhaps the most interesting and influential product of Mantuan agriculture, at least in a social and cultural sense, was not these noble crops of wheat, rice, or mulberries; rather, it was grass and hay. The natural meadows, which filled the bottom lands along the many waterways, were too wet for most domesticated plants but provided abundant grasses. Still in the sixteenth century, farmers lacked the capability of planting their own artificial meadows. To feed sheep, goats, oxen, cows and other animals, they principally relied upon these natural supplies of hay.

By virtue of these meadows, Mantua could export both hay and animal products to its neighbors. Moreover, large flocks and herds, many of them from the region of Pavia in the upper Po valley, came during winter to graze upon Mantua's still verdant pastures. In a description of governmental revenues, prepared in 1554, the ducal officers were collecting a substantial tax from these foreign *bestie*, which came to feed on Mantua's green meadows. The same report shows that the duke's own extensive estates were well stocked with sheep, cattle and horses. His gifts to his courtiers and servants always included great quantities of meats (pork and veal predominantly) and of cheese. And Mantua also exported raw wool, to be made into cloth in Verona, Vicenza and other cities.

Finally, the countryside with its abundant grasses could feed a large population of horses. Abundant hay, it is no exaggeration to say, helped make the elite of Mantua a society of cavaliers and ladies. In the fourteenth and fifteenth centuries, the Gonzaga rulers supplemented their income and enhanced their reputations by organizing armed and mounted companies, and by selling their services to foreign states—Milan, Venice, the papacy and others. They were, in sum, *condottieri*, mercenary captains. In 1495, a League of the principal Italian powers, the king of Aragon and the Emperor, organized to drive King Charles VIII of France out of Italy, chose the marchese Francesco II Gonzaga as the commander of its combined army. In the assessment of the Venetians, he was "young, inexperienced and treacherous," but the food and hay he could collect from his Mantuan lands apparently absolved him of these flaws. Francesco challenged the French king at Fornovo in the Romagna, in July, 1495, as he was seeking to retreat from Italy. After a day of bloody but indecisive combat, the French army, beset by dwindling stores of food and fodder, elected to break off the fighting and resume the march to France. Francesco did not win a decisive victory, but at least he showed the French that conquests in Italy would not be easy. And in large part, his achievement and his glory were built on hay.

Francesco, we might mention in passing, has two other titles to fame. He was the husband of Isabella d'Este, perhaps the most famous woman patron of arts and letters in the Renaissance period. And it is said that he was the first Italian since the ancient Romans to sport a beard. Allegedly, his tonsorial style changed the faces of gentlemen throughout the peninsula.

From the last decades of the fifteenth century, the breeding of fine horses was becoming a major industry at Mantua, and chief among the entrepreneurs were the Gonzaga themselves. Francesco, who died in 1519, reputedly kept a stable of more than one thousand horses. One of these noble animals was supposedly worth its weight in silver; others he gave as presents to the kings of France and of England, and to other great princes, whose favor he was cultivating. His successor, Federico II, the first Gonzaga to acquire the title of duke, commissioned the court architect and painter Giulio Romano to build the famous Palazzo del Te, just outside the walls of the city. A vast pleasure palace, it also contained the principal stables; it was designed, it seems fair to say, as much for horses as for people. Through the sixteenth century and beyond, the lure of bridle paths drew prince and courtiers for extended periods into the countryside, particularly during Mantua's humid and unhealthy summers. The courtly enjoyment of horses dotted the Mantuan landscape with pleasant villas and their indispensable stables.

The tax report, dated 1554, which we have previously cited, includes a census not only of the gentlemen and ladies in attendance at the Gonzaga court, but also of the most esteemed horses in the ducal stables. Apart from fillies and colts, and low-bred animals, they numbered 83. They included horses imported from Austria, Spain, Turkey, and "Barbery," presumably the steppes of eastern Europe. The census records the names of the animals, and the names themselves convey a taste of the courtly culture, in which the exercise of riding played so large a part. Some of the equine names proclaim the nobility of the animals; there were, for example, steeds called Captain, Caesar, even Archbishop. One horse is called Cacciapensiero, "Worry-chaser," and this hints at the solace and delight his riders found in him. Some names have a touch of whimsy: one horse is called "Moon in the Head." Was it, we inquire, stable under the reins? Another is called Gonzaga; what qualities, we wonder, earned it the name?

Mantua was, in sum, an agricultural rather than a commercial and industrial center, and the products of the countryside largely sustained the economy of the town. By 1300 there were already two specialized guilds of butchers; shoemakers, tanners and furriers were by then also recognized corporations. The large flocks of sheep which grazed on Mantuan meadows provided abundant wool, and a woolen industry took early root within the urban economy. But perhaps because of its defective communications, Mantua never became a large industrial center, after the manner of Florence or Milan. Still in the sixteenth century, it was an exporter of raw wool. Even its silk industry, its chief employer of the poor, was of middling size.

How many Mantuans could be supported by these resources? Population in both city and countryside shows substantial shifts, from the Middle Ages, into the sixteenth and seventeenth centuries. Although our evidence is indirect, the urban population seems to have expanded substantially from about the year 1000 until about 1300, across the central Middle Ages. The city constructed its last circle of walls in 1242, and never thereafter perceived a need for additional residential space. It may be that the population of the medieval city was then larger than it was again to be, until our own century.

From the middle fourteenth century, a shocking sequence of epidemics, famines and wars radically reduced Italian populations everywhere, in both cities and countrysides. In this grim panorama, the Black Death of 1348 holds a special notoriety, but it was only the first of many natural and social disasters. At Mantua, the Black Death allegedly carried off two-thirds of the town's inhabitants. Plagues again struck the city in 1361–62, 1373, and 1399. By 1372—the date of our earliest surviving census—the city contained 28,700 persons. The urban population thereafter remained stable at low levels for more than a century. In 1463, the town counted a little more than 26,000 persons (26,407), and in 1491, still only 23,000 (23,185).

In contrast to these years of stability, the city experienced an authentic demographic boom during the opening decades of the sixteenth century. From a paltry 23,000 persons in 1491, Mantua attained by 1560 nearly 38,000 inhabitants. In 1564, the Venetian ambassador reported that the city included between 40 and 45,000 residents. In fewer than 70 years, the town had grown by 63 percent. The cultural efflorescence at Mantua in the first half of the sixteenth century thus rode the tides of substantial demographic and economic expansion, the latter presumably based on the heightened production of rice and silk. About 1560, the town was at or near its peak size; population then remained stable at high levels for the next half century.

Once again, in the seventeenth century, disasters struck Mantua. By 1615, in the report of the Venetian ambassador, the population had slipped to 30,000. There ensued a disastrous war, during which the city was twice besieged, and a devastating epidemic followed hard behind. The urban population dipped to only 7000, and never rose above 20,000 during the course of the century. The inhabitants of the entire principality declined from 170,000 to 43,000—a staggering drop of 70 percent. The duke's own revenues fell by nearly two-thirds, lavish patronage of the arts ended, and life at court took on austere and somber tones. These serried disasters effectively ended the Renaissance at Mantua, stomping out the cultural splendor of the sixteenth-century city.

It is worth noting that as late as 1901, Mantua claimed a population of only 31,000; by 1928, it still contained only 36,300. Four hundred years, in other words, would pass, before the town would again attain the size it had held, during the glistening middle years of the sixteenth century.

Who ruled this small state of Mantua? The political and constitutional changes which the town experienced between the thirteenth and the sixteenth centuries follow an almost classical sequence: from free and popular commune in the thirteenth century, to despotism under the Gonzaga in the fourteenth, to signory or principality in the fifteenth and sixteenth centuries, ruled first by marchesi and then by dukes.

The Gonzaga family itself, more appropriately called the Corradi da Gonzaga, derived from the class of petty knights and landholders, who had immigrated into the town from their ancestral rural castle in the twelfth century. They participated actively in the politics of the communal government, but never lost their close ties with the countryside. They seem never to have had significant mercantile interests but remained faithful to their original calling, as landlords and cavaliers.

In 1328 Luigi Gonzaga eliminated a principal rival and secured his own election as captain general of the people; later he became also vicar general of the empire. The coup d'état of 1328 ended free and popular government at Mantua, and established despotic rule over the city. The Gonzaga governed Mantua under various titles until 1707; their line was among the most tenacious and durable of the petty dynasties of Italy.

After 1328, for the first century of their regime, Luigi and his successors ruled as despots, that is, they had no permanent and hereditary claim to the powers they exercised, but based their dominance on rigged elections or naked usurpation. Sensing danger in their illegitimate office, they assiduously cultivated the favor of the Holy Roman emperors, who had the authority to declare Mantua a fief of the empire and bestow on the Gonzaga a legal title to its rule. Finally, in 1433, in return for a payment of 12,000 florins, Emperor Sigismund conferred on Gianfrancesco Gonzaga the title of marchese. After 100 years, the Gonzaga clothed their despotism with the robes of legal office. The size of the payment indicates the considerable wealth of the family, and also the importance the Gonzaga attached to a recognized and heritable title. The dynasty's rise to dignity among the princes of Europe reached its culmination another century later, in

1530, when Emperor Charles conferred on Federico II, son of Francesco and Isabella d'Este, the exalted title of duke.

Even as dignities accumulated, the properties and income of the Gonzaga house expanded, and so also their expenditures. To be sure, styles differed from ruler to ruler. The bearded marchese Francesco appears relatively austere, with an income of about 100,000 gold ducats. His successors, Isabella as regent and Federico the first duke were, in contrast, lavish in supporting a "great court," as the Venetian ambassador notes, in stocking their stables, constructing palaces, and patronizing letters and arts. Their effective successors, Cardinal Ercole Gonzaga as regent and Duke Guglielmo returned to more austere ways. As a Venetian ambassador described him, Guglielmo, duke from 1550 to 1587, was an *ometto*, a misshapen little man, who took no delight in the frivolities of court and was even cool to horses, the reigning passion of his lineage. His one diversion was music. "He composes," the ambassador wrote of him, "every sort of musical thing more than competently, and it is a pleasure to hear the things he has written." Guglielmo's handsome and dissolute son, Vincenzo, who became duke in 1587, once more changed styles, enlarged the court and the stables, and squandered fortunes on court festivals. He was a notorious womanizer in his youth, and age did not dampen his sexual appetites. His disgruntled father-in-law, the Grand duke of Tuscany, said of him: "The youth of Lord [Vincenzo] is indeed prolongued, since he still abandons none of the appetites and pleasures he cultivated in his early years."

The moneys flowing through his treasury ranged upwards of 200,000 ducats per year from Mantua alone—about twice what they had been 100 years before. A few figures may illustrate Vincenzo's taste for conspicuous consumption. At his coronation in 1587, he wore a suit of white silk and a mantle which cost 36,000 scudi. This consumed about 18 percent of the duke's yearly income. His ducal crown cost 150,000 ducats—a price which of itself equaled about three-quarters of a year's revenue. There is little wonder that Vincenzo carried the government and community to the brink of bankruptcy. Perhaps, as his father-in-law suggested, he never grew up.

Hardly less in importance than the personality of the prince, in shaping culture at Mantua, were the composition and character of his court. Mantuan culture of the epoch was "courtly" in the basic significance of the term: it was primarily intended to sustain the morale and enrich the lives of those who served the prince.

What was this court, and what kind of political and social functions did it serve? In a strict sense, the court consisted of the officials, counsellors, administrators, guards and servants, who attended the prince and the members of his family. But it also included visitors, who might in fact remain for extended periods. The Gonzaga court at Mantua in the sixteenth century was distinct within the genre for at least three principal reasons.

First, at Mantua no distinction was made between the public officials employed in the service of the state and the personal servants of the duke and his family. Both were equally courtiers. Analogously, no distinction was drawn between the public revenues of the government and the private income of the dukes. Both streams of money were collected and dispersed at the duke's behest and in his perceived interest.

The conflation of public and private service had one important social result. It gave women a prominence in public and social life they might not otherwise have obtained. Women could not ordinarily aspire to careers as bureaucrats or public officials, but they were traditionally the dominant figures in domestic affairs and in the management of the household and family. In republics such as Venice, or even at Florence in the fifteenth century, women, excluded from the high bureaucratic circles, played a minimal role in public life. Where, on the other hand, household management and public administration were merged, women acquired full social visibility and much influence, even in the conduct of public affairs. This perhaps explains why women—let us recall again Isabella d'Este—enjoyed prominence and influence at the princely courts of Mantua, Ferrara and Urbino, which they did not attain in the republican cities.

Secondly, the court of Mantua experienced an extraordinary growth between the fifteenth and sixteenth centuries. The bearded marchese Francesco reputedly supported at his court only sixty nobles, and he earned thereby a reputation for thrift. If later ratios hold good, these 60 nobles would represent a total court population of about 480 persons. Under Francesco's son, the first duke Federico, the court population shot upwards, reaching, in the estimate of the Venetian ambassador, "800 and more." Surely this swelling of his entourage prompted Duke Federico to construct the huge Palazzo del Te. The succeeding governments of Cardinal Ercole and the mis-shapened Duke Guglielmo constituted, as we have mentioned, a return to austerity. The number of permanent courtiers sank to only 350 paid or pensioned members. But after 1587, Duke Vincenzo loosened all restraints. He doubled the size of his personal body-guard, to the delight of job-hungry nobles. The population of the court once more surpassed 800 persons. And a constant stream of visitors flowed through Mantua, sampling or consuming the duke's hospitality. A festival held in 1608, to honor his new daughter-in-law, brought to the city 12,000 visitors.

Did this sixteenth-century inflation in the numbers of courtiers reflect the growing needs of government? Did the swarming atten-dants at court earn their way by performing necessary services? The answer is a distinct no. Descriptions of the court repeatedly note the presence of idlers, *uomini poco utili,* men of little use. According to the Venetian ambassador, the spendthrift Vincenzo kept on pension "the principal women of the city and men, who have no other func-tion but to cater to the tastes of the duke." His words are not alto-gether clear, but the implication is certain: Vincenzo's court was crowded with parasites. Moreover, it would be hard to understand how the numbers of courtiers could fluctuate sharply from duke to duke, if their services were essential to the state.

The size of the court thus primarily reflects not the requirements of government, but the liberality of the prince. The manuals, offer-ing instruction on proper behavior at court, which proliferate in the sixteenth century, leave the strong impression that courtiers every-where were for most of the day unemployed or underemployed in any practical task. In the best known of these manuals, Castiglione's *Book of the Courtier,* the gentleman of court seems to possess, apart from a general literacy, no special skills. The successful courtier, in Castiglione's image, is the one who by his grace and charm holds the benevolence and favor of the prince. His principal duty is to per-suade the prince to do good and to avoid evil, and to advise him without provoking displeasure. The courtier's day—at least at the court of Urbino, which Castiglione describes—is given over not to bureaucratic labors but to efforts at self-improvement, to "honorable and pleasant exercises, both of the body and the mind." The evening in turn was devoted to "sweet conversations and clean jokes." The courtly culture of the sixteenth century appears to be, in significant measure, the creation of the unemployed.

Why, at Mantua and elsewhere, did the size of the court grow so dramatically between the fifteenth and sixteenth centuries? The answer seems to lie with the general population expansion of the epoch, which affected the upper classes as much as, perhaps even more than, the lower orders of society. The Venetian ambassadors at Mantua noted two things about the region's nobles in the sixteenth century; their numbers, and their poverty. "There is a large number of nobles," one of them reported in 1564, "most devoted to their prince." "There are in Mantua," another commented in 1615, "a considerable number of gentlemen and knights, who, except for those of the house of Gonzaga and a few others, hold the remnants of mediocre and inadequate fortunes." It seems, in other words, as if the growth of noble ranks in the sixteenth century, the resultant division of their patrimonies, threatened many of them with impoverishment. Where could they turn to repair their damaged fortunes? What career might they pursue? At Mantua, the answer was obvious: they must seek the favor and the pensions of the duke.

The third distinguishing characteristic of the Gonzaga court in the sixteenth century is the enormous wealth it collected and dispersed. It was far and away the largest economic enterprise in the territory. The income of 200,000 ducats per year, which came to Duke Vincenzo, would have supported more than 13,000 persons, at the modest but sufficient salary of 15 ducats a year. Although we have no exact figures, the court must have absorbed a substantial proportion of the total social product of the Mantuan state.

If the hard-pressed son of a noble family wished to earn a living, he could not, at Mantua, join a great banking house, or seek his fortune as a merchant. His one hope was a court appointment; his one strategy was to win the favor of the duke. Daughters too of noble families too poor to provide an adequate dowry might still look to a career at court, to improve their status. The favor of the prince might provide dowries and suitable husbands; or they might at least attract a propertied and supportive paramour. Descriptions of court life in the sixteenth century usually present a picture of gracious men and beautiful women, talking, playing, dancing, singing, in an atmos-

phere of sweet serenity. In fact there seems to have been little serenity. Competition for place at court was intense, bitter, ruthless. The
successful courtier more often than not had recourse to lying flattery
rather than moral philosophy in advising the prince, and he had to
be expert too at concocting calumnies with which to denigrate and
discredit rivals and enemies. Court life was a continuous battle, in
which the chief weapons were sycophancy and slander.

The prince in turn invited this competition. At the court of
Urbino, for example, according to the description of a Venetian
ambassador, the Duke expected his subjects to vie with one another,
to win through effort and talent a place at court. At Urbino as at
Mantua, the court offered to ladies and gentlemen virtually the only
honorable career, outside of religion. "By doing this," the ambassador explained, "he gives incentive to his subjects to trod the paths
of virtue. And thus the subjects pay heed to different exercises, in
order to improve their position with his Excellency [the Duke], who
for this reason is well served in every office." Moreover, by inviting
ruthless competition among the nobles for his favor, the shrewd
prince divided their numbers, prevented the formation of cabals
against him, and thus reinforced his own authority.

The terms of this competition for place at court influenced culture as well as behavior. The runners in this race had to cultivate
and excel in the courtly arts. The young courtier must know how to
manage a horse well, fence, dance, sing on tune, play a musical
instrument, and hold his own in witty conversation. His female
counterpart must similarly display charm, skill in dancing and
singing, and wit in conversation; she must also be, in the real world
if not in Castiglione's idyllic vision, an accomplished flirt. And both
cavaliers and ladies had to practice these arts with a kind of effort-
less excellence. That art which conceals art was basic to the
courtly style.

The same sense of superiority and separation from the common
herd infuses the courtly literature of the epoch. Ariosto, greatest
master of the romantic epic, declares, for example, that the vulgar
will not understand *Orlando Furioso*, his tales "of loves and ladies,
knights and arms ... of courtesies, and many a daring feat." In
Canto VIII of his great poem, he complains that the "misjudging vul-

gar, which lies under the mist of ignorance" will not believe his fabulous stories. But then he addresses his noble listeners:

> But this be great or small, I know not why
> The rabble's silly judgment I should fear,
> Convinced *you* will not think the tale a lie,
> In whom the light of reason shines so clear.
> And hence to you it is I only try
> The fruit of my fatigues to render dear.

Finally, the social functions at court—the festivals and balls,
recitations, plays and musical performances—also reinforced the
courtier's sense of his own innate excellence. These activities were
far more than the diversions of the idle, although courtiers did
indeed have many idle hours to fill. Rather, they were a kind of ritual, in which nature's noblemen both displayed and celebrated their
superiority to the common run of people. We might look upon these
fetes as a type of liturgy, which confirmed the faith of courtiers, that
the privileges they enjoyed were their justly merited deserts.

How well does the experience of the community and court of
Mantua fit the now current assumptions, concerning the Renaissance and its social foundations? One commonplace assumption in
interpretations of the Italian Renaissance is that this cultural renewal
was somehow rooted in the wealth of cities and in the values, attitudes and aspirations of the great merchants who dominated them.
Was Renaissance culture truly the expression of the rising and rebellious bourgeoisie? The thesis might be defensible, if applied to the
history and achievements of Florence or of Venice. But it hardly
seems applicable at Mantua. Neither the dukes nor most courtiers at
Mantua were middle class in origin, and they show little skill or
interest in commercial affairs. The conspicuous consumption and
lavish display, essential qualities of Mantuan court life, hardly reflect
the tastes and mentality of calculating, grasping bankers.

More important than the origins of wealth in commerce or in
agriculture seems to have been its distribution in society. In several
cities of Italy—Florence, Pistoia, Perugia—it can be shown that
wealth came to be concentrated in far fewer hands, between the
thirteenth and the fifteenth centuries. We witness the formation of
what the fifteenth-century humanist, Poggio Bracciolini, called
"barns of money" within society. At Mantua, the growth of the lands

and revenues of the Gonzaga family suggests that a similar process was occurring. At the same time, moral philosophers and humanists came to develop and to preach a new ethic of affluence—essentially, instructions to the enormously wealthy on their responsibilities to society. According to the Neapolitan humanist Giovanni Pontano, who wrote between 1493 and 1498, the affluent must practice liberality, beneficence, magnificence, splendor (by which he meant the maintenance of a large and elegant home) and hospitality. They must favor with their benefactions the destitute, the sick, girls in need of dowries, and promising but poor young men. They should stage magnificent weddings and funerals, and be prepared to entertain throngs. Their liberality will assure support to the meritorious, and jobs to the poor.

In 1497, a courtier by the name of Giovanni Sabadino degli Arienti wrote a similar tract for the benefit not of all the rich, but for the wealthy prince. Its misleading title is "The Triumphs of Religion," but it is in fact a description of the virtues of Duke Ercole I d'Este, prince of Ferrara. Ercole is, in candor, an unlikely model of religious virtues, but our author in fact says little about religion. Central to the ethics of princely behavior are rather liberality and magnificence. Ercole has built temples, endowed poor girls, and aided the deserving but shame-faced poor. He has also liberally distributed among his courtiers and servants "money, palaces, possessions, clothes, jewels, horses, offices and dignities." The prime duty of the wealthy prince was thus to recognize and reward merit, especially at his own court.

The growing concentrations of wealth in few hands led directly to the appearance of the private or princely patron—individuals with the means and the moral obligation to rescue the virtuous needy, and to favor society with costly buildings and splendid festivals.

Finally, the most recent research in social history—still not far advanced, still tentative in its conclusions—suggests that the composition of social elites was changing in Italy between the thirteenth and the sixteenth centuries. In the thirteenth century, the urban aristocracies were recruited from two principal sources: from the old, established families, and, in important measure, from ambitious, talented newcomers. The aristocracies were, in other words, fairly open, and vertical social mobility fairly common. Moreover, the newcomers, with no established family traditions to influence their behavior, were psychologically conditioned to seek their fortunes in new, untried ways, especially in commerce and industry. The marketplace and the counting house directed their ambitions.

By the sixteenth century, on the other hand, the relative contribution of newcomers to the social elites appears to have diminished. Social mobility, never entirely precluded, became more difficult. There was still much competition for preferment, but the competitors were in the main the sons of older families. Many of them were, to be sure, poor. The tendency of the old families to divide into numerous branches inevitably reduced many to poverty. Even the house of Gonzaga had come to contain, by 1588, no fewer than 85 "lords and cavaliers," although, given their exceptional status, their wealth kept pace with their numbers. Still, even an impoverished son of an old lineage did not readily forget his name, nor the pretenses of his family. He was thus prone to seek his fortune in ways congenial with his traditions, through the profession of courtier and cavalier, through winning the favors of the prince. The court replaced the counting house as the focus of youthful ambition, especially in small towns such as Mantua. Economically, socially, and culturally, the court dominated society. The values it nurtured and disseminated were not those of the commercial bourgeoisie, but of cavaliers and their ladies, struggling to hold place upon a slippery social ladder.

The social system we have described at sixteenth-century Mantua may appear to many distasteful, even obnoxious. Many idle courtiers lived by the blood and sweat of the laboring poor. Still, this incontrovertible fact ought not to spoil our appreciation of the literature, art and music, which these courtiers cultivated and developed. These great monuments, we must recognize, were not simply the frivolous entertainments of the indolent. Rather, through these celebrations of beauty and grace, the courtiers sought to prove, to themselves, to their contemporaries, and to us, that their privileges were justified. They brought to this important task wealth and commitment, and the monuments in turn reflect the exquisite tastes and refinements of their daily lives. The court of sixteenth-century Mantua is not, by modern standards, an altogether admirable human society, but still it has bequeathed us an admirable legacy.

15

CITY AND COUNTRYSIDE
IN RENAISSANCE TUSCANY

✦ ✦ ✦

The relationships between city and countryside in Italian history, or European history, have long been studied, and yet remain today a lively and provocative topic. Present interest arises in part from past disappointments, from the failure, really, of the great masters of urban history to offer a full and convincing analysis of the social interactions between town and country, bourgeois and peasant. The work of two of these masters can illustrate this point. They are the German sociologist Max Weber, whose extended treatment of the city was published in 1921; and the Belgian historian Henri Pirenne, whose numerous writings on the medieval city fill the earlier part of this century.

Weber was and remains the peerless master of comparative social institutions. In brilliant displays of erudition, he moved easily from Peking to Pittsburgh, from the temple towns of the ancient Near East to the mill towns of industrial Europe. Weber stressed the originality and distinctiveness of the late-medieval town, particularly in northwest Europe. It differed radically from the surrounding rural society, and from all earlier urban forms. Ancient and Asiatic cities had fulfilled, in the main, administrative or religious functions. They were, in essence, mere extensions, simple microcosms, of the dominant, primarily rural society.

The Western town of the late Middle Ages was, in contrast, dominated by merchants and by artisans. The primacy of commercial concerns nurtured the growth of new cultural attitudes, which the countryside did not share: realism, rationalism, the habit of making decisions not on instinct, not on tradition, but on algorithms aimed at profit. Moreover, contract and private agreements, not birth, knitted the fabric of urban social relations. *Stadtluft macht frei*, and in Weber's interpretation of this famous phrase, the air of towns freed the resident from the bonds of inherited status, from the ties of the feudal order, even from the meshes of kinship. In promoting individualistic behavior and the rationalistic calculus, these towns of the late Middle Ages broke the constraints of rural medievalism, and prepared the society of the modern West.

Henri Pirenne also emphasized the separateness and distinctiveness of the medieval towns, in the Mediterranean as well as the north. Long-distance trade created them, and in long-distance trade the peasants had little part. From small beginnings in the late tenth century, this trade swelled to significant volumes in the eleventh and twelfth centuries. The earliest merchants were recruited from the ranks of "footloose adventurers," village drop-outs, who had no established place in rural or feudal society. Why would anyone, he argued, pioneer a new way of life, if he already possessed stake and status, however humble, in the traditional order? The new medieval towns were a revolt against the old economy, the old way of life; they were new plantings, soaring skyward, seemingly without roots.

The assumption of a sharp division between town and country has also marked the work of many historians, writing on medieval and Renaissance Tuscany. Robert Davidsohn published his monumental *Geschichte von Florenz* between 1896 and 1925. In it he affirmed without close examination that during the central Middle Ages the population of the growing city was recruited primarily from escaped serfs, fugitives from the countryside. Like Lot fleeing Sodom, they left their rural homes, and presumably never looked back.

Still other historians of Tuscany have elaborated upon this notion of a wide chasm between town and countryside, and have posited that the two maintained a kind of adversary relationship. The progressive city, fostering modern social relationships and attitudes, was allegedly also the oppressive city. The urban community ruthlessly exploited the peasantry, through rents, taxes, controlled prices, uncontrolled usury. This lacrimose theory of town-country ties found perhaps its most passionate advocate in the Italian historian Romolo Caggese. Writing shortly before the first World War, he claimed that the society of Dante and of Giotto lacked a social conscience. Pious, it was not piteous; it had little feeling for the poorer members of society, especially the peasants. The grinding poverty of Tuscany's rural masses hangs like a dark backdrop behind its brilliant cities.

This theory of the exploitive city still today commands a following. A recent, able book by Frank McArdle examines the experience of the little village of Altopascio, between Lucca and Pistoia. The period he considers is late, running from 1587 to 1784. But the theme is familiar: the theme is oppression. If we are to believe McArdle, over the entire length of these years, the peasants of Altopascio groaned under an "unending burden of indebtedness." To be sure, other scholars take exception to this view that the city mistreated the countryside. Chief among the dissenters is the Italian scholar Enrico Fiumi, the indefatigable historian of small Tuscan cities, of San Gimignano, Volterra and Prato. The policy of cities towards the villages, he has argued, was even-handed, even benign, and not consciously exploitative. "No other topic in Tuscan history," he concludes, "is more deserving of reconsideration [than this one]." And reconsideration, he is sure, will mean revision.

In this paper, we too shall reconsider relations between city and countryside in Tuscany from about 1250—with some backward glances—to about 1500. The novelty, and the risk, of this our enterprise is the following. We shall attempt to apply in our analysis certain concepts drawn from sociology and urban geography. Recently, sociologists and geographers have emphasized the unity, rather than the division, of town and country within a regional community. The city, they maintain, is not a self-contained and intelligible unit of analysis; there is, in consequence, no such thing as urban history. A recent collection of studies devoted to historic towns, published in 1978, argues the case in its title, *Towns in Societies*. Towns, these words imply, can be studied only as parts of larger societies.

Geographers too have shown that the location and even the size of historic towns are crucially dependent upon factors exogenous to the towns themselves, as, for example, the lay of the land, lines of communications, and distances from other urban centers. We cannot explain where cities grew, why they grew, by how much they grew, if our gaze is limited to within the city walls.

One tool which geographers and sociologists now productively utilize in the study of towns goes under the forbidding name, "general systems theory." What is a system? Its most characteristic feature is movement. A system is a continuous flow of persons, objects, energy or information among permanent nodes or focal points, within a limited spatial area. Systems can function within particular geographic regions such as Tuscany. These regional systems are necessarily "open," in the sense that new persons, goods, units of energy or information are constantly added to them, and also constantly escape. Persons are born and die, for example, or immigrate or emigrate into or out of the system; energy and information are generated and utilized, gathered or dispersed.

Within the regional system, cities have particular functions. They can be described as fixed nodes or loci, in which social processes intersect. They are fields of concentrated action. People, after all, come to cities, occasionally or permanently, to participate in some social process and to interact with other people—to buy and sell, appeal to bureaucrats, consult with experts, pray or play. Moreover, the regional system tends to be homeostatic —self-regulating and self-adjusting over time. For example, if a plague or other disaster radically reduces the population, incentives will arise to stimulate marriages and births, in order to restore the losses and to return the system to its former state. If too many or too few goods are produced in one year, the system will also intervene to reduce or raise output, and so to assure stable supplies. The system is also said to operate "equifinally," in the sense that it aims at fulfilling certain fixed goals and purposes, which are typically set by traditional cultural values and supported by a social consensus. It will strive to achieve these final purposes under all conditions, in spite of exogenous shocks or disturbances.

This concept of the town as a locus of intersecting processes within a regional system offers substantial analytical advantages. The researcher no longer must attempt to define what a town is, in terms of absolute numbers of inhabitants. He does not have to formulate evocative but vague definitions of the town, that it is, for example, a set of attitudes or a state of soul. Not a fixed size, not a distinct mentality, but movement, the relative frequency and intensity of human contacts, identify the town. While the analysis makes cities readily identifiable within regions, it avoids the dubious assumption that urban residents really were or are radically divergent, in their society or culture, from those living in areas of dispersed settlement. Life in the sense of human interactions, is not different within the towns; it is only more intense.

A further advantage of this definition of towns is that it directs our attention towards the relationship between social process and space. If activity defines the town, so the activity will impose certain spatial requirements. To understand the use or organization of space in an urban settlement is first to inquire who is using the space, and for what purposes. We shall later say some further words on the spatial implications of these regional processes, for the towns of medieval and Renaissance Tuscany.

Here, we shall informally apply these concepts of "general systems theory" to Tuscan towns from the central to the closing Middle Ages. Let us stress the word, informally. We cannot pretend to develop here an elaborate systems model of medieval Tuscan towns. Our data are not sufficiently abundant, sufficiently precise, sufficiently clean, for truly hard analysis. Moreover, we limit our attention to only two types of flows between city and countryside: the movement of money, and the movement of people. In other words, we shall examine the financial, and then the demographic interactions of city and countryside in the period of our interest.

What then were the financial and fiscal relationships between the Tuscan cities and their countrysides? Moneys of course constantly flowed from villages to the town. The city governments actively encouraged the concentration of capital within the urban populations, with apparent success. According to the Florentine Catasto— the great tax survey of 1427—the 100 wealthiest families in Florence alone held more wealth than the 37,000 peasant families settled in the extensive Florentine domains, outside of towns. By then Florence—and in lesser measure the other towns—had absorbed virtually the entire savings of the regional community. The channels by which the towns drained money from rural areas are evident: payments for urban goods and services, rents on rural properties leased from urban landlords, usury on, and repayments of, loans from city moneylenders, and taxes paid to the communal governments. Historians have long studied these channels through which money from the countryside entered the cities. But systems theory affirms that in the absence of rural savings there would have to be an equal and opposite flow of money from town to countryside. Otherwise, there would be no flow at all. In other words, if the peasant was to pay rents, taxes and interest, maintain the productive capacity of his farm, and support his family with the necessities of life, he had to acquire money. This requirement, that equivalent flows of money move into and out of the countryside, seems not to have occurred to historians, and they have not systematically studied the manner in which urban wealth was recycled back into rural areas. This we shall attempt to do here, although in preliminary and crude fashion.

Here then is our principal hypothesis. In the period of our interest, from about 1250 to 1500, the principal flow of money from town to country two times jumped channels. Insofar as we can judge, money first flowed largely as payments to independent peasants for agricultural commodities, then as remissions by urban investors for the purchase of rural lands, then finally as investments and loans needed to keep up the productivity of the rural lands already owned by urban residents. These shifts had profound effects on town-country relations.

In the thirteenth century, the typical Tuscan peasant was an independent cultivator. He lived in a large nucleated village, and worked many, widely scattered plots, usually without the aid of cattle. Under this system, money flowed from city to countryside primarily as remittances for agricultural produce. This system entered into profound crisis from the late thirteenth century. The city, anxious to provide its burgeoning population with cheap food, imposed controls of various sorts on commodity markets, and this obstructed or diminished the recycling of money back to the countryside.

Fiscal relations between city and countryside were also changing. From about 1250, the urban budget was climbing steeply. In May and June, 1240, for example, the treasurers of Florence accounted for some 4300 pounds in revenue. In May and June, 1301, the comparable figure was 130,000 pounds—an increase of thirteen times in terms of the real value of the money. The city government did not however wish to deplete through taxes the great urban fortunes—the "barns of money," as Poggio Bracciolini later called them, on which it depended to meet the mounting costs of war. In 1315, Florence abolished direct taxes, the so-called estimo, within the city, and henceforth, with rare exceptions, relied on interest-bearing loans to meet extraordinary expenditures. But it retained the direct tax in the countryside, as well as many indirect taxes, which weighed primarily upon the humble in both city and villages. The Florentine fiscal system was thus savagely regressive. It took money from the rural population and from the urban poor, and channeled it through interest remissions and the repayment of loans into the coffers of the urban rich. The "barns of money" had to be replenished, and the government helped in the harvest.

In concentrating wealth within the city, the system conferred numerous advantages on Florentine urban society. In swelling private fortunes, it made money available for large-scale commercial ventures. In the early fourteenth century the Bardi and Peruzzi of Florence may have been the richest merchants in Europe; they were at all events, in Giovanni Villani's famous phrase, pillars of Christendom. But these fiscal policies also worked to transform economic and social relations between city and countryside. Many propertied residents of the contado—substantial peasants, middlemen, managers of estates, notaries, moneylenders—emigrated to the city, to take advantage of the favorable tax climate prevailing within it. To have remained in the fiscally oppressed rural areas would have courted ruin. It can be shown how villages, such as Impruneta, fifteen miles south of Florence, were losing their wealthier members during the early decades of the fourteenth century. Those rural residents who did not emigrate were likely to sell their properties to urban investors. Ownership migrated to the towns even when the owners did not.

Money, in other words, continued to be, had to be, recycled into the countryside, but in the fourteenth century it was decisively shifting channels. Instead of coming as payments for produce to independent cultivators, it returned as investments in agricultural lands, which could be purchased at low prices from the desperate contadini. The emigration of substantial rural residents to the city had the same result: the ever increasing urban ownership of rural lands.

This trend is indirectly but dramatically reflected at Florence in the sinking capital value of the rural direct tax, the Estimo. The Estimo, to be sure, was not a direct assessment of the worth of the taxpayers' property, only a measure of his comparative ability to pay. Still, the collapsing value of the Estimo shows the shrinking property and resources, which the inhabitants of the countryside could marshal. In 1289, the total value of the Estimo in the Florentine *contado* was about 448,000 pounds; by 1364, it had sunk to 60,000 pounds, less than one-sixth its former size. And debasement was simultaneously sapping the value of Florentine money. The slide continued in the latter half of the century. According to an index constructed by Elio Conti, reflecting the assessments borne by four villages, the Estimo fell from a base index of 100 in 1350 to only 23 by 1415. The collapse reflected in part the abandonment of agricultural lands under conditions of acute depopulation. But it also indicates that urban owners were claiming an ever larger proportion of rural lands. In fact in 1427 their holdings overspread the most fertile and productive Tuscan fields, especially in the vicinity of cities. Independent cultivators survived in large numbers only in rough, swampy or infertile regions, remote from the urban centers.

The march of urban ownership across the countryside was associated with a basic change in patterns of settlement. Rather than living in nucleated villages and working scattered plots, the peasants now were coming to reside on dispersed, compact farms, the classical *podere* of rural Tuscany. Urban capital fueled this process of "poderization," as it is called in the Italian literature. And the peasant working the *podere* usually had the use of *bestie*, to plow the fields and fertilize the land—also supplied by urban capital. By 1500, the *podere* had become the characteristic form of settlement in the most fertile and productive regions of Tuscany.

Still, even this channel—the remissions by urban investors for the purchase of agricultural land—could not continuously recycle money from the town to countryside. By 1427, as the Catasto clearly shows, urban investors already claimed the best of Tuscany's agricultural lands. There were no more worlds to conquer. The flow of urban moneys once more shifted channels, from the purchase of lands to improvements in farms and stock. The cornerstone of this new system of investment was the *mezzadria* lease, the famous share-cropping contract of late medieval and modern Tuscany. Under the terms of the *mezzadria* contract, the landlord, almost always an urban resident, leased for a short period of time a *podere,* in return for one-half the harvest paid in kind. The landlord provided not only the farm, but most or all of the considerable capital needed to maintain it or to work it: the costs of repairing farmhouse and physical structures, ditches and walls; the costs of the *bestie* and sometimes too of fertilizer purchased off the farm. Tuscan agriculture under the *mezzadria* system was quite capital-intensive, at least by medieval standards. And almost always the landlord would extend loans to the sharecropper or *mezzadro.* These loans are peculiar; they seem rarely to have been repaid. Even the tax assessors in the Catasto of 1427 did not recognize them as authentic obligations. In the fifteenth century, when population was low and labor scarce, the offer of a loan helped attract and retain tenants. "He wanted the loan and not the land," says a disgruntled landlord of Pistoia in 1427, in reference to his sharecropper. In the same year, Palla di Nofri Strozzi, Florence's richest citizen according to the Catasto survey, lists in his declaration hundreds of loans to sharecroppers, totalling thousands of florins. Then he gives up, explaining that he does not want to bore the tax assessors, as the loans were worth so little.

The extension of the *mezzadria* thus stabilized financial relationships between the towns and the close-in, most populated, most productive regions of the countryside. The system proved to be remarkably stable, persisting from the late Middle Ages into the twentieth century. Historians differ as to how the peasants fared as sharecroppers. The English historian Philip Jones claims that the *mezzadri,* almost without capital and without security of tenure, lived in misery. I do not myself believe this. *Mezzadri* inhabited Tuscany's most productive farms, and had the aid of capital with which to work them. They consistently appear in the tax records with large families. In their demographic characteristics they more closely resemble substantial peasants, than the small, independent cultivators, who struggled to earn a living on poor soil, usually without capital.

To be sure, the *mezzadria* manifests several, substantial faults. It seems to have discouraged productive effort in the countryside. If the peasant worked hard and raised output, he would have to surrender a substantial part to the landlord, in increased rent or repayment of loans. Why should he increase his exertions? Moreover, the new system drained off capital from the city and also claimed the close attention of the urban landlords. Its triumph helped transform Florence from a city of great merchants and bankers competing on international markets to one of small property-owners resembling squires. Historians have long spoken of a "return to the land" on the part of wealthy Florentines in the fifteenth and sixteenth centuries; allegedly they gradually abandoned the commercial activities of their forebears in favor of agricultural investments. The trend has surely been exaggerated, but not entirely misapprehended. It should, however, be noted, that the decision to invest in agriculture was not altogether free, spontaneous, personal. The Florentine affluent bent to powerful forces, and acted as the system demanded.

Having considered the flow of money across Tuscan society, we shall now look at movements of population—births, deaths and migrations—and their role in defining relations between town and countryside. To clarify our analysis, we shall construct a formal model of the Tuscan community, and divide it initially into two principal sectors, rural and urban. The exact numerical distributions between the two sectors need not concern us. We shall initially assume that the proportions of city dwellers and rural inhabitants are constant and stable. Later, we can relax this assumption, in order to bring our model closer to historical reality. Still in the interest of clarity, we shall assume that our ideal community is closed, that is, that its population is not affected by in- or out-migration.

What happens to the urban-rural balance over time? If replacement rates in city and countryside are equal, then the two sectors will remain in equilibrium indefinitely. In fact, however, evidence from Tuscany and from many other regions of traditional Europe indicates that replacement rates were not equal in city and countryside. Rather, cities everywhere did not reproduce themselves as successfully as rural lands; they ran a constant "demographic deficit."

There were several reasons for this. Death rates in traditional societies seem to have been consistently higher in cities than in rural areas. Why else did those Tuscan citizens who could do so flee the towns, at the earliest signs of approaching epidemic? Giovanni Botero, the great Piedmontese social philosopher, observed in 1588 that plagues were likely to be deadlier, and famines more severe, in large urban communities. The high mortalities of cities were one principal reason why, in his estimation, the human population had not grown at all over the last 3000 years.

Within cities too, birth rates were too low to compensate for the high mortalities. Again several factors lowered the fertility of urban populations. In rural areas, the young peasant who possessed a farm almost always married early, as he needed the help of a wife and eventually children in his agricultural labors. In the city, on the other hand, the merchant, artisan, and professional usually could not marry until they were well established in their professions and mature in age. Productive assets in the countryside, a wife and children, were more truly burdens in the city. In the urban environment, marriage and a family were rewards for economic achievement; in peasant communities, they were its prerequisite.

For analogous reasons, widows living on a farm almost always remarried, as they needed help in working the soil. In the city, on the other hand, many widows preferred not to remarry; the dowry, which was returned to them at the death of their husbands, gave them a measure of financial independence. At Florence, more than one-half the adult population were living without a spouse in 1427. The majority of urban adults was formed of bachelor males waiting to marry, and widowed women who chose not to take a new husband.

Besides residence in town or country, another social factor strongly influenced rates of reproduction: wealth, or access to material resources. Death rates were surely higher among the destitute than among the comfortable rich. Plague and famine made deep inroads into the ranks of the wretched, while a better diet, better nursing, and greater physical mobility gave the wealthy a partial defense against disease and want. Birth rates too seem to have been higher among affluent families than among the poor in the Tuscan cities and widely in traditional societies. The poor often could not afford to marry or to support large families. Whenever we have surveys of the population, the advantaged families consistently appear with more children than their poor neighbors, both in rural and in urban populations. It is not always clear whether higher birth rates or lower death rates among the wealthy families explain the larger numbers of children, but the social repercussions would at any rate be the same. With each new generation, the upper levels of the social hierarchy, in both city and country-side, would tend to expand more rapidly than its base.

We can now introduce this further refinement into our formal model of Tuscan society. We now reclassify our community into four sectors: the urban rich, the urban poor, the rural rich, and the rural poor. We can further estimate whether the rates of replacement or growth in each sector will be positive (that is, higher than the mean for the community as a whole) or negative (that is, lower than the mean). Of the four sectors the rural rich should be the most prolific. The rural poor, on the other hand, will be influenced by one positive factor (residence) and one negative factor (poverty), and their rates of replacement will converge toward the community mean, depending on the relative strength of the two factors. The urban rich will also be influenced by one positive and one negative factor, and their rates of replacement should similarly move toward the community mean. The urban poor, influenced by two negative factors, will show the lowest replacement rates, and will tend most rapidly to decline in numbers over generations.

In sum, over time, each new generation will not be an exact replication of the generation which produced it. Some sectors of the community will tend to gain in relative numbers, and some to lose. The relative numbers of urban dwellers will fall, and the poorest urban classes will suffer the largest losses. On the other hand, the privileged classes everywhere will increase in relative size. Obviously, however, the system cannot allow these distortions to proceed unchecked, as it is self-regulating and "equifinal"—that is, it aims at preserving stable numbers within the various social sectors, which in turn will assure a constant level of needed and desired services. The system, therefore counters this generational redistribution of the population by pushing or attracting persons from the sectors of positive replacement to those of negative replacement, specifically from rural areas into the towns, and from the richer to the poorer levels of society.

These flows will have important sociological repercussions. The cities compensate for their "demographic deficit" by attracting immigrants from the countryside, and this immigration is likely to be selective on the basis of talent, skill or energy. The system thus favors the town with a steady stream of gifted, active people, and this may partially explain the high creativity of urban cultures. How-ever, there is also the risk that great cities in particular might over time drain off and consume the human capital of the region, the available pool of talented people. For these gifted persons are drawn into a milieu where their own reproduction will be obstructed. The old assumption, that traditional cities ran in a cycle from brilliance to decadence, from neapolis to necropolis, may not be entirely fatuous.

Moreover, the numerous offspring of the wealthy families—patri-cians, we shall call them—face an uncertain future. They may have to accept a position on the lower, less populated rungs of the social ladder. To avoid this downward slippage, some sons would, through emigration, leave the system altogether and seek their fortunes in foreign lands. Gregorio Dati, a Florentine chronicler writing proba-bly in the first decade of the fifteenth century, perceptively describes this phenomenon:

> [The inhabitants of Florence] have multiplied greatly because of the temperate air, which is very generative in that locale. For that reason, for some time back it has been necessary for the Florentines, because they are so many, to seek their livelihood through entrepreneurial endeavors. Therefore, they have departed from their territory to search through other lands, provinces and countries, where one or another has seen an opportunity to profit for a time, to make a for-tune, and to return to Florence.

Gregorio, it should be noted, is not thinking of humble artisans, few of wham wandered far abroad, few of whom made fortunes. He has the sons of patricians foremost in mind. The threatened status of patrician sons also exacerbated competition among them for offices and heiresses, kindled factional feuds, and helped sustain that vio-lent tenor of life, characteristic of the Tuscan towns.

We can now put some further questions to our formal model of Tuscan society. What will happen if births come significantly to exceed deaths, and the community as a whole experiences sub-stantial growth. There are three likely consequences: (1) The towns will grow more rapidly than the total population. The system, resist-ing disturbances, tries to dampen the high birth rate by transferring population from sectors of positive rates of growth in the country-side to those of negative rates in the city. In periods of general growth, cities will therefore expand more rapidly than the commu-nity as a whole, primarily through increased immigration. (2) The sector which will feel initially and most intensively the pressures of increased births will be the wealthier rural classes; they will therefore figure prominently in the quest for new resources and in the early phases of the incremented movement into the towns. (3) The immigration of increased numbers of formerly rural inhabitants into towns will work to impose rural institutions and values upon the society and culture of the city.

Conversely, if deaths exceed births and the total size of the community declines, then we would predict: (1) Cities will drop in size more rapidly than the total population, as the system encourages the retention of persons in sectors of positive rates of reproduction, that is, in the countryside, and may even stimulate some emigration out of the cities. (2) The declining flow of immigrants from country to town will, however, diminish rural influences upon the cities and leave room for the development of authentically urban social and cultural forms. (3) This "deurbanization" will also favor the extension of some urban cultural values and tastes into the countryside.

Let us now interpret in the light of the preceding speculations the historical experiences of town and countryside in Tuscany, up to 1500. In the eleventh and twelfth centuries, Tuscany, as many European regions, witnessed a substantial growth in population. Our model predicts that the patrician, propertied families of the countryside would initially feel the strongest pressures. Threatened with downward social slippage, they had to search aggressively for new resources and opportunities. Some found them by emigrating to distant frontiers, joining crusades, and so forth. But the towns also offered opportunities, in service to the resident bishop or count, and above all in long-distance commerce. Our model predicts, in other words, that in Tuscany the first wave of substantial immigration to the towns in the eleventh and twelfth centuries would be patrician or magnate in character; and the town formed or reformed by this immigration would reflect the style of an essentially rural aristocracy.

Within the twelfth-century Tuscan towns, the center of magnate habitation remained the town or castle, often the property of a "tower society" or *consorteria*. Much as they did in rural areas, the casate or magnate families built their fortress homes at strategic points within the city—the harbor areas of maritime and river towns, intersections of important streets, at gates, bridges and markets. The houses of collateral lineages clustered around the central tower, and were at times physically joined to it. According to Benjamin of Tudela, a Spanish Jew who visited Tuscany about 1159, Pisa then contained no fewer than 10,000 towers. A description of Florence claims that the city then included numerous, densely constructed stone towers of marvelous height, so that the town seemed to approaching travelers like a stone forest. Some were allegedly as high as the present tower of Giotto. Today of course, within Tuscany, San Gimignano best preserves this aspect of the magnate forest-city. In its use of space, this town might well be viewed as a cluster of castles, which still retained their rugged, rural character.

Our model further predicts that as population growth continues, the middle and lower classes of rural society will likewise be pressed, like the magnates before them, to immigrate in large numbers into the urban centers. In the thirteenth century, this wave of popular immigration further transformed the Tuscan cities—politically, culturally, architecturally. Borrowing a term which Max Weber used in a different context, we can call this reformed, partially rebuilt thirteenth-century Tuscan town the plebeian city.

The plebeian city reached its full efflorescence under the political regime of the Popolo, which was established in most of the principal Tuscan cities from 1250. The *popolani* retained close ties with their villages of origin, in which they were often property owners and small rentiers. They were not typically organized into large *consorterie*. Immigrants from the same villages seem to have settled together in the same urban neighborhoods, often close to the principal routes which connected with their rural homes. Some immigrants seem to have moved back and forth between village and city, depending on where, at any given time, they could find the most attractive opportunities. If the patricians brought their castles with them to the towns, the *popolani* brought their villages.

Individually and collectively, the *popolani* changed the style of urban living. They typically inhabited modest dwellings, rarely more than two stories in height, and sometimes only sheds (*capanne*). Their multiplying houses formed new *borghi*, stretching out along the principal roads beyond the second circle of walls, the limits of the patrician towns. Eventually the large size of these popular *borghi* prompted the governments to construct a third circle of walls, which marks the maximum physical expansion of the medieval town.

At the same time, the popular commune sought to reduce the number and strength of the magnate towers, even as it repressed the violent social habits of the patrician families. Working primarily as artisans and small shopkeepers, the *popolani* depended upon the free movement of foodstuffs and commodities, to and from the urban markets. The popular governments accordingly straightened, often widened and usually paved the principal urban thoroughfares. The *popolani* also had need for open, common spaces, where they could hold markets; assemble for political purposes; participate in religious festivals; watch tournaments and carnivals; and so forth. Large churches, as well as large piazzas, marked the style of the plebeian city. The new mendicant orders took as their principal apostolate the preaching of Christ's message to the urban masses, and the mendicants built churches of imposing dimensions, in which their large flocks could gather. Great public buildings also reflected this need to facilitate social interactions on a massive scale. In sum, the forest city of the magnates gave way to what we might call the park city of the popular commune.

In the late Middle Ages, between the early fourteenth and early fifteenth centuries, population numbers collapsed in Tuscany, by approximately two-thirds. Between about 1410 and 1460, Tuscan population remained stable at very low levels, and not until after 1460 did it begin to register even a modest growth.

Our model predicts that in periods of population decline cities would fall even more rapidly than the total population, and a process of "deurbanization" would ensue. The prediction would seem certainly true for the small Tuscan towns, for Pisa, Pistoia, or San Gimignano, but not for Florence itself. Within the Florentine *contado*, the proportion of urban dwellers seems to have dropped only minimally from the thirteenth to the fifteenth centuries, from 26 to 24 percent of the population. On the other hand, many urban families were quick to flee the city at the first rumor of plague; others, especially the wealthy, took to spending months every year in a rural setting, in *villeggiatura*. These phenomena too might be called a kind of deurbanization.

Perhaps the waning strength of rural influences may have facilitated the growth of a purely urban set of cultural values—the cultivation of "urbane" manners and a new refinement of tastes. Moreover, the highly skewed distribution of wealth, to which we have made prior allusion, allowed the rich urban dwellers to pursue luxury and elegance in clothes, entertainment, and habitation. They could build for themselves comfortable houses and *palazzi*. They could, in sum, cultivate a seigneurial way of life, and the city they partially transformed we can call the seigneurial city.

These same *signori* further carried their polished mode of life into the countryside, where they constructed and enjoyed formal gardens and elegant villas. Writing in the early fifteenth century, Gregorio Dati noted how, "beyond the walls of [Florence] there are the most beautiful gardens and parks, with residences and numerous palaces; the countryside appears to be an entire city; if one took all the lovely villas, or palaces of the citizens, which surround Florence for ten miles, one could make two other Florences." His words, to be sure, echo those of Giovanni Villani in his description of Florence in 1338, who also claimed that two Florences could be formed from the elegant villas built within six miles of the city. But both authors presumably allude to the same process—the diffusion in the countryside of urban styles—which began when the voluminous immigration from country to town was ebbing. In sum, the altered relations between town and country allowed room for the elaboration of an authentically urban style of life—the culture in fact of the Renaissance town.

These remarks constitute no more than an experiment, and offer no more than a crude sketch of the relations between city and countryside in medieval and Renaissance Tuscany. All parts of this paper will doubtlessly have to be rethought, reargued, restated. I hope only to have shown the advantages of a particular approach to city-town relationships in the past. The town is not a static aggregation of persons, implanted within but sealed from a strange and uncomprehending environment. The city, I have argued, is the locus where social processes intersect, and these processes in turn link the urban population to a regional community larger than itself. The city is a field of intensified human movement. City and countryside have been in history sometimes adversaries and more often partners, but always they have interacted. Historians ought to examine for every epoch of urban history the terms of that interaction, the ways in which town and country, bourgeois and peasant, cooperated, collided, behaved, the one facing the other.

16

THE PROBLEM OF THE "RETURN TO THE LAND" IN TUSCAN ECONOMIC HISTORY OF THE FOURTEENTH AND FIFTEENTH CENTURIES

✦ ✦ ✦

In the economic history of medieval Europe, Tuscany is chiefly celebrated for the number, precocious growth, and dazzling wealth of its cities. According to the most recent estimates, Tuscany was probably, in the late Middle Ages, the most urbanized region of Europe.[1] Still, for all the splendor of its cities, about 75 percent of the population in the fourteenth and fifteenth centuries—three out of four persons—lived outside the region's principal urban centers, in small villages or on isolated farms. The chief support of this large majority of the medieval Tuscan population was of course agriculture. Moreover, even those families settled within the cities maintained a large part of their fortunes in rural properties, and drew a comparable share of their sustenance from agricultural rents. The patriciate of the medieval Tuscan towns never committed its resources exclusively to commerce or to manufacture.

1. In 1427, out of 264,210 persons resident in the areas of Tuscany subject to Florentine rule, the city of Florence contained 37,245 inhabitants and the six secondary cities (Pisa, Pistoia, Prato, Arezzo, Volterra and Cortona) contained 26,315 residents. The number of Tuscans settled in these seven cities thus represented 24 percent of the total population. The percentage may have been slightly higher in the thirteenth century. On the levels of urbanization in various regions of medieval Europe, including Tuscany, see J. C. Russell, *Medieval Regions and Their Cities* (Bloomington, Indiana, 1972).

What proportion of their wealth did urban investors place in agricultural activities, and what in trade or industry? Did the balance between these two types of investment shift over time? The one historian who has dared to give a forthright answer to these difficult questions was Niccolo Rodolico, initially in a short study published more than forty years ago.[2] In the eyes of this perceptive scholar, investment in business enterprises was the preferred tactic of Tuscans—and Italians—in periods of economic growth and prosperity. In historical terms, with a view to the Tuscan experience, the leading urban families of the twelfth and thirteenth centuries took capital out of land and out of agriculture, and directed it toward building a vast commercial empire, which soon became the wonder of the medieval world. But times changed from approximately the middle of the fourteenth century, and so also did the collective psychology of the Tuscan investors and businessmen. The companies of the Bardi and the Peruzzi, those pillars of Christendom according to Giovanni Villani, collapsed in the 1340's; plagues, wars, and social unrest followed hard upon this business disaster. Amid a contracting economy, Tuscan investors beat a headlong retreat into real estate. They withdrew their capital from the now hazardous ventures of commerce, and consigned it to the safety of fixed, indestructible land. The merchants of Tuscany's heroic age, or at least their sons and grandsons after them, transformed themselves into landlords and rentiers. The "return to the land" thus marked a fundamental shift in the psychology of Tuscany's investors, and heralded the end of a brilliant period of entrepreneurial daring and economic growth.

This claim, that Tuscan investors in the late fourteenth century were retreating into agriculture, has never, to my knowledge, been systematically examined and tested. But a large number of prominent historians—Gino Luzzatto, Armando Sapori, Robert S. Lopez, Enrico Fiumi, among others—have commented favorably upon it[3] It

2. "Il ritorno alla terra nella storia degli italiani," *Atti dei Georgofili* (1933), 111, pp. 323ff. See also *idem, La democrazia fiorentina nel suo tramonto* (Bologna, 1905), p. 149.

3. A. Sapori, *Studi di storia economica (secoli XIII-XIV-XV)*, 3rd edition (Florence, 1955), I, p. 645. G. Luzzatto, "Per la storia dell'economia rurale in Italia nel secolo XIV," *Hommage à Lucien Febvre. Eventail de l'histoire vivante* (Paris, 1953) II, p. 112: "... è indubitato che gli Alberti, in misura anche maggiore di molte altre casate di mercanti fiorentini, investirono una parte crescente dei guadagni della mercatura e della banca negli acquisti di terre ..." R. S. Lopez, "The Trade of Medieval Europe: The South," in *The Cambridge Economic History of Medieval Europe*, Vol. II: *Trade and*

is particularly congenial to those who detect depression or decadence in the Tuscan and Italian economy from the late fourteenth century. "Moreover", writes Robert Lopez, in one of his several depictions of the economic depression of the Renaissance, "a growing number of merchants retired from business, invested in real estate, lavished huge sums in magnificence, and became members of the new 'Bourgeois nobility' ...".[4] Investment in land allegedly appealed to those who had lost the entrepreneurial spirit, or discerned little room for its exercise.

Still, neither the concurrence of distinguished historians, nor the inherent plausibility of the argument, can erase lingering doubts, that the direction of investment really was changing across the fourteenth century. With his usual fine critical sense, Philip Jones pointed out some years ago that no one has yet advanced sure documentary evidence, that agricultural investments were growing in popularity as the fourteenth century progressed.[5] To read the memoirs of Florentine household heads is rather to be struck by the abiding interest which these men manifest, in their farms, their animals, their tenants, harvests and rents. If shifts were occurring, they have left few visible traces across the vast extent of Tuscan documentation. More recently, Charles de la Roncière has examined the career of a Florentine money-changer, Lippo di Fede del Sega, who lived from about 1285 to about 1363,.[6] Counter of coins, money lender, merchant who spent some thirty years in France, Lippo still paid consistent attention to acquiring, rearranging, and managing his landed possessions, most of which were located in the rural *popolo* of Santa Maria a Pontanico, not far from Settignano. According to La Roncière, he brought to this activities as landlord and rentier the "true qualities of a businessman".[7] Lippo's career, in other words, gives no firm support to the thesis of a "return to the land". Were

---

Industry in the Middle Ages, ed. M. Postan and E. E. Rich (Cambridge, 1952), p. 344. E. Fiumi, "Fioritura e decadenza della economia fiorentina," Archivio Storico Italiano, 116 (1958), p. 500.

4. Cambridge Economic History of Medieval Europe, II, p. 344.

5. P. J. Jones, "Florentine Families ard Florentine Diaries in the Fourteenth Century," Papers of the British School of Rome, 24 (1956), pp. 183-205, especially pp. 197ff.

6. Un changeur florentin du trecento: Lippo di Fede del Sega (1285 env.–1363 env.). Ecole Pratique des Hautes Etudes—VIième Section. Centre de Recherches Historiques, Affaires et Gens d'Affaires, 36 (Paris, 1973).

7. Ibid., p. 108: "... la constitution d'une propriété foncière exige de véritables qualités d'homme d'affaires ..."

urban investors truly returning to the land in the fourteenth century? Or had they ever really departed from it?

In the light of present knowledge, Rodolico's thesis must be judged neither proved nor refuted. But this much at least is certain: the behavior or Tuscan investors, the decisions they made, the motives which prompted them, were considerably more complex than the thesis envisions. We here can offer no comprehensive or profound examination of that behavior. Our hope is only to illuminate certain aspects of a central problem in the history of medieval Tuscan society—a problem which could easily occupy and richly deserves the attention of many scholars, over many years to come.

Several factors seem to have influenced the behavior of Tuscan investors, and thus to have bent the flow of moneys into or away from business or agriculture. We shall examine four of them here: the place of residence of the investor; his position upon the ladder of wealth; his age, or location along the path of his life; and the secular or long-term economic trend, the prevailing conditions of prosperity or depression in which he was operating.

How did the residence of the investor affect his preferences in the placing of his capital? One source which can throw light on this and the other questions is the Florentine Catasto of 1427, that inexhaustible mine of data on almost every aspect of Tuscan economic and social life.[8] The Catasto surveys the population of those areas of Tuscany then subject to Florentine rule—some 60,000 households, containing 260,000 persons. It also provides a detailed inventory of properties owned, whether in real estate, in movable goods, or in shares in the Florentine public debt, known as the *Monte*. The redactors of the survey did not, to be sure, include in the assessment properties considered essential for the survival and support of the taxpayer and his family. The family dwelling, its furnishings, and the tools utilized in the trade of the household head, were either not recorded or, if recorded, went unassessed. In rural areas, the peasant proprietor was allowed to deduct one-half the harvest of lands worked by his own hand. The belongings included in the survey were thus regarded as surplus and disposable capital, which could

---

8. On the redaction of the Catasto and for an analysis of its content, see D. Herlihy and C. Klapisch-Zuber, *Les Toscans et leurs familles. Une étude du Catasto florentin de 1427* (Paris, 1978).

be assessed without impairing the capacity of the taxpayer to earn his living, support his family, and pay his taxes.

The total, surplus capital owned by Tuscan households in 1427 was valued at approximately 15 million gold florins, before allowable deductions.[9] Of this sum, about 8 million florins, or 53 percent, consisted of holdings in real estate. Unfortunately, the manner by which this information was collected (in aggregated amounts for each household) does not now allow us to distinguish the value of urban properties from those in rural areas. It is, however, certain that the substantial part of the evaluated real estate consisted of rural or agricultural holdings. The majority of urban families either inhabited their own houses, which were not assessed, or lived without paying rent in the homes of relatives.[10] The exemption, in other words, of the family domicile removed a substantial part of urban properties from the tax rolls, including the most luxurious city palaces.

It is interesting to observe that different residential groups held different proportions of their wealth in land, movables, or the Monte. Residents of the countryside, for example, characteristically retained the largest share of their assets in real property. Among the rural households, holdings in land account for 91 percent of all taxable property. In the small towns of Tuscany, places such as San Gimignano, Colle, Empoli, San Miniato al Tedesco, Montevarchi, and the like—the same percentage drops to 78 percent.[11] In the six large towns—Pisa, Pistoia, Prato, Volterra, Arezzo and Cortona—the proportion of wealth in real estate falls still further, to 64 percent. Finally, at Florence itself, only 41 percent of the total wealth of the citizens was comprised of landed holdings.

This conclusion seems obvious: the larger the community, the greater the concentration of movable wealth found within it. And the reason for this seems obvious too: the larger the community, the greater dependency of the population upon non-agricultural activities, upon manufacture and commerce. But manufacture and com-

9. In exact figures the total assessed wealth was 15,085,331 florins, of which 8,058,189 florins was in real property; 4,447,101 in movables; and 2,580,041 in shares in the public debt.

10. At Florence, out of 9,946 households, 4,134 owned their own dwellings, and 1,524 lived with relatives.

11. In analysing the data from the Catasto, we have divided the region surveyed into four groups: Florence, the six cities, fifteen towns, and the remaining countryside.

merce both required and generated large amounts of movable wealth—raw materials, finished products, cash and credit instruments.

This high correlation between the size of the community and the concentration of movable wealth within it suggests this further speculation. Florence in 1427 counted only 37,000 inhabitants. Less than a century before, in 1336–38, according to the famous description of the city written by Giovanni Villani, the city possessed somewhere between 90,000 and 120,000 residents.[12] The economy of this substantially larger city must have required and generated a comparably larger concentration of movable wealth. Villani himself claims that the woolen cloths manufactured in the 200 shops of the city numbered 70,000 or 80,000, and were valued at 1.2 million gold florins. This cloth industry alone employed some 30,000 workers. The twenty or more shops associated with the guild of Calimala, finished every year 10,000 cloths imported from France, worth another 300,000 florins. In 1336–38, these two industries produced goods valued at 1.5 million gold florins. In 1427 the cloth industry was certainly much smaller. Movable wealth of every kind, associated with all industrial and commercial activities within the city, amounted to the comparatively modest sum of 3.5 million gold florins in 1427.

It is therefore very likely that the great fall in the urban population induced a corresponding decline in the output of the Florentine economy, and in the concentrations of movable capital within the city. It is, for example, well known that the capitalization of the great banking houses of the Bardi and Peruzzi, before their failure in the 1340's, surpassed the assets of fifteenth-century banking houses, notably the several Medici companies.[13] The reduced concentrations of liquid capital found at Florence in the fifteenth century may not reflect a new preference for investment in agriculture, but the smaller absolute size of the urban community and the economy which supported it.

The Catasto also shows that the composition of family fortunes was not consistent across all social levels. To judge how the com-

12. *Cronica di Giovanni Villani* (Florence, 1823), pp. 183-88. Villani states on the basis of the amount of bread consumed in the city that Florence then contained upwards of 90,000 mouths, but the number of recorded births (5500 to 6000) suggests a higher figure, in the neighborhood of 120,000. The estimates are reexamined in D. Herlihy and C. Klapisch-Zuber, *Les Toscans*, Ch. 6.

13. On the enormous sums of money managed by the Bardi and Peruzzi, see the contents of Y. Renouard, *Les hommes d'affaires italiens du Moyen Âge* (Paris, 1949), pp. 123-25.

position of fortunes changed as we move up or down the social hierarchy, we shall here examine only the population of Florence itself in 1427—some 10,000 households. We shall first rearrange these urban households in the order of ascending wealth (based on the total of all taxable assets, before deductions), and then divide the households into centiles—100 groups composed of approximately 100 households each. We can exclude from further consideration here the lowest 13 centiles, comprising approximately 13 percent of the urban households, as these *miserabili* held no property at all. Table 1 shows the composition of Florentine fortunes for selected centiles on a descending scale of wealth.

Table 1

Composition of Household Wealth in the City of Florence, 1427.

Centile*	Percent Real	Percent Movables	Percent Monte
1	20.8	37.5	41.7
5	41.6	29.1	29.2
10	49.2	31.9	18.9
25	63.0	27.5	9.4
50	63.6	32.2	4.3
75	56.9	42.0	0.0
80	31.8	67.1	1.1

*100 urban households, with centiles ranked in descending order of wealth.

Among those urban households with some possessions, the composition of Florentine fortunes shows interesting shifts, as we progress from poor to rich up the scale of wealth. The poorest, but still propertied households have the largest part of their possessions in movables. They rarely own land, and never shares in the Monte. These are the small artisans and shopkeepers, working in rented shops and living in rented quarters, who own only the goods they produce or offer for sale. However, as we move upward on the scale of wealth, the proportion of holdings in real estate substantially increases. At the level of the eightieth centile, real property still constitutes less than one-third of the household fortunes; at the seventy-fifth centile, more than one-half; and at the fiftieth, nearly two-thirds. These proportions then remain fairly constant for the next twenty-five centiles—a quarter of all the households of the city—as we continue to move upward on the scale of wealth. Thereafter, the importance of shares in the public debt increases rapidly, and also, though less dramatically, the proportion of wealth held in movables. Among the wealthiest citizens, holdings in real estate are comparatively small, accounting for only about one-fifth of their enormous fortunes.

These conclusions follow from our analysis. A strong preference for investments in real estate is characteristic of the middle levels of Florentine society. In contrast, the fortunes of both the greatest and the humblest property owners of Florence show a curious similarity, in that they are principally composed of movable wealth. This fact may justify a further speculation. The humble artisan or shopkeeper held most of his assets in movables. However, if fortune favored him and his wealth accrued, he was prone to place a growing part of his capital in real estate. As the level of his wealth mounted, so also did his appetite for land. On the other hand, if his fortune increased spectacularly, so as to carry him into the ranks of the richest urban households, then he was likely to turn his incremented capital into business ventures or into shares in the public debt. The Florentine citizen, if and as he grew richer, showed an initial appetite for land, but that appetite was not unlimited.

The importance of landed holdings for Florentine investors of the middle class may help explain certain apparent inconsistencies, in the history of rural investments. It has, for example, been noted that Lippo di Fede del Sega, the money-changer of modest position studied by La Roncière, showed more interest in rural investments than his contemporaries, three rich and powerful brothers of the Alberti family.[14] In 1309 the brothers seem to have derived only 22 percent of their income from their rural holdings.[15] Lippo, on the other hand, apparently invested over several decades of the Trecento (1311-1356) 58.6 percent of his moneys in his agricultural interests.[16] But the Alberti were among the greatest of the Florentine families, and Lippo was a man of middling status. The data from the Catasto suggest that they were acting in ways consistent with their social position.

14. *Un changeur florentin*, p. 125.

15. Luzzatto, "Per la storia dell' economia rurale," p. 106. According to the accounting of January 1, 1309, the amount of income from their rural holdings was 17,966 florins out of a total revenue of 83,022 florins.

16. La Roncière, *Un changeur florentin*, p. 125.

Another factor which affected the propensity to invest in land was the age of the investor. In Table 2 we give the composition of the fortunes of male Florentines according to categories of age.

Table 2

Composition of Household Wealth According to Age of Male Head in the City of Florence, 1427.

Age	Avg. Wealth	Percent Real	Percent Movables	Percent Monte	Percent Debts*
0-22	1164.89	46.11	28.21	25.68	19.88
23-32	960.72	45.91	26.58	27.51	27.01
33-42	935.64	42.45	37.52	20.03	33.31
43-52	1260.27	38.89	37.09	24.02	28.85
53-62	1461.58	35.18	39.90	24.92	27.58
Over 62	954.32	39.77	32.49	27.74	23.95

*Expressed as a percentage of total wealth.

The age group in Florentine society with the largest relative investment in land consists of young, male household heads under age 23. Most of these household heads are fatherless boys, and many hold their property together with brothers or sisters who are also minors. The frequency of joint households, based on undivided inheritances, in this age category also explains their large, average wealth. As these male household heads grow older at Florence, the proportion of their holdings in real property tends to fall, and their holdings in movables increase. Their debts increase at an even more rapid pace during the years of young adulthood.

The tendency here seems to be clear. As the male Florentine entered adulthood, he was likely to make three decisions in regard to his capital. He tended first of all to divide the common patrimony and claim his separate share of the paternal inheritance. This explains the falling average wealth of the urban households as their heads grow older. At the same time, in order to increase his wealth, he was likely to embark upon a commercial or professional career. To do this he needed liquid assets above all, and to gain them he was prone either to mortgage his real properties (which accounts for his mounting debts) or to sell them outright (which explains the growing proportion of his movable capital). During his years of active engagement in a career, he retained a substantial proportion of his capital in movables. After age 63, in old age, the Florentine household heads were likely to convert their wealth into land or into shares in the public debt. This suggests that the Florentines preferred to bequeath to their heirs real property rather than movables (apart from shares in the public debt, which were easily managed). The favored way of packaging the wealth of the family and of transferring it across generations was to convert it into real estate. The assumption seems to have been that only mature and active persons could manage and defend large amounts of liquid capital.

Conversion of assets into movables across the years of young adulthood, and reconversion back into real property in old age— this seems to have been the common tactic of Florentine investors. There was, in other words, a "return to the land" across the life cycle of the individual citizen. The careers of many Florentines of the late Middle Ages seem to adhere to this pattern. Guido Filippi dell'Antella, born in 1254, has bequeathed us one of the earliest set of *ricordi* or memoirs.[17] He spent his years of young adulthood in an active mercantile career, visiting Genoa, Venice and Provence. We do not know the sources of the capital he used in his commercial enterprises, but his surviving account book gives no hint of an interest in real estate. He married in 1291, at the age of 37, and from about the same time he began to acquire considerable amounts of real property. The first of his recorded purchases dates from 1285, when he was 31 years old, but the bulk of his acquisitions were made during the 1290's, when he was a settled *paterfamilias* with a growing family. In 1297, at the age of 43, he made his largest single purchase: a *podere* or farm, which cost him 900 pounds. In the following years he invested another 300 pounds in improving the same *podere*.[18] Guido tells us that he acquired many properties in compensation for outstanding debts, which implies that he was converting liquid assets, that is, the money owed, into real property. He further remarks that he was purchasing land "as a way of defense".[19] He does not identify whom he was defending, but we may presume

17. "Ricordanze di Guido Filippi dell'Antella," in *Nuovi Testi Fiorentini del Dugento,* ed. A. Castellani (Florence, 1952), pp. 804-13.
18. *Ibid.,* p. 808: "poi v'oe ispeso i lavori di chase e di corte da lb. ccc, sin' a dì ***di novembre anno xxxlxviiii."
19. *Ibid.,* p. 812: "Tutte altre compere e vendite che fatte si trovaseno sin' a dì xxvii di marzo anno Mcccii sono fatte o per modo di difensione o per debiti ch'io debo avere d'altrui."

that it was his wife and growing family, whom he wished to protect against the risk of his own death. Holdings in real estate best defended the interests of the widow, the orphaned and the aged.

Matteo di Niccolò Corsini, born in 1322, left Florence for England in 1344, at the age of 21, and remained abroad for the following 22 years.[20] We do not know the composition of his fortune at this period of his life, but it would seem obvious that liquid capital primarily supported him in his career as a merchant. In 1358, at the age of 36, while still abroad, he arranged his first purchase of real estate within the city of Florence, and thereafter began to acquire both urban and rural properties. To pay for the land, he sent furs and cloth to his brother at Florence The acquisitions of real estate were in evident preparation for his return to Florence in February, 1366, and for his marriage the following May, when he was *39* years of age. In 1365 Matteo placed 2000 florins in a wool ship; this seems to have been his last commercial investment, and it turned out badly.[21] For the remainder of his long life (he died in 1402) he concerned himself with purchases and sales of real estate. Again, there seems to have been an association between advancing years and a preference for investments in land.

In our examination of the "return to the land" in Tuscan economic history of the late Middle Ages, the last factor to be considered is the long-range, economic trend. Did the hard times of the fourteenth century provoke a retreat from commercial ventures into agriculture? Unfortunately, of all the factors we are considering, the long-range economic trend is the most difficult to evaluate. We have argued that a "return to the land" consistently characterized individual Tuscan investors in the last phases of their life cycles. If true, this phenomenon would necessarily obscure the direction of the long-term movement of investments. Moreover, there is not, to my knowledge, any consistent run of documents, which might illuminate for us the changing behavior of Tuscan investors.

Still, we do possess some evidence, which indirectly reflects the flow of urban capital into agricultural lands. One of the few possible indicators of this movement is the size of the rural *Estimo*, the assessment imposed upon the rural parishes or *popoli* by the

---

20. *Il libro di ricordanze dei Corsini (1362–1457)*, ed. A. Petrucci, Fonti per la Storia d'Italia, 100 (Rome, 1965), pp. 3–4.

21. *Ibid.*, p. 39. Armando Petrucci (p. xvii) notes that the sum was "meno di quanto ha finora investito in terre."

Florentine government.[22] Each *popolo* was assigned a particular sum, expressed in lire, which was in turn divided among its resident families. The Estimo was periodically revised, often at five-year intervals. In taxing the countryside, the government would declare that the rural parishes and households must pay so many *solidi* per *lira* of assessment. It is important to note that the figure given by the Estimo does not represent the absolute wealth of the *popolo* or the household, but only its relative ability to pay, in relation to other parishes and families. Still, the Estimo does give a rough indication of the resources held by the rural inhabitants.

Between the thirteenth and the fifteenth century, the total size of the rural Estimo declined steadily and precipitously. It seems to have been as high as 448,000 lire in 1289, but was only 12,500 lire in ca. 1470.[23] Several factors account for this continuous deterioration in the rural assessment. Between these two dates, the rural population declined, in some areas by as much as two-thirds. But population decline cannot be the principal reason for this apparent rural impoverishment. As we shall presently see, the average assessment of the remaining rural households, as well as the total sum of the Estimo, was also drastically falling in the fourteenth and fifteenth centuries. Besides the diminishing numbers of rural residents, immigration of propertied families into the city helped concentrate the ownership of rural lands in the hands of urban dwellers. But even more important seems to have been the purchase by citizens of fields and farms, the outflow of urban capital into the countryside. The decline in the Estimo reflects, in other words, the steady dispossession of the Tuscan peasants, their conversion in large numbers from independent cultivators working their own lands into tenants and *mezzadri.* The dispossession of the peasantry is the reverse image of urban investments in rural holdings. By investigating when the decline in the Estimo principally occurred, it may be possi-

22. On the character of the Estimo see E. Fiumi, "L'imposta diretta nei comuni medioevali della Toscana," in *Studi in onore di Armando Sapori* (Milan, 1957), pp. 329-53.
23. For the basis of the early figure, see D. Herlihy, "Santa Maria Impruneta. A Rural Commune in the Late Middle Ages," in *Florentine Studies. Politics and Society in Renaissance Florence,* ed. N. Rubinstein (London, 1968), p. 286. The "Tavola Antica" published by Ildefonso di San Luigi, *Delizie degli eruditi toscani,* XIII (Florence, 1780), p. 246, gives as the total number of households in the Florentine countryside 24,818, and the total value of the Estimo borne by them, 12,466 pounds, 6 solidi and 3 denarii. The date of the Tavola is uncertain, but it may represent the results of the survey of 1470.

ble, in sum, to locate the period when urban capital moved in particularly large amounts into agriculture. Perhaps we can determine when, if ever, there occurred a return of capital to the land.

Table 3 gives for various years the size of the Estimo of a Florentine village, the *populus plebis,* or chief parish, of Santa Maria Impruneta.

Table 3
Estimi of the *Populus Plebis* of Santa Maria Impruneta.

Year	Hhlds	Total (lire)	Avg.	Annual Rate of Change
1307	122	1925	15.78	-4.25%
1319	115	1078	9.37	-1.93%
1330	123	930	7.56	-6.48%
1350	(101)	200	1.98	-0.95%
1427	71	67	9.95	-6.61%
1470(?)	122	87	0.73	

Sources: For the assessments of 1307, 1319 and 1330, see D. Herlihy, "Santa Maria Impruneta. A Rural Commune in the Late Middle Ages", *Florentine Studies. Politics and Society in Renaissance Florence,* ed. Niccolai Rubinstein (London 1968), p. 259. The Estimo for 1350 is taken from ASF, Estimo, reg. 303. The figure of 101 households is taken from an Estimo of 1356, and is given in E. Fiumi, "La demografia fiorentina nelle pagine di Giovanni Villani", *Archivio Storico Italiano,* CVIII (1960), p. 148. The figures for 1470 are taken from the "Tavola Antica", published by Ildefonso di San Luigi *Delizie degli eruditi toscani,* XIII (Florence, 1780), pp. 290ff. The date, 1470, is uncertain.

The highest rates of decline in the Estimo of Santa Maria Impruneta are found in the years before 1350. Between the earliest surviving Estimo, dated 1307, and the assessment of 1350, the annual rate of decline, calculated according to the rules of compound interest, was -4.71 percent. After 1350, the rate moderates considerably, and does not surpass -1 percent per year. The conclusion must be that, at Impruneta, the great influx of urban capital into the countryside anticipated the Black Death (1348) and corresponded with the period of assumed prosperity, in the early decades of the fourteenth century.

Estimi from other rural areas of the Florentine countryside confirm this conclusion that the return of urban capital to rural lands was occurring well before the 1340's, before the advent of the "economic depression of the Renaissance". In 1319, the 34 households of San Donato a Torre bore an assessment of 116 pounds—an average of 3.41 pounds per household.[24] In 1350, the amount had shrunk to 23 pounds, and the number of households to 30, for an average of 0.77 pounds per family. The yearly rate of decline between 1319 and 1350 was therefore—4.69 percent, nearly the same as we observed at Impruneta. Over the same period (1319-1350), the Estimo of the *populus plebis,* the chief parish, of Antella fell from 1232 pounds to only 197, while the number of households declined from 137 to 118.[25] The average annual rate of decline between the two dates was—5.29, even higher than the rates registered at Impruneta and San Donato. The neighboring parish of San Pietro a Ema experienced a decline in the average assessment of its households, between 1319 and 1350, of —4.90 percent.[26] All these examples suggest a range of loss, in the average assessments of households in the Florentine countryside, of somewhere between—4.0 and—5.0 percent per year, over the first half of the fourteenth century. This period of commercial prosperity, in other words, witnessed an authentic conquest of the countryside by urban capital.

This rate of change in the Estimo falls considerably in the last half of the fourteenth century; surviving Estimi suggest a loss ranging below—2.5 percent per year.[27] The economic troubles of the late

24. Archivio di Stato di Firenze (henceforth, ASF), Notarile A.C., M 39 (2), 17 September 1319. The values for 1350 come from ASF, Estimo, reg. 303, and E. Fiumi, "La demografia fiorentina nelle pagine di Giovanni Villani," *Archivio Storico Italiano,* 108 (1950), p. 120.

25. ASF, Notarile A.C., A 435, 69v, 22 August 1319; ASF, Estimo, reg. 303 and Fiumi, "La demografia," p. 139.

26. In 1319, according to the Estimo copied in ASF, Notarile A.C., A 435, 66r, dated 19 August 1319, the popolo di San Pietro contained 56 households and bore an assessment of 231 pounds 10 solidi. In 1350 the assessment was 40 pounds and in 1356 the number of households was 46. See ASF, Estimo, reg. 303, and Fiumi "La demografia," p. 139.

27. In 1350 the 33 households of the populus plebis of San Giovanni in Soana bore an assessment of 65 pounds, or an average of 1.97 pounds per household. According to the Estimo copied in ASF, Notarile A.C., N 125, 107v, dated 16 December 1394, 34 households in the parish bore an assessment of 21 pounds 3 solidi—an average of 0.62 pounds per household. This represents an average annual rate of decline of -2.59 percent. In 1404 (*ibid.* 112r, 17 February 1403, Florentine style) 20 households in the parish bore an assessment of 11 pounds 5 solidi, an average of 0.56 pounds per household. The annual rate of decline for these ten years was -1.01 percent. The parish of Santa Maria alla Rombola in the same pieve shows an average assessment per household in 1350 of 2.35 pounds (34 households, 80 pounds of assessment). In 1394 the average was 0.75 pounds (28 households, 21 pounds of assessment). See ASF, Notarile A.C., N 125 (1), 108r, 21 December 1394. The average annual rate of decline was -2.56 percent. Over the following ten years the rate falls to -1.89. See ASF, Notarile

fourteenth century did not enlarge, but rather diminished the flow of urban capital into agriculture.

These then are the conclusions, or rather the observations, which our examination of Rodolico's thesis suggests. Investments in business and investments in real property in city or in countryside did not represent opposed or contrary movements. In periods of an expanding economy and growing wealth, capital sought outlets both in new business ventures and in agriculture. In the early four-teenth century, urban money flowed in large amounts into rural properties, even as it was swelling the assets of such great commercial companies as the Bardi or Peruzzi. Although this was a period of abundant business opportunities, investment in real estate still retained a powerful attraction, as, for example, among those citizens who, late in their careers, wished to guarantee the eco-nomic security of their families. Similarly, the hard times of the late fourteenth century did not bring with them a "return to the land", but a general reduction in the flow of capital, simultaneously into business and into agriculture.

Rodolico's thesis, in sum, seems to rest upon the fallacious assumption that investment in commerce and investment in agri-culture moved in contrary directions. Our partial review of the evi-dence suggests that investments of all kinds grew or declined in phase with the long-term economic cycle of prosperity and decline. There were strong reasons why, even under prosperity, investors might prefer to place their savings into agriculture. There were also strong reasons why, even in bad economic times, citizens were will-ing to assume the risks of commercial investments.

Although these arguments cannot be considered conclusive, nowhere do we find evidence of a "return to the land" in quite the manner Rodolico defined it. Yet, to his credit, he posed a question which well deserves intensive and continuing examination. This pre-sent essay is itself a tribute to the perspicacity of a gifted historian.

A.C., N 125 (2), 111r, 9 February 1403, Florentine style, "Distributio libre populi sancte Marie," 13 houses with a total assessment of 8 pounds 2 solidi 8 denarii.

SALUTO DELL'ASSESSORE PROVINCIALE ALLA CULTURA

Porgo a tutti i partecipanti a questo convegno il saluto dell'Amministrazione provinciale. Non mi dilunghero anche perché vedo che questo pomeriggio ci sono ancora delle relazioni da tenere, cui seguiranno le conclusioni di questo convegno. Mi auguro che i lavori che sono stati svolti, le relazioni, i dibattiti che sono awenuti in questi giorni possano aprirsi e continuare ad essere vivi anche in futuro all'interno della societa pistoiese, anche perché il tema che e stato affrontato e che e stato portato al dibattito e un tema estremamente importante e interessante, soprattutto nel momento in cui andiamo ad una riorganizzazione, ad un rilancio, che induce anche in noi, come Amministrazione, un particolare interesse al mondo dell'agricoltura dal punto di vista culturale, sociale ed economico. E soprattutto anche nel momento in cui vediamo nella nostra societa pistoiese un ritorno, da parte soprattutto dei giovani, di alcuni giovani, alle campagne e quindi un tentativo di rendere ancora vive e proficue le nostre terre e soprattutto i paesi, le citta, che purtroppo sono visti per lungo tempo abbandonati e spopolati. Io auguro a questo convegno, che sta per terminare, un buon lavoro e mi auguro anche che l'edizione di questi convegni e il lavoro del Centro Studi di Storia e d'Arte possano avere sempre maggiore successo, ancora piu grande di quello ottenuto anche quest'anno.

17

TUSCAN NAMES, 1200–1530

✦ ✦ ✦

"A name," Bernardine of Siena declares, "is a *famosa notitia*," a public statement.[1] In this paper I review the stock of personal names, and, implicitly, the public statements, associated with the men of women of Florence and of Tuscany, between the thirteenth and sixteenth centuries. The justifications for this enterprise are two. The surviving sources give overwhelming attention to the rich and powerful; they pay little heed to the poor and lowly. Inevitably, they yield an unbalanced view of Tuscan society. But if in most respects the humble are voiceless, they do bear personal names; they do make, in Bernardine's phrase, public statements.

Moreover, as Bernardine implies, a name is far more than a bland identifier. It is rather a pointer, that directs our gaze in three directions. Its principal and unvarying function is to identify a particular man or woman. It bestows individuality; it ensouls. But names may also recall the past; often, they convert living persons into memorials to the dead. They may also predict the future, express a hope, augur a destiny. They carry, in sum, multiple messages. Through names, we eavesdrop as the old instruct the young, prepare them to carry the culture, and bless them on their way.

Florence and Tuscany offer an exceptional opportunity for studying names of the Middle Ages and Renaissance. The city and region possess many, lengthy nominal lists, both surveys and registrations. The oldest survey we shall utilize here comes not from Florence

---

1. "Pernomen famosa notitia designatur." *S. Bernardini senensis ordinis fratrum minorum Opera omnia*, 4 (Florence, 1956), p. 514.

itself but its near neighbor Pistoia, some 20 miles distant. In 1219, over 3000 male citizens of the city swore to uphold a peace with Bologna.[2] The countryside of Pistoia also possesses, from about 1244, a list of family heads, called the *Liber focorum* or Book of Hearths.[3] It contains over 7300 names, and about 12 percent of the named heads are women. Florence itself has preserved, in the *Libro di Montaperti*, a muster of its army that marched against Siena in 1260. The *Libro* contains in fact many documents, and the total of names recorded within them is over 6000; the Swedish scholar, Olaf Brattö, has devoted to them two invaluable studies.[4] The largest of all Tuscan surveys is the great Florentine Catasto of 1427–1430 It contains over 60,000 households distributed all across the Florentine domains, then nearly the entire province of Tuscany; it names 260,000 persons.[5] When I and Christiane Klapisch-Zuber more than ten years ago redacted the Catasto into a form that computers could read, we recorded only the names of the family heads, some 60,000, but not those of the household members. The omission of any data is always regrettable, even though at the time it seemed necessary if our analysis of this huge document was ever to be finished. In particular, this decision reduced the number of female names, as women headed only a little more than 11 percent of the Tuscan households. That yields 6810 women's names in the machine-readable edition. Still, the 53,000 male names and nearly 7000 women's names surely constitute a representative sample of those preferred in Florentine Tuscany in the early fifteenth century.

---

2. The oath, dated June 1–4 and now preserved at Bologna, was published in *The liber censuum comunis Pistorii*, ed. Q. Santoli, Fonti storiche pistoiesi, 1 (Pistoia, 1915), pp. 509–27

3. *Liber focorum districtus Pistorii (a. 1226). Liber finium districtus Pistorii (a. 1255),* ed Q. Santoli, Fonti per la storia d'Italia, 91 (Rome, 1955). The date of 1226 which Santoli applied to the survey is surely wrong. For the date of 1244, see D. Herlihy, *Medieval and Renaissance Pistoia* (New Haven, Conn., 1968), pp. 61-62.

4. *Studi di antroponimia fiorentina: Il Libro di Montaperti (an. mcclx)* (Göteborg, 1953) and *Nuovi studi di antroponimia fiorentina: i nomi meno frequenti del libro di Montaperti (an. mcclx),* Acta Universitatis Gothoburgensis, 61 (Stockholm, 1955). The *Libro di Montaperti* includes besides the muster of the army many administrative directives, grain requisitions, and the like. Brattö collected names from all these and other records, to arrive at a total of 6,203. The soldiers mustered seem to be only 1954. This latter set of names, drawn out of the same example, I use here to determine frequencies.

5. D. Herlihy and C. Klapisch-Zuber, *Tuscans and Their Families: A Study of the Florentine Catasto of 1427* (New Haven, Conn., 1985).

Among registrations, the oldest used here is the matriculations of Florentine citizens—regrettably all male—into the guild of the silk merchants, the Por Santa Maria, which begins in 1225. Next in chronological line is the necrology of those buried at the Dominican church of Santa Maria Novella between 1296 and 1526—especially valuable because it also includes women. The largest of our registrations is a list of male citizens scrutinized for or elected to communal or guild offices between the establishment of the priorate in 1282 and the end of the Republic in 1530. The work of collecting and entering the names is not yet complete, but it is already substantial—it includes some 120,000 names—and is surely representative of the male names displayed by the office holding class of Florence.

The task of counting and interpreting Tuscan names in the tens of thousands would have been impossible 30 years ago, and hard and expensive even 10 years ago. But information technologies have since become ever more powerful, ever more accessible, and ever cheaper. Today, these technologies make possible analyses of a range and power not doable before. We should express our gratitude to those who have designed, built and know how to use these technical wonders.[6] Names may be only whispers from the past, but the new technologies can lend them amplitude.

Between the thirteenth and the fifteenth centuries, a revolution occurs in the number and nature of Tuscan names. There is a radical reduction in the variety of names displayed. It is, to be sure, hard to make precise counts of the names of Pistoiese citizens in 1219. They are recorded in Latin, and the different notaries may have transcribed the same name differently. Here, for example, somewhat arbitrarily, I count Iunta and Zunta as the same name, but not Giovanni and Zagni. Some strange appearing names may have been misread or misprinted.[7] Though precision is elusive, there is no doubt that at Pistoia and throughout Tuscany, the stock of names declines radically between 1219 and 1427. The 1157 Pistoiese names used in 1219 shrinks to only 220 in the Catasto of the same city in 1427.[8] An aver-

---

6. I would like to thank my son Gregory P. Herlihy, who analysed the data through a data management system called The Fourth Dimension.

7. For example, should the one citizen called Cuidetto be Guidetto?

8. The males taking the oath in 1219 are 3,190, the male household heads in 1427, 918.

age of 2.8 persons share the same name in 1219, but 4.4 persons do so in 1427. Moreover, by 1427, some few names attract an extraordinary following. In 1219, 109 of the leading names are required to cover one-half the population: in 1427, only the first eleven leading names account for one-half the male household heads. The most popular single name among Pistoia's citizens is Iacopo (93 appearances), and it is displayed by slightly under 3 percent of the population. In 1427 in the same city, Iacopo and Antonio are tied for first place, but each now includes 6.5 percent of the males.

Our properly Florentine names show the same radical fall in numbers over the same period; they further establish that the trend continues right across the fifteenth century. In 1225 at Florence, in a list of the members of the silk merchants' guild, 611 males report 338 names, a ratio of about two persons per name. Among the Florentine soldiers who marched against Siena in 1260, the ratio of names to persons has not much changed—715 distributed over 1954 soldiers. In 1225, 71 of the most popular names cover one-half the guild members. In 1260, the number embracing one-half the army is about the same, 76. Then, between 1290 and 1348, among males buried at Santa Maria Novella, the number of leading names needed to cover one-half the population falls from roughly 70 to only 27. In 1427, among the male household heads of the city of Florence, one-half their number can be grouped under only fourteen names. By then, the most popular name, Giovanni in place of Iacopo, includes fully 8 percent of the male household heads. In all the Florentine domains, fifteen leading male names include one-half the population of 53,000 family heads. In the Florentine electoral scrutinies taken across the fifteenth century, the number of male names accounting for one-half the population falls to only thirteen.

The Florentine data would locate the sharpest reduction in the number of preferred names as occurring between about 1280 and 1320, although the trend then established continues across the late Middle Ages.

The stock of women's names, though more difficult to measure shows the same strong tendencies to contract and to cluster. The 244 women buried at Santa Maria Novella before 1349 display 123 names—an average of two women per name. The 589 women buried there after 1348 show 187 names—an average of 3.1 women per name. Among Florentine women in 1427, the number of leading names needed to encompass one-half the population is 17, slightly higher than the 14 names required to cover one-half the males.

The names used at Pistoia and in Tuscany change in nature too. The names of the thirteenth century come from a great variety of sources, and carry a great variety of meanings. Some are clearly nonsensical. Two Pistoiesi in 1219, and a member of the Florentine silk guild in 1225, are called Senzanome, "Without a name." A citizen in 1219, and a peasant in ca. 1244, are simply called Nome, "Name."[9] What can we make of names such as Medlialtri, "among others", Trincamusta, "Wine-drinker," or Mezovillano, "Half a peasant"? Other names, such as Guido or Cambio for men or Beatrice or Matilda for women, were traditional in the region, pointing back to important figures in its history.

Medieval philosophers have much to say about names, and we can look to them for guidance in our interpretations. "Names," writes Thomas Aquinas, "must respond to the properties of things, as is evident in the names of genera and species."[10] Bernardine of Siena concurs: "A thing is only truly named when its nature is expressed through its name."[11] Antoninus of Florence repeats: "Names are conferred on things according to their properties."[12] For all these philosophers, this necessary correspondence between signifier and object extended to personal names as well. "The names of individual men," Aquinas affirms, "are always imposed out of some property of the person to whom the name is given."[13]

The first property that, according to Aquinas, determines names is time of birth. Frequently, he observes, "the names of some saints are given to those born on their feast days."[14] To name a baby after a

9. *Liber focorum*, p. 71, Bernardus quondam Nome.

10. *Summa theologica*, III.37.2, in *Opera omnia*, 11 (Rome, 1903), p. 377: "Respondeo dicendum quod nomina debent proprietatibus rerum respondere. Et hoc patet in nominibus generum et speciarum."

11. *Opera omnia*, 4, p. 496: "Hoc siqudem solummodo vere nominatur cuius natura vere per nomen exprimitur; unde, Gen. 2, 20, Adam omnes res nominavit, quia omnium rerum naturas novit."

12. Nomina enim imponuntur rebus secundum proprietatem earum." *Summa theologica*, III.37.2, in *Opera omnia*, 11 (Rome, 1903), p. 377.

13. *Ibid.* "Nomina autem singularium hominum semper inponantur ab aliqua proprietate eius cui nomen imponitur."

14. *Ibid.* "Vel a tempore, sicut imponuntur nomina aliquorum Sanctorum his qui in eorum festis nascuntur."

saint, whether born on the feast or not, is an ancient Christian practice. According to the fourth-century Church historian Eusebius, St. Dionysius of Alexandria explained as follows the popularity among Christians of the name John:

> Many, I imagine, have had the same name as John the Apostle, men who because they loved, admired and esteemed him so greatly, and wished to be loved as he was by the Lord, were more than glad to be called after him, just as Paul and Peter were favorite names for the children of believers.[15]

That colorful chronicler, Salimbene of Parma, born in 1221, says that of the names he bore—he went through four, as we shall see—he at first preferred Dionysius, as he had been born on Dionysius' feast.[16] (Four citizens of Pistoia bear that name in 1219.) But if many Pistoiesi were christened with a saint's name, remarkably few retained it in later life. Of the more than 1100 names recorded in 1219, 39, barely 3 percent, recall an early saint or a Biblical figure, such as Adam, Isaac or Solomon.[17] To be sure, one such name, Iacopo, led all others. Even so, the conclusion stands: the great majority of names displayed at Pistoia in 1219 did not honor a saint.

Under Thomas' category of time we might place personal names taken from the months, like Gennaio or Maggio in 1219. Many names express contentment with a person's arrival: Benvenuto (30), Bonaventura (12), Bencivenni (12), Benivieni (5), Ventura (35), or Venuto (5). Such names may also be regarded as augurative, that is, as expressing a hope for the person's future welfare. Many other names are unmistakably augurative, as they expressly call on God for aid or help: Diologuardi (22), Dietaiudi (1), Dietaiuti (4), Dietiguardi (2), and Dietisalvi (10).

Many Pistoiesi are hailed as gifts from God: Diofeci (I), Diolafeci (1), Diolporta (1), Diomildiedi (6), Deodato (14), Dondidio (4), Dono (3), Graziadio (1) and probably Grazia (8). Some names even comment on the time, presumably of arrival or meeting: Bonanno (1),

15. *The History of the Church from Christ to Constantine*, trans. G. A. Williamson (Baltimore. 1965), p. 311.

16. Salimbene, *Cronica*, ed. F. Bernini, 1 (Bari, 1942), p. 344.

17. They are Adamo, Alissandro, Ambrogio, Anastasio, Andrea, Anselmo, Antone Bartolomeo, Benedetto, Bernardo, Bonifazio, Cristofano, Dainisio, Dainele, Domenico, Filippo, Galgano, Giovanni, Giuliano, Gregorio, Isaac, Lazaro, Leonardo, Leone, Marco, Marsilio, Matteo, Michele, Miniato, Niccolaio, Paolo, Piero, Salamone, Salvestro, Simone, Stefano, Tommaso, Vincenzo and Vittorio.

Bondì (17), Bonora (2), Bonricolto (1), Vendemmia, "wineharvest" (used for both men and women). Or, seemingly, they refer to the weather: Beldì (1), Bonasera (9), Bontempo (2). Many of these names, like Bonaventura or Beldì , are also androgynous, in the sense that both men and women bore them.

Aquinas does not mention place or locale as one of the proper-ties that inspire names, but a large number of Pistoia's early names contain either generic allusion to travel or references to specific places. Two men are named Passalacqua; one, Passamonte; three, Cavalcante. Two are called Tramontano, and two again, Trans-mondino, "across the mountains" and "across the world." One cit-izen is called Montaltissimo, "highest mountain." Five citizens are called Pelegrino and ten Romeo, alluding to pilgrimage. Twelve citizens are named Negozante and eight Mercadante, names that also suggest travel.

The many references to specific places are hard to decode. The men named Milanese or Milano were not necessarily born in Milan. Francis of Assisi, for example, was not born in France. But personal names taken from geography do show some awareness of the indi-cated place. Francis' father, the merchant Pietro Bernardone, was away in France at his son's birth. Upon his return he called his baby Francis, and this replaced his baptismal name, Giovanni.

Ten names refer to Pistoia itself, but no name points to its imme-diate big neighbors in Tuscany, Florence and Lucca, though little Prato appears five times. These first two cities were Pistoia's bitter rivals, and relationships were often disturbed by war. On the other hand, Pistoia was a station on a principal highway that linked it to the sea and to Lombardy beyond the mountains. This route ran from Pisa up the Arno valley, over the waters of the swamp of Fucecchio, across the Monte Albano at the pass of San Baronto, and into Pistoia. It continued over the Apennine passes to Bologna or to Modena. From there travelers could disperse to the principal towns of the Lombard plain.

In 1219, many stations along this route are recalled in Pistoia's personal names: Pisa, Bologna, Modena, Parma, Cremona, Milan, Pavia, Genoa, Verona, Venice, Treviso and perhaps Turin.[18] Three

18. Pisano (2), Bologno (1), Modenese (1), Parmisano (1), Milano (5), Milanese (4), Pavese (3), Genovese (3), Veronese (3), Trivisano (1) and Veneto (2).

citizens are called Lombardo. A further scattering of names refers to even more distant places, to which this highway gave initial approach. Does the popular Romeo mean Roman or pilgrim? A "Siena" appears in the rural Book of Hearths; Napoli, Napolino, and Salerno are recorded in 1219; and two other citizens are named Sardo.[19] What are we to make of the seven citizens named Saracino, or the four named Turco in the oath of 1219?

The northern lands beyond the Alps are also well represented. "Alamanno" probably does not point to Germany, but seven men are named Tedesco. France is even better represented, a region with which the merchant bankers of Pistoia were establishing a lively exchange. Ten citizens are named Francesco—in 1219 the name points to the land and not the saint. Five are called Parisio; one Leonese after Lyons; and one Mergolese, from Melgueil, a mint town in southern France. A citizen in 1219 is called Provincia, and a peasant in the Book of Hearths is named Provinziano, surely after Provence.[20] A peasant woman bears the name Francia.[21]

Geographic names can also have cultural overtones. Many names of 1219 evoke the great pilgrim highway to Sant' Iago de Compostela in Spain, the tomb of the apostle St. James the Greater. Antoninus, bishop of Florence, once remarked that "[James'] body is held in greater veneration than that of any other apostle," even presumably Peter's at Rome.[22] James the Greater, or Iacopo, was also the patron saint of Pistoia, who allegedly saved the city from the Saracens in 866. In the twelfth century, a Spaniard named Atto, born at Badajoz, became Pistoia's bishop; his greatest service for the city was his acquisition of a relic of James' body; it became the town's most prized possession.[23] The local relic did not divert but rather directed pilgrimages to the apostle's tomb. The pilgrims on the way must have heard the tales of Roland and Oliver and of the massacre at Roncesvalles. A citizen is even called Roncivalle in 1219, and a peasant bears the same name about 1244.[24] Spagna and Spagnese

19. *Liber focorum*, p. 183.
20. *Ibid.*, p. 238.
21. *Ibid.*, p. 189.
22. *Summa theologica* (Verona, 1740), III, col. 1587, "... quia in majori veneratione est corpus ejus quam alicuius apostoli."
23. See Herlihy, *Pistoia*, p. 254.
24. *Liber focorum*, p. 187, Roncivallis de Campillio.

also appear among both citizens and peasants.[25] Thirteen citizens bear the name Roland or Orlando, and seven the more respectful Orlandino. Nine citizens are named Oliver, one Charles and two Pepin, and a peasant woman is called Pepina. The names of Alexander (appearing three times), Amadeus (also three times), Cazare (once) and perhaps even Saladino (two appearances) may also reflect this largely French chivalric culture. And could the name Campidore, borne by one of Pistoia's citizens in 1219, recall the title of Spain's great chivalric hero, El Campeador, the Cid? Perhaps too, Pistoia's leading name of Iacopo points to the saint's body in distant Spain as much as to his spirit in heaven. Iacopo, we should note, is also the leading name among the Florentine soldiers of 1260; Giovanni, the patron of Florence, ranks only a poor third, after Guido.[26]

Among Pistoia's early names, the conceits of courtly love are represented too. One peasant woman is named Diadamore, "goddess of love," and another Finamore, and two others Dolceamore, "sweet love." Two are named Cortese, "courteous." French and Spanish chivalric values and the sentiments of courtly love caught the fancy of Pistoia's burghers and even peasants in this early thirteenth century.

Aquinas further observes that names may be imposed "out of some quality of the person to whom it is given."[27] He surely means by this both physical and moral attributes. At Pistoia, many citizens' names in 1219, and peasants' names about 1244, allude to physical, moral or social characteristics, but it is not usually possible to know whether the names expressed a reality or a wish. A comparison of male and female names yields a kind of spectrum of qualities, considered appropriate for each sex. Only men, in reality or aspiration, are strong (Forte, 14) or strong-armed (Fortebraccio, 3; Bracciaforte, 3) or simply "arm" (Braccio, 7); guide the army (Guidaloste, 11) or guide others (Guidaglialtri, 1); massacre felons (Matafellone, 2); conquer castles (Vinciacastello, 1) or capture booty (Vinciproa, 6). Both men and women can be good or beautiful, but men more commonly the former, women the latter. Twelve citizens are called simply Bono, and only five are Bello. Bono is also often combined with other male names—Bonaccorso (47), Bongiovanni (9),Bonfilippo (1).

25. Once each in 1219. *Liber focorum*, pp. 47, Spagna, and 134, Spagnus.

26. The names and appearances are Iacopo (163), Guido (70), and Giovanni (61).

27. *Summa theologica*, III.37.2, in *Opera omnia*, 11 (Rome, 1903) p. 377: "Vel etiam ex aliqua qualitate eius cui nomen imponitur."

On the other hand, only women can be Piubella (5), "more beautiful," Bellassai (1), "pretty enough," Bellafina, Dolcebella, Bellina, or Bellamipare, "I think she's pretty." Four peasant women are called Belladonna and one Bellafemina. And femininity is surely emphasized in the names Tuttadonna, "all woman," and Sempredonna, "always a woman." Both men and women can be named for flowers; two citizens are called Fiore, and another, Belgiglio, "beautiful lily." But four peasant women are called Fiore and others Belfiore and Fiorita; among the women there are also five Roses, a Palm, and a Green Palm (Verde palma). Women also more than men bear the names of small, precious or at least lovely objects: Gemma (2), Diamante, Gioletta, Stella (4).

Names can allude to exalted social station: for men, Barone (3), Bonsignore (12), Bonvasallo (2), Principe (1), Rico (3), Ricomo (3), Signorante (1), Signorato (1), Signore (1), Signoretto (1), Signorile (1); Duchesa, Imperera, Cignorina, Ricadonna, Rigina, or Gentedonna for women. But humble stations are mentioned too: Villano (8), Bonvillano (1) among the men; Serva among the women.

Finally, Aquinas mentions that names may be imposed *a cognatione*, from the family: "as when there is imposed on a child the name of the father or of anyone of his lineage."[28] The *cognatio* included spiritual relationships; Salimbene, for example, received at baptism the name of Baliano, after his godfather. In Tuscany, on the other hand, it was very rare to bestow on a child the name of a living parent. Of the 3344 Florentines inducted into the silk merchants' guild between 1225 and 1432, only 53, about 1.5 percent, bear their father's name. And of the 53 fathers, 33 are explicitly described as deceased; it is likely that most fathers were in fact dead at the time their sons were christened with their names.

To bear the name of an ancestor was of course to commemorate him or her, a sentiment also reflected in these names: Ricordato (3) "remembered"; Ricordante (1), Ricordino; and, among peasant women, Ricordanza. But other names imply recovery even more than remembrance: Coppia (6), Ricoverato (2), Ricovero (3), Ristoro (1); or, among the Florentine soldiers, Reddito (3), "come back."

28. *Ibid.* "Vel a cognatione: sicut cum filio imponitur nomen patris vel alicuis de cognatione ejus."

They suggest that in some mysterious way a name might restore, remake or bring back the deceased.[29]

Even this hint at reincarnation rings strange within a Christian culture, but traces of these or similar sentiments appear in several contexts over the long centuries of Italian history. In the middle eleventh century, Peter Damian, in his Book of Gomorrah, condemns the zeal with which allegedly carnal persons "desire to leave the memory of their name behind them through succeeding generations of offspring."[30] "They desire this," he explains, "with the whole affection of their minds because they believe that they will never completely die to this world if they perpetuate the title of their names through the offshoot of their surviving offspring." Peter is not talking about family names, still very uncommon in the middle eleventh century, or about the desire to perpetuate a lineage. Rather, he speaks of personal names and their perpetuation in family lineages.

This expectation was of course in Peter's view misguided. Names were likely to survive only over a few generations. How much happier are the celibate and childless! Their names are permanently entered into the Book of Life. The celibate make up the 144,000 saints who follow the Lamb wherever he goes and sing a canticle no others can. But Peter's denunciations still establish a capital fact: his contemporaries, some of them at least, thought that to reuse a name was to save an ancestor from total annihilation. In some mysterious way, reused names undid death.

The same sentiment seems present at Florence in the late Middle Ages, when fathers in their memoirs explain why they apply the name of a dead child to a newborn baby. "He died and I remade him," a Florentine father inscribed in his tax declaration in 1469 or 1470.[31]

29. See the comments on "remaking" a name by C. Klapisch-Zuber, "The Name 'Remade': The Transmission of Given Name in Florence in the Fourteenth and Fifteenth Centuries," in the collection of essays by the same author, Women, Family and Ritual in Renaissance Italy, trans. L. G. Cochrane (Chicago and London, 1985), pp. 283-309. See also idem, "Constitution et variations temporelles des stocks de prenoms," in Le prénoms: Mode et histoire. Entretiens de Malher, 1980, ed. J. Dupâquier, A. Bideau, and M. Ducreux (Paris, 1984), pp. 37–47; "Compérage et clientélisme à Florence (1360-1520)," Ricerche Storiche, 15 (1985), pp. 51-76.

30. Liber Gomorrhianus. Book of Gomorrah. An Eleventh Century Treatise against Clerica Homosexual Practices, trans. P. J. Payer (Waterloo, Ontario, 1982), pp. 84–85.

31. Words of Bernardo Lanciani in 1469–1470, cited in C. Klapisch-Zuber, "The Name 'Remade'", p. 300 n. 40. But was the hope to remake (rifare) the name or, somehow, the person?

In 1685, a petty lord of Cilento in southern Italy, Giovan Battista del Mercato, explained in his memoirs the source of his own name: "My parents gave me the name of my grandfather, Giovan Nicola: for the custom of mortals is to give to descendants the names of ancestors. They believe that with the continuation and return of the name, there will also return their *fortuna*."[32]

But if Tuscans often reused the name of a dead child, they seem not to have reused it more than once. For the fortuna imbedded in the name could be good or bad, and the death of a second baby made the name seem a carrier of adverse fortune.

One further characteristic of these early names should be noted: they were highly unstable. People changed their names with seeming ease. Salimbene, as we have mentioned, at his christening in 1221 was named after his godfather Baliano. But he preferred to be called Dionysius. His family, on the other hand, called him Ognibene, "every good." Ognibene entered the Franciscan order in 1238. A year later, he met an aged friar, the last survivor of Francis' original disciples. The saintly old man expressed dismay when he heard Ognibene's name. "Son," he chided, "no one is good except God. From now on let your name be Fra Salimbene, as you climbed well in entering a good order."[33]

In the following century, the relatives and neighbors of Catherine of Siena called her as a child not Catherine but Euphrosyna, Greek for Letitia or Happiness. Her biographer, Raymond of Capua, cannot explain why. Catherine herself believed that she was called this because she was determined to imitate St. Euphrosyna. "But I think," says Raymond, "that this little child in her speech made certain sounds that resembled or sounded like the word Euphrosyna, and for this reason the others, repeating her little sounds, called her thus."[34] Raymond's explanation of Catherine's childhood name is not particularly edifying, but it is doubtlessly realistic. Names in this age were formed from many fonts, even from the babblings of infants.

32. Cited in G. Delille, *Famille et propriété dans le Royaume de Naples (XVe-XIXe siècle)*, Bibliothèque des Ecoles Françaises d'Athènes et de Rome, 259 (Rome-Paris, 1985), pp. 309–10.

33. *Cronica*, ed. F. Bernini, 2 vols, 1 (Bari, 1942), p. 53.

34. Vita Fr. Raimundo Capuano, *Acta Sanctorum, III Aprilis*, 869: "Ego autem puto, quod infans haec in suis locutionibus infantilibus utebatur quandoque quibusdam vocabulis, quae appropinquabant vel concordabant cum hoc vocabulo Euphrosyna, et idcirco quasi eius verbula repetentes, ipsam sic nominabant."

These then are the salient characteristics of thirteenth century Tuscan names: they were many in number, derived from many sources, and unstable. In contrast, by the fifteenth century, the number of visible names has diminished sharply, and the names themselves have changed in character. We could add parenthetically that diminishing numbers of personal names favored the spreading use of surnames or family names, to assure umambiguous identification.

To what did the fewer personal names of the fifteenth century point? Chivalric legends retain a faint echo. Among the 53,000 male household heads in the Catasto, Turpin joins his fellow heroes, Roland and Oliver; Lancelot is there, and perhaps Priam too should be reckoned a chivalric name. The contemporary revival of classical learning shows little influence. There is no Aeneas or Enea among the 53,000 household heads in 1427, but seven appear in the later list of citizens scrutinized for office, alongside twenty Caesars and three Juliuses. Nineteen candidates for office are named Hannibal, but only one Cato; no candidate is named Scipio, Tullio, or Vergil. The best example of classical influence is probably Girolamo or Jerome; the name first appears in the electoral lists in 1395 and achieves across the fifteenth century a count of 35. But Jerome was a saint as well as a humanist. The prestige of the ancient world affected Tuscan naming conventions only belatedly and slightly.

Contemporary literature makes no notable impression. If we look at women's names, there is not a single Laura among the 7000 Tuscan women household heads in 1427; patient Griselda, supposedly a model for Tuscan wives, is not there. The name of Boccaccio's lady, Fiammetta, appears once, in the unlikely town of Volterra. Even Beatrice, a traditional Tuscan name, is recorded only four times; the name had done better among the peasant women of Pistoia in 1244. The poets, in choosing names for their ladies, neither recognized nor bestowed popularity.

The real winners in this shift of Tuscan names are saints. In 1219 at Pistoia, of the twenty most popular names, only five recall a Christian saint: Iacopo, Giovanni, Benedetto, Bartolomeo and Matteo. In 1427 at the same town, fully eighteen of the twenty leading names do so; only Nanni and Meo—hypocoristics of Giovanni and Bartolomeo respectively—do not. Of the names in the *Libro di Montaperti* of 1260, again fewer than one in five bear the name of a Christian saint.[35] Thereafter saints dramatically enlarge their presence. Among men buried at Santa Maria Novella between 1290 and 1348, twelve of the twenty leading names are those of saints. Among the men buried there after 1348, that number increases to eighteen out of the leading twenty. For all of Florentine Tuscany in 1427, of the fifteen leading names that account for half the male population, thirteen point to a celestial sponsor.[36]

Women's names evolve in comparable fashion. In the burial lists after 1349, nine of the ten leading women's names refer to saints; in the Catasto of the city of Florence, seven out of ten do so. For all women in 1427, of the seventeen leading names that include one-half the population, fifteen refer to saints.[37] It is worth noting that of the seventeen, nine are feminized forms of male names: Antonia, Giovanna, Francesca, Piera, Bartolomea, Agnola, Mattea, Iacopa and Niccolosa. This doubtlessly reflects a shortage of recognized women saints, but it also shows that Tuscans were not very sensitive to sex in appointing celestial patrons.[38]

Compound names, still rare in the period of the Catasto, grow continuously more common through and beyond the fifteenth century, and they seem always to refer to saints. Either, like Michelangelo or Gianbattista, they specify the saint more explicitly, or like Pierfrancesco or Pierpaolo, they appoint two spiritual sponsors. Maria, as in Francescomaria, also becomes fairly common as an element in male compound names, even though the name as yet does not claim much popularity among women. Again, in choosing spiritual patrons, Tuscans seem rather indifferent to gender.

Tuscan names did not cease to evolve when our own list runs out in 1530. Classical names were doubtlessly destined to become more

35. The estimate comes from Brattö, *Nuovi studi,* p. 7; names with five or more appearances represent by his count 17.9 percent of all names.

36. The rank and appearances are as follows: Antonio (4767), Giovanni (3144), Piero (2711), Nanni (2352), Domenico (2081), Iacopo (1707), Francesco (1442), Bartolomeo (1374), Michele (1241), Andrea (1223), Matteo (1146), Cecco (1034), Niccolò (933), Meo (913), and Agnolo (883), adding up to 50.51 percent of the Catasto's male household heads.

37. They are Caterina (537), Antonia (396), Giovanna (366), Margherita (350), Francesca (226), Piera (226), Bartolomea (187), Agnola (179), Cecca (169), Nanna (146), Lucia (143), Mattea (126), Iacopa (122), Niccolosa (122), Mea (112), Maddalena (101) and Lisa (96), adding up to 51.06 percent of the women household heads.

38. On male and female names in the baptismal registrations, see C. Klapisch-Zuber, "Patroni celesti e rapporti di sesso dei battezzati fiorentini (secc. XIV-XV)," to appear in *La ragnatela dei rapporti: "Patronage" e reti di relazione nella storia delle donne.*

frequent, and the names of Jesus' relatives, Mary, Joseph and Ann, would gain enormous popularity in the late sixteenth and seventeenth centuries. These are the preferred saints of the Counter-Reform. But if the stock of Tuscan names was still evolving in 1530, the principle, in place from about 1300, held firm: names should not be whimsical and shifting and should refer to known figures, preferably to saints.

The biographies of many great Florentines faithfully reflect this evolution. The greatest Christian poet of the Middle Ages, Dante, born in 1260, does not bear a Christian name. Presumably it is an hypocoristic for Durante, but neither Dante nor Durante exudes an odor of sanctity and neither name ever gained much popularity. So also, Cino, as in Cino of Pistoia, or Brunetto, the name of Dante's teacher, are typical of their age—uncommon and religiously neutral. But names of the next generation of great Florentines are already very different. Francesco Petrarch, born in 1304, provides an example. His father's name, Petrarco or Petrarca is again secular, uncommon, and doomed to virtual extinction. Not one of the 53,000 male heads of family in the Catasto of 1427 bears it. The name "Francesco," on the other hand was only beginning in 1304 its tremendous surge in popularity. Among the Florentines scrutinized for office between 1450 and 1500, it is the most popular of all names, surpassing even the name of Florence's patron, Giovanni. Giovanni Boccaccio, who was born in 1313, offers a similar example. His father's and grandfather's names, Boccaccino and Chelo, are again uncommon and secular; his own, religious.[39]

The pattern is the same for women. The genealogy of Catherine of Siena reflects the shift. Her mother's name was Lapa, presumably a hypocoristic for Iacopa; it is the most popular woman's name among those buried at Santa Maria Novella before 1349. After that date, it drops to nineteenth, while Caterina itself rises to eighth position. In the Catasto of 1427, at Florence and all across Tuscany, Caterina reigns supreme as the most popular female name.

Wealth or residence had only trivial effects on name choices. Among the richest Florentine women—those heading households in the wealthiest quarter of the population—six of the ten leading names are those of saints; the number is seven among the poorer

39. T. G. Bergin, *Boccaccio* (New York, 1981), p. 29.

three-fourths of the female household heads.[40] This may suggest that the rich were slightly more conservative in name choices than the poor. In the mountains of Pistoia—one of the poorest and most remote areas of Tuscany—the saints account for seven of the ten leading male names in 1427.[41] There were not two cultures in Tuscany, at least in regard to names.

Superficially read, the evolution of name use in Tuscany suggests that the thirteenth century was much less religious than is usually assumed, and the Renaissance of the fifteenth less secular than supposed. In truth the evidence rather indicates that we do not understand very well the piety, the culture, or the spirit of either epoch.

Why did Tuscan names change so dramatically in number and nature between the thirteenth and fifteenth centuries? It may not have been entirely the result of changing personal preferences. Both the communal governments and the Church objected to the use of numerous, unstable names. Both institutions wanted to track people better, in order to enforce rules or collect taxes. As early as 1288, the commune of Bologna imposed a penalty on anyone who changed his name, and required that, when asked, the citizen "must state his name and *cognomen* by which he is publicly named."[42] Even the statutes of a little village of Frignano in the Apennines between Pistoia and Modena, dated 1334-1338, insist that in all criminal indictments the name, *pronomen* and residence of the accused must be accurately recorded.[43] The modernizing bureaucracies of Tuscany were insisting on the modern practice of fixed and stable names. In the fifteenth century, in his discussion of baptism, Antoninus, Archbishop of Florence, says this: "And care must be taken that there is imposed a name of some male or female saint, not the names of pagans, such Pyramides or Palamides, Lancelot

40. For the rich the names and appearances are Caterina (17), Nanna (11), Bartolomea (9), Lisa (9), Lena (8), Niccolosa (7), Gostanza (6), Margherita (6), Piera (5), Sandra (5); for the lower three quartiles they are: Caterina (131), Antonia (73), Margherita (57), Piera (48), Giovanna (38), Nanna (38), Bartolomea (37), Cecca (36), Lisa (36), and Francesca (33).

41. They are Antonio (32), Giovanni (32), Iacopo (74), Nanni (24), Domenico (22), Piero (20), Bartolomeo (15), Menico (15), Cecco (14), and Michele (11).

42. *Statuti di Bologna dell'anno 1288,* ed. G. Fasoli and P. Sella, Studi e Testi, 85 (Vatican City, 1939), 1, p. 214: "De pena eius qui mutaverit sibi nomen ... Et si interrogatus fuerit dicere debeat suum nomen et cognomen quo publice denominatur."

43. *Statuti dell Apennino Tosco-Modenese, Secoli XIII-XIV,* ed. Q. Santoli, A. Sorbelli and F. Jacoli (Rome, 1913), p. 226. I owe this reference to Dr. Jane Fair Bestor.

and of that sort, or shortened names, such as Nanni, Meo, Thoma, Maso, Pippo, or meaningless names, like Blando, Lapo, Ginevra, and of that kind."[44] But clearly, Antoninus is attempting to standard-ize a common practice, which had become implanted in Tuscany perhaps two centuries before. His admonition did not so much direct as reflect a much older change.

A profound reorganization of family structures also influenced names. Tuscans were showing from the thirteenth century a new consciousness of ancestry, perhaps best reflected in family memoirs. A growing tendency to name children after ancestors should have reduced the stock of names, as it would have excluded the entirely whimsical and the new. Clearly too, at least by the fifteenth century, the name of a saint often pointed to an ancestor as well as to a heavenly sponsor. This double service meant in turn that certain saints developed a traditional association with certain lineages.

But if genealogical consciousness worked to reduce and stabilize the stock of names, it clearly cannot explain the growing preference, from about 1300, to adopt or impose the names of saints. In fact, the reuse of ancestral names should, at least initially, have obstructed any change at all.

Why did Tuscans across the late Middle Ages change the culture of their names? The easiest explanation is this: they were seeking spiritual favor and protection. Saints undoubtedly liked to have their names adopted by their clients and sometimes insisted on it, in return for favors. About 1246, a barren couple pray at Monte Gargano to Michael the Archangel. They ask the favor of a child. Michael appears to them, grants their request, but commands that the baby be called Angelo.[45]

Several saints of the late Middle Ages gained reputations as won-derworkers or as guardians, and thereby, apparently, won popular-ity for their names. Perhaps the best example of the wonderworker is Anthony. The name may refer to the ancient father of hermits. Even a disease, St. Anthony's fire, was named for him. But the name

---

44. *Summa theologica* (Verona, 1740), 11, col. 645: "Ad hoc tamen debet attendi, ut imponitur nomen alicujus sancti vel sanctae non nomina paganorum, ut Pyra-mides, vel Palamides, Lancelottus et hujusmodi, vel nomina diminuta, ut Nanni, Meo, Thoma, Maso, Pippo, vel nomina nil significantia, ut Blando, Lapo, Ginevra et hujusmodi."
45. *ASS*, I *Februarii*, 937, *Life of Angelus a Furcio*.

appears only two times at Pistoia in 1219 and not at all among the Florentine soldiers of 1260. Anthony is not a popular saint in the thirteenth century, but thereafter his climb is spectacular. The name's soaring popularity surely reflects mendicant influence, and probably points not only to the hermit but also to a follower of Francis who died in 1231, Anthony of Lisbon or of Padua. He preached to fishes and played with the child Jesus. He shares in Francis' human appeal and in his popularity. Perhaps because of his association with the great medical center of Padua, he acquired prominence as a healing saint. As another Franciscan, Bernardine of Siena, would say of him: "God gives to certain saints particular powers of patronage in particular causes, as to St. Anthony of Padua, by whose patronage every day graces and miracles are obtained."[46] Probably, the combined references to the Egyptian hermit and to a recent miracle worker explain the name's appeal. At Florence, the name appears among the matriculants into the silk guild in 1332 and becomes common after 1374. In 1427, it is the most popular name in all of Florentine Tuscany.

Some saints were known to be curers, surely an attractive quality in this age of ferocious epidemics. Cosmas or Cosimo is a physician; his name is totally unknown in the thirteenth century lists. At Florence, the name first appears in the electoral scrutinies in 1416. And its close associations with the Medici family surely enhanced its popularity. Cosimo's brother Damiano is also a physician but apparently never a Medici. At Florence, its frequency of appearance is about a fourth that of Cosimo.

The protector saints of Tuscan cities also protected individuals, and this helps explain the popularity of Giovanni at Florence or Iacopo at Pistoia, the leading names in both these respective cities in 1427. At Pisa, the recent and local saint Ranieri holds a respectable tenth position in 1427, though, with 38 appearances, far below the two leaders, Antonio and Giovanni, both with 118 clients.

A newer type of spiritual protector, much cultivated in the late Middle Ages, is the angel. St. Michael is the only angel with an official cult in the early medieval period; his shrines at Mont-Saint-Michel in Normandy and Monte Gargano in Italy were famed

---

46. *Opera omnia* , 6 (Florence, 1959), p. 82. "Nam quibusdam sanctis divinitus datus est in aliquibus causis praecipue patrocinari, sicut sancto Antonio de Padua ordinis Minorum quotidie eius patrociniis gratias et miracula impetrare."

throughout Europe. He registers an impressive nineteen appear-ances at Pistoia in 1219, earning him twenty-first position, and he is also present among the Florentine matriculants of 1225. But this early Michael is much more the aggressive warrior than the watchful guardian. His name actually declines in popularity in the Florentine electoral lists across the fifteenth century. Angels also rep-resented purity and innocence, with special concern for protecting the pure and innocent. Raphael is the model of the guardian angel. His name first appears in the Florentine electoral surveys in 1387, and in the last half of the fifteenth century he holds fifteenth position among the leading names; by then, the name has actually surpassed Michael in popularity, though Michael is also losing to a new, more explicit compound: Michelangelo.

In this age when the grasp on life was everywhere precarious, churchmen such as Jean Gerson, chancellor of the University of Paris, or Antoninus himself, actively promoted devotion to angel guardians, the individual angels appointed to watch over every human being. Even pagans, says Antoninus, have angel guardians.[47] The guardian angel had a particular importance in the protection of children, particularly threatened by the ravishing epidemics. St. Francesca of Rome—we should note her name—who died in 1434 and is today regarded as patroness of the city, had a particular rap-port with angels. According to witnesses testifying at her beatifica-tion, she enjoyed the company of two angelic companions in succession, not common angels but dispatched from the most pres-tigious choirs. They appeared, when they could be seen, as beauti-ful boys about nine years old. Each shed so much light that Francesca could read at night in her cell, without need of a lamp. The second of her angelic companions was so temperamental that he slapped her when she did not reveal her spiritual secrets to her confessor.[48] His mission was apparently one of correction as well as protection. And yet a quest for heavenly favor and protection in times of adversity is not a complete or adequate explanation for the popularity of the saints. The change becomes visible roughly about

47. J. Gerson, *Oeuvres complètes*, ed. Msgr. Glorieux, 5 (Paris, 1963), pp. 320–24, on the services rendered by angels; Antoninus, *Summa theologica*, 4, p. 1158, "De Angelis."

48. *I processi inediti per Francesca Bussa Ponziani (Santa Francesca Romana)*, ed. P. T. Lugeno, O.S.B., Studi e Testi, 120 (Vatican City, 1945), p. 98.

1300 fifty years before the first of the great epidemics. If Tuscans wanted powerful spiritual protectors, why were they so late in cultivating such exalted personages as Mary, Ann or Joseph? Maria appears only once among the 244 women buried before 1349 at Santa Maria Novella, and even after the plague, she holds with seven appearances only a dismal twenty-second position. In the entirety of Tuscany in 1427, she ranks nineteenth with 83 appearances, and is displayed by only 12 percent of the Tuscan women. Even the totally secular name, Fiore, surpasses her with 94 appearances. Among the 7000 Tuscan women, Anna appears only five times, borne by only 0.07 percent of women. Joseph appears only once among the 53,000 male household heads. This was not a gesture of deference before august powers; if it were, the names would have had no representation at all. The neglect of these saints in bestowing names indicates that the choice of a saint's name was not primarily in return for past or future favors. What did this association between saint and namesake really mean?

It is helpful here to consider the relationship between one prominent Tuscan saint, Catherine of Siena, and her namesake, the martyr Catherine of Alexandria. The Tuscan Catherine shows no particular devotion toward, and receives no special help from, the ancient martyr. The Egyptian Catherine is not even invited to the mystical wedding of Catherine with Christ. There come to the wedding the Virgin Mary, John the Evangelist, Paul, Dominic and, from out of the Old Testament, David with his harp, to provide the music.[49] The relationship between the two Catherines is not especially close, and clearly not that of patron and client. Raymond of Capua has an explanation for the relationship: the first Catherine, after her baptism, was betrothed to Christ. "Do you not conclude," Raymond asks the reader, "that now you have a second, most happy Catherine, who after so many victories over the flesh and the devil was solemnly betrothed by the same Lord?" In her marriage with the Savior, the little Tuscan girl is a second Catherine; she replicates the fortune of the first. If, in secular thought, an ancestor could be remade, why not a saint?

A desire not to cultivate the most powerful patrons, but to replicate experiences, to recapture a *fortuna*, best explains the new, most

49. *ASS, III Aprilis*, p. 891.

popular Tuscan names. Thus, Francis of Assisi had no particular reputation as a wonderworker. But here was a humble man raised in a
troubled society; he knew the tensions of life, and yet had found his
way to peace, joy and salvation. A salient characteristic of many
popular saints of the late Middle Ages was victory over suffering.
The two saints directly associated with the plague are Sebastiano, or
in its Florentine form, Bastiano, and Roq or Rocco, the modern
Rocky. Bastiano first appears in the electoral scrutinies in 1383;
Rocco is known in the thirteenth century, then seemingly disap-
pears, to come back as a consoling saint in the sixteenth century.[50]
So Sebastian, a Roman soldier, cleaves to his Christian faith. The
emperor Diocletian first orders him shot with arrows, but the arrows
do not kill him. Rather, a pious widow nurses him back to health.
He again defies the emperor and is now successfully executed,
beaten to death by clubs. Arrows are ancient symbols of infectious
disease, but they do not harm Sebastian. Numerous paintings from
all over Europe show him bound to a column in relative ease, while
the ineffectual arrows dangle from his torso. He is immune to their
menace, and so may be those who take his name.

In his own confused legend, St. Roq, born at Montpellier in
southern France, sets forth on a pilgrimage to Rome, aiding plague
victims along the way. He contracts the plague himself at Piacenza,
and is expelled from the town. He suffers physical pain and social
exclusion for reason of plague but does not fall victim to it. He
understands the plight of those sickened by it. And those who bear
his name may also share his triumph.

Of course, the death of every martyr was a triumph over pain,
and this may explain the great popularity of other ancient martyrs
such as Bartholomew or Lawrence. Plague was also a disease man-
ifested on the skin through buboes and blotches, and those martyrs
tortured on their skins may have had a particular relation to it. The
apostle St. Bartholomew preached in India and was there flayed
alive. In the thirteenth-century Florentine lists, the most common
form of the name is the hypocoristic Bartolo. Bartolo gives way to
Bartolomeo over the course of the late Middle Ages, surely because
it created a more intimate association with the martyred apostle.
Lawrence was the deacon of the Roman church. Since he kept the

50. On Rocco see Brattö, *Nuovi studi*, p. 189.

church's treasury, he may have had special appeal at Florence, a city of money changers. At least he was in 1427 more popular there than in other Tuscan cities. Lawrence was roasted alive under Emperor Valerian. The name first appears in the Florentine lists in 1320, and holds ninth place among male household heads in 1427, sixteenth in the whole of Florentine Tuscany.

The great change in the culture of personal names, evident in all sectors of Tuscan society from about 1300, has analogues all over Europe. Surely this shift is linked to other developments in cultural history. It is, however, not easy to recognize what they were, still less to explain them. Clearly, however, preachers or teachers, the mendicants primarily, were successfully collecting and publicizing the legends of the saints. They were also instilling veneration for them, among rich and poor, urban and rural, men and women.

The shift in names also hints at a profound reorientation in religious psychology. In spite of their religiously indifferent names, the Tuscans of the early thirteenth century could hardly have been religiously indifferent. But their multitudinous and shifting names did not point steadily and did not carry clear and compelling cultural messages. The later, fewer, borrowed, stable names had, in contrast, deeper cultural resonance. Often simultaneously, names now pointed to a near ancestor; pointed deep into the historical or legendary past; and augured a destiny. The name was now a lecture, given to the young.

Raymond of Capua expounds at length on the mystic, historic and prophetic meanings of the name, Catherine.[51] The name resounded. And deeper resonances of meaning surely explains why at Florence in the fourteenth century, Giovanni surpasses the older favorite Iacopo as the most popular male name, why the feminine form, Giovanna, comes out of nowhere to become the third most popular woman's name in all of Tuscany in 1427, surpassed only by Caterina and Antonia. Iacopo was a wonderworker, whose body lay in Spain, but he remained a somewhat shadowy figure. John the Evangelist, on the other hand, was the disciple whom, according to the New Testament, "Jesus loved" (John 13:23); of John the Baptist, Christ himself reportedly declared, "among those born of women there is not a greater than John" (Mark 11:11). The names Giovanni

51. *ASS, III Aprilis,* p. 864.

and Giovanna pointed to both. To be loved like the Evangelist; to be exalted like the Baptist: what more could one wish for one's child?

Perhaps paradoxically, the repeated name, the name remade, the stable name emphasized individuality by giving the person not only firm identity in the present but ties with the past and prospects for the future. It bestowed on Tuscan men and women a unique set of relationships. The change in names at about 1300 marks the arrival of a finer religious and cultural sensibility and of a deeper sense of place in time and in society.

To decode the names of old populations is not an easy task. We must count them, sort them, and puzzle over their mysterious meanings. The work is laborious, and its conclusions are always touched by uncertainties. But the study of personal names still promises a way of conversing with the largely inarticulate members of this distant society, whose values and beliefs, fears and aspirations, we cannot otherwise share.

18

THE RULERS OF FLORENCE, 1282–1530

✦ ✦ ✦

Like the Roman Republic in antiquity, the republic of Florence in the late Middle Ages called to its offices significant numbers of its citizens. In this chapter, I attempt to survey Florence's governing class from the commune of the *popolo* in the thirteenth century to the establishment of the grand duchy of Tuscany in 1530. As I hope to illustrate, the numbers of citizens considered for office increased continuously, even spectacularly, from the early fourteenth to the late fifteenth centuries. This observation is by no means new. Many historians have noted that the size of the officeholding class grew in Florence from the latter half of the fourteenth century.[1] This growth

---

1. See, for example, G. A. Brucker, *Florentine Politics and Society, 1343–1378* (Princeton, 1962) who, after reviewing the legislation of the 1340s that aimed to limit the numbers entering office, notes (p. 123) that "in 1350 the trend actually shifted in the opposite direction, toward a more popular regime." G. A. Brucker, *The Civic World of Early Renaissance Florence* (Princeton, 1977), p. 73, sees a reinforcement of aristocratic rule after 1393, but even this is questioned by G. Guidi, *Il governo della città-repubblica di Firenze del primo quattrocento*, I: *Politica e diritto Pubblico*, II: *Gli istituti "di dentro" che componevano il governo di Firenze nel 1415*; III: *Il contado e distretto*, Biblioteca Storica Toscana, 20 (Florence, 1981), 1, p. 240. D. V. Kent, "The Florentine *Reggimento* in the Fifteenth Century," *Renaissance Quarterly*, 28 (1975), pp. 575–638, notes a continuing expansion through the end of her study, up until 1449. R. P. Cooper, "The Florentine Ruling Group under the *Governo Popolare*," *Studies in Medieval and Renaissance History*, 7 (1984-85), pp. 71–181, accepts these conclusions but argues that only the expulsion of Piero de' Medici in 1494 led to a partial closure of the officeholding class; however, even by her figures the size of the class remained large. For further discussion of the changing complexion of Florentine governments (a subject of seemingly limitless fascination for historians), see, besides Brucker, *Florentine Politics* and *The Civic World*, and Guidi, *Il governo*; A. Molho, "The Florentine Oligarchy and the *Balìe* of the Late Trecento," *Speculum*, 43 (1968), pp. 23-51; and A. Molho, "Politics and the Ruling Class in Early Renaissance Florence," *Nuova Rivista Storica*

has proved puzzling, particularly because the city's population was simultaneously in drastic decline. How could the number of citizens considered for high office constantly increase in a shrinking or stagnant city, under regimes commonly regarded as oligarchic?

By measure of the sources illuminating its citizenry, Florence for this period may well be the best-served city in Europe. It claims several large surveys of its inhabitants, dating from 1352 and including the famous Catasto of 1427–1430.[2] The Florentine state archives further possess numerous registers of guild matriculations and of elections to guild offices and huge deposits of fiscal records and collections of notarial chartularies. Especially valuable for the prosopographical study of the city's rulers is the deposit known as the Tratte (drawings). From November 1328, Florence chose nearly all of its governing officials—its policy makers, its "inside" administrators serving within the city, and its "outside" administrators resident in the subject territories—by lottery or sortition.[3] Our interest is confined here to the policy makers and specifically to those who filled the three highest offices of the Florentine government, called traditionally the *Tre maggiori*.[4] The most prestigious and powerful office was that of prior; the priors numbered three, six, twelve, or most commonly eight, and they bore the title *domini* or *signori* (the priorate itself was the signoria). The priors were assisted by a notary and presided over by the standard-bearer of justice, the titular head of

52, (1968), pp. 401–20; R. G. Witt, "Florentine Politics and the Ruling Class, 1382–1407," *Journal of Medieval and Renaissance Studies* 6, (1976), pp. 243–67; and, more recently, J. Najemy, *Corporatism and Consensus in Florentine Electoral Politics* (Chapel Hill, N.C., 1982), though the last work is more concerned with the general character of Florentine government than its personnel. F. Gilbert, *Machiavelli and Guicciardini, Politics and History in Sixteenth-Century Florence* (Princeton, 1965), depicts the changes at the end of the republican regime and offers a masterful analysis of their effects upon Machiavelli and Guicciardini. S. Bertelli, *Il potere oligarchico nello stato-città medievale* (Florence, 1978), provides a useful overview.

2. The so-called Libro della Sega, ASF. Estimo., reg. 306, names the head and assigns a tax estimate for 9,899 households of the city. Our own study of the Catasto, first published in French in 1978 and in English in 1985, has recently appeared in Italian translation: D. Herlihy and C. Klapisch-Zuber, *I toscani e le loro famiglie. Uno studio sul catasto fiorentino del 1427*, trans. M. Bensi (Bologna, 1988).

3. G. Guidi, "I sistemi elettorali agli uffici del comune di Firenze nel primo Trecento: il sorgere delle elezioni per squittino," *Archivio Storico Italiano*, 130 (1972), pp. 345–407, surveys the government's provisions (*provvisioni*) regarding elections. The chief chronicle source for the reform is G. Villani, *Cronica*, ed. Magheri (Florence, 1823–25), X, ch. 108.

4 The many complex regulations governing these offices are reviewed in G. Guidi, *Il governo*, II, pp. 129–344.

the Florentine state. The priors, the standard-bearer, and their notary all served for two months. Two colleges, made up of "twelve good men" (*dodici buonuomini*) and of sixteen "standard-bearers of the companies" (*sedici gonfalonieri delle compagnie*) respectively, advised the priorate and approved its decisions. The dodici held office for four months and the sedici for three. When set and stable from 1343 the system called each year a minimum of 150 citizens (156 if the notary is included) to high office.

I can summarize only briefly the complex and evolving methods by which the Florentines by lottery chose their governors. Special commissions first carried out a scrutiny (*squittino*) of the adult male citizens. The commissions were composed of incumbent officials, representatives of the guilds, and specially appointed adjuncts (*arroti*), and they sometimes numbered more than two hundred persons. The commissions voted on the qualifications of each citizen; to be successful, the scrutinized citizen usually needed a two-thirds majority of the votes cast. He could not be a magnate and had to be enrolled in a guild, even when he was *scioperato*, that is, he did not practice the particular art. From some year, perhaps 1406, the eligible citizen also had to own shares in the Florentine public debt, that is, he had to be a creditor of the government. The government frequently collected sums of money from its citizens, but it regarded payments above a certain amount as loans (even if forced), entitling the citizen to shares in one of the several funded debts. Poorer citizens who paid less than the threshold amount gave their money ad *perdendum*, "to be lost." The government sometimes allowed even those wealthier citizens who could not meet their full assessment to contribute a reduced sum *ad perdendum*.[5]

5. The contemporary chronicler Iacopo Salviati mentions "una legge, che era fatta, che chi non havea pagato le sue prestanze, non potesse essere imborsato, per la qual legge moltissimi huomini buoni e guelfi venivano ad essere esclusi." The law was then revised the same year to give the delinquents further time to pay, "per forma che quasi ogniuno pagò." (The passages are cited in *ibid.*, I, p. 254.) I take this to mean that the citizens who could pay only the small sums *ad perdendum* were not represented in the purses. *Ibid.*, I, p. 106, notes that in 1404 those citizens whose fathers or grandfathers had not paid the *prestanze* ("notare solo le prestanze," he adds) should not be admitted to office. The law of 1406 surely represented a change in policy (why otherwise would so many citizens have been taken by surprise?). Payment of *gravezze* (taxes in general) alone was not enough to qualify for office; candidates must also have given money to the Monte (*prestanze*). The law of 1406 seems to be the first excluding the noncreditors even from the purses.

Scrutinies of this sort were first held at short intervals, but after 1382 rather regularly every five years. The selected names were written on slips of paper (*polizze, cedole*) and entered into purses, one for each office and for each electoral district (the urban quarters for the priors and the *dodici;* the sixteen *gonfaloni* or wards for the *sedici*). Members of the seven greater and fourteen lesser guilds also had their names entered into separate purses. In May 1387, four special officials known as *accoppiatori*, in collaboration with the standard-bearer of justice, chose from those citizens who had passed the scrutiny for the priorate the names of the ones they regarded as especially qualified for office. These names they entered into "little purses," (*borsellini*). Tow (later three) of the priors were chosen from the "little purses," the remaining six (or five) from the "general purse."[6]

At the intervals set by the city statutes, in the presence of the sitting government, the podesta (in this period always a foreigner called in to serve as an impartial judge) read names drawn from the appropriate purses, beginning with the oldest and continuing until the offices were filled. The signoria and the colleges then determined whether or not the candidate was subject to a *divieto*, or disqualification, from the office. The exclusions might be either temporary or permanent; in the first case, the slip was returned to the purse (*rimesso*); in the second, it was destroyed (*stracciato*). Reasons for temporary exclusion included insufficient age (those selected had to have completed thirty years) or recent service in the same office (within two years for the priorate, six months for the two colleges, according to the regulations of 1328). Also, close relationship with a recent incumbent was reason for temporary exclusion; a father, brother, or son could not have served within one year as prior or within six months as a member of the two colleges.

The slip could be destroyed for several reasons. The candidate might be dead, an enemy of the Guelf regime (a Ghibelline), a cleric, a magnate, exiled, imprisoned, bankrupt, or in tax arrears (*in speculo*, "in the mirror," in the language of the registers). During the plague year of 1374, the signoria ruled that even those citizens who had fled the city should have their slips destroyed if their names

6. See *ibid.,* I, pp. 220–23, for this reform.

were drawn from the purses in their absence.[7] All the citizens whose names were publicly considered before the signoria and the colleges were regarded as *veduti*, "seen," and those awarded the office were *seduti*, "seated." The public pronouncement of the name showed that the citizen had been judged worthy in the original scrutinies, was represented in the purses, and (unless his slip was destroyed) was likely to be called to office at some future date. To be seen even if not seated was an honor. As Giovanni Rucellai about 1457 explained to his two sons, "[It pleases] me that you are in the purses and honored as the other citizens, if only for the reason that it shows that you are not under suspicion by the government but are accepted and in the good grace of the citizens."[8] For my purposes, these *veduti* define the circle of active Florentine citizens.

The complicated manipulations of the electoral system form an integral part of the Florentine political history from the system's origin in 1328 to the end of the republic in 1530. The manipulations affected at various times the preliminary scrutinies of the citizenry, the composition of the purses, and the drawings themselves. Several scholars have followed this history in close detail. For the fifteenth century, in a classic study, Nicolai Rubinstein has meticulously reconstructed how the Medici through fine-tuned management over the years between 1434 and 1494 sought to assure themselves of friendly governments.[9] But as his book also shows, at least until the year of the Pazzi conspiracy against Medici hegemony in 1478, the Medici did not do real violence to the electoral system. Management more than muscle marked the Medici manner. The years between 1328, when election by sortition was first adopted, and 1478, the date of the Pazzi conspiracy, may well be regarded as the golden age of Florentine republicanism.

For some years now, I have been editing selected Tratte registers and other related deposits into machine-readable form. To my knowledge, the original *giornali*, or registers, recording the scrutinies for the three greater offices begin in June 1376.[10] I have partly

7. M. Stefani, *Cronaca*, ed. N. Rodolico, *Rerum Italicarum Scriptores*, 30 (Città di Castello, 1903), p. 290.

8. G. Rucellai, *Giovanni Rucellai ed il suo Zibaldone, I: Il Zibaldone quaresimale*, ed. A. Perosa (London, 1960), p. 39: "Non dico che non mi piaccia che voi siate nelle borse e onorati come gli altri cittadini, se non fosse per altro che per mostrare non esser a sospetto al reggimento, ma esser accetti e in gratia de' cittadini."

9. N. Rubinstein, *The Government of Florence under the Medici (1434 to 1494)* (Oxford, 1966).

10. ASF, Tratte, 193, with entries dated from 1376 to 1381.

edited these registers for computer processing (to lighten the labor, I did not enter names excluded without a stated reason). The machine-readable edition has been carried forward until 1530, but gaps remain in the 1460s and 1480s. The parallel series of elections to the guild consulates until 1530 has been finished in its entirety.[11] In August 1429, the government also required that candidates for office (or their fathers) present for official registration proof of age, usually in the form of entries in the father's book of *ricordi*, or memoirs. These "confirmations of age" (*approbationes etatum*) have also been rendered machine-readable, giving us the birth dates of Florentine citizens of the officeholding class from 1429 to 1530. Finally, I have the registrations of emancipations, based on transcriptions of the original registers supplied by Thomas Kuehn.

The total number of assorted observations on Florentine citizens so far collected amounts to well over 150,000 names. As should be apparent, the difficulty in studying the Florentine ruling elite is not the collection of information, but its efficient analysis. Even with the help of computers—and this project would be inconceivable without them—the task of linking all these many observations into a coherent and readily usable data bank is formidable. Here, I only attempt to skim the surface of this sea of data. I will make particular use of still another archival series, which is internally coherent and thus more easily analyzed than observations drawn from many different sources.

Although they are late compilations, apparently redacted in the seventeenth century, registers eight through eleven in the Tratte series yield information very useful for our purposes. That information is of two kinds.[12] The registers first give lists of priors and members of the colleges for the period 1349 to 1374 for each of the city's four quarters. The names are entered in a clear and elegant script and were probably meant to serve as a formal record of officeholders. These registers of *seduti* (those awarded office) are followed in the same volumes by much longer lists of *veduti*, the citizens whose names were drawn from the purses and considered for office.

The redactors of the registers collected their names from the original *giornali*, or day books, of the Office of the Scrutiny (Tratte). They were evidently seeking to determine who were members of the office-

11. These registers form part of the *Mercanzia* deposit in the *ASF*.
12. ASF, Tratte, reg. 8 (quarter of Santa Croce), 9 (Santo Spirito), 10 (Santa Maria Novella) and 11 (San Giovanni).

holding class at various times. To do this, the compilers divided the time between 1349 and 1478 into twenty-four periods, from one to more than ten years in duration, as shown in Table 1. Under each of these periods, they entered the names of those "seen" for high office in a rough alphabetical order. For each of the twenty-four periods, the compilers recorded only the first appearance of an individual citizen and not the total number of times he might have been viewed for offices. The dates appended to the names accordingly cluster strongly under the early years in each of the twenty-four periods.

Some years are altogether missing from the series. For example, the years from 1375 to 1381 are skipped for three of the four quarters; only the lists from San Giovanni include those years. These were troubled times for Florence, during which the city fought a disastrous war against the papacy (1375–1378) and then endured an uprising of wool workers (called the Ciompi) and a short-lived popular regime (1378–1382). It is hard to know whether the redactors of the lists of the three missing quarters did not have the original registers before them or simply had no interest in these years of political turmoil.

The compilers of the lists of *veduti* often added comments to the names. They occasionally allude to missing folios in the *giornali*. In seeking to avoid repetitions of the same name, they sometimes added, when two names in the same period looked alike, "non è il medesimo" (it is not the same). They place an *F* perhaps for "fatto" (made), in front of some names, presumably of those awarded an office. The redactors also mark a cross in front of other names, presumably indicating that they were then deceased.[13] Often, they place after the name the comment, "morto" (deceased), together with a date when the death was noted in the original registers. They also single out citizens who were subsequently viewed for the government's highest office, the standardbearer of justice. The redactors of these registers make a concerted effort to identify the persons named more precisely than in the original *giornali*. They quite frequently add a family name, the name of an occupation, or of an ancestor, and even cite the basis for the emendation. The emendations are valuable, as the redactors of the list were clearly devoting close study to the citizens' names and recognized those that were incomplete or in error.

13. But the deaths of some citizens marked with a cross seem to have occurred only later.

Table 1

Florentine Citizens Viewed for Office
Quarters of Santa Croce and Santo Spirito, 1349–1478

Period of citizens		Number name	With family families	Number of families & members	New index (1)	Cluster index (2)	Cluster
Aug.	1349	148	95	74	74	36.49	32.42
Sep.	1351			95			
Mar.	1352	129	97	73	25	34.25	37.98
Dec.	1354						
Feb.	1355	155	109	85	14	34.47	35.48
Dec.	1356						
Feb.	1357	151	94	74	11	37.84	31.79
Apr.	1358						
Jun.	1358	130	88	64	8	32.81	34.62
Jun.	1359						
Feb.	1362	188	131	85	15	30.59	35.11
Jun.	1363						
Jun.	1363	176	122	88	13	31.82	35.23
Dec.	1364						
Apr.	1365	125	86	63	12	33.33	35.20
Feb.	1366						
Feb	1366	204	145	95	10	28.42	35.78
Feb	1367						
Apr.	1367	189	148	100	9	28.00	39.68
Dec.	1368						
Feb.	1369	138	102	69	3	27.54	37.68
Apr.	1370						
Jun.	1370	140	101	72	9	30.56	36.43
Mar.	1371						
Apr.	1373	177	124	82	7	28.05	35.59
Mar.	1374						
Apr.	1381	646	361	168	79	22.02	28.17
Sep.	1392						
Dec.	1392	651	422	166	31	18.67	32.57
Sep.	1401						
Feb.	1402	544	381	147	26	19.73	35.29
Dec.	1409						
Feb.	1410	803	596	162	24	20.99	37.36
Dec.	1417						
Dec.	1417	1097	807	198	33	18.69	37.19
Mar.	1428						
Mar.	1428	1557	1248	214	43	17.78	40.27
Mar.	1435						
Apr.	1435	1313	1132	237	62	14.78	43.18
Mar.	1444						
Apr.	1444	1530	1312	220	33	15.00	43.53
Mar.	1454						
Mar.	1454	1655	1520	244	36	14.34	46.52
Mar.	1464						
Apr.	1464	915	729	146	29	15.09	45.77
Aug.	1470*						
Feb.	1474	975	904	234	32	17.52	46.6
Aug.	1478						

*Santa Croce only

Source: ASF, Tratte, regg. 8 and 9.

The registers, in sum, show rather well the number of individual citizens who formed the officeholding class of late-medieval Florence. True, the count of citizens viewed for office is defective for the last years in every period, because the compilers were not interested in repeated names. On the other hand, the counts for early years in each period yield a fairly complete picture of the numbers actually considered in filling the offices. In spite of faults, it is reasonable to assume that the copyists accomplished what they sought: the drawing up of reasonably comprehensive lists of citizens viewed for high office for each of the twenty-four periods between 1349 and 1478.

These compilations, though not contemporary, have a special value for two reasons. They include some years (1349-1374) for which no original registers for the three great offices have apparently survived. And their emendations of the names facilitate what is always the most difficult task in research of this kind: the linking of records, the tracking of the same persons over vast documentary runs.

The work of converting these lists of *veduti* into machine-readable form has been completed for two quarters of the city, those of Santa Croce and Santo Spirito, and the work moves forward on the remaining two. Even the two quarters provide abundant data concerning our principal interest: how the Florentine political class changed from the middle fourteenth to the late fifteenth century.

The analysis of Florentine electoral lists is both aided and obstructed by the period's naming conventions. The greatest help is the Florentine practice of supplying for citizens both a patronymic and a family name; sometimes, particularly in the late-fifteenth century, the names of grandfather, greatgrandfather, and even more distant ancestors are given. Ambiguities, however, remain. Names are still unstable, particularly in the early decades; the same person may be Gianni or Giovanni, Giacomo or Iacopo, Geri or Ruggieri, Goro or Gregorio. The same occupations, even when given in Latin, have different forms: *beccarius* (butcher) or *tabernarius*; *campsor* (money changer) or *tavolerius*. As many of the lists are in Latin, it is impossible to determine whether a Nicolaius is a Niccolò, Nicola, or Niccolaio in the vernacular (I treat them all as Niccolò). Standardization of name spellings is nearly indispensable if the computer is to link observations efficiently. Very often, the grandchild bears the same name as his paternal grandfather, even the same patronymic. It is easy to mistake grandson for grandfather and to attribute to one citizen the life span of two. On the whole, however, Tuscan personal names, which usually carry short genealogies, are more easily linked than medieval names anywhere else in Europe.

From the origin of the priorate in 1282, until at least the 1340s, high offices in Florence were dominated by a narrow even if shifting oligarchy.[14] It is hard, of course, to arrive at firm conclusions regarding the first ten years of the priorate, between its beginnings in 1282 and 1292, the date of the Ordinances of Justice, which redefined eligibility for office. In that decade, 267 citizens filled the 445 terms of office, an average of 1.6 terms for each incumbent—not an easy figure to interpret, as ten years is much shorter than the duration of an average political career.[15] Bartolo di messer Iacopo di Ricco Bardi, from the great banking house, served five times as prior (1283–1291).[16] His younger brother Cino was elected three times between 1285 and 1290; and two other brothers, Simone and Giovanni, also served one term each. The Bardi family was clearly a presence. The Ordinances of Justice in 1292 excluded some seventy magnate families from the priorate, the Bardi among them, and the oligarchy seems to have been somewhat loosened.[17] The numbers of citizens serving for the first time as priors can be used as an index of the relative openness of the office. Table 2 gives the result of such a count by decades, from 1290 to 1409.

The priorate did become relatively more open to new men over the roughly two decades following the Ordinances of Justice, but for several decades after 1310, its composition swung strongly in the

14. The continuing oligarchic character of communal governments in the late thirteenth century even under regimes of the so-called *popolo* was emphasized by N. Ottokar, *Il Comune di Firenze alla fine del dugento* (Florence, 1926); as opposed to G. Salvemini, *Magnati e popolani in Firenze dal 1280 al 1295* (Florence, 1897).

15. This count includes the notaries serving the priorate. A. Molho, "Politics and the Ruling Class," counts 223 persons serving as priors from 1282 to 1292 and arrives at the figure of 1.8 terms per incumbent.

16. The names of the priors are taken from the published *priorista* in M. Rastrelli, *Priorista fiorentino istorico pubblicato e illustrato*, 3 vols (Florence, 1783).

17. For the later history of a magnate lineage, see the recent study of the Buondelmonti by R. Bizzocchi, "La dissoluzione di un clan familiare: i Buondelmonti di Firenze nei secoli XV e XVI," *Archivio Storico Italiano*, 140 (1982), pp. 3–46.

Table 2
**Florentine Citizens Elected to the Priorate for the First Time,
by Decade, 1290–1409**
(count includes notaries, and after 1292, the standard-bearers of justice)

1290–1299	248	1350–1359	402
1300–1309	281	1360–1369	300
1310–1319	268	1370–1379	511
1320–1329	222	1380–1389	519
1330–1339	154	1390–1400	475
1340–1349	345	1401–1409	196

Source: Rastrelli, 1783.

direction of restricted access. The grip that relatively few citizens exerted on the priorate and other offices was in fact a principal motivation for the reform of 1328 and the recourse to selection by lottery. But the new method seems not to have opened the priorate to many new men; rather the contrary. In the 1330s Florence lived under the narrowest government it had ever experienced since 1292.[18]

For the entire period between 1282 and 1328, 1,217 citizens filled the 2,295 available seats in the priorate (including notaries)— an average of slightly less than two terms per citizen. Many citizens—682, or 55 percent of all who served—were priors (or notaries) for only a single term. But this group was outweighed by many who returned frequently to office. The record for service belongs to Boninsegna di Agnolino Machiavelli, twelve times prior between 1283 and 1326; his extraordinary political career ran over 44 years. Anselmo di Palla di Bernardo Anselmi served eleven times as prior between 1304 and 1338. The notary Ser Matteo Biliotti was three times notary of the priorate and eight times prior, between 1297 and 1316. It seems not unreasonable to assume that these long-serving and experienced officials dominated the government. Those who served three terms or more account for 53 percent of all the incumbencies.

From December 1328, lists of the membership of the colleges also survive and allow us to judge the number of citizens who actually served in the high councils of government. Between that year and August 1342, the number of offices filled was 2,153, and the

18. This analysis is in substantial agreement with the study of the priorate by Molho, "Politics and the Ruling Class."

persons who filled them were 675.[19] The average number of terms the active citizen filled within a period of eleven years was slightly more than three. Florence in the 1330s had a population that I would estimate at 120,000. If we assume that men over thirty constituted 20 percent of the population, then the number of adult male citizens seemingly eligible for election was 24,000.[20] But only 675 actually served. Two citizens, Spinello di Primerano da Mosciano and Vanni Donnini, each served thirteen terms in various offices—in apparent defiance of the rules governing the divieto.[21] Unmistakably, the 1330s were the decade of tight oligarchic government in Florence.

From the 1340s on the political pendulum swings in the direction of open governments. The early signs are, to be sure, not auspicious. The chronicler Giovanni Villani describes a scrutiny held in 1343, immediately after the expulsion of the despotic duke of Athens. A commission of 206 men scrutinized 3,346 citizens, but, says Villani, "not a tenth remained."[22] He implies, in other words, that the names of fewer than 340 citizens reached the purses.

From 1349 on we can take advantage of the surviving lists of *veduti*. Table 3 shows, for two of the city's four quarters (Santa Croce and Santo Spirito respectively), representing about 45 percent of its population, the raw count of citizens viewed for the *tre maggiori* (but not for the office of notary). Table 4 shows the number of citizens viewed in the first complete years of various periods.

The numbers of *veduti* surges from 65 in 1350 to nearly 400 in 1428. It is notable that the hegemony of the Medici family from 1435 had no visible impact on the numbers of citizens considered for the greater offices. Indeed, the high point in the entire series is reached in 1454, when 452 citizens from these two quarters had

19. The members of the *dodici* and *sedici* are given in Ildefonso di San Luigi, *Delizie degli eruditi toscani*, 24 vols. (Florence, 1770–89), vols. 12 and 13, as notes to his edition of the chronicler Marchionne di Coppo Stefani.

20. See our discussion on the population of Florence in D. Herlihy and C. Klapisch-Zuber, *I toscani e le loro famiglie*, pp. 236–43. In 1427 men aged 30 or over numbered 8,112 (including 435 men for whom no ages are given but who were presumably adult). The population of the city was 38,027. Men aged 30 or over thus constituted 21.3 percent of the population.

21. Vanni Donnini was chosen a member of the *dodici* on 24 March 1337 and again on 21 September.

22. Villani, *Cronica*, VII, ch. 72: "E andarono allo squittino tremilatrecento-quarantasei uomini ma non rimasono il decimo."

Table 3
Citizens Viewed for the Three Higher Offices
Quarters of S. Croce and S. Spirito
(Initial Complete Years of Various Periods)

1350	65	1373	163
1353	69	1382	109
1355	83	1393	157
1357	132	1402	156
1358	99	1410	220
1362	153	1418	277
1363	203	1428	399
1364	84	1435	282
1367	222	1444	340
1369	109	1454	452
1366	165	1475	354
1370	159		

Source: ASF, Tratte, regg. 8 and 9.

their names read out before the signoria. The projected number for the entire city is 1,000 names, viewed for a maximum of 150 offices, in this single year.

This expansion in numbers of the *veduti* is all the more surprising, as the governments, before and after the Medici period, had instituted several policies clearly aimed at reducing the number of candidates for office. The creation of the special "little purses" for the selection of some priors in 1387 was followed by other limitations on the admission of names into the purses.[23] After 1434, in the Medici period, those preparers of the purses, the *accoppiatori*, were authorized to select a portion of the priors *a mano*, that is, without recourse to drawings with their uncertain outcomes.[24] But, as Figure 1 suggests, these restrictive policies did not reduce the number of *veduti*. Perhaps these limitations were not strictly imposed. It may also be that the lineages that could pass these tests had so many branches and offspring that they alone could supply this surfeit of eligible candidates.

23. See G. Guidi, *Il governo* I, p. 106, for the requirement from 1404 that a father or grandfather in the male line had to have made loan payments for at least 25 years.

24. N. Rubinstein, "Oligarchy and Democracy in Fifteenth-Century Florence," in *Florence and Venice. Comparisons and Relations*, ed. S. Bertelli, N. Rubinstein and C.H. Smyth (Florence, 1979), pp. 99–112, considers the work of the *accoppiatori* the cornerstone of Medici effort to pack the governments with their supporters.

Table 4

**Dates of Purses Supplying Names of Citizens Considered
for the Three Great Offices, Entire City***

1348	226	1393–98	1766
1351	795	1400	184
1354	694	1406	119
1357	1027	1411	51
1360	904	1416	28
1363	842	1421	2
1366	123	1433	300
1371	13	1434	2743
1378	719	1439	2227
1381(2)	5079	1444	2203
1391	6660	1471	701

*Dates are in Florentine style (year begins on March 25)
Sources: ASF, Tratte, reg. 192 and ff.

It would be useful to know the size of the purses supplying these names. Unfortunately, the Ciompi regime in 1378 burned the contents of all existing purses, and the slips in its own purses were similarly burned in 1382. Both the exile of Cosimo de' Medici in 1433 and his return in 1434 led to similar purges and reconstitutions of the purses. Nonetheless, the original *giornali* of the Tratte office frequently cite the date and type of purse from which the name was drawn. These references we can count. It must be emphasized, however, that our edition of the original *giornali* does not include disqualifications for office when no reason was stated. Sometimes, in a practice known as *rimbotto*, younger purses were simply emptied into the older ones, confusing their true dates. Thus, a citizen named Agnolo di Bartolomeo Carducci came to be represented in the combined purses of 1393 and 1398, though he was not born until April 8, 1403.[25] Many other factors influenced the numbers of appearances. Purses prepared right before purges were necessarily poorly represented in the elections, as their years of use were few. At best, the sums reached by adding the references to purse dates in the actual drawings do no more than identify years when a major change in electoral policy occurred.

The scrutiny of 1382 registers a kind of quantum jump in the admission of citizens' names into the electoral purses.[26] The purses

25. His birthday is given in ASF, Tratte, reg. 1093, f. 42.
26. The antiquarian friar Ildefonso di San Luigi, in the late eighteenth century, published an unfortunately incomplete copy of the scrutiny of the city's male popu-

of 1391 seem to have been even larger. The governments that took and held power after the Ciompi uprising are traditionally regarded as oligarchic, but the term does not accurately represent their electoral policies, at least during the first decade after the suppression of the wool workers. Seemingly shaken by the Ciompi uprising, these regimes may well have been trying to coopt into the government as many middle-class and presumably conservative citizens as possible. Moreover, after 1391, the size of the purses seems to decline, only to grow again in the middle years of the fifteenth century.

In 1427, according to the Catasto, 6,283 out of 9,780 households, or 64 percent, held shares in the public debt; their adult male members were presumably eligible for office. Although these richer households contained more members than the poor, it seems not unreasonable to estimate that 64 percent of the 8,112 males age thirty or over were eligible for office. In this small city of fewer than 40,000 inhabitants, the potential active participants in government numbered as many as 5,200.

When the government, in 1429, insisted that those who wished to claim eligibility for office had to register and prove their true ages, 5,414 names were entered.[27] Many of the males registered were of course underage at the time; the conclusion must be that many, but not all, of the well-to-do Florentine citizens viewed government office as a possible career for their sons.

There is no indication that the circle of those competing for government jobs grew smaller under Medici rule, at least up to 1478. It may even have grown larger. According to the chronicler Benedetto Dei, Florence in 1472 boasted 365 "houses or family alliances,"

---

lation in 1382. See Ildefonso di San Luigi, *Delizie degli eruditi toscani*, 16, pp. 125–260. The first two gonfaloniers of the quarter of S. Spirito are missing; the third gonfalonier of the quarter, Ferza, lists 443 names. According to a survey of the city made only two years before, in 1380, Ferza, with 4,929 *bocche*, or residents, accounted for 9 percent of the city's population of 54,747. (These figures are also from Ildefonso di San Luigi, p. 123.) The complete scrutiny must have contained 4,900 names and could be compared with the figure of 3,346 citizens scrutinized in 1343, in a city then two times larger than in 1382. (For the reference, see n, 21). It is difficult to know from the scrutiny of 1382 which citizens were entered into what purses, or how many were excluded altogether. The surviving entries give numbers after the names, apparently registering the votes of the scruinizers, and letters, chiefly *O* and *R*, in front of some names, the exact meanings of which are to me inexplicable.

27. These represent the combined totals of ASF, Tratte, 1093 and 39. I have tried to exclude duplicated entries.

each with 200 "or more" citizens able to bear arms and, presumably, stand for office.[28] While clearly a boast, his estimates imply an active male and adult citizenry of perhaps 7,300 citizens. Figure 2 illustrates by year the numbers of citizens who proved (or their fathers proved for them) their ages and had their claims approved by the "conservators of the laws."[29] The figure shows that with every important change of regime, citizens, or their fathers for them, rushed to register and to claim for themselves or for their sons eligibility for office. Figure 2 displays rather well when regimes changed in Florence. It shows even better the growing competition for posts in the government.

Who were these throngs of office seekers? The Tratte registers allow us to view the family connections of the *veduti*. The total number of families appearing in the two quarters is 638. To be sure, the count cannot be perfectly exact. Although the compilers were committed to identifying families, ambiguities remain. The names are given in Latin, and it is sometimes hard to distinguish a patronymic in the genitive case (e.g., Iohannes Rossi) from a true family name (Giovanni Rossi). On the other hand, the size of the lists usually allows us to see many examples of the same name and hence to make a reasonable determination as to whether it is or is not a true family name.

Were the growing numbers of office seekers "new men," in the sense of new arrivals in the city? Were they the newly successful, vertically mobile individuals who succeeded in penetrating the officeholding class? Table1 identifies for each of the twenty-four periods the "new" citizens. They are new only in the sense that their family names do not appear in the lists for any earlier periods. The data do indicate a strong infusion of "new men" into the governing circles in the late fourteenth century. This influx reaches its apex in the period 1381 to 1392. Nearly one-half of the family names (79 out of 168, 47 percent) then appear for the first time, and these families account for nearly one-third (117 out of 361, 32 percent) of all citizens who carry a family name. In the wake of the Ciompi uprising (1378), the Florentine government does seem

28. See B. Dei, *La cronica dall'anno 1400 all'anno 1500*, ed. R. Barducci, Istituto per la storia degli antichi stati italiani, Fonti e studi, 1 (Florence, 1984), p. 80. He calls them "chasati e parentele."

29. The chart represents the citizens registered in ASF, Tratte, reg. 40, 41, 43, and 44.

committed to broadening its political and social base. But thereafter the number of new families markedly declines, as the figures in Table 1 trace out. By the decade 1454–1464, when the citizen body had reached its largest recorded size, new families constituted only 15 percent of all families represented (36 out of 244), and they accounted for only 3 percent (46 out of 1520) of the citizens who show a family name.

By the middle of the fifteenth century, those viewed for office seem to have been drawn chiefly from the proliferating branches of older houses. To illustrate this phenomenon, Table 1 shows two "cluster indices," which measure the tendency for a smaller number of families to provide greater numbers of *veduti*. The indices are initially constructed by arranging the families for each period in descending order on the basis of size. It can then be calculated how many of the larger families account for one-half of the total population of *veduti* with family names. Thus, in the period 1349–1351, 27 larger families out of 74 include one-half of the population. This is 36.5 percent of the set of families, and this is our first cluster index. These same families provide 32 percent of all citizens viewed for office, including those without a family name. This is our second cluster index.

Over the period of our interest, the number of the greater families needed to account for one-half of the population sharply declines. The index drops from 36.5 in 1349–1351 to only 14.3 percent (35 out of 244 families) by 1454-1464. Between the same two periods, the percentage of *veduti* drawn from the larger families grows from 32.4 to 46.5. By then, the big houses were providing nearly one-half of all citizens viewed for office. Rather oddly, even as the governing class was growing larger, it was becoming socially more restricted.

The growth in the citizens competing for office (even if drawn from fewer families) cannot but surprise. For the liberal admission of citizens to office inevitably undermined the ability of any oligarchic clique to hold on to power. The rotations in office in 1434 led directly to the overthrow of Rinaldo degli Albizzi and his faction, after only one year of seeming dominance.[30] Why had he allowed this to happen? What factors pried and kept the offices open?

---

30. For a close analysis of the contending factions, see D.V. Kent, *The Rise of the Medici. Faction in Florence, 1426–1434* (Oxford, 1978).

To answer these questions we must first ask another: why was the Florentine government encountering such difficulties in finding among the *veduti* citizens eligible for office? Why were 800 drawings required in 1428, or 1,000 in 1454, to fill 150 seats? We must look at the *divieti*, the disqualifications that barred office to many *veduti*, and in doing so opened them to others.

One common reason for disqualifying candidates was age: they had not yet attained the thirty years required for most high positions. The electoral purses were seemingly stuffed with the names of underage citizens. As early as 1387, an anonymous chronicler reported that "many youths of little age" had been introduced into purses of 1382.[31] The government never strictly and consistently prohibited the inclusion of underage boys in the purses but regulated the practice in complex ways; the regulations imply that some of these many youths had barely reached five years of age when their fathers persuaded those conducting the *squittino* to place their names in the purses.[32] It can further be shown that many young Florentines pretended to be older than they really were, in order to pass the threshold of thirty years, which qualified them for the most important offices.[33] The government attempted to counter this fraud by insisting, from 1411 and several times thereafter, that candidates declare under oath their true ages. In August 1429, as mentioned, it set about systematically compiling a register of its male citizens showing their ages, and the practice was continued across the fifteenth century.[34]

Figure 3 shows for the entire city the numbers of citizens viewed for the three great offices who were disqualified for reason of insufficient years. The number soars after 1427, and thereafter it was not unusual for 200 and more citizens to be barred from office in one year because of their youth. The picture is rather bizarre. The august signoria in solemn session hears and ponders the qualifications of boys who will remain ineligible for decades; the same names are

31. G. Guidi, *Il governo,* I, p. 300, citing the *Cronaca volgare di anonimo fiorentino* of pseudo-Minerbetti.

32. *Ibid.,* I, pp. 300–03, for these regulations.

33. For examples of male citizens younger than 30 who pretended that they were above that age, see D. Herlihy and C. Klapisch-Zuber, *I toscani e le loro famiglie,* pp. 486–89.

34. ASF, Tratte, reg. 1093, is the original rough draft of these proofs of age, subsequently copied with additions into ASF, Tratte, reg. 39.

pronounced aloud again and again, as the slips of the underage candidates were returned to the purses only to be drawn again at future sessions. Why was the signoria wasting so much of its time?

Figure 4 shows the numbers of underage citizens excluded in the elections of the captains or consuls of the guilds. Here, the exclusions for reason of insufficient years were even more numerous than with the communal offices. Fathers seem to have matriculated their sons into the guilds and to have had their names entered into electoral purses soon after birth. One citizen, Andrea di Benedetto Bonsi, was viewed 36 times between 1472 and 1497 for the consulship of the wine merchants' guild.[35] He finally was awarded the office on 24 April 1509. He must have been entered into the guild purses soon after his birth. Why did the officials of the guild not become bored with hearing the name of this flagrantly ineligible candidate for more than 25 years? But seemingly not here, nor in the purses of communal councils, was the exclusion of the underage citizens required.

This seems an odd procedure. However, there is an apparent reason for the government's toleration of padded purses. The mature men who sat in the government wanted the names of their own sons read aloud before the council, and often. And why were Florentine fathers so eager to have their young sons viewed for offices that they could not possibly attain?

This paternal zeal is the more puzzling, as in the culture of Florentine merchants a marked antagonism existed toward the *statuali*, those who held government office. The sage Giannozzo Alberti, as represented in Leon Battista Alberti's *Books on the Family* from the late 1430s, reckons that gifts of fortune (a family, property, honor, and friendship) constitute happiness—but not state offices. Officeholders were public slaves, and the life of such officials was *molestissima*. "Imagine yourself in office," he demands from his young interlocutors; "what good do you gain apart from this: to be able to rob and coerce with some freedom?"[36] Officeholders are mad, haughty, bestial, and cruel little tyrants. "My children," Giannozzo exhorts, "let us remain happy with our little family, let us enjoy the goods that fortune bestows on us, sharing them with our

---

35. Based on ASF, Mercanzia, reg. 86 to 88. His first appearance is 22 December, 1472.
36. Alberti, 1960 [incomp. cit.], I, pp. 179–180. "Eccoti sedere in ufficio. Che n'hai tu d'utile se none uno solo: potere rubare e sforzare con qualche licenza?"

friends, for that person is sufficiently honored who lives without vice and dishonesty."[37]

The Alberti were, to be sure, exiles, and had reason to hate *statuali*. But even Giovanni Rucellai, in instructions on the "civil life" written about 1457 to instruct his two sons, borrows passages from Alberti in composing his own diatribe against the officeholders.[38] Do not seek public office, he advises his sons, and perhaps his advice had some influence. His two sons, Bernardo and Pandolfo, seem not to have served as communal officers though they were consuls in the money changers' guild (Cambio).[39] But perhaps the pressures to enter government eventually worked on this lineage, too. Bernardo's son Palla was chosen standard-bearer of justice on 20 February 1520.[40]

As the fifteenth century progressed, few citizens apparently wished (or could afford) to limit their lives to their "little families," in Giannozzo's idyllic phrase. Rather, they were scrambling to gain for their sons' representation in the electoral purses. Why?

Florentine merchants in the heroic age of the city's commercial expansion, up to the troubled 1340s, seemingly could ignore government with impunity. Florentine merchants of the fifteenth century could not. As even the diatribes against the *statuali* confirm, government by then controlled important patronage and wielded destructive powers. Patronage, in the form of paid offices, became ever more attractive, for two reasons. The jobs in the government's largess had multiplied, even as the state expanded its sway over a large part of the territory of Tuscany. Indeed, the chief means by which Florence exploited its subject territories was to impose on them gov-

37. *Ibid.* I, p. 182: "Figliuoli miei, ... stiànci lieti colla famigliuola nostra, godiànci quelli beni ci largisce la fortuna faccendone parte alli amici nostri, ché assai si truova onorato chi vive senza vizio e senza disonestà."

38. Rucellai, *Giovanni Rucellai ed il suo Zibaldone*, pp. 39–43, "La vita civile."

39. Bernardo on 12 August 1479 was viewed for the *sedici* but disqualified for reason of being *in speculo* (ASF, Tratte, 203, unpaginated). He was elected on 27 February 1490 to be a member of the "Six of the Mercanzia," a powerful office that oversaw Florence's commercial situation, and on 19 August 1491 he was chosen as consul of the money changers. Pandolfo was viewed twice for the priorate, on 12 December 1454 and on 28 April 1469, and his name bears an *F* in the latter entry. He was elected consul of the money changers twice, on 16 December 1467 and on 16 August 1469 (ASF, Mercanzia, reg. 85, f. 167 and 274).

40. ASF, Tratte, 342, f. 93.

ernors and staffs, the salaries of which the subjects had to pay. And the bigger Florentine state nurtured a bigger bureaucracy at home.

The second reason was that in troubled economic times, the great families had no assurance that careers as long-distance merchants could engage and support all their usually numerous offspring. Government service offered alternative careers that could not be dismissed out of hand. Jobs in the government were secure and reasonably remunerative. But they were not easily obtained without visibility and influence. To have one's name read aloud before the signoria and the colleges and regarded for high office conferred visibility; to be chosen brought influence.

The destructive powers that the government could wield were chiefly associated with taxes. We can measure the fiscal burdens of the citizen by counting, for the entire city, the number of citizens excluded from office for reason of tax arrears. Figure 5 illustrates, for the entire city, the numbers of citizens barred for this reason from the three great offices. Figure 6 shows the same exclusions in regard to elections to the guild consulships. The exclusions show a marked upsurge in the period of the first Catasto, and a second period of acute fiscal difficulties at century's close.

State expenditures and, necessarily, revenues had grown enormously from the mid-fourteenth into the fifteenth century.[41] Locked in frequent and costly wars, the state was desperate for funds, and, to facilitate their collection, it offered concessions to the citizenry it was bleeding. As mentioned, those who were assessed and who contributed sums above a threshold amount were promised repayment with interest on their moneys, when peace and prosperity returned. And, in a kind of trade off, those who paid the high assessments were offered access to public offices, the ones that paid salaries and the ones that did not. The desperate fiscal needs of the government thus prompted it to open its offices to all who could pay.

Fiscal policy worked in another way to enlarge the government. The shaming mirror of tax delinquency caught the faces of large numbers of citizens. Many high dignitaries are, at one time or another,

41. A phenomenon noted by many. Marvin Becker saw the growing fiscal weight of government in Florence a decisive factor in changing the political, social, and even cultural life of the city. See his older now but still interesting works, M. Becker *Florence in Transition*, I: *The Decline of the Commune*; II: *Studies in the Rise of the Territorial State* (Baltimore, 1966–67), and our own comments, D. Herlihy and C. Klapisch-Zuber, *I toscani e le loro famiglie*, pp. 21–24.

found among them: Palla di Nofri Strozzi, the city's richest citizen in 1427; and even Cosimo when he supposedly dominated the government.[42] These exclusions, even when temporary, inevitably made room in the offices for new citizens, with new moneys.

The prospects of ruin through high tax assessments weighed upon all citizens. The prudent Florentine paterfamilias could not relax, as Giannozzo recommended, in domestic tranquility. He had to defend both his property and his family against the voracious demands of government. He must cultivate the *statuali*, or, perhaps better, join their ranks. He thus could influence who assessed the taxes, and how much would be imposed upon him, his relatives, and his friends. The power to tax is the power to destroy: this was never more true than in fifteenth-century Florence.

Between the fourteenth and the fifteenth centuries, the government made unprecedented tax demands upon its citizens, but also offered to them the opportunity to share in the benefits and powers of office. Inevitably, government loomed ever larger in the lives of the people. Some years ago, Marvin Becker sensed this change and attributed to it major cultural repercussions. The terms he used to describe this cultural shift—from "gentle paideia" in the earlier age to "stern paideia" in the following—are problematic, but his basic instinct was not faulted.[43] To survive in this world, young Florentines had to learn to live and interact civilly. In his memoirs written for his descendants, Giovanni Morelli does not envision that they will pursue political careers, but they still must learn how to interact with the *statuali* and how to ingratiate themselves to them. They must acquire the skill to cultivate all factions, while joining none. Be agreeable, he tells his descendants, be pleasant, evasive if you must, invite the powerful to dinner, cultivate them "even if it costs you a little." And "always hold with whoever possesses the palace and the Signoria."[44]

42. Palla was listed in *speculo* in a drawing for the Sei della Mercanzia, ASF Mercanzia, reg. 83, f. 133 on 30 August 1431, and again on September 29 in a drawing for the same office. He was still in tax arrears on 29 August 1434 in a drawing for the *sedici* (ASF, Tratte, reg. 198, f. 163). Cosimo was also found to be in tax arrears on 28 April 1436 in a drawing for the *sedici* (ASF, Tratte, reg.199, f. 22), on 28 April 1440 (*ibid.*, not paginated, office of the *sedici*); on 12 December 1440 (*ibid.*, office of the *dodici*); and on 20 December 1448 (ASF, Mercanzia, reg. 84, f. 28, office of the Sei della Mercanzia).

43. M. Becker, *Florence in Transition.*

44. G. Morelli, *Ricordi*, ed. V. Branca, new edition (Florence, 1969), p. 274.

In a social environment where government counted for so much, sons had to be trained to function effectively in a tumultuous world, to parry, if not to participate in, political power. Giovanni Rucellai, while serving with the humanist Donato Acciaiuoli on the priorate in 1463, engaged him in a discussion on the topic of "whether it was more difficult to do good or evil." What seems to us an idle issue clearly concerned Giovanni, as he further elicited from Giovanni da Viterbo, a Dominican friar, an answer to the same question. He incorporated both answers, from the friar and from the humanist, into his *Zibaldone*, for the benefit of his sons.[45] The friar averred that it was more difficult to do evil than good, but Giovanni clearly preferred the humanist's answer, that evil behavior was both easier and more common. The pervasive penchant of men to do evil had cultural repercussions. It required that the state through education instill "good customs" in its citizens; if the state failed to do so, the paterfamilias must take on this charge and train his children in appropriate moral behavior. Implicitly, he must educate them for the active life, teach them the good customs but also instruct them how to counter the machinations of the evil majority. Fra Giovanni's argument was rejected, because it did not offer logical support for education in moral philosophy. Giovanni regarded such education as critical for his age.

The moral counsels of Morelli and the educational philosophy of Rucellai are echoed many times in the vast didactic literature of the Florentine Renaissance. These counsels were meant to promote survival in the active life. Do not their goals and their content reflect the essence of what we now call civic humanism? One had to *vivere civile* if one was to live at all.

But if the unprecedented intrusion of government into private affairs recommended new standards of behavior and, beyond them, new educational goals, there were practical costs too in keeping powerful offices accessible to the many. How could high officials with limited experience manage the many crises that Florence confronted in the late fourteenth and fifteenth centuries? The creation of the special, small purse for priors, the *borsellino*, in 1387, could be interpreted not as an oligarchic ploy but simply as a method of bringing

---

45. G. Rucellai, *Giovanni Rucellai ed il suo Zibaldone*, p. 85 ff., with the Latin version of Donato's statement, dated 15 August 1464, pp. 125–33.

more "suitable," that is, experienced, citizens into the priorate. Recognition of the need for experience seems, however, best reflected in the repeated creation of *balie*, committees usually of ten members, who served for six months, one year, or more. Between 1363 and 1478, forty-one committees of this sort served for six months, one year, or longer.[46] Clearly the composition of these *balie* put an emphasis on experience. They included magnates, who, though excluded from the three great offices, often served the commune as delegates and ambassadors to foreign states. Citizens viewed for the commune's highest office, the standard-bearer of justice, were also favored, even if they had never actually served. And the committees routinely included one or more doctors of law, to provide legal expertise.

Over this long period of time, 357 citizens held the 574 places on the forty-one *balie*, an average of 1.6 terms per citizen. But several citizens appeared with much greater frequency. Messer Lorenzo di Antonio Ridolfi, *decretorum doctor*, served on ten commissions from 1396 to 1440, over a long political life of 44 years. Tied with him for most appearances was Cosimo di Giovanni Medici, who also served on ten *balie* between 1427 and 1453. His father, Giovanni di Bicci, served twice (1414 and 1423). His son Piero served three times (1453–1468), and his grandson Lorenzo, "Il Magnifico," twice in the brief period between 1471 and 1478.

Cosimo also served twice in the *dodici*, twice in the *sedici*, twice as prior, and three times as standard-bearer—a total of two years in elected office. Quite clearly, the rule he exerted over the Florentine state was based more on service on *balie* than in the three great offices, and that service too earned him his eventual title of *pater Patriae*.

After 1478, a central issue in Florentine political thought was the very survival of its republican government. The chief argument that theorists advanced against it, and in favor of the Medici principate, was that traditional republicanism bred instability and civil war; only a principate could ensure peace at home and the pursuit of effective policy abroad.[47] A Venetian observer, Marco Foscari, in

46. The names of the citizens serving on these *balie* are given in Ildefonso di San Luigi, 1770–1789, 14, p. 284 ff. The practice was older than 1363 but never used as frequently as in this period.
47. The literature on Florentine political speculations in the last years of its republic into the Medicean principate is of course vast. I cite here only the works regarded

1527 offered a perspicacious summary of the Florentine political experience.[48] Florence in the past had either been subject to various princes (the Medici preeminently) or been free. But when the Florentines were free, they were battered by civil wars. He goes on to describe the parties or factions of the city. He notes that the Medici supporters, called the "grays," or *bigi*, were few in number but composed of politically experienced persons. He thus links support of the principate with a premium placed upon experience in government. And experience in office was the one quality that fifteenth-century Florentine republicanism, with its programed high turnovers in powerful positions, could not supply.

Figure 1
Veduti, Quarters of Santo Spirito and Santa Croce 1349–1478.

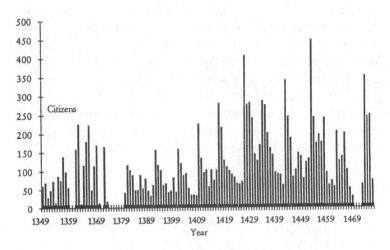

Figure 2
Citizens Disqualified for Reason of Age, Drawings of the Three Great Offices, 1363–1500.

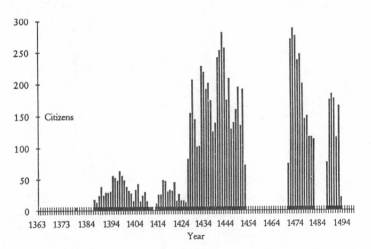

Figure 3
Citizens Disqualified for Reason of Age, Drawings for the
Guild Consulates, 1391–1500.

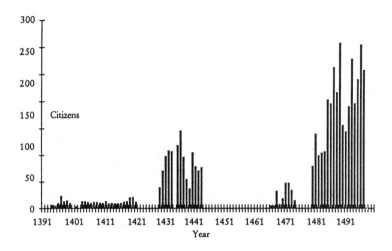

Figure 4
Citizens in Tax Arrears, Three Great Offices, 1350–1530.

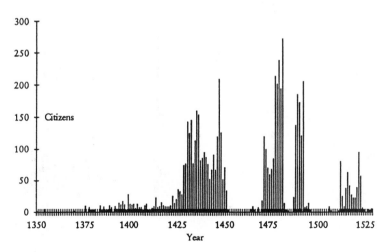

Figure 5
Citizens in Tax Arrears, Guild Consulates, 1394–1530.

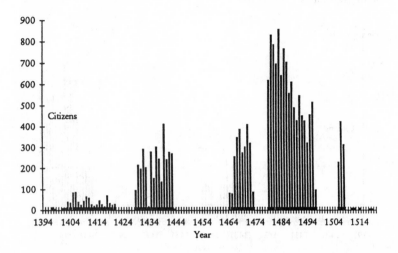

Figure 6
Citizens Presenting Proof of Age, 1429-1530.

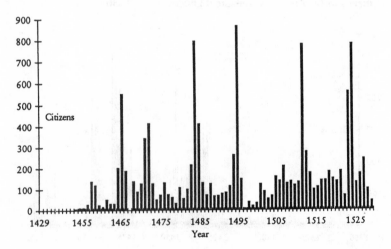

THE AMERICAN MEDIEVALIST

A Social and Professional Profile

——— ✦ ✦ ✦ ———

In becoming medievalists and members of the Academy, we assumed a commitment to promote the study of the European Middle Ages on this continent. But to do this well, we ought on occasion to study ourselves, to discover who we are, who we were, and who we are likely to become in the near and distant future. Our arts are long and our lives are short, and we ought frequently to inquire how the changing composition of our profession may be affecting the arts we uphold.[1]

In this paper I propose to survey the current membership of the Medieval Academy of America. My chief source may appear singularly pedestrian; it is the Academy's mailing list for 1982, used pri-

This presidential address was delivered at the annual meeting of the Medieval Academy of America at the University of California, Berkeley, on 9 April 1983. The author would like to express his gratitude to Dr. Luke Wenger for permission to consult the archives and the mailing list of the Medieval Academy and to Mrs. Emily Vogt, the Academy's Executive Manager, for much help in the preparation of this address. All conclusions are exclusively my own.

1. Recent and useful surveys of medieval studies in the United States and their recent history may be found in the collection of essays *Medieval Studies in North America: Past, Present, and Future*, ed. F.G. Gentry and C. Kleinhenz (Kalamazoo, 1982). For the early history of the Medieval Academy, see especially the contributions by W.J. Courtenay, "The Virgin and the Dynamo: The Growth of Medieval Studies in America (1870–1930)," pp. 5–22; and by L. Wenger, "The Medieval Academy and Medieval Studies in North America," pp. 23–40. See also K. Morrison, "Fragmentation and Unity in 'American Medievalism,'" in *The Past before Us: Contemporary Historical Writing in the United States*, ed. M. Kammen (Ithaca, 1980), pp. 49–77, with abundant bibliography.

marily for the distribution of its flagship publication, Speculum. I shall look at the names and addresses of Academy members resident in the United States, with a glance also at institutional subscribers to Speculum. These remarks, in sum, do not apply to the many members and subscribers in Canada and overseas.[2] Because the list of Academy members in the United States is long—3,060 names— and because the questions put to it are somewhat involved, I enlisted the aid of a computer to gather the responses. The computer does this work well. Given the right data to scrutinize, it is an exact observer and an implacable judge.

The information which the mailing list offers is admittedly limited. The register of North American medievalists compiled for the Academy's Committee on Centers and Regional Associations by the Medieval Institute of Western Michigan University at Kalamazoo contains some 7,924 names, better than twice the number of the Academy's 3,289 North American members. That is to say, only 41.5 percent of those who consider themselves to be in some sense medievalists are members of the Academy. Moreover, the Academy's list does not systematically identify members by their discipline. To be sure, of the 3,060 members resident in the United States, 1,460 have their issues of Speculum delivered to them at an academic department. Disciplinary allegiances are thus revealed for some 48 percent of the membership. Slightly more than one-half of the members—52 percent—do not display through their addresses their special interest in the Middle Ages.

Still, the mailing list invites and rewards close study. Though forming only a minority of practicing medievalists, members of the Academy still make up a substantial proportion of the profession, and contribute perhaps even more than their numbers suggest to the ongoing work of teaching, investigating, and promoting the Middle Ages. The labels tell much about the subscribers, more than might at first be realized. To begin with, first names are almost always spelled out, and the gender of the members is therefore evident. So also is their place of residence. But perhaps the most interesting information the labels supply is the following. The address labels note when the subscriber first joined the Academy, and what has been and is now his or her type of membership, whether active, contributing, life,

---

2. Residents of Canada in the 1982 mailing list number 229.

honorary, or Fellow. The list for 1982 reflects, of course, the composition of a single year, but the inclusion of these dates opens a wide door into the past, and offers a vista stretching back to the very beginnings of the Academy in 1925 and 1926. Not even the larger register maintained at Kalamazoo offers the opportunity for studying not only the current composition of the American community of medievalists, but also the current directions of change.

Where do members of the Academy live in the United States? To answer this question we can take advantage of the fact that the list is arranged in order of zip codes, identifying postal districts across the country. The districts begin in Puerto Rico and make their continental landfall in Massachusetts. After wandering around New England, they proceed down the Atlantic coast to Florida; they then swing north again along the western slopes of the Appalachians. Next they turn down and up the Mississippi valley. They cover the far west by a similar path, tracing out great sweeping coils. They come to an end, at least for our purposes, in Washington. They thus progress in a general sense from east to west, with broad oscillations south and north.

If we divide the 3,060 address labels exactly in half, and thus find the midpoint of the distribution, where in continental America do we find ourselves? The median value, as statisticians would call it, in the distribution of zips is 30329; we are at Atlanta, Georgia. The spatial distribution of the 89 Fellows—the Academy's elite—is even more skewed to the east; the midpoint of those resident in the United States is University Park, Pennsylvania.[3] On the assumption that the postal districts contain roughly the same numbers of people, then the eastern seaboard from Maine to Georgia, in which reside 50 percent of the Academy membership, holds only some 30 percent of the American population. If we test to see where the first quartile of the distribution is found, then the zip value of the distribution places us in Mount Vernon, New York. One-fourth of the membership lives to the east of the Hudson river.

In 1968, the number of Academy members from eleven far-western states was 340, or 13.98 percent of all members; the compara-

3. The Fellows resident in the United States currently number 79. Of the remainder, 6 live in Canada (all in Toronto) and 4 in Europe.

ble figure in 1982 was 490 persons, or 13.64 percent.[4] The geographical distribution of Academy members (or at least the representation among them of residents of the far west) seems to have remained remarkably stable over the past fifteen years.

The concentration of Academy members in New England and the eastern seaboard is in itself not surprising, but the degree of this concentration, which our figures emphasize, is nonetheless disconcerting. To offer one further illustration, we can compare these results with the distribution of the institutional subscribers to Speculum, which ought to show objectively where interest in the Middle Ages is located across the country. The median code for institutional subscribers is 39210, which carries us all the way along the trail of zips to Jackson, Mississippi. To be sure, there is evident even here a bias toward the east. Among institutional subscribers, 50 percent are apparently found in eastern areas containing slightly less than 40 percent of the population. But the tilt toward the east is much less pronounced among institutional subscribers than among Academy members.

I would draw from these figures the following conclusions. Out west—and the meaning here is west of the Appalachians—medievalists rely in large measure on libraries to secure copies of Speculum, on the assumption that they read it at all. They manifest comparatively little personal loyalty to the Academy. Clearly, the Academy must strive to enlarge its national influence: the west has yet to be won.

What is the relative size of the disciplines which make up the Academy? I have prepared a table showing the distribution across disciplines of the 1,460 members whose scholarly specializations can be identified in 1982. To lend these figures a temporal dimension, I include in the same table the comparable distribution as found in the directory of its members which the Academy published in 1973. In fact I utilize here the figures based on that directory which an ad hoc committee on the governance of the Academy prepared in 1978.[5] The chair of that committee was our incoming president, Fred

4. The figures for 1968 are taken from a report dated 5 April 1968 in the Academy's archives. The states, the number of members in 1968, and the number in 1982 are as follows: Washington (26, 41); Oregon (29, 26); California (224, 316); Nevada (2, 6); Arizona (17, 25); Idaho (1, 5); Montana (1, 1); Wyoming (0, 2); Utah (7, 15); (Colorado (27, 40); New Mexico (6, 13).

5. The report of the committee is dated 11 January 1978; the committee members were James D. Breckenridge, Robert J. Brentano, Virginia Brown, Robert E. Kaske, and Fred C. Robinson. The report may be found in the Academy's archives.

C. Robinson. To facilitate comparisons I use in the table the professional groupings contained in the committee's report.

Table 1

**Members of the Medieval Academy
by Academic Discipline, 1973 and 1982**

	1973		1982	
	Number	Percent*	Number	Percent*
English	786	33	456	31
History	690	29	413	28
Modern Languages	408	17	258	18
Art History	115	5	98	7
Classics	79	3	39	3
Philosophy	58	2	41	3
Music	33	1	31	2
Other	183	8	106	7
Unspecified	1,380	—	1,600	—
Total	3,732		3,060	

*Based on total numbers for whom profession is known.

The distribution of members across disciplines has not changed significantly between 1973 and 1982. The largest discipline then and now is English language and literature, which claimed 33 percent of the members in 1973 and 31 percent in 1982. In second position are the historians, scoring 29 percent in 1973 and 28 percent in 1982. Modern languages and literatures take third position: 17 percent ten years ago and 18 at present. Art history, classics, philosophy, and music follow, each today with less than 8 percent of the membership. The distribution across disciplines thus shows a considerable stability over the past decade. In these years of acute retrenchment in higher education, no one discipline has suffered worse than the others.

The comparison of the two lists does, however, show two differences worth noting. In all fields today there were more medievalists listed in 1973 than can be found today. To be sure, the directory included all members, whatever their residence, and some non-members (3,732 names, as against the official membership figure of 3,314 in 1973), while for 1982 my sample includes only members resident in the United States (3,060, as against a total membership of 3,590). Accordingly, the table exaggerates what was in fact a smaller decline in numbers. The second difference may therefore be of greater significance. More members—2,352 to be exact, or 63 percent of the total—gave an academic address in 1973; only 1,460, or 48 percent, did so in 1982. This slippage may well indicate that diminishing numbers of the membership now hold stable academic jobs. Reduced numbers of subscribers and smaller proportions of members giving proof of permanent academic appointment are ominous signs for the future.

The mailing labels also allow us to calculate sex ratios, among the members as a whole, across the various disciplines, and for the various types of membership. We can also judge how sex ratios have been changing in the recent past.

As conventionally defined, the sex ratio of a population states the number of men per 100 women. In 1982, the Academy membership included 1,975 men and 1,085 women, for a ratio of 182. They are not, however, distributed in the same fashion across the different disciplines and categories of membership. We first look at fields. To be sure, the calculations of sex ratios according to fields cannot be regarded as precise. Of male members of the Academy, 1,057 out of 1,975, or 54 percent, show a profession; the comparable figures for women are 403 out of 1,085, or 37 percent. Women prefer to have their copies of Speculum delivered at home, either for reasons of convenience—they may be caring for children—or because more women than men are without an academic post. Table 2, giving sex ratios according to discipline, substantially understates the true numbers of women actually associated with the respective fields.

Even if women are underrepresented in the Table, still it is clear that the sexes are not evenly distributed across the disciplines. The category with the largest relative number of women is "modern languages," but used here in a special way. Essentially, it includes those who teach in departments of modern languages or foreign languages with no further specification; these departments are usually found in smaller schools or community colleges throughout the country. The standard discipline, if such it may be called, with the largest relative number of women is French language and literature, and it is closely followed by art history. In ascending order of sex ratios, there come music, English, classics, "Romance languages" not further defined, history, and German. With a sex ratio of 450, German is the discipline with the highest percentage of men, but history, which scores at 410, is not much below it. In relative terms, there are nearly twice the number of women in English literature than are found in history.

Table 2

**Sex Ratios, by Academic Discipline,
of Medieval Academy Members, 1982**

Discipline*	Men	Women	Sex Ratio
"Modern Languages"	30	23	130
French	23	16	144
Art History	61	37	165
Music	20	11	182
English	310	146	212
Classics	29	10	290
"Romance Languages"	46	19	242
History	332	81	410
German	36	8	450

*Only disciplines with 30 or more members are included.

Women, in sum, are especially numerous in most languages and literatures and in art history, but are comparatively few in history.

An uneven distribution of the sexes also marks the special categories of members—life, contributing, honorary, and the Fellows. Life members include 40 men and 13 women, for a sex ratio of 308, much higher than the 180 found among the active members. Women are less likely than are men to make the single, large investment required to attain life membership. Contributing members, who donate to the Academy more than the annual dues, are 543 men and 236 women, for a ratio of 230. Males are slight more likely than females to make a contribution to the Academy. Honorary members are those now retired who have belonged to the Academy for thirty years; they include 83 men and 36 women, for a ratio of 231. By far the sharpest imbalance between the sexes is found within the Academys elite, the Fellows. The mailing list for 1982 identifies 89 Fellows—82 men and 7 women, for a ratio of 1171, nearly 12 men for every woman. Men have traditionally dominated the older, richer, and most prestigious cadres of the Academy.

We can now consider how the membership in the Academy has been changing over time. The annual reports of the executive director give for every year since 1926 the total number of members, though not unfortunately a breakdown by sex and discipline.[6] Still, even these bald numbers are intriguing. The Academy's common experience since its foundation in 1925 has been growth, and it has had to endure only two protracted periods of retrenchment. From 1926 until 1931, the number of members grew continuously, from 761 to 1,062. But amid the Great Depression of the 30s, the membership fell by more than 10 percent, to a low of 931 members in 1935. The exodus of scholars from Europe and the outbreak of the Second World War increased the membership after 1939, although the number remained erratic across the war years. From 1945, the Academy embarked on a period of sustained growth, and membership reached its historic high in 1978, with 3,901 members. Since 1978 the trend has been consistently downward, to a figure of 3,590 today, a loss of 311 members in five years. Not since the Great Depression has the Academy endured so protracted a period of decline.

Still, the recent and continuous expansion means that the present membership is quite young. In 1982, one-fourth of the members had joined since 1978, and one-half the members since 1972. The average length of membership for males is 14.9 years and for females 11. On the assumption that most members join between 25 and 30 years of age, the average male member of the Academy is in his early forties, and the average woman in her late thirties.

Even as the total membership has been shifting, so also its gender composition has been changing, and in quite dramatic fashion. Table 3 shows the sex ratio of the members according to the year they joined, as registered in the mailing list for 1982.

Over time, the sex ratio of the Academy membership shows only two major swings, but these are very powerful: a movement from relative equality between the sexes in the earliest years to an extraordinary male preponderance, which peaks in the early 1950s; and, after the 1950s, an equally powerful turn in the other direction, to virtual equality today.

Those who joined the Academy before 1939 and remained as members in 1982 number 41, and form a little more than 2 percent of the membership. They include 35 men and 26 women, for a ratio of 135. To be sure, superior longevity enjoyed by women doubt-

6. The report of the executive director is published yearly in the July issue of *Speculum*. See also L. Wenger, "The Medieval Academy," on the Academy's changing membership.

lessly affects these figures, to an indeterminable extent. It is nonetheless true to say that female medievalists were relatively numerous in the years before World War II, and were represented even among the first Fellows.

The Second World War emptied colleges and graduate schools of men, and yet from 1939 to 1946 the sex ratio was swinging in their favor. Fifty men then joined the Academy, but only 13 women, for a ratio of 385. The chief reason would seem to be the influx into the ranks of the Academy of refugee scholars, driven out of Europe by politics, persecution, and war. They more than compensated for the small number of young male Ph.D.'s produced under wartime conditions.

This swing toward masculine predominance gained further momentum in the immediate postwar years. New members between 1946 and 1953 include 136 men and only 22 women, for a ratio of 618. In 1952, 19 men joined the Academy, and only a single woman. Over the five years from 1949 to 1952 the sex ratio of new members is an astounding 970. Women had virtually disappeared from the profession, at least from among its youngest members.

What was happening? We can, of course, only speculate, and the following explanation seems the most likely. Returning veterans, aided by generous government support, filled the colleges and graduate schools, to pursue the education that the war had delayed. The war for many of them had also forced postponement of marriage. They now married quickly, and their brides were content to work

Table 3

Sex Ratios of Academy Members by Decade

Year Joined	Men	Women	Sex Ratio
1926–38	35	26	135
1939–45	50	13	385
1946–53	136	22	618
1954–63	295	70	421
1964–73	728	362	201
1974–82	717	662	108
Unknown	14		
Totals (1982)	1,975	1,085	182

while the male veterans earned their degrees. The veteran in school and his working wife—was this not a common couple on university campuses in the immediate postwar years? The pattern probably also affected the life styles and career choices of those men who were not veterans, and of their fiancees and wives. The mores of the time recommended early marriage, and recommended too that the wife support her husband over his long years of training. The result was a string of *années creuses*, of empty years, for the higher education of women, in the medieval disciplines and doubtlessly other fields too.

It should be noted, too, that the generation of medievalists trained in the immediate postwar years today forms the leadership of the Academy and the profession. There is little wonder that women are few among them.

After about 1952, the pendulum begins to swing the other way, quite powerfully and consistently. The sex ratio of new members drops from 618 to 421 in the decade 1954 to 1963, and down to 201 in the ten years from 1964 to 1973. Since 1974, the sex ratio of new members has been 108. In 1975, surely for the first time in the history of the Academy, more women joined than did men. In 1982 the sex ratio of entering members, 92, dropped to its historic low. There are no indications that this fall in sex ratios is abating.

The low sex ratios of new members of course also mark the separate disciplines. If we calculate ratios for the older members who joined in 1972 or earlier, and for the younger members who entered since 1973, then all the disciplines show a precipitous drop: in English literature, from 315 to 131; in history, from 534 to 235; in Romance languages, from 428 to 125; in art history, from 253 to 95. And these figures, as I have mentioned, certainly understate the true proportions of women in the separate subjects.

The conclusion seems certain: we are witnessing a major increase in the proportion of women among medievalists in this country. The trend is especially visible in a field such as art history, but in fact it is affecting all disciplines, without exception. How are we to explain it? By the early 1950s, many of the veterans were successfully launched on their careers; now their wives were free to continue their own education. Doubtlessly affirmative action has played a role, though the swing toward larger numbers of entering women and falling numbers of men began well before affirmative action became national policy. Doubtlessly, too, the women's movement has been influential, but here again the trend began in the middle 50s, well before the women's movement had become established.

Changing styles of personal and professional life are surely crucial. The young, college-educated woman of 1982 is expected to pursue a career and not be content, as was her mother, with marriage and a family but no life outside the home. And young women have shown exceptional energy in realizing this ambition.

This trend to lower sex ratios within our profession is satisfying to anyone who believes that all Americans ought to have equal access to education and to professional careers. And yet this sexual revolution in medieval studies, coupled as it is with shrinking membership, has some disturbing aspects. Let me explain, in careful words, what troubles me about it. It is possible that this phenomenon may not at all indicate growing equality between the sexes and the suppression of differing sex roles in society. Rather, it may point to a redefinition of sex roles. As many observers of contemporary higher education in America have noted, college-educated young men are not now entering graduate education in the humanities in large numbers. The male flight from graduate education in the humanities seems especially pronounced in our finest schools. Rather, the young men are entering professional and technical schools, in evident search for a money-making skill. Men seem still to study primarily to find a job when their days of training are over. Women seem less deterred by economic uncertainties. The typical campus couple of the postwar years—the male graduate student and his working wife—is today replaced by another couple, the male student in medical, law, or business school, and the female student in the humanities. Differing sex roles in regard to the professions may not have been eradicated, only redefined.

These powerful trends may also indicate that the teaching and study of the humanities in a college setting is becoming more and more a second-income job, acceptable to women, but not attractive to males. To profess the humanities at a university requires years of training no less protracted and exacting than that required of lawyers or doctors, but much less remunerative in terms of lifelong earnings. Then, too, the humanities enjoyed great prestige in the immediate postwar years, when they seemed to offer guidance in a troubled world; they seem to have less appeal in our present times, to our present young.

This then is the crucial, still unanswerable question: to what extent does the continuing, marked increase in the percentage of

women in the medieval disciplines represent the enhanced recruitment of women, or rather the growing failure of those same disciplines to attract young men? If that failure is real and growing, then
we must worry that our disciplines are not enlisting the best students, regardless of sex. And recruitment of the finest must of
course remain our goal.

These then are the trends hidden within the Academy mailing list
for 1982. The computer detects their presence; it is an accurate
observer. It remains for us to judge how well its conclusions correspond with our own memories and perceptions of what has been
happening, in the long and recent past. Many current members of
the Academy lived through, and were trained during, the immediate
postwar years, and many more have been witness to the ensuing
changes in the profession, in the tumultuous 60s and 70s. Is the
computer right in what it finds in the Academy mailing list for 1982,
and what do its figures portend? Even if we cannot now flesh out the
answers, we must at a minimum continue to monitor these movements, in order to know better than we know today how they are
affecting us and the disciplines we profess.

INDEX

✦ ✦ ✦

Hanawalt, B., 168
Hartman, M., 41n
Harvard University, xii, 195n
Heers, J., 194n
Heirat, 144n
Heist, W.W., 43n, 51n, 107n
Hellas, 6
Hengge, P., 171
Henrion, R., 114n
Henry IV, German emperor, 48
Henry IV, king of England, 79
Herlihy, D., ix–xx, 14n, 23–24n,
    45n, 54n, 77n, 89n, 107n,
    141n, 145n, 149n, 151n,
    157n, 162, 167, 168 and n,
    169, 170 and n, 177–180n,
    182n, 194n, 196–197n,
    201–202n, 207n, 210n,
    221–222n, 234n, 259n,
    263–264n, 273–274n, 276n,
    317n, 319n, 325n, 326, 331n,
    337n, 354n, 364n, 370n, 373n
Herlihy, G.P., 332n
Herlihy, I.F., 9
Herlihy, M., 7
Herlihy, P., 7
Herlindis, St., 50
Hermann of Steinfeld, St., 168–169,
    171
Herod, king, 153
Herodotus, 139
Hewitt, M., 217 and n
Hildebrand, German warrior,
    225
Hilpisch, F., 44n
Hincmar of Reims, 51n, 98, 104,
    109n, 156n
Holy Land, 53
Holy Roman Empire, 281
Hopkins, K., 96n
Horace, xviii
Hörzinger, M., 133n
Howell, M.C., 76n, 83n
Hudson, river, 383
Hugh of St. Victor, 125 and n
Hugh, king of Italy, 47, 166
Hughes, D.O., 13n, 20n, 49n
Hughes, S., 19n
Humbert, M., 142n, 156n
Hungary, 43

Iacoba, donna, 88–89
Iacobus, 89
Iacometti, F., 177n
Iacoma, donna, 88
Iacopa, widow, 88
Iacopo, St., 337, 347, 351; see also
    James the Great, St.
Iberia, 84
Ibrahim ibn-Iakub, Arab geographer,
    60–61
Ida of Louvain, St., 170
Idaho, 384n
Ildefonso di San Luigi, 23n,
    325–326n, 364n, 366–367n,
    376n
Impruneta, 327
India, 253, 350
Ingund, Merovingian queen, 106,
    164
Innocent II, pope, 233
Innocent III (Lotario di Segni), pope,
    233 and n, 262
Iohanna, donna, 88
Iohannes de Fregano, ser, 88
Iohannes of Padua, 88
Irons, W., 249n, 253n
Irvine, H.D., 55n
Isabella d'Este, marquise of Mantua,
    284, 288–289
Isidore of Seville, 46, 118, 138,
    144, 237
Islam, 154, 256
Israel, 119, 256
Italy, x, 3–7, 13, 15n, 16, 19, 22,
    27, 33n, 61, 76–77, 84, 87, 90,
    151, 168, 171–172, 175, 184,
    188, 190, 193, 218, 257, 284,
    287, 293, 341, 347; central,
    224n; northern, 280

Jackson, Mississippi, 384
Jackson, W.T.H., 241–242n
Jacquin, A.M., 227n
James II, king of Aragon, 76
James the Greater, St., 337
Jannssen-Peigné, S., 154n
Jaqueline, wife of Morise the
    Breton, 70

Tramontano ("across the mountains", 336; Transmondino ("across the world"), 336; Trincamusta ("wine-drinker"), 334; Trivisano, 336; Tullio, 342; Turco, 337; Turpin, 342; Tuttadonna ("all woman"), 339; Vendemmia ("wineharvest"), 336; Veneto, 336n; Ventura, 335; Venuto, 335; Verde Palma ("green palm"), 339; Veronese, 336n; Villano, 339; Vincenzo, 335n; Vinciacastello ("conquer castles"), 338; Vinciproa ("capture booty"), 338; Virgilio (Vergil), 342; Vittorio, 335n; Zagni, 332; Zunta, 332
Nardi, P., 18n
Near East, 296
Negroni, C., 18n
Nevada, 384n
New England, 383–384
New Mexico, 384n
Nobilis, wife of Iohannes de Fregano, 88
Noonan, J.T., 157
Normandy, 71, 347
Nuremberg, 61, 83

O'Malley, J., 18n
Oberman, H.A., 241n
Oeschger, J., 31n
Oesterle, G., 31n, 96n
Olivi, Petrus, 151
Olschki, C., 198n
Oregon, 384n
Orgetorix, Helvetian chief, 116
Origen of Alexandria, 122 and n, 123, 125, 126 and n, 127, 131
Origo, I., 18n, 28n
Osterveen, K., 133n
Ottokar, N., 362n
Oudet, "valet", 72
Ozment, S., 167

Padua, 281, 347
Palencia, 64

Palmerina, 182
Palmieri, Matteo, 235
Paolo da Certaldo, 118 and n, 131 and n, 206 and n
Pardi, G., 177n, 179n
Paris, 69, 70 and n, 71–76, 79–82, 91, 93, 126, 130n, 131, 133, 148, 171, 262, 348; abbey and monastery of Saint-Germain-des-Prés, 60, 141, 223; hospital of Saint-Esprit en Grèves, for children, 233
Parma, 89, 336
Passavanti, Iacopo, 18
Passerini, L., 197n
Paternus, 100
Patlagean, E., 154n
Patricius, father of St. Augustine, 220
Patrick, St., 51, 100, 107
Patrick, St., council of, 105
Paul, St., 159, 172, 349
Paula, donna, 89
Paulus de Regio, poor, 88
Pauly, E., 107n
Pavia, 233, 283, 336
Pavone, C., 14n
Payer, P.J., 340n
Pazzi, family, 357
Peking, 296
Pepin the Short, 36n, 37, 101
Perels, E., 98n
Perosa, A., 14n, 357n
Perpetua of Carthage, St., 42
Perrot, M., 113n
Perugia, 293
Peruzzi, company, 315, 319 and n, 328; family, 302
Pescia, 23
Peter, son of Bernard, 23
Peter, son of Mathilda, 23
Peter, St., 36, 337
Peter Damian, St., 45 and n, 46–48, 144–145, 340
Peter Lombard, bishop of Paris, 126–127, 132
Peter of Blois, 126n
Petrarch, Francesco, 344
Pétré, H., 123n
Petrucci, A., 198n, 276, 324n